Microsoft

Microsoft
Outlook 2016
Step by Step

Joan Lambert

PUBLISHED BY
Microsoft Press
A division of Microsoft Corporation
One Microsoft Way
Redmond, Washington 98052-6399

Library of Congress Control Number: 2015934881
ISBN: 978-0-7356-9778-2

Printed and bound in the United States of America.

First Printing

Microsoft Press books are available through booksellers and distributors worldwide. If you need support related to this book, email Microsoft Press Support at mspinput@microsoft.com. Please tell us what you think of this book at http://aka.ms/tellpress.

This book is provided "as-is" and expresses the author's views and opinions. The views, opinions, and information expressed in this book, including URL and other Internet website references, may change without notice.

Some examples depicted herein are provided for illustration only and are fictitious. No real association or connection is intended or should be inferred.

Microsoft and the trademarks listed at www.microsoft.com on the "Trademarks" webpage are trademarks of the Microsoft group of companies. All other marks are property of their respective owners.

Acquisitions and Developmental Editor: Rosemary Caperton
Editorial Production: Online Training Solutions, Inc. (OTSI)
Copyeditors: Kathy Krause and Val Serdy (OTSI)
Indexer: Susie Carr (OTSI)
Cover: Twist Creative • Seattle

Contents

Part 1: Get started with Outlook 2016

Give us feedback
Tell us what you think of this book and help Microsoft improve our products for you. Thank you!
http://aka.ms/tellpress

2 Explore Outlook modules 31

Part 2: Manage email messages

Part 3: Manage contacts

Part 4: Manage appointments and tasks

e efficiency

13

14 Manage email automatically 479

Give us feedback
Tell us what you think of this book and help Microsoft improve our products for you. Thank you!
http://aka.ms/tellpress

Introduction

Welcome! This *Step by Step* book has been designed so you can read it from the beginning to learn about Microsoft Outlook 2016 and then build your skills as you learn to perform increasingly specialized procedures. Or, if you prefer, you can jump in wherever you need ready guidance for performing tasks. The how-to steps are delivered crisply and concisely—just the facts. You'll also find informative, full-color graphics that support the instructional content.

Who this book is for

Microsoft Outlook 2016 Step by Step is designed for use as a learning and reference resource by home and business users of Microsoft Office programs who want to use Outlook to manage email messages, calendaring, contact records, and task lists. The content of the book is designed to be useful for people who have previously used earlier versions of Outlook, and for people who are discovering Outlook for the first time.

The *Step by Step* approach

The book's coverage is divided into parts representing general Outlook skill sets. Each part is divided into chapters representing skill set areas, and each chapter is divided into topics that group related skills. Each topic includes expository information followed by generic procedures. At the end of the chapter, you'll find a series of practice tasks you can complete on your own by using the skills taught in the chapter. You can use the practice files that are available from this book's website to work through the practice tasks, or you can use your own files and Outlook items.

Download the practice files

Although you can complete the practice tasks in this book by using your own Outlook items and files, for your convenience we have provided practice files for some of the tasks. You can download these practice files to your computer from *http://aka.ms /outlook2016sbs/downloads*. Follow the instructions on the webpage to install the files on your computer in the default practice file folder structure.

 IMPORTANT Outlook 2016 is not available from the book's website. You should install that app before working through the procedures and practice tasks in this book.

As you work through the practice tasks in this book, you will create Outlook items that you can use as practice files in later tasks.

The following table lists the practice files supplied for this book.

Chapter	Folder	File
Part 1: Get started with Outlook 2016		
1: Outlook 2016 basics	Ch01	None
2: Explore Outlook modules	Ch02	None
Part 2: Manage email messages		
3: Send and receive email messages	Ch03	AttachFiles.docx
4: Enhance message content	Ch04	ApplyThemes.docx
5: Manage email security	Ch05	None
6: Organize your Inbox	Ch06	None
Part 3: Manage contacts		
7: Store and access contact information	Ch07	None

Chapter	Folder	File
8: Manage contact records	Ch08	JJProfile.png
		SBSContacts.csv
Part 4: Manage appointments and tasks		
9: Manage scheduling	Ch09	None
10: Manage your calendar	Ch10	None
11: Track tasks	Ch11	None
Part 5: Maximize efficiency		
12: Manage window elements	Ch12	None
13: Customize Outlook options	Ch13	None
14: Manage email automatically	Ch14	None

Ebook edition

If you're reading the ebook edition of this book, you can do the following:

- Search the full text
- Print
- Copy and paste

You can purchase and download the ebook edition from the Microsoft Press Store at *http://aka.ms/outlook2016sbs/detail*.

Get support and give feedback

This topic provides information about getting help with this book and contacting us to provide feedback or report errors.

Errata and support

We've made every effort to ensure the accuracy of this book and its companion content. If you discover an error, please submit it to us at *http://aka.ms/outlook2016sbs/errata*.

If you need to contact the Microsoft Press Support team, please send an email message to *mspinput@microsoft.com*.

For help with Microsoft software and hardware, go to *http://support.microsoft.com*.

We want to hear from you

At Microsoft Press, your satisfaction is our top priority, and your feedback our most valuable asset. Please tell us what you think of this book at *http://aka.ms/tellpress*.

The survey is short, and we read every one of your comments and ideas. Thanks in advance for your input!

Stay in touch

Let's keep the conversation going! We're on Twitter at *http://twitter.com /MicrosoftPress*.

Part 1

Get started with Outlook 2016

Outlook 2016 basics

Electronic messaging keeps many of us in contact with colleagues, clients, friends, and family members. For people who are dependent on electronic communications—and even more so for those who work in enterprises that use Microsoft Exchange Server, SharePoint, and Skype for Business to manage collaboration—Outlook 2016 offers an ideal solution. From one place, you can quickly create, store, organize, manage, and retrieve messages, address books, calendars, task lists, and more. More importantly, Outlook makes this information available to you when and where you need it.

The elements that control the appearance of Outlook and the way you interact with it are collectively referred to as the user interface. Some user interface elements, such as the color scheme, are cosmetic. Others, such as toolbars, menus, and buttons, are functional. You can modify cosmetic and functional user interface elements to suit your preferences and working style.

This chapter guides you through procedures related to starting Outlook, working in the Outlook user interface, and managing Office and Outlook settings.

> ⚠️ **IMPORTANT** The content in the chapters of this book assumes that you have already connected Outlook to one or more email accounts. If you haven't yet connected to an email account, see Appendix A, "Get connected" for information about connecting to email accounts and troubleshooting connection issues.

In this chapter

- Start Outlook
- Work in the Outlook user interface
- Manage Office and Outlook settings

Practice files

No practice files are necessary to complete the practice tasks in this chapter.

Start Outlook

The way that you start Outlook 2016 is dependent on the operating system you're running on your computer. For example:

- In Windows 10, you can start Outlook from the Start menu, the All Apps menu, the Start screen, or the taskbar search box.

- In Windows 8, you can start Outlook from the Apps screen or Start screen search results.

- In Windows 7, you can start Outlook from the Start menu, All Programs menu, or Start menu search results.

You might also have a shortcut to Outlook on your desktop or on the Windows taskbar.

When you start Outlook, it checks your default app settings on the computer. If Outlook isn't the default email app, it displays a message and an option to set it as the default so that any email you initiate from outside of Outlook—for example, from a Microsoft Word document or from File Explorer—is created in Outlook from your primary Outlook account.

 **TIP** If you have a different default email app and don't want Outlook to display the message box, you can turn off the function that checks whether Outlook is the default app. For information, see "Configure general Office and Outlook options" in Chapter 13, "Customize Outlook options."

To start Outlook on a Windows 10 computer

1. Click the **Start** button, and then click **All apps**.

2. In the app list, click any index letter to display the alphabet index, and then click **O** to scroll the app list to the apps starting with that letter.

3. Scroll the list if necessary, and then click **Outlook 2016** to start the app. (If Outlook 2016 isn't in the list, it might be in a Microsoft Outlook folder in the M section.)

To start Outlook on a Windows 8 computer

1. From the **Start** screen, display the **Apps** screen.

2. Sort the **Apps** screen by name, and then click any index letter to display the alphabet index.

3. In the alphabet index, click **O** to scroll the app list to the apps starting with that letter. Then click **Outlook 2016** to start the app.

Work in the Outlook user interface

The Outlook user interface provides intuitive access to all the tools you need to manage your email, calendar, contacts, and tasks. You can use Outlook 2016 to do the following:

- Send, receive, read, respond to, organize, and archive email messages.

- Create attractive business graphics and incorporate and edit external images in your communications.

- Send documents, spreadsheets, presentations, pictures, and other files as message attachments, and preview attachments you receive from other people.

- Schedule events, appointments, and meetings; invite attendees; and reserve conference rooms, projectors, and other managed resources.

- View upcoming appointments and tasks, and receive reminders for them.

- Share schedule information with other people, inside and outside your organization.

- Store contact information in a transferable and easily accessible format.

- Keep track of tasks you need to complete, schedule time to complete your tasks, and assign tasks to co-workers.

- Organize and easily locate information in messages, attachments, calendars, contact records, tasks, and notes.

- Filter out unwanted and annoying junk messages.

- Have information from favorite websites delivered directly to you.

About Office

Outlook 2016 is part of the Microsoft Office 2016 suite of apps, which also include Microsoft Access, Excel, PowerPoint, and Word. The apps in the Office suite are designed to work together to provide highly efficient methods of getting things done. You can install one or more Office apps on your computer. Some apps have multiple versions designed for different platforms. For example, you can install different versions of Word on a computer, a smartphone, an iPad, and an Android device; you can also work in a version of Word that is hosted entirely online. Similarly, you can install the desktop version of Outlook on your computer or work in Outlook Online. Although the core purpose of an app remains the same regardless of the platform on which it runs, the available functionality and the way you interact with the app might be different.

The app that is described and depicted in images throughout this book is a standard desktop installation of Outlook 2016 on a Windows 10 computer, configured to connect to a Microsoft Exchange account. It is available as part of the Office 2016 suite of apps, as a freestanding app, or as part of an Office 365 subscription.

Until recently, the standard way of acquiring Office software was to purchase a disc, packaged in a box, and install the software from the disc. The standard distribution model recently changed to an online installation, often as part of an Office 365 subscription licensing package.

1

Office 365, which was originally available only to businesses, now has many subscription options designed for individual home and business users, students, households, small businesses, midsize businesses, enterprises, government agencies, academic institutions, and nonprofits; in other words, whatever your needs may be, there is an Office 365 subscription option that will be a close fit. Many of the Office 365 subscription options include licensing for the desktop Office apps, and permit users to run Office on multiple devices, including Windows computers, Mac computers, Windows tablets, Android tablets, iPads, and smartphones.

If you have an Office 365 subscription that includes Outlook 2016, you'll also have access to Outlook Online. You can manage email, calendar items, contacts, and account settings in Outlook Online, which runs directly in your browser instead of on your computer, and is therefore available to you from any location in which you have Internet access. Office Online apps are installed in the host online environment and are not part of the desktop version that you install directly on your computer.

Outlook Online displays email message content very much like the desktop app does, and offers a limited subset of the commands and content formatting options that are available in the full desktop app.

Outlook has multiple modules—Mail, Calendar, People, Tasks, Notes, and Folders—in which you display and manage specific types of information. All of the modules are displayed within an app window that contains all the tools you need to add and format content.

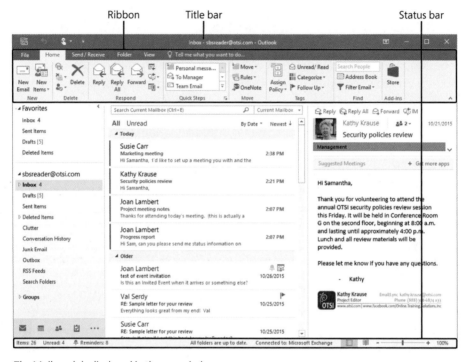

The Mail module displayed in the app window

Individual Outlook items such as email messages, appointments, contact records, and tasks are displayed in item windows. Like the app window, an item window has a title bar and ribbon, but it doesn't have a status bar. The title bar and ribbon content is specific to the type of item displayed in the window.

Identify app window elements

The Outlook app window contains the elements described in this section. Commands for tasks you perform often are readily available, and even those you might use infrequently are easy to find.

Title bar

At the top of the app window, this bar displays the name of the active account, identifies the app, and provides tools for managing the app window, ribbon, and content.

Quick Access Toolbar   Account   Window Management

Folder   Ribbon Display Options

The title bar elements are always on the left end, in the center, and on the right end of the title bar

The Quick Access Toolbar at the left end of the title bar can be customized to include any commands that you want to have easily available. The default Quick Access Toolbar in the Outlook app window displays the Send/Receive All Folders and Undo/Redo buttons. In the item windows, the Quick Access Toolbar includes the Save, Undo, Redo, Previous Item, and Next Item buttons. On a touchscreen device, the Quick Access Toolbars also include the Touch/Mouse Mode button.

>
>
> **SEE ALSO** For information about Touch mode, see "Work with the ribbon and status bar" later in this topic.

You can change the location of the Quick Access Toolbar and customize it to include any command you want to have easy access to. You're more likely to do this in the app window than in the item windows, but in Outlook, you can customize user interface elements for each window and view.

> **TIP** You might find that you work more efficiently if you organize the commands you use frequently on the Quick Access Toolbar and then display it below the ribbon, directly above the workspace. For information, see "Customize the Quick Access Toolbar" in Chapter 12, "Manage window elements."

Four buttons at the right end of the title bar serve the same functions in all Office apps. You control the display of the ribbon by clicking commands on the Ribbon Display Options menu, temporarily hide the app window by clicking the Minimize button, adjust the size of the window by clicking the Restore Down/Maximize button, and close the active item window or exit the app by clicking the Close button.

Ribbon

Whereas other Office apps have one app window ribbon, Outlook has multiple ribbons: one for each module, and one for each item type window. (There are many item type windows, including windows specific to creating messages, appointments, meetings, contact records, and so on, and another set for editing each of those item types.) The content of each item window ribbon is appropriate to the content of that type of item. The basic functionality of every ribbon is the same, however.

You can customize the Quick Access Toolbar and ribbon for each item type. This is more common in Word, Excel, and PowerPoint than in Outlook because Outlook has individual ribbons that contain commands focused on the item type. For information about customizing Outlook functionality and command interfaces, see Chapter 12, "Manage window elements," and Chapter 13, "Customize Outlook options."

In any window, the ribbon is located below the title bar. The commands you'll use when working with Outlook items are gathered together in this central location for efficiency.

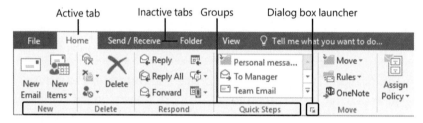

Your ribbon might display additional tabs

> **TIP** The available ribbon tabs and the appearance of the commands on the ribbon might differ from what is shown in this book, based on the apps that are installed on your computer, the Outlook settings and window size, and the screen settings. For more information, see the sidebar "Adapt procedure steps" later in this chapter.

Across the top of the ribbon is a set of tabs. Clicking a tab displays an associated set of commands arranged in groups.

Backstage view

Commands related to managing Outlook (rather than item content) are gathered together in the Backstage view, which you display by clicking the File tab located at the left end of the ribbon. Commands available in the Backstage view are organized on named pages, which you display by clicking the page tabs in the colored left pane. You redisplay the active Outlook module and the ribbon by clicking the Back arrow located above the page tabs.

You manage app settings in the Backstage view

Commands related to working with items and item content are represented as buttons on the remaining tabs of the ribbon. The Home tab, which is active by default, contains the most frequently used commands.

When a graphic element such as a picture, table, or chart is selected in an item window, one or more *tool tabs* might appear at the right end of the ribbon to make commands related to that specific object easily accessible. Tool tabs are available only when the relevant object is selected, and are differentiated from other tabs by a *Tools* heading above the tab name.

> **TIP** Some older commands no longer appear as buttons on the ribbon but are still available in the app. You can make these commands available by adding them to the Quick Access Toolbar or the ribbon. For more information, see "Customize the Quick Access Toolbar" and "Customize the ribbon" in Chapter 12, "Manage window elements."

On each tab, buttons representing commands are organized into named groups. You can point to any button to display a ScreenTip that contains the full command name (which is often longer than the button label), a description of its function, and its keyboard shortcut (if it has one).

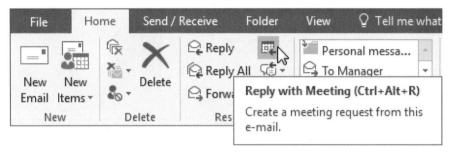

ScreenTips are particularly helpful with minimized, unlabeled buttons

> **TIP** You can control the display of ScreenTips and of feature descriptions in ScreenTips. For more information, see "Configure general Office and Outlook options" in Chapter 13, "Customize Outlook options."

Some buttons include an arrow, which might be integrated with or separate from the button. To determine whether a button and its arrow are integrated, point to the button to activate it. If both the button and its arrow are shaded, clicking the button displays options for refining the action of the button. If only the button or arrow is shaded when you point to it, clicking the button carries out its default action or applies the current default formatting. Clicking the arrow and then clicking an action carries out the action. Clicking the arrow and then clicking a formatting option applies the formatting and sets it as the default for the button.

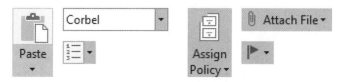

Examples of buttons with separate and integrated arrows

When a formatting option has several choices available, the choices are often displayed in a gallery of images, called *thumbnails*, that provide a visual representation of each choice. When you point to a thumbnail in a gallery, the Live Preview feature shows you what the active content will look like if you click the thumbnail to apply the associated formatting. When a gallery contains more thumbnails than can be shown in the available ribbon space, you can display more content by clicking the scroll arrow or the More button located on the right border of the gallery.

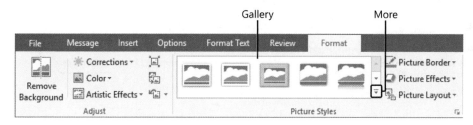

Tool tabs frequently include galleries of formatting options

Related but less common commands are not represented as buttons in a group. Instead, they're available in a dialog box or pane, which you display by clicking the dialog box launcher located in the lower-right corner of the group.

> **TIP** To the right of the groups on the ribbon is the Collapse The Ribbon button, which is shaped like a chevron. For more information, see "Work with the ribbon and status bar," later in this topic.

Status bar

Across the bottom of the app window (but not the item windows), the status bar displays information about the current presentation and provides access to certain Outlook functions. You can choose which statistics and tools appear on the status bar. Some indicators, such as Filter, Unread Items In View, and Reminders, appear on the status bar only when specific conditions exist.

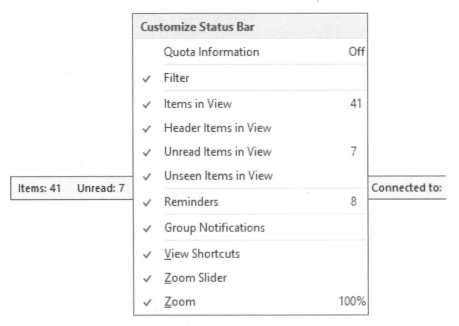

You can specify the information that the status bar displays

The View Shortcuts toolbar, Zoom Slider tool, and Zoom button are at the right end of the status bar. These tools provide you with convenient methods for changing the display of module content.

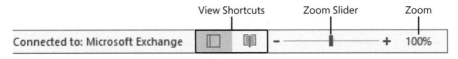

Change content views and magnification from the status bar

 SEE ALSO For information about changing the content view, see "Work in the mail module" in Chapter 2, "Explore Outlook modules."

Tell me what you want to do

Entering a term in the Tell Me What You Want To Do box located to the right of the ribbon tabs displays a list of related commands and links to additional resources online. Or you can press F1 to open the Help window for the current app.

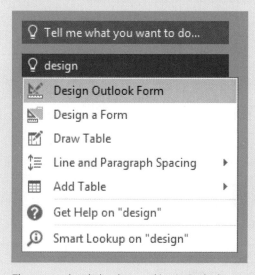

The easy path to help when working in Outlook

Work with the ribbon and status bar

The goal of the ribbon is to make working with items and item content as intuitive as possible. The ribbon is dynamic, meaning that as its width changes, its buttons adapt to the available space. As a result, a button might be large or small, it might or might not have a label, or it might even change to an entry in a list.

For example, when sufficient horizontal space is available, the buttons on the Home tab of the Outlook app window are spread out, and you can review the commands available in each group.

At 1024 pixels wide, most button labels are visible

If you decrease the horizontal space available to the ribbon, small button labels disappear and entire groups of buttons might hide under one button that represents the entire group. Clicking the group button displays a list of the commands available in that group.

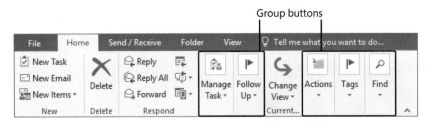

When insufficient horizontal space is available, group labels disappear and groups collapse under buttons

When the ribbon becomes too narrow to display all the groups, a scroll arrow appears at its right end. Clicking the scroll arrow displays the hidden groups.

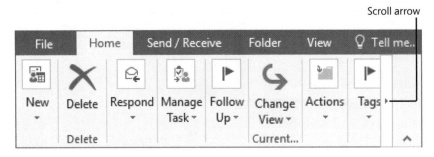

Scroll to display additional group buttons

The width of the ribbon depends on these three factors:

- **Window width** Maximizing the app window provides the most space for the ribbon.

- **Screen resolution** Screen resolution is the size of your screen display expressed as pixels wide × pixels high. The greater the screen resolution, the greater the amount of information that will fit on one screen. Your screen resolution options are dependent on the display adapter installed in your computer, and on your monitor. Common screen resolutions range from 800 × 600 to

2560 × 1440 (and some are larger). The greater the number of pixels wide (the first number), the greater the number of buttons that can be shown on the ribbon.

- **The magnification of your screen display** If you change the screen magnification setting in Windows, text and user interface elements are larger and therefore more legible, but fewer elements fit on the screen.

You can hide the ribbon completely if you don't need access to any of its buttons, or hide it so that only its tabs are visible. (This is a good way to gain vertical space when working on a smaller screen.) Then you can temporarily redisplay the ribbon to click a button, or permanently redisplay it if you need to click several buttons.

If you're working on a touchscreen device, you can turn on Touch mode, which provides more space between buttons on the ribbon and status bar. (It doesn't affect the layout of dialog boxes or panes.) The extra space is intended to lessen the possibility of accidentally tapping the wrong button with your finger.

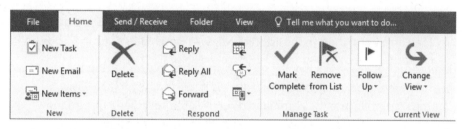

Touch mode has a greater amount of space on the ribbon and status bar

The same commands are available in Touch mode, but they're often hidden under group buttons.

 SEE ALSO For information about working with a modified ribbon, see the sidebar "Adapt procedure steps" later in this topic.

You can switch between Touch mode and Mouse mode (the standard desktop app user interface) from the Quick Access Toolbar. Switching any one of the primary Office apps (Access, Excel, Outlook, PowerPoint, and Word) to Touch mode turns it on in all of them.

Adapt procedure steps

This book contains many images of user interface elements (such as the ribbons and the app windows) that you'll work with while performing tasks in Outlook on a Windows computer. Depending on your screen resolution or window width, the Outlook ribbon on your screen might look different from that shown in this book. (If you turn on Touch mode, the ribbon displays significantly fewer commands than in Mouse mode.) As a result, procedural instructions that involve the ribbon might require a little adaptation.

Simple procedural instructions use this format:

1. On the **Folder** tab, in the **Clean Up** group, click the **Run Rules Now** button.

If the command is in a list, our instructions use this format:

1. On the **Send/Receive** tab, in the **Server** group, click the **Mark to Download** arrow and then, in the list, click **Mark to Download Message Copy**.

If differences between your display settings and ours cause a button to appear differently on your screen than it does in this book, you can easily adapt the steps to locate the command. First click the specified tab, and then locate the specified group. If a group has been collapsed into a group list or under a group button, click the list or button to display the group's commands. If you can't immediately identify the button you want, point to likely candidates to display their names in ScreenTips.

Multistep procedural instructions use this format:

1. Display the module view that you want to modify.

2. On the **View** tab, in the **Current View** group, click the **View Settings** button to open the Advanced View Settings dialog box for the selected module view.

1

3. In the **Description** section, click the **Sort** button to open the Sort dialog box.

4. In the **Sort items by** section, expand the list, and then click **Size**.

On subsequent instances of instructions that require you to follow the same process, the instructions might be simplified in this format because the working location has already been established:

1. Display the module view that you want to modify.

2. Open the **Advanced View Settings** dialog box, and then click the **Sort** button.

3. In the **Sort items by** list, click **Size**.

The instructions in this book assume that you're interacting with on-screen elements on your computer by clicking (with a mouse, touchpad, or other hardware device). If you're using a different method—for example, if your computer has a touchscreen interface and you're tapping the screen (with your finger or a stylus)—substitute the applicable tapping action when you interact with a user interface element.

Instructions in this book refer to user interface elements that you click or tap on the screen as *buttons*, and to physical buttons that you press on a keyboard as *keys*, to conform to the standard terminology used in documentation for these products.

When the instructions tell you to enter information, you can do so by typing on a connected external keyboard, tapping an on-screen keyboard, or even speaking aloud, depending on your computer setup and your personal preferences.

To maximize the window

1. Do any of the following:

   - Click the **Maximize** button.

   - Double-click the title bar.

   - Drag the borders of a non-maximized window.

   - Drag the window to the top of the screen. (When the pointer touches the top of the screen, the dragged window maximizes.)

To change the screen resolution

 TIP Methods of changing screen resolution vary by operating system, but you should be able to access the settings in Windows 10, Windows 8, and Windows 7 by using these methods.

1. Do any of the following:

   - Right-click the Windows 10 desktop, and then click **Display settings**. At the bottom of the **Display** pane of the **Settings** window, click the **Advanced display settings** link.

   - Right-click the Windows 8 or Windows 7 desktop, and then click **Screen resolution**.

   - Enter screen resolution in Windows Search, and then click **Change the screen resolution** in the search results.

   - Open the **Display** Control Panel item, and then click **Adjust resolution**.

2. Click or drag to select the screen resolution you want, and then click **Apply** or **OK**. Windows displays a preview of the selected screen resolution.

3. If you like the change, click **Keep changes** in the message box that appears. If you don't, the screen resolution reverts to the previous setting.

To completely hide the ribbon

1. Near the right end of the title bar, click the **Ribbon Display Options** button.

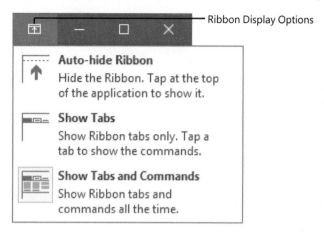

The Ribbon Display Options button is on the title bar so that it is available when the ribbon is hidden

2. On the **Ribbon Display Options** menu, click **Auto-hide Ribbon**.

 TIP To redisplay the ribbon, click the Ribbon Display Options button and then click Show Tabs or Show Tabs And Commands.

To display only the ribbon tabs

1. Do any of the following:

    *   Double-click any active tab name.

    *   Near the upper-right corner of the app window, click the **Ribbon Display Options** button, and then click **Show Tabs**.

    *   In the lower-right corner of the ribbon, click the **Collapse the Ribbon** button.

    *   Press **Ctrl+F1**.

To temporarily redisplay the ribbon

1. Click any tab name to display the tab until you click a command or click away from the ribbon.

To permanently redisplay the ribbon

1. Do any of the following:

   - Double-click any tab name.

   - Near the upper-right corner of the app window, click the **Ribbon Display Options** button, and then click **Show Tabs and Commands**.

   - Press **Ctrl+F1**.

To optimize the ribbon for touch interaction

1. On the Quick Access Toolbar, click or tap the **Touch/Mouse Mode** button, and then click **Touch**.

To specify the items that appear on the status bar

1. Right-click the status bar to display the Customize Status Bar menu. A check mark indicates each item that is currently enabled.

2. Click to enable or disable a status bar indicator or tool. The change is effected immediately. The menu remains open to permit multiple selections.

3. When you finish, click away from the menu to close it.

Manage Office and Outlook settings

You access app settings from the Backstage view; specifically, from the Office Account page and the Outlook Options dialog box. This topic discusses the information you can configure from the Office Account page of the Backstage view.

 SEE ALSO For information about working in the Outlook Options dialog box, see Chapter 13, "Customize Outlook options."

The Office Account page displays information about the account you use for Office, not for your email account

The Office Account page of the Backstage view displays information about your installation of Outlook (and other apps in the Office suite) and the resources you connect to. This information includes:

- Your Microsoft account and links to manage it.

- The current app window background and theme.

- Storage locations and services (such as Facebook and LinkedIn) that you've connected Office to.

- Your subscription information and links to manage the subscription, if you have Office through an Office 365 subscription.

- The app version number and update options.

Microsoft account options

If you use Office 365, Skype, OneDrive, Xbox Live, Outlook.com, or a Windows Phone, you already have a Microsoft account. (Microsoft account credentials are also used by many non-Microsoft products and websites.) If you don't already have a Microsoft account, you can register any existing email account as a Microsoft account, sign up for a free Outlook.com or Hotmail.com account and register that as a Microsoft account, or create an alias for an Outlook.com account and register the alias.

TIP Many apps and websites authenticate transactions by using Microsoft account credentials. For that reason, it's a good idea to register a personal account that you control, rather than a business account that your employer controls, as your Microsoft account. That way, you won't risk losing access if you leave the company.

You can quickly personalize the appearance of your Outlook app window by choosing an Office background and an Office theme. (These are specific to Office and aren't in any way associated with the Windows theme or desktop background.) The background is a subtle design that appears in the title bar of the app window. There are 14 backgrounds to choose from, or you can choose to not have a background.

Backgrounds depict a variety of subjects

1

At the time of this writing, there are three Office themes:

- **Colorful** Displays the title bar and ribbon tabs in the color specific to the app, and the ribbon commands, status bar, and Backstage view in light gray

- **Dark Gray** Displays the title bar and ribbon tabs in dark gray, and the ribbon commands, status bar, and Backstage view in light gray

- **White** Displays the title bar, ribbon tabs, and ribbon commands in white, and the status bar in the app-specific color

There are rumors that another theme will be released in the near future, but it hasn't yet made an appearance.

 TIP The images in this book depict the No Background option to avoid interfering with the display of any user interface elements, and the Colorful theme.

From the Connected Services section of the page, you can connect Office to Facebook, Flickr, and YouTube accounts to access pictures and videos; to SharePoint sites and OneDrive storage locations; and to LinkedIn and Twitter accounts to share information. To connect Office to one of these services, you must already have an account with the service.

Until you connect to storage locations, they aren't available to you from within Outlook. For example, when inserting a picture into an email message, you will have the option to insert a locally stored picture or to search online for a picture. After you connect to your Facebook, SharePoint, or OneDrive accounts, you can also insert pictures stored in those locations.

The changes that you make on the Office Account page apply to all the Office apps installed on all the computers that are associated with your account. For example, changing the Office background in Outlook on one computer also changes it in Outlook on any other computer on which you've associated Office with the same account.

Some of the settings on the Office Account page are also available in the Outlook Options dialog box, which you open from the Backstage view. This dialog box also contains hundreds of options for controlling the way Outlook works. Chapter 13, "Customize Outlook options," provides in-depth coverage of these options. It's a good idea to familiarize yourself with the dialog box content so you know what you can modify.

To display your Office account settings

1. Start Outlook.

2. In the app window or in any item window, click the **File** tab to display the Backstage view, and then click **Office Account**.

To manage your Microsoft account connection

1. Display the **Office Account** page of the Backstage view.

2. In the **User Information** area, click any of the links to begin the selected process.

To change the app window background for all Office apps

1. Display the **Office Account** page of the Backstage view.

2. In the **Office Background** list, point to any background to display a live preview in the app window, and then click the background you want.

To change the app window color scheme for all Office apps

1. Display the **Office Account** page of the Backstage view.

2. In the **Office Theme** list, click **Colorful**, **Dark Gray**, or **White**.

To connect to a cloud storage location or social media service

1. Display the **Office Account** page of the Backstage view.

2. At the bottom of the **Connected Services** area, click **Add a service**, click the type of service you want to add, and then click the specific service.

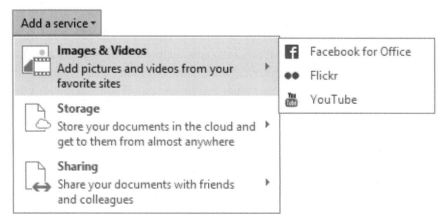

The menus display services that you're not yet connected to

1

To change or remove a social media service connection

1. Display the **Office Account** page of the Backstage view.

2. In the **Connected Services** area, click the **Manage** link to the right of the service you want to modify. A webpage opens and displays information about the account you're connected to and the information that is available from that account.

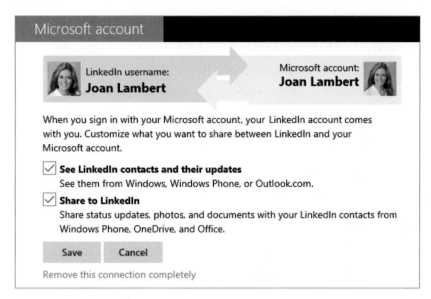

Additional information on the page provides information and links to the service

3. Modify or remove the connection from this page, or close the page to return to Outlook.

To disconnect from a cloud storage location

1. Display the **Office Account** page of the Backstage view.

2. In the **Connected Services** area, click the **Remove** link to the right of the storage location you want to modify.

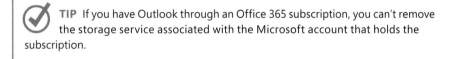

> **TIP** If you have Outlook through an Office 365 subscription, you can't remove the storage service associated with the Microsoft account that holds the subscription.

3. In the confirmation message box, click **Yes**.

To manage your Office 365 subscription

1. Display the **Office Account** page of the Backstage view.

2. In the **Product Information** area, click the **Manage Account** button to display the sign-in page for your Office 365 management interface.

3. Provide your account credentials and sign in to access your options.

To manage Office updates

1. Display the **Office Account** page of the Backstage view.

2. Click the **Update Options** button, and then click the action you want to take.

You can install available updates from the Backstage view before the automatic installation occurs

To open the Outlook Options dialog box

1. In the left pane of the Backstage view, click **Options**.

Skills review

In this chapter, you learned how to:

- Start Outlook

- Work in the Outlook user interface

- Manage Office and Outlook settings

Practice tasks

No practice files are necessary to complete the practice tasks in this chapter.

Start Outlook

Perform the following tasks:

1. Using the technique that is appropriate for your operating system, start Outlook.

Work in the Outlook user interface

Start Outlook, maximize the app window, and then perform the following tasks:

1. On each tab of the ribbon, do the following:

    *   Review the available groups and commands.

    *   Display the ScreenTip of any command you're not familiar with. Notice the different levels of detail in the ScreenTips.

    *   If a group has a dialog box launcher in its lower-right corner, click the dialog box launcher to display the associated dialog box or pane.

2. Change the width of the app window and notice the effect it has on the ribbon. When the window is narrow, locate a group button and click it to display the commands.

3. Maximize the app window. Hide the ribbon entirely, and notice the change in the app window. Redisplay the ribbon tabs (but not the commands). Temporarily display the ribbon commands, and then click away from the ribbon to close it.

4. Use any of the procedures described in this chapter to permanently redisplay the ribbon tabs and commands.

5. Display the status bar shortcut menu, and identify the tools and statistics that are currently displayed on the status bar. Add any indicators to the status bar that will be useful to you.

Manage Office and Outlook settings

In Outlook, perform the following tasks:

1. Display the **Office Account** page of the Backstage view and review the information that is available there.

2. Expand the **Office Background** list. Point to each background to display a live preview of it. Then click the background you want to apply.

3. Apply each of the Office themes, and consider its merits. Then apply the theme you like best.

   > 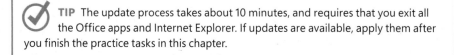 **TIP** If you apply a theme other than Colorful, your interface colors will be different from the interface shown in the screenshots in this book, but the functionality will be the same.

4. Review the services that Office is currently connected to. Expand the **Add a service** menu and point to each of the menu items to display the available services. Connect to any of these that you want to use.

5. Click the **Update Options** button and note whether updates are currently available to install.

   > **TIP** The update process takes about 10 minutes, and requires that you exit all the Office apps and Internet Explorer. If updates are available, apply them after you finish the practice tasks in this chapter.

6. On the **Update Options** menu, click **View Updates** to display the *What's New and Improved in Office 2016* webpage in your default browser. Review the information on this page to learn about any new features that interest you.

7. Return to Outlook and open the **Outlook Options** dialog box.

8. Explore each page of the dialog box. Notice the sections of each page and the settings in each section.

9. Review the settings on the **General** page, and modify them as necessary to fit the way you work. Then close the dialog box.

Explore Outlook modules

The Outlook 2016 user interface includes many features and tools to help you easily store, find, and display information. Outlook functionality is divided among several modules that are specific to the items you work with in them. You work with messages in the Mail module; with appointments, events, and meetings in the Calendar module; with contact records in the People module, and with tasks and to-do items in the Tasks module.

You display and work with one module at a time in the app window. The functionality of the ribbon, status bar, and content area in each module is specific to the items you manage in the module, and sometimes to the view of the module that you display.

The ribbon in each Outlook module displays commands for managing the types of items you create in that module, and the status bar displays indicators relevant to the module. Similarly, the ribbon of each type of item window has a unique tab that displays commands specific to that item type. The result of all this is that the relevant commands are easy to access.

This chapter guides you through procedures related to working in the Outlook app window, and working in the Mail, Calendar, People, and Tasks modules.

In this chapter

- Work in the Outlook app window
- Work in the Mail module
- Work in the Calendar module
- Work in the People module
- Work in the Tasks module

Practice files

No practice files are necessary to complete the practice tasks in this chapter.

Work in the Outlook app window

The first time you start Outlook, the app window displays your Inbox in Compact view. When you subsequently start Outlook, the app window displays the view and arrangement of the Mail module that was active when you closed Outlook.

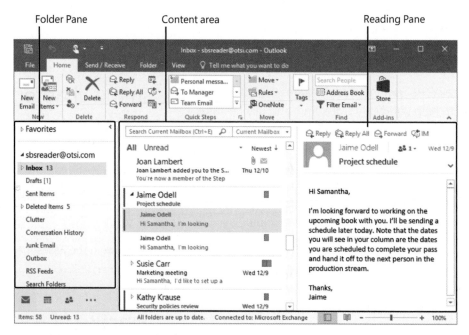

Areas of the app window for working with Outlook items

Work with items

You can individually control the display, and in some cases the location, of app window elements from the View tab.

In addition to the title bar, ribbon, and status bar that are common to all Microsoft Office apps, the Outlook app window includes three areas in which you work with Outlook items: the Folder Pane, the content area, and the Reading Pane.

- **Folder Pane** This collapsible pane appears on the left side of the Outlook app window in every module. Its contents change depending on the module you're viewing—it might display links to email folders, calendars, address books, or filtered views. The Folder Pane can be minimized to display only favorite folders. The Folder Pane setting (Normal or Minimized) remains the same as you switch among modules.

- **Content area** The content area is the part of the app window bordered on the left by the Folder Pane and on the right by the To-Do Bar, when the To-Do Bar is displayed, or by the right side of the app window when it is not displayed. The content area displays the content of the selected module—your message list, calendar, contact records, or tasks—and can also host the Reading Pane.

- **Reading Pane** This optional pane can be displayed vertically or horizontally within the content area. Within the Reading Pane, you can preview and work with the content of a selected item, or display a full-featured preview of a file that is attached to an Outlook item (including Microsoft Word documents, Excel worksheets, PowerPoint presentations, and PDF files). The Reading Pane can also host the People Pane.

> **SEE ALSO** For information about working with the Reading Pane, see "Display messages and message attachments" in Chapter 3, "Send and receive email messages."

The Folder Pane and content area are standard in every Outlook module; the Reading Pane can be displayed in any Outlook module but is displayed by default only in the Mail and Tasks modules.

Switch among modules

The Navigation Bar, which is located on the left side of the app window above the status bar, displays the controls you use to navigate between modules. The Navigation Bar can take the form of a compact vertical or horizontal bar that displays buttons labeled with module icons, or as a larger horizontal bar with text labels.

The standard Navigation Bar is separate from the Folder Pane and does not change orientation. The compact Navigation Bar is incorporated into the Folder Pane, and its orientation depends on whether the Folder Pane is minimized or expanded.

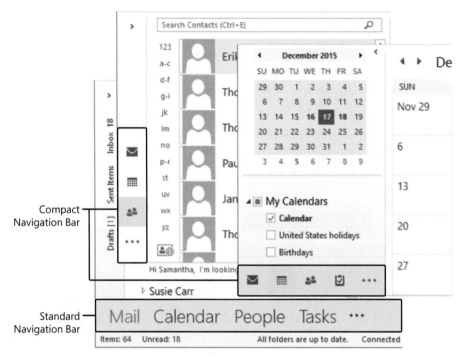

The different forms of the Navigation Bar

> **SEE ALSO** You can specify the maximum number of buttons that appear on the Navigation Bar and the order in which they appear. For information about modifying the Navigation Bar and its contents, see "Personalize the Outlook app window" in Chapter 12, "Manage window elements."

To display an Outlook module

1. On the Navigation Bar, click the module button, or click the **Options** button (...) and then click the module name.

Or

1. Use any of the following keyboard shortcuts:

   - **Ctrl+1** for Mail

   - **Ctrl+2** for Calendar

   - **Ctrl+3** for People

   - **Ctrl+4** for Tasks

   - **Ctrl+5** for Notes

> **SEE ALSO** For more information about keyboard shortcuts, see Appendix B, "Keyboard shortcuts."

> **TIP** If you want to work in two modules at the same time, you can open a module in a second instance of Outlook by right-clicking the module button on the Navigation Bar and then clicking Open In New Window.

Work in the Mail module

The Mail module is displayed by default when you start Outlook. Content that is specific to the Mail module includes the Favorites list at the top of the Folder Pane, and the message list in the content area. The Home tab displays commands specific to working with messages.

Content that is unique to the Mail module

Folder Pane content

In the Mail module, the Folder Pane displays the Favorites list and the folder structure of your mailbox (or mailboxes, if you have set up multiple email accounts). The folders you add to your Favorites list are displayed at the top of the Folder Pane when it is open, and on the minimized Folder Pane when it is minimized.

When you are connected to a Microsoft Exchange account, the Favorites list automatically includes the Inbox, Sent Items, Drafts, Deleted Items, and Clutter folders.

If you have Outlook configured to connect to multiple email accounts, you might find it convenient and efficient to add the Inbox folders of each account to the Favorites list, so you can easily access all your messages in one location. If you experience connection issues with an account, you can add the account's Outbox folder to the Favorites list so you can easily observe whether messages are being sent.

When you connect to any type of email account, these nine folders are available in each mailbox:

- **Inbox** By default, Outlook delivers new messages to this folder.

- **Drafts** Outlook stores temporary copies of in-progress messages in this folder, which is created the first time you save a message without sending it. Outlook might also create a draft for you while you work, if you don't send the message immediately.

> **SEE ALSO** For information about creating and working with message drafts, see "Create and send messages" in Chapter 3, "Send and receive email messages."

- **Sent Items** When you send a message, Outlook stores a copy of it in this folder. You can change this setting if you would prefer to store sent messages elsewhere or if you prefer to not store sent messages, but the safest option is to stick to this default setting.

- **Deleted Items** Outlook items that you delete from other folders are held in this folder. They are not deleted permanently until you empty the folder.

- **Clutter** Outlook monitors the messages that you routinely delete and those that you respond to. Based on these patterns, Outlook delivers messages that it thinks you will ignore to this folder.

- **Junk E-Mail** Outlook delivers messages blocked by the spam filter to this folder.

- **Outbox** Outlook holds outgoing messages in this folder while establishing a connection to your mail server.

- **RSS Feeds** Website information feeds that you subscribe to are available from this folder. When you first start Outlook, you might find information feeds recommended by Microsoft here.

- **Search Folders** These folders contain up-to-date results of searches you've conducted for messages that match specific search criteria.

If your organization uses Microsoft Skype for Business, the default installation includes a Conversation History folder in which you can locate, review, and restart instant message exchanges (and other Skype communications). Other folders might be installed by your email service provider or third-party email security apps. You can view additional folders by displaying the Folders list in the Folder Pane of the current module.

The full folder structure for an Exchange account is displayed in the Folders list and is significantly more complex than that shown in the standard Mail module view. The Folders list includes these additional folders for Exchange account mailboxes:

- **Calendar** Contains the contents of the Outlook Calendar module
- **Contacts** Contains the contents of the Outlook People module
- **Journal** Contains the contents of the Outlook Journal module
- **Notes** Contains the contents of the Outlook Notes module
- **Sync Issues** Contains a list of conflicts and communication failures on your mail server or in your mailbox
- **Tasks** Contains the contents of the Outlook Tasks module
- **User-created folders** Contains any calendar, contact, or task folders you create

The folders in the Folder Pane are displayed in a specific order that is somewhat by priority—or perhaps just a programmer's idea at the time that's stuck around. If you prefer, you can display the folders in alphabetical order.

Outside of the account folder structure, the Folders list also displays the Groups, Group Calendars, and Public Folders nodes, if your organization uses these Office 365 and Exchange features.

If you connect or subscribe to any Microsoft SharePoint lists or Internet calendars, links to these groups appear at the same level as your mailbox.

To add a folder to the Favorites list

1. Display the Mail module, and then do any of the following:

   - Drag the folder to the **Favorites** list.
   - Right-click the folder, and then click **Show in Favorites**.
   - Click the folder, and then on the **Folder** tab, in the **Favorites** group, click the **Show in Favorites** button.

IMPORTANT The Show In Favorites commands are not visible when you are displaying the Folders list or a module other than the Mail module.

2

To display the Folders list in the Folder Pane of any module

1. Do any of the following:

   - On the Navigation Bar, click the **Options** button (...), and then click **Folders**.

   - If the Navigation Bar has been modified to include the Folders button, click the **Folders** button.

   - Press **Ctrl+6**.

To display folders in alphabetical order

1. On the **Folder** tab, in the **Clean Up** group, click **Show All Folders A to Z**.

To display subfolders in alphabetical order

1. Click the folder that contains the subfolders to select it.

2. Right-click the folder, and then click **Sort Subfolders A to Z**.

Ribbon tabs

The ribbon in the Mail module includes the File tab (which displays the Backstage view) and the four command tabs that appear in all modules: Home, Send/Receive, Folder, and View. The Home and View content is module-specific. The Mail module includes the following tabs:

- **Home** Includes commands you need for creating and managing email messages (but not message content). For an Internet email account, this tab also includes a Send/Receive group.

The Home tab of the Mail module

- **Send/Receive** Includes commands for synchronizing data in Outlook with data on your mail server. You can control how Outlook sends and receives messages, whether Outlook automatically downloads full messages or only message headers, and manual download processes. You can also choose to disconnect Outlook from the active Internet connection if you want to work offline—for example, to stop sending and receiving messages while connected to the Internet.

The Send/Receive commands are the same in all modules

> **TIP** The Work Offline button is available for Internet accounts that download content to your computer, and for Exchange accounts when you specify that Outlook should use Cached Exchange Mode for the account connection.

- **Folder** Includes commands for creating and managing folders in which you can store messages, calendar items, contact records, notes, tasks, and other Outlook items, in addition to Search Folders in which you can display up-to-date collections of messages that meet specific criteria. You can manage the contents of a folder and recover inadvertently deleted items; add a folder to the Favorites list; view messages that have been archived to an Exchange server; and control archive settings, folder access permissions, and the folder properties.

Some commands on the Folder tab are common to all modules

> **TIP** Many of the Actions commands are available only when you select a custom folder (a folder that you create, rather than the folders created by Outlook).

- **View** Includes commands for changing the way items are displayed in the content area; displaying, hiding, or changing the location of app window panes; and opening or closing secondary app windows.

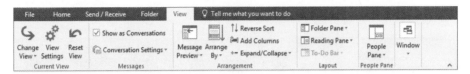

Views and view settings are specific to each module

Content area views

In the Mail module, the content area displays the message list. Messages that you haven't yet read are indicated in the message list by vertical blue lines on the left edge and bold blue header text. When you open a message, Outlook indicates that you have read it by removing the blue indicators and changing the header font in the message list from bold to normal.

There are three standard views of the message list:

- **Compact** This view displays two lines of message properties, including the read status, subject, sender, time received, whether files are attached to the message, and any color categories or follow-up flags associated with the message. This is the default view.

- **Single** This one-line view displays the importance, reminder, item type or read status, whether files are attached to the message, sender, subject, date received, size, category, and follow-up flags. The Reading Pane is open by default in this view.

- **Preview** This view displays the first 255 characters of each unread message, which might give you enough information to make a quick decision about whether to delete or open it, and the first line of each read message. The Reading Pane is closed by default in this view.

    Because more lines of each unread message are displayed, fewer messages are visible on your screen at one time than in the default Messages view.

Single view and Preview view are list views. When the content area width supports it, they display information in columns. You can add, remove, and resize columns in these views to display only the information you want.

Column headings

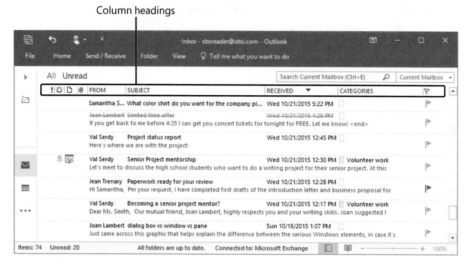

You can hide panes to make room for columnar list views

 SEE ALSO For more information about view features and read/unread messages, see "Display and manage conversations" in Chapter 6, "Organize your Inbox."

If you want to concentrate on reading messages without the distraction of other information typically presented in the Outlook app window, you can switch from Normal view to Reading view. Reading view maximizes the content area by minimizing the Folder Pane and closing the To-Do Bar, if it is open.

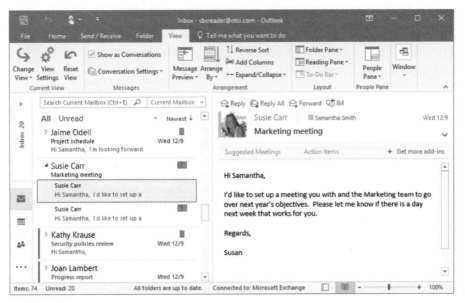

Reading view is available from the status bar, not from the View tab

Reading view does not affect the display of the ribbon. Any modifications you make to the display of elements in the Outlook app window while working in Reading view remain in effect in Normal view.

To display a different view of the Mail module

1. On the **View** tab, in the **Current View** group, click **Change View**, and then click **Compact**, **Single**, or **Preview**.

To add columns in a list view of any module

1. Right-click any column heading, and then click **Field Chooser** to display the floating Field Chooser pane.

2. If the field you want to add doesn't appear in the default **Frequently used fields** list, click the list, and then click any of the field categories.

3. Drag a field from the **Field Chooser** to the column heading area.

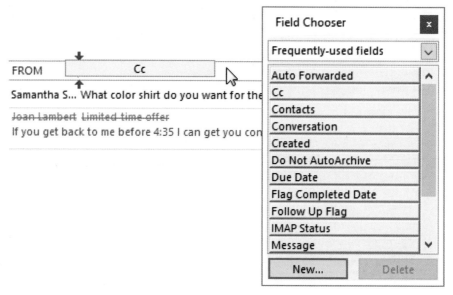

Add any field to the list view columns

4. When red arrows appear above and below a column break, release the mouse button to add the column in that location.

Or

1. On the **View** tab, in the **Arrangement** group, click **Add Columns** to open the Show Columns dialog box.

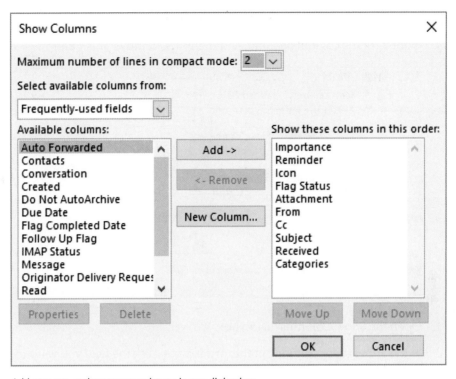

Add, remove, and rearrange columns in one dialog box

2. If the field you want to add isn't shown in the **Available columns** pane, expand the **Select available columns from** list, and then click any of the field categories.

3. Click any field in the **Available columns** pane, and then click **Add** to add it to the list view.

4. When you finish modifying columns, click **OK**.

To remove columns from a list view of any module

1. Right-click the column heading, and then click **Remove This Column**.

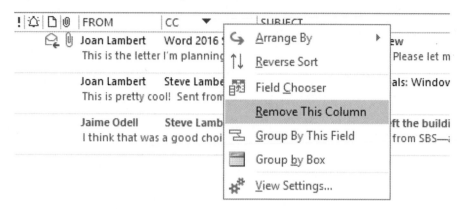

You can perform many actions from the shortcut menu

Or

1. Open the **Show Columns** dialog box.

2. In the **Show these columns in this order** pane, click the field you want to remove. Then click **Remove**.

3. When you finish modifying columns, click **OK**.

To reorder columns in a list view of any module

1. Drag the column heading to the left or right.

2. When red arrows appear above and below a column break, release the mouse button to move the column to that location.

Or

1. Open the **Show Columns** dialog box.

2. In the **Show these columns in this order** pane, click the field you want to move. Then click **Move Up** or **Move Down**.

3. When you finish modifying columns, click **OK**.

To display any module in Reading view

1. On the status bar, to the left of the Zoom Slider, click the **Reading** button.

2

Display conversations

Conversation view is a way of grouping a series of received messages that stem from the same original message. This feature makes it easy to locate current message responses and to identify separate branches of a conversation (referred to as *message threads*). The original Conversation view has been expanded to present an even clearer method of tracking message threads and to include not only received messages but also sent messages. Conversation view is a useful organizational tool that you can use to more easily manage all the information associated with a particular subject, but it is not turned on by default in Outlook 2016.

SEE ALSO For more information about Conversation view, see "Display and manage conversations" in Chapter 6, "Organize your Inbox."

Message windows

Outlook displays email messages (in addition to meeting requests and task assignments received from other Outlook users) in the Mail module. When you start Outlook, it displays the Inbox of your default email account. When you create a new message or open an existing message, it opens in a separate message window. The message window has its own ribbon and Quick Access Toolbar, separate from those in the Outlook app window (and from those in other types of item windows).

The layout of all message windows is similar; each has a title bar, Quick Access Toolbar, and ribbon. By default, all message windows have the same Quick Access Toolbar, featuring the Save, Undo, Redo/Repeat, Previous Item, and Next Item buttons. (The Previous Item and Next Item buttons are enabled only in message reading windows.) The Save command is also available in the Backstage view, but the other commands are available only from the Quick Access Toolbar.

On a touchscreen device, the Quick Access Toolbar also includes the Touch/Mouse Mode button that you can use to switch between the standard interface and a more touch-friendly interface.

You can customize the Quick Access Toolbar for message composition windows or for message reading windows.

 SEE ALSO For information about customizing the Quick Access Toolbar, see "Customize the Quick Access Toolbar" in Chapter 12, "Manage window elements."

The commands on the ribbon in an outgoing message window (a *message composition window*) differ from those in a received message window (a *message reading window*). In each case, the message window ribbon content is specific to the actions that you take when working in that window.

Message composition windows

In the message composition window, you can insert and format outgoing message content and modify the settings of outgoing messages.

Message header   Message body

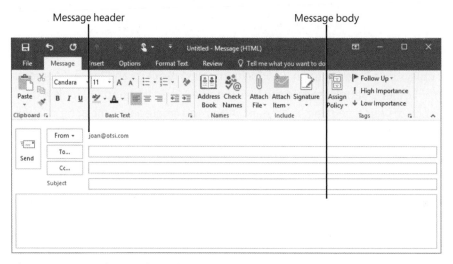

The message composition window ribbon includes tabs specific to content creation

The message composition window interface includes the following elements:

- **Ribbon** This includes the File tab (your link to the Backstage view) and the Message, Insert, Options, Format Text, and Review tabs.

- **Message header** This area includes the To and Cc address fields and the Subject field, by default. If you configure Outlook to connect to multiple accounts, a From field appears above the To field. You can click the From button to select the account from which you want to send the message. You can also display the Bcc field in the message header by clicking that button in the Show Fields group on the Options tab.

 SEE ALSO For information about the From field, see the sidebar "Send from a specific account" in Chapter 3, "Send and receive email messages."

- **Message body** This is the area in which you create message content. The message body can include text, images, tables, charts, screen clippings, hyperlinks, and other types of content. An email message created in Outlook 2016 can include virtually any element that you can insert into a standard electronic document, such as a Word document.

- **People pane** When turned on, this optional pane appears after you enter at least one message recipient. It displays information about the message recipients. Clicking a recipient's icon displays information about previous communications with that person.

 SEE ALSO For more information about the Bcc field, message header, message body, and People pane, see "Create and send messages" in Chapter 3, "Send and receive email messages."

Commands on the ribbon of a message composition window are organized on these five tabs:

- **Message** Includes a selection of the commands you are most likely to use when creating a new message, some of which are also available on other ribbon tabs. Specific to this tab are commands for inserting and validating email addresses, marking an outgoing message for follow-up, and indicating the importance of an outgoing message to the message recipient.

You can compose and send most messages by using the commands on the Message tab

- **Insert** Includes commands that are standard to all item-creation windows, for attaching items such as files and contact cards to the message, and for inserting specialized content such as email signatures, tables, images, links, and artistic text into the message body. In addition to the standard commands, the Insert Calendar command is available in the Include group on the Insert tab of the message composition window ribbon.

All command groups are active when the cursor is in the content pane

■ **Options** Includes commands that are specific to the message composition window, for applying thematic formatting to message content, displaying less-frequently used address fields in the message header, and setting specialized message delivery options.

The Options tab of the message composition window ribbon

■ **Format Text** Includes commands that are standard to all item-creation windows, for manipulating and formatting characters and paragraphs; applying and working with Quick Styles and style sets; finding, replacing, and selecting text and objects within a text box; and magnifying text. In addition to the standard commands, commands for changing the message format are available in the Format group on this tab.

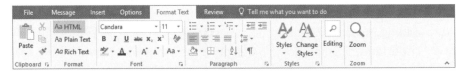

Additional formatting commands are available on the Format Text tab

> **SEE ALSO** For information about formatting fonts, using styles, inserting various types of illustrations, setting permissions, and tracking messages, see Chapter 4, "Enhance message content."

2

- **Review** Includes commands that are standard to all item-creation windows, for working with the text in the message body, including checking spelling and grammar; researching word choices; tracking message content statistics (pages, words, characters, paragraphs, and lines); and translating content either directly or through an online service.

The Review tab of the message composition window ribbon

The Insert, Format Text, and Review tabs appear in other item windows that contain rich text fields.

> ✅ **TIP** Other apps that you install on your computer might install tabs that appear on the ribbon in Outlook and other Office apps so that you can interact with the installed app from within Office. You can hide those tabs if you don't use them. For information about hiding ribbon tabs, see "Customize the ribbon" in Chapter 12, "Manage window elements."

Message reading windows

In the message reading window, you can take action with received messages.

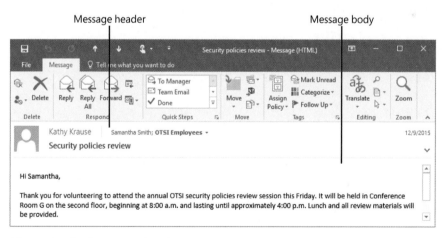

Message header elements are inactive

The message reading window interface includes the same elements as the message composition window, but the content differs:

- **Ribbon** Includes the File tab and a Message tab that contains a set of commands different from the commands on this tab in a message composition window. This tab includes commands for working with the active message, including deleting, responding to, moving, tagging, editing, and viewing it. The Message tab also includes the Quick Steps gallery of command combinations that you can use to accomplish multiple tasks with one click.

   SEE ALSO For information about Quick Steps, see "Manage messages by using Quick Steps" in Chapter 14, "Manage email automatically."

- **Message header** Displays the names and online status (if available) of the message sender and message recipients (those entered in the To and Cc boxes), along with the message subject and any message notifications, categories, or flags. Content in this area can't be edited.

- **Message body** Displays the content of the message and of any subsequent responses.

Draft responses in the Reading Pane

When you respond to an existing message from within the Reading Pane, the response message is drafted within the Reading Pane, and a Message tool tab that contains a limited selection of commands appears on the Mail module ribbon. You can draft and send the response from the Reading Pane, or if you'd prefer to work with it in a separate window with a full set of commands, you can open the draft in its own window.

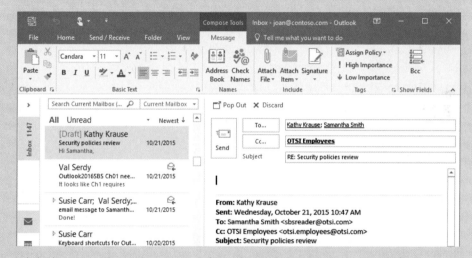

A hybrid Message tab provides commands for working with the response message draft

If you need to use commands that aren't available on the Message tool tab, click Pop Out in the upper-left corner of the Reading Pane to move the message draft from the Reading Pane to a message composition window.

SEE ALSO For information about changing the way Outlook handles new and original messages when you reply to or forward a message, see "Configure message options" in Chapter 13, "Customize Outlook options."

The Backstage view of a message

When opened from a message composition window, the Backstage view includes commands related to managing the outgoing message, such as saving, moving, printing, or closing the draft, restricting the actions that recipients can take, and displaying message properties. Some of these commands are also available on the Options tab of the message composition window.

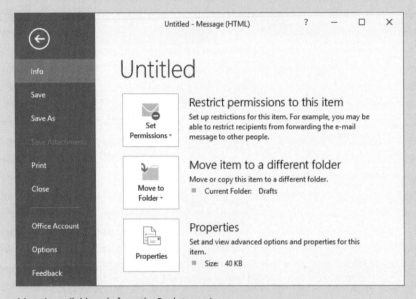

Move is available only from the Backstage view

The Backstage view also includes access to your Office Account (discussed in Chapter 1, "Outlook 2016 basics"), and the Outlook Options dialog box (discussed in Chapter 13, "Customize Outlook options").

When opened from a message reading window, the Backstage view also includes commands for displaying a delivery report, resending the message as a new message, and recalling the message from the recipients. Only the message sender can recall a message.

Work in the Calendar module

In the Calendar module, the Folder Pane displays the Date Navigator and a list of the calendars that you have connected to Outlook. The list might include only the calendar of your default email account, or it might include custom calendars you create, calendars that are shared with you by other Outlook users, and Internet Calendars or SharePoint Calendars that you connect to.

The Calendar module in Month view, with the ribbon closed

The content area displays appointments, meetings, and events that you've added to the calendar, for a period of time that you select. The default time period is one month; however, you will frequently find it more useful to display only a day or a week at a time, to have a closer look at your activities for those time periods. You can display a single day, your specified work week, a seven-day period, a month, or a schedule view that shows a close-up view of a short time period.

 SEE ALSO For information about Calendar module views, see "Display different views of a calendar" in Chapter 9, "Manage scheduling."

Ribbon tabs

The ribbon in the Calendar module includes the File tab and the four standard module tabs: Home, Send/Receive, Folder, and View.

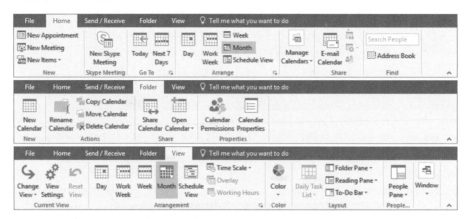

The ribbon includes commands that are specific to the Calendar module

Commands that are relevant to calendar items are displayed on the following tabs:

- **Home** Includes the commands you need for creating calendar items, displaying specific views of the calendar, managing other calendars and calendar groups, and sharing the calendar with other people.

> **TIP** The Home tab includes the Skype Meeting group only if Microsoft Skype for Business is part of your organization's collaboration environment. Skype provides the capability not only to commence real-time text, audio, video, and collaboration sessions with other people in your organization, but also to invite internal and external attendees to online meetings.

- **Folder** Includes commands for creating and working with calendars. From this tab, you can create a new calendar, manipulate an existing calendar, share a calendar with other Outlook users and specify what each user can do with the shared calendar, open a calendar that you're not currently connected to, and control the behind-the-scenes behavior of a calendar.

> **TIP** From a structural point of view, a calendar is simply a folder that contains calendar items. When you specify that a folder is of the Calendar type, that folder is subject to the display options allocated to calendars and is managed with other calendars. For information about creating calendars, see "Work with multiple calendars" in Chapter 10, "Manage your calendar."

- **View** Includes commands for viewing and arranging calendar items, changing the layout and appearance of the Calendar module, displaying missed reminders, opening multiple calendars in separate windows, and closing open calendar item windows.

The Send/Receive tab content is the same in all modules.

> 🔍 **SEE ALSO** For information about calendar views, see "Display different views of a calendar" in Chapter 9, "Manage scheduling." For information about changing default settings for the Calendar module, see "Configure calendar options" in Chapter 13, "Customize Outlook options."

Calendar item windows

A window in which you create an appointment is an appointment window, one in which you create or respond to a meeting request is a meeting window, and one in which you create an event is an event window; collectively, these are *calendar item windows*. Like the message windows, the calendar item windows each contain relevant commands arranged on the ribbon.

Each calendar item window includes two pages. The primary page is the Appointment page. You can set up an appointment by using only the commands on this page.

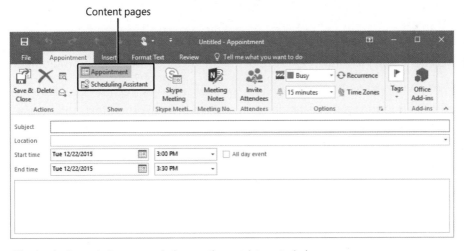

All calendar item windows are variations on the appointment window

The second page is the Scheduling Assistant page (for an Exchange account) or the Scheduling page (for other account types). On this page, you can view the schedules of people and resources in your organization who you want to invite to a meeting or event. You can visually locate a time when attendees are available, or Outlook will suggest times based on the attendees' calendars.

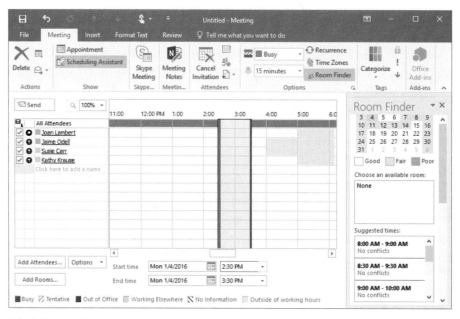

Scheduling people in an appointment window creates a meeting

The calendar item window interface includes the Quick Access Toolbar, the ribbon, and the content area that displays the appointment, message, or event information.

Commands on the ribbon of a calendar item window are organized on four tabs: a main tab specific to the type of calendar item and the Insert, Format Text, and Review tabs. The latter three tabs are identical to those of other item windows.

The commands you use to create and manage calendar items are available on the main tab. The tab name is Appointment, Meeting, Event, or a variation on one of those, depending on the type of item you're creating and whether it's a series. Regardless of the tab name, commands are organized on the tab in six groups: Actions, Show, Attendees, Options, Tags, and Add-ins. The tab includes groups for Microsoft Skype for Business and Microsoft OneNote if these apps are installed on your computer; you can use the commands in these groups to facilitate the relationship between Outlook calendar items and those apps.

> **SEE ALSO** For information about creating appointments, meetings, and events, see "Schedule appointments and events" and "Schedule and change meetings" in Chapter 9, "Manage scheduling."

Work in the People module

In the People module, the Folder Pane displays your available address books—the Contacts address book, any custom address books you create, address books shared with you by co-workers, and address books containing contacts from social networks that you connect to. The content area includes the contact list and, in some views, the Reading Pane.

Contact index

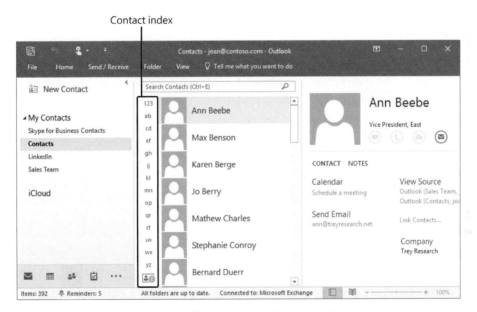

The default view of the People module displays contact information in People cards

> **TIP** Clicking a letter or letter pairing on the contact index scrolls the Contacts pane to display contact records that begin with that letter. You can add a second contact index that displays the Arabic, Cyrillic, Greek, Thai, or Vietnamese alphabet by clicking the button at the bottom of the contact index and then clicking the language you want.

The content area of the People module displays the contact records saved in the currently selected address book. The default view of contact records in Outlook 2016 is a format named People cards, but you can choose from several standard views, including business cards, text-only cards, and various lists.

 SEE ALSO For more information about contact record views, see "Display different views of contact records" in Chapter 7, "Store and access contact information."

TIP In earlier versions of Outlook, the People module was named the Contacts module. Remnants of the previous naming convention can be found throughout the app. In this book, I frequently refer to people whose contact information you have stored in Outlook as *contacts*. I assure you, however, that contacts are people too!

Ribbon tabs

The ribbon in the People module includes the File tab and the four standard module tabs: Home, Send/Receive, Folder, and View. The Home tab includes the commands you need for creating, managing, and viewing contact records, and for initiating communication with contacts. You can select contacts for a mail-merge process, send contact information to OneNote, share contacts with other Outlook users, and tag contact records in ways that enable you to better locate or manage them.

Commands for managing contact records and groups

The Send/Receive, Folder, and View tabs include the standard functionality as in the other modules. On the View tab, the Arrangement gallery includes fields that are specific to contact records.

Arrangements are available in the Phone and List views

2

Contact record windows

When you create a contact record or display the contact record for a person or group of people, the record opens in a contact record window. The contact record window has its own ribbon and Quick Access Toolbar, separate from those in the Outlook app window and other types of item windows. You can insert, format, and work with information in a contact record or contact group record by using the commands on the contact record window ribbon.

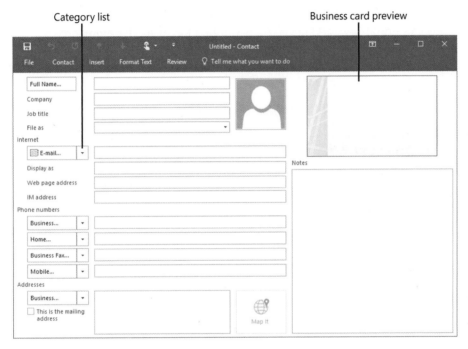

A blank contact record

> ✓ **TIP** You save information in a field by entering it into the corresponding text box. Outlook saves the information you enter as data attached to the item, and uses it in various ways. Some types of fields have special rules attached that affect the appearance of the data in the field. For example, phone number fields in contact records automatically format the numbers you enter to match a standard (123) 456-7890 format.

The contact record window interface includes the Quick Access Toolbar, the ribbon, and the optional People Pane, in addition to the content area that displays the contact record information.

When opened from a contact record window, the Backstage view includes commands related to managing contact records, such as saving contact records and contact record attachments and closing, moving, and printing contact records.

> **TIP** The commands available in the Backstage view of a contact record window are identical to those in the Backstage view of an appointment window. For more information, see "Work in the Calendar module" earlier in this chapter.

Commands on the ribbon of a contact record window are organized on four tabs: Contact, Insert, Format Text, and Review. The Contact tab includes commands that are specific to managing and working with contact records.

Content pages

Manage contact records from the Contact tab

Commands include those for managing the contact record, switching among the contact record pages, communicating with the contact, accessing and verifying saved contact information, and personalizing a contact's electronic business card. This tab also includes commands for assigning a category or follow-up flag to a contact record, preventing other Outlook users from viewing the contact record when connected to your account, and changing the magnification level of the notes pane within the contact record window.

The Insert, Format Text, and Review tabs include the same standard commands as those in a message composition window. Most of the commands apply only to the content of the notes pane.

> **SEE ALSO** For information about creating contact records, see Chapter 7, "Store and access contact information."

Work in the Tasks module

In the Tasks module, the Folder Pane displays the two built-in task list views: the default To-Do List view and the Tasks view. (These views are represented as folders although both display different views of the same tasks, much like a Search Folder.) It also contains any custom task folders you create. The content area displays the selected view of the tasks.

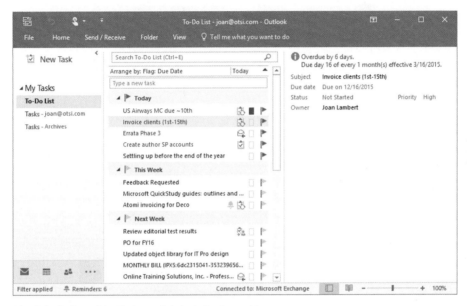

The default view of the Tasks module includes flagged items

To-Do List view displays tasks organized by default in groups by due date (you can reorder the tasks any way you want), and the Reading Pane, in which you can preview the details of any selected task. This is the default view.

Tasks view displays a list of task details in columns. Each task is preceded by a check box so that you can easily indicate when the task is complete. The Reading Pane is hidden by default, so you must open a task item (or display the Reading Pane) to display additional details.

> ✓ **TIP** In addition to these standard views, you can display tasks filtered and organized in many other ways, by selecting a view from the Change View gallery. For more information, see "Display different views of tasks" in Chapter 11, "Track tasks."

Ribbon tabs

The ribbon in the Tasks module includes the File tab and the four standard module tabs: Home, Send/Receive, Folder, and View. The Home tab includes the commands you need for creating, managing, and viewing tasks. You can assign tasks to co-workers and work with tasks assigned to you, send task information to a OneNote notebook, and tag tasks in ways that enable you to better locate or manage them.

Commands for managing tasks

The Send/Receive, Folder, and View tabs include the standard functionality as in the other modules. On the View tab, the Arrangement gallery includes fields that are specific to tasks.

Task windows

The window in which you create or manage a task is a task window. Like the message, contact record, and calendar item windows, the task window includes the Quick Access Toolbar, a unique set of commands arranged on the ribbon, and the content area that displays the task information.

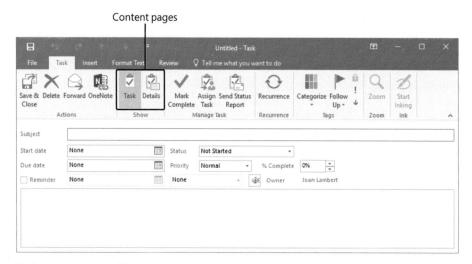

Task windows have multiple content pages

Commands on the ribbon of a task window are organized on four tabs: Task, Insert, Format Text, and Review. The commands you use to create and manage most tasks are available on the Task tab. Commands include those for managing and assigning the task, sending the task to a OneNote notebook, and switching among the task pages. This tab also includes commands for assigning a category or follow-up flag to a task, preventing other Outlook users from viewing the task details when connected to your account, and changing the magnification level of the notes pane (not of the task window).

The Insert, Format Text, and Review tabs are identical to those of other item windows. The commands for inserting, modifying, and formatting elements apply only to content in the notes pane of the Task window.

Skills review

In this chapter, you learned how to:

- Work in the Outlook app window
- Work in the Mail module
- Work in the Calendar module
- Work in the People module
- Work in the Tasks module

Practice tasks

No practice files are necessary to complete the practice tasks in this chapter.

Explore Outlook modules

Start Outlook, display your Inbox, and then perform the following tasks:

1. In the Mail module, display the **Folders** list in the **Folder Pane**.

2. Notice the folders that are available to you in the Folders list that aren't available in the standard Folder Pane.

3. Return to the standard Mail module Folder Pane.

4. Add a folder from the **Folder Pane** to the **Favorites** list.

5. Display the Mail module in Reading view. Consider the advantages and disadvantages of this view.

6. Display the Calendar module.

7. Notice the information that is available in the default view of the Calendar module. Then display each of the other built-in module views.

8. In a list view of the Calendar module, do the following:

   - Remove a column that doesn't contain information.

   - Add a column that wasn't previously in the view.

   - Change the order of the columns.

9. Review the commands on the **Home** tab, and note those that are unique to the Calendar module.

10. For the People and Tasks modules, do the following:

    - Display the module.

    - Notice the information that is available in the default view of the module. Then display each of the other built-in module views, and consider when each view would be most useful.

    - Review the commands on the **Home** tab, and note those that are unique to the module.

Part 2

Manage email messages

Send and receive email messages

Although Microsoft Outlook 2016 is an excellent tool for managing your schedule, contact records, and task lists, the primary reason most people use Outlook is to send and receive email messages. Over the past decade, email has become an important method of communication for both business and personal purposes. Outlook provides all the tools you need to send, respond to, organize, find, filter, sort, and otherwise manage email messages for one or more email accounts.

When creating email messages in Outlook, you can format the text, include images, attach files, and set message options such as voting buttons, importance, sensitivity, reminders, and message receipts.

Outlook has many features that make it easy to display and track information about the people you correspond with, particularly if your organization uses technologies that interact with Outlook such as Microsoft Exchange, SharePoint, and Skype for Business. These features include presence icons that indicate whether a person is online and available, and information cards that provide a convenient starting point for many kinds of contact.

This chapter guides you through procedures related to creating, sending, and displaying messages and message attachments; displaying message participant information; and responding to messages.

In this chapter

- Create and send messages
- Attach files and Outlook items to messages
- Display messages and message attachments
- Display message participant information
- Respond to messages

Practice files

For this chapter, use the practice file from the Outlook2016SBS\Ch03 folder. For practice file download instructions, see the introduction.

71

Create and send messages

If you have an Internet connection, you can send email messages to people within your organization and around the world by using Outlook, regardless of the type of email account you have. Outlook can send and receive email messages in three message formats:

- **HTML** Supports paragraph styles (including numbered and bulleted lists), character styles (such as fonts, sizes, colors, weight), and backgrounds (such as colors and pictures). Most (but not all) email programs support the HTML format. Programs that don't support HTML display these messages as Plain Text.

- **Rich Text** Supports more paragraph formatting options than HTML, including borders and shading, but is compatible only with Outlook and Exchange Server. Outlook converts Rich Text messages to HTML when sending them outside of an Exchange network.

- **Plain Text** Does not support the formatting features available in HTML and Rich Text messages, but is supported by all email programs.

Email message content isn't limited to simple text. You can create almost any type of content in an email message that you can in a Microsoft Word document. Because Outlook 2016 and Word 2016 share similar commands, you might already be familiar with many processes for formatting content.

You can personalize your messages by using an individual font style or color and add a professional touch by inserting your contact information in the form of an email signature. (You can apply other formatting, such as themes and page backgrounds, but these won't always appear to email recipients as you intend them to, and they can make your communications appear less professional.)

> **TIP** You can specify different email signatures for new messages and for replies and forwarded messages. For example, you might want to include your full name and contact information in the signature that appears in new messages, but only your first name in the signature that appears in replies and forwarded messages. For more information, see "Create and use automatic signatures" in Chapter 4, "Enhance message content."

You can format the text of your message to make it more readable by including headings, lists, or tables, and you can represent information graphically by including charts, pictures, and other types of graphics. You can attach files to your message and link to other information, such as files or webpages.

> **SEE ALSO** For information about attaching files and other content to email messages, see "Attach files and Outlook items to messages" later in this chapter.

For the purposes of this book, I assume that you know how to enter, edit, and format content by using standard Word techniques, so I don't discuss all of them in this book.

> **SEE ALSO** For extensive information about entering and editing content and about formatting content by using character and paragraph styles, Quick Styles, and themes, refer to *Microsoft Word 2016 Step by Step*, by Joan Lambert (Microsoft Press, 2015).

Creating an email message is a relatively simple process. You will usually provide information in the following fields:

- **To** Enter the email address of the primary message recipient(s) in this field. This is the only field that is absolutely required to send a message.

- **Subject** Enter a brief description of the message contents or purpose in this field. The subject is not required, but it is important to provide information in this field, both so that you and the recipient can identify the message and so that the message isn't blocked as suspected junk mail by a recipient's email program. Outlook will warn you if you try to send a message with no subject.

- **Message body** Enter your message to the recipient in this field, which is a large text box. You can include many types of information, including formatted text, hyperlinks, and graphics in the message body.

> 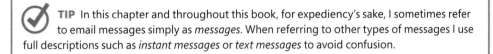 **TIP** In this chapter and throughout this book, for expediency's sake, I sometimes refer to email messages simply as *messages*. When referring to other types of messages I use full descriptions such as *instant messages* or *text messages* to avoid confusion.

Create messages

Addressing an email message is easy: just insert the intended recipient's email address (or name, if he or she is in your address book) into an address box in the message header of a message composition window.

You can enter email recipients into any of three address boxes:

- **To** Use for primary message recipients. Usually, these are the people you want to respond to the message. Each message must have at least one address in the To box.

- **Cc** Use for "courtesy copy" recipients. These are usually people you want to keep informed about the subject of the email message but from whom you don't require a response.

- **Bcc** Use for "blind courtesy copy" recipients. These are people you want to keep informed, but whom you want to keep hidden from other message recipients. Bcc recipients are not visible to any other message recipients and therefore aren't included in message responses unless specifically added to one of the address boxes in the response message.

The To and Cc address boxes are always displayed in the message header. The Bcc address box is not displayed by default. You can display it in the message header by clicking the Bcc button, located in the Show Fields group on the Options tab of the message composition window.

 TIP Replying to or forwarding a received message automatically fills in one or more of the address boxes in the new message window. For information, see "Respond to messages" later in this chapter.

If your email account is part of a Microsoft Exchange network, you can send messages to another person on the same network by entering only his or her email alias—for example, *joan*; the at symbol (@) and domain name aren't required. If you enter only the name of a person whose email address is in your address book, Outlook associates the name with the corresponding email address, a process called *resolving the address*, before sending the message.

 TIP Press Ctrl+K to initiate address resolution. For more information about keyboard shortcuts, see Appendix B, "Keyboard shortcuts."

Depending on the method you use to enter a message recipient's name or email address into an address box, Outlook either resolves the name or address immediately (if you chose it from a list of known names) or resolves it when you send the message.

The resolution process for each name or address has one of two results:

- If Outlook successfully resolves the name or address, an underline appears below it. If the name or address matches one stored in an address book, Outlook replaces your original entry with the content of the Display As field in the contact record, and then underlines it.

> **SEE ALSO** For information about contact record fields, see "Save and update contact information" in Chapter 7, "Store and access contact information."

- If Outlook is unable to resolve the name or address, the Check Names dialog box opens, asking you to select the address you want to use.

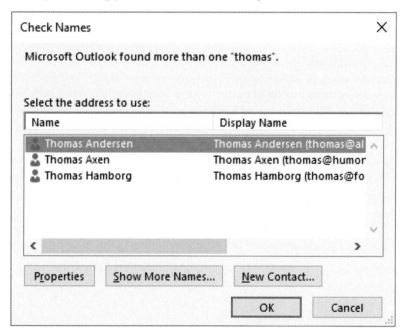

The Check Names dialog box might display No Suggestions, names that match the entry, or saved contact options

In the Check Names dialog box, you can select from the suggested options, or do any of the following:

- Click **Properties** to learn more about the selected option.
- Click **Show More Names** to display your default address book.
- Click **New Contact** to create a new contact record in your default address book, directly from the dialog box.

To open an email message composition window

1. Do either of the following:

   - In any module, on the **Home** tab, in the **New** group, click the **New Items** button, and then click **E-mail Message**.

   - In the Mail module, on the **Home** tab, in the **New** group, click the **New Email** button.

To enter an email address into an address box

1. In the message composition window, click in the **To**, **Cc**, or **Bcc** box, and then do any of the following:

   - Enter the entire address.

   - Enter part of a previously used address and then select the address from the **Auto-Complete List** that appears.

   - Click the address box label to display the Select Names dialog box, in which you can select one or more addresses from your address book(s).

   > **SEE ALSO** For information about the Auto-Complete List, see "Troubleshoot message addressing" later in this topic. For information about address books, see "Save and update contact information" in Chapter 7, "Store and access contact information."

To enter a subject for an email message

1. In the message composition window, in the **Subject** box, enter the subject of the email message.

To enter content for an email message

1. In the message composition window, in the message body field, enter the content of the email message.

To format the content of an email message

1. In the message composition window, in the message body field, select the content you want to format.

2. Apply basic font and paragraph formatting from the **Mini Toolbar** that appears when you select the content, or from the **Basic Text** group on the **Message** tab.

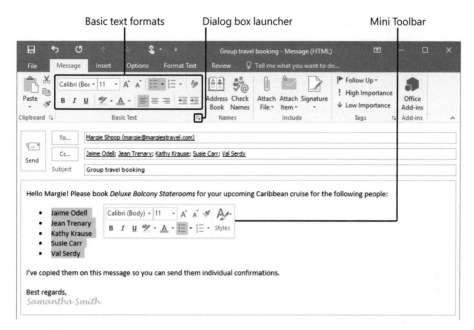

You can format message content in the message composition window just as you can in Word

Or

Do any of the following:

- Apply an extended range of font and paragraph formats from the **Format Text** tab.

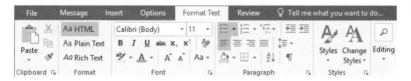

The Format Text tab provides additional font and paragraph formatting options

- On the **Message** tab, click the **Basic Text** dialog box launcher, or on the **Format Text** tab, click the **Font** dialog box launcher to open the Font dialog box. Apply the full range of font formatting, including character spacing, from this dialog box.

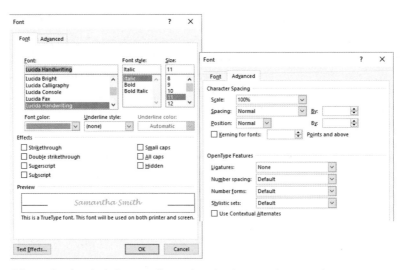

Advanced options include expanding and condensing space between characters

Troubleshoot message addressing

Outlook 2016 includes many features intended to simplify the process of addressing messages to recipients. As with any tool, these features can sometimes be more difficult to use than you'd like. In this topic, I discuss troubleshooting tips for some common problems.

Troubleshoot the Auto-Complete List

As you enter a name or an email address into the To, Cc, or Bcc box, Outlook displays matching addresses in a list. You can insert a name or address from the list into the address box by clicking it or by pressing the arrow keys to select it and then pressing Tab or Enter.

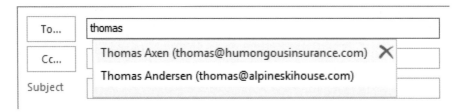

You can insert a recipient for the message from the Auto-Complete List

Sometimes the Auto-Complete List might contain incorrect or outdated addresses—for example, if you have previously sent a message to an incorrect email address, or if a person changes his or her email address. The list might also contain people with whom you no longer correspond. If you don't remove incorrect or outdated addresses from the list, it can be easy to mistakenly accept Outlook's suggestion and send a message to the wrong address.

You can modify the Auto-Complete List settings in the Outlook Options dialog box.

Troubleshoot address lists

When resolving email addresses, Outlook first searches your Global Address List (the corporate directory provided with an Exchange account, if you're working with one), and then searches the contact records stored in the People module of your default account.

If you have multiple address lists, such as those in custom contact folders that you create or associated with additional email accounts that are configured in Outlook, you can specify the order in which Outlook searches for names and addresses, or you can exclude an address list from the search if you don't want to accidentally resolve to an email address from that list.

Troubleshoot multiple recipients

By default, Outlook requires that you separate multiple email addresses with semi-colons. If you separate multiple addresses by pressing the spacebar or the Enter key, Outlook replaces the space or return with a semicolon before sending the message. If you separate multiple addresses by using a comma (which might seem to be the more natural action), Outlook treats the addresses as one address and displays an error message when you try to send the message.

You can instruct Outlook to accept commas as address separators in the Outlook Options dialog box.

 SEE ALSO For more information, see "Configure message options" in Chapter 13, "Customize Outlook options."

To remove a name or email address from the Auto-Complete List

1. In the **To**, **Cc**, or **Bcc** box, enter the first letter or letters of a name or email address to display the Auto-Complete List of matching names and addresses.

2. In the list, point to the name or address you want to remove.

3. Click the **Delete** button (the X) that appears to the right of the name or address.

To open the Outlook Options dialog box

1. In any module, click the **File** tab to display the Backstage view, and then click **Options**.

To change the Auto-Complete List settings

1. Open the **Outlook Options** dialog box, and then click the **Mail** tab.

2. On the **Mail** page, scroll to the **Send messages** section.

3. Do any of the following:

   - To prevent the Auto-Complete List from appearing when you enter an address, clear the **Use Auto-Complete List to suggest names...** check box.

   - To remove all entries from the Auto-Complete List (and start the list from scratch) click the **Empty Auto-Complete List** button, and then click **Yes** in the dialog box that appears.

4. Click **OK** to apply the changes and close the dialog box.

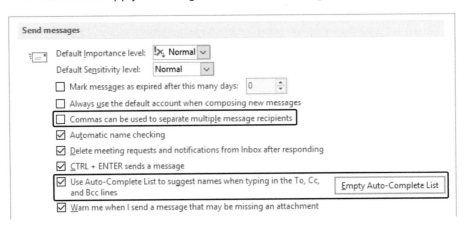

You can customize how Outlook resolves addresses

To use commas as a separator between email addresses

1. Open the **Outlook Options** dialog box, and then click the **Mail** tab.

2. On the **Mail** page, scroll to the **Send messages** section.

3. Select the **Commas can be used to separate multiple message recipients** check box.

4. Click **OK** to apply the changes and close the dialog box.

To change the order in which Outlook searches the address books

1. On the **Home** tab of any module, in the **Find** group, click **Address Book** to open the Address Book displaying your default address list.

2. In the **Address Book** window, on the **Tools** menu, click **Options**.

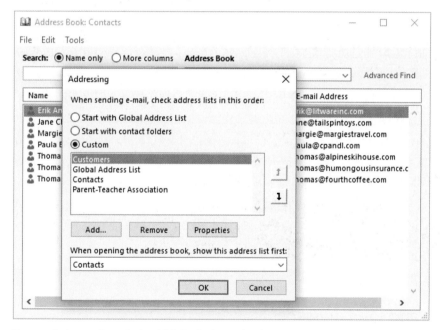

You can designate the order in which Outlook searches for contacts in existing address books

3. In the **Addressing** dialog box, do one of the following:

- Click **Start with Global Address List** to have Outlook search first in your default Exchange account directory.

- Click **Start with contact folders** to have Outlook search first in the contact records in the People module of your default account.

- Click **Custom**, and then reorder address lists by clicking the list and then clicking the **Move Up** or **Move Down** button, to specify a custom search order.

4. In the **Addressing** dialog box, click **OK**. Then close the **Address Book** window.

To modify the address lists that Outlook searches

1. On the **Home** tab of any module, in the **Find** group, click **Address Book**.

2. In the **Address Book** window, on the **Tools** menu, click **Options**.

3. In the **Addressing** dialog box, click **Custom** to activate the buttons below the list. Then do any of the following:

- To search additional address lists, click **Add**. In the **Add Address List** dialog box, click the address list you want to add, click **Add**, and then click **Close**.

- To prevent Outlook from searching an address list, click the address list, and then click **Remove**.

- If you're uncertain of the source of an address list, click the address list, and then click **Properties** to display the server address or account name and folder name of the address list.

4. In the **Addressing** dialog box, click **OK**. Then close the **Address Book** window.

Save and send messages

At regular intervals while you're composing a message (every three minutes, by default), Outlook saves a copy of the message in the Drafts folder. This is intended to protect you from losing messages that are in progress. If you close a message that hasn't yet had a draft saved, Outlook gives you the option of saving one. You can manually save a message draft at any time, and you can resume working on it later, either in its own window or directly in the Reading Pane. When you save a draft, the number in the unread message counter to the right of the Drafts folder in the Folder Pane increases. If the draft is in response to a received message, [Draft] appears in the message header of the received message.

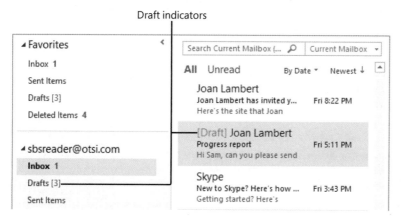

Locate a message draft in the Drafts folder or message list

When you send a message, Outlook deletes the message draft, if one exists, and moves the message temporarily to the Outbox. After successfully transmitting the message, Outlook moves it from the Outbox to the Sent Items folder. If a connectivity issue prevents Outlook from transmitting the message, it remains in your Outbox.

> **TIP** Each account you access from Outlook has its own Drafts folder and its own Sent Items folder. Outlook automatically saves draft messages and sent messages in the folders associated with the email account in which you compose or send the message. You can change the location in which Outlook saves message drafts from the Mail page of the Outlook Options dialog box. For more information, see "Configure message options" in Chapter 13, "Customize Outlook options."

Send from a specific account

If you have configured Outlook to connect to multiple email accounts, a From button appears in the header area of the message composition window. The active account appears to the right of the From button.

By default, Outlook assumes that you intend to send a message from the account you're currently working in. If you begin composing a message while viewing the Inbox of your work account, for example, Outlook selects the work account as the message-sending account. If you reply to a message received by your personal account, Outlook selects the personal account as the message-sending account.

To change the active account when you're composing a message, click the From button, and then click the account from which you want to send the message.

The From list displays all types of email accounts

TIP If Outlook is configured to connect to only one account, you can display the From button by clicking From in the Show Fields group on the Options tab of a message composition window.

If you have permission to send messages from an account that you haven't configured in Outlook—for example, a generic Customer Service email account for your company—you can click Other E-mail Address in the From list, enter the email address you want to send the message from, and click OK.

Clicking the From button displays the Address Book window in which you can choose a sending address

To save a draft of an email message

1. In the message composition window, do either of the following to save a draft without closing the message:

   - On the **Quick Access Toolbar**, click the **Save** button.

   - Press **Ctrl+S**.

Or

1. At the right end of the title bar, click the **Close** button.

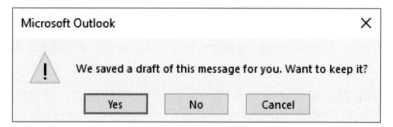

If you close a message before sending it, Outlook prompts you to save a draft

2. In the **Microsoft Outlook** message box, click **Yes** to save a draft and close the message window.

To change how often Outlook automatically saves email message drafts

1. Open the **Outlook Options** dialog box, and then click the **Mail** tab.

2. On the **Mail** page, scroll to the **Save messages** section.

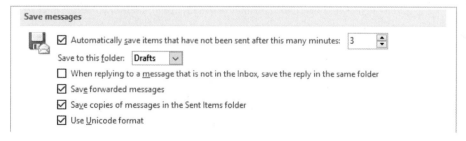

You can customize how often and where Outlook saves message drafts

3. Do either of the following:

- To save drafts more or less often, in the **Automatically save items that have not been sent after this many minutes** box, enter or select the number of minutes.

- To turn off the automatic saving of message drafts, clear the **Automatically save items that have not been sent after this many minutes** check box.

4. Click **OK** to apply the changes and close the dialog box.

To modify an email message draft

1. Do either of the following in the Mail module to display the message draft in the Reading Pane:

- In the **Folder Pane**, click the **Drafts** folder, and then click the message you want to continue composing.

- If the draft is a response, right-click the received message in the **Inbox**, click **Find Related**, and then click **Messages in this Conversation**. Then click the message draft in the search results.

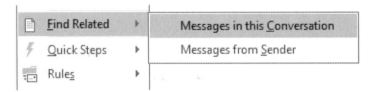

You can find messages that are related to the selected message by conversation or sender

 TIP If you have a lot of message drafts in your Drafts folder, this can be the simplest method of locating a specific draft.

When you click the message in either message list, the message becomes active for editing in the Reading Pane, and a Message tool tab appears on the ribbon.

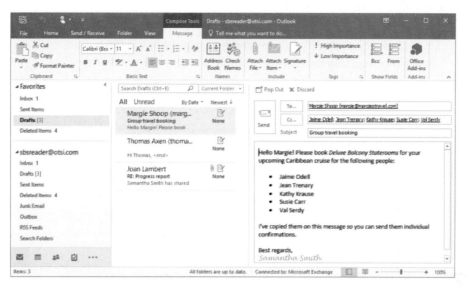

You can edit message drafts directly in the Reading Pane

2. Do any of the following:

   - Edit the message in the **Reading Pane**. The Message tool tab contains the most frequently used commands from the message composition window ribbon.

   - In the upper-left corner of the **Reading Pane**, click the **Pop Out** button to open the message in a message composition window (with the full ribbon).

   - In the message list, double-click the message header to open the message in a message composition window.

3. After you edit the message, you can send it or close it. If you close the message, it remains in the Drafts folder.

To send an email message

1. In the message composition window, do either of the following:

   - In the message header, click the **Send** button.

   - Press **Ctrl+Enter**. (The first time you press this key combination, Outlook asks whether you want to designate this as the keyboard shortcut for sending messages.)

2. The message window closes and the message is sent. If the message was saved in the Drafts folder, sending it removes it from the Drafts folder.

To verify that an email message was sent

1. In the **Folder Pane** of the Mail module, click the **Sent Items** folder to verify that the message is in the folder.

2. If the message is not in the Sent Items folder, check the **Outbox** folder.

> **TIP** If you want to send personalized copies of the same email message to several people, you can use the mail merge feature of Word 2016. For more information, refer to *Microsoft Word 2016 Step by Step*, by Joan Lambert (Microsoft Press, 2015).

Attach files and Outlook items to messages

A convenient way to distribute a file (such as a Microsoft PowerPoint presentation, Excel workbook, Word document, or picture) is by attaching the file to an email message. Message recipients can preview or open the file from the Reading Pane, open it from the message window, forward it to other people, or save it to their computers.

When Outlook is set to your default email app, you can email files by using several different methods:

- **From Outlook** You can create a message, and then attach the file to the message. If the file you attach is stored in a shared location such as a OneDrive folder or SharePoint library, you have the option of sending a link rather than a copy of the file.

- **From an Office app** You can send a document from Word, a workbook from Excel, or a presentation from PowerPoint while you're working in the file. You have the option of sending a copy of the file as a message attachment or, if the file is stored in a shared location, you can send a link to the file.

- **From File Explorer** You can send any file as an attachment directly from File Explorer. When sending pictures from File Explorer, you have the option of resizing the pictures to reduce the file size.

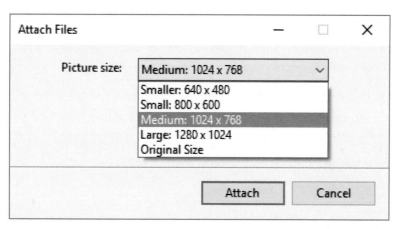

The picture size options are always the same, so they might be larger or smaller than your original picture

After you attach a file to an email message by using any of these methods, and before you send the message, you can modify or remove the attachments. When you attach files that are from shared locations, a cloud symbol on the file icon indicates that the attachment is a link, rather than a copy of the file. If you want to send a copy of the online file, you can easily do so.

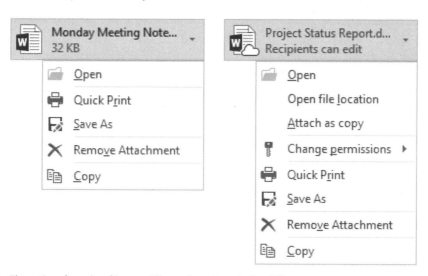

The options for online files are different from those for local files

In addition to sending files, you can send Outlook items, such as email messages or contact records.

To attach a file to an outgoing email message

1. In the message composition window, do either of the following to display the Attach File menu:

   - On the **Message** tab, in the **Include** group, click the **Attach File** button.

   - On the **Insert** tab, in the **Include** group, click the **Attach File** button.

   The Attach File menu includes a list of files you've worked with recently, and that are stored in locations Outlook can connect to.

Cloud overlays indicate files that are stored online

2. On the **Attach File** menu, do any of the following:

- If the file you want to attach is in the list, click the file.

- At the bottom of the **Insert File** menu, click **Browse Web Locations**, and then click a connected online storage location to open the Insert File dialog box displaying the storage structure of that location. Browse to the file you want to attach, select it, and then click **Insert**.

- At the bottom of the **Insert File** menu, click **Browse This PC** to open the Insert File dialog box displaying your local storage structure. Browse to the file you want to attach, select it, and then click **Insert**.

The attached file or files appear at the bottom of the message header. If the file that you attached is stored online, the file icon includes a cloud.

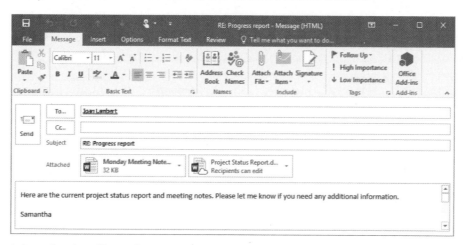

Information about file attachments is visible to the sender and to the recipient

To create an email message with an attachment from within an Office file

1. In the document, workbook, or presentation, click the **File** tab to display the Backstage view.

2. On the **Share** page of the Backstage view, click **Email** to display the email options.

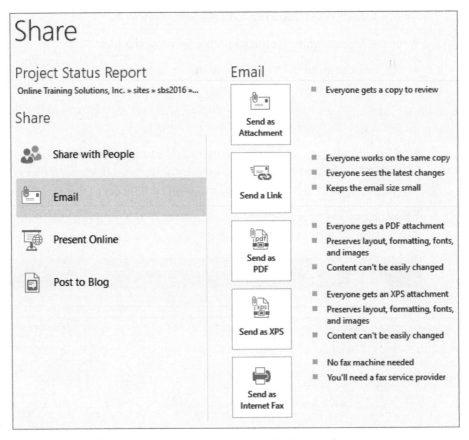

You can share an Office document as an attachment to an Outlook email message

3. In the **Email** pane, click **Send As Attachment**, **Send a Link**, **Send as PDF**, or **Send as XPS** to create an email message and attach the specified version of the file.

> **TIP** If you have an account with a fax service provider that permits the transmission of fax messages by email, you can click the Send As Internet Fax option and provide the fax number to address the message in the format required by the fax service. For example, if your fax service provider is Contoso and the fax number is (425)555-0199, the email might be addressed to 14255551212@contoso.com. The fax service relays the message electronically to the recipient's fax number.

To create an email message with an attachment from File Explorer

1. Select the file or files you want to send.

2. Right-click the selected file or files you want to email, click **Send to**, and then click **Mail recipient**.

3. If the files are pictures, the Attach Files dialog box opens and provides the opportunity to reduce the file size. In the **Picture size** list, click a size to display an estimate of the total file size of the pictures at those maximum dimensions.

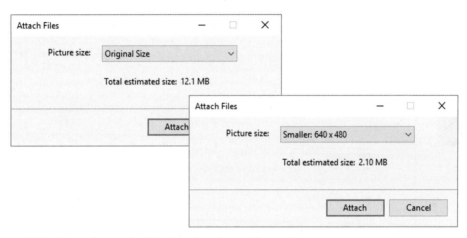

Reducing picture size can significantly reduce the attachment size

4. After you specify the picture size if necessary, click **Attach** to create the message.

To attach a copy of an online file

1. Attach the file to the email message.

2. In the **Attached** area, point to the file attachment, click the arrow that appears, and then click **Attach as copy** to download a temporary copy of the file to your computer and attach that copy to the message.

To remove an attachment from an outgoing email message

1. In the **Attached** area, point to the file attachment, click the arrow that appears, and then click **Remove Attachment**.

To attach an Outlook item to an outgoing email message

1. In the message composition window, do either of the following to open the Insert Item dialog box:

   - On the **Message** tab, in the **Include** group, click the **Attach Item** button, and then click **Outlook Item**.

   - On the **Insert** tab, in the **Include** group, click the **Outlook Item** button.

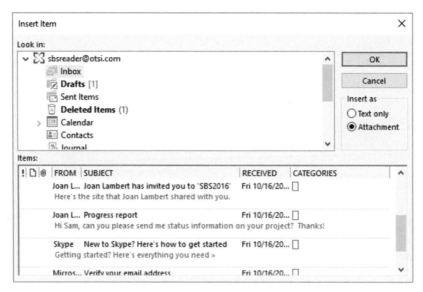

The Insert Item dialog box displays all the items in the folder, so it can be difficult to locate a specific item by using this method

2. In the **Insert Item** dialog box, browse to the message, calendar item, contact record, note, or task you want to send.

3. Click the item, and then click **OK**.

Or

1. In the Outlook program window, locate the item you want to send.

2. Right-click the item, and then click **Forward**.

 SEE ALSO For information about sending calendar information by email, see "Share calendar information" in Chapter 10, "Manage your calendar."

New mail notifications

When new messages, meeting requests, or task assignments arrive in your Inbox, Outlook alerts you in several ways so that you can be aware of email activity if you're using another application or you've been away from your computer.

These are the default notifications:

- A chime sounds.

- A desktop alert appears on your screen for a few seconds, displaying the sender's information, the message subject, and the first few words of the message.

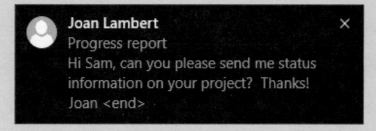

You can open the message by clicking the desktop alert

- A closed envelope icon appears on the Outlook taskbar button and, in versions of Windows earlier than Windows 10, in the notification area of the taskbar.

- In Windows 10, the Action Center icon in the notification area changes from hollow to white, and the new message is available in the Action Center.

You can configure the notification options from the Mail page of the Outlook Options dialog box. The only optional notification that isn't turned on by default is for Outlook to briefly change the shape of the mouse pointer to an envelope.

SEE ALSO For information about modifying new mail notifications, see "Configure message options" in Chapter 13, "Customize Outlook options."

Display messages and message attachments

Each time you start Outlook and connect to your email server, any new messages received since the last time you connected appear in your Inbox. Depending on your settings, Outlook downloads either the entire message to your computer or only the message header, which provides basic information about the message, such as:

- The item type (message, meeting request, task assignment, and so on)
- Who sent it
- When you received it
- The subject

Icons displayed in the message header indicate optional information such as:

- The most recent response action taken
- Whether files are attached
- If the message has been digitally signed or encrypted
- If the sender marked the message as being of high or low importance

The message list displays the message header information. You can open messages from the message list or display message content in the Reading Pane.

> **SEE ALSO** For information about changing the display of the message list or configuration of the program window elements, see "Work in the Mail module" in Chapter 2, "Explore Outlook modules."

Display message content

You can display the content of a message by opening it in a message window. However, you can save time by reading and working with messages (and other Outlook items) in the Reading Pane. You can display the Reading Pane to the right of or below the module content pane.

If a message contains external content, which many marketing email messages do, the external content will be automatically downloaded only if your security settings are configured to permit this. Otherwise, you must give permission to download the external content.

> **TIP** If you find it difficult to read the text in the Reading Pane at its default size, you can change the magnification level of the Reading Pane content by using the Zoom controls located at the right end of the program window status bar. Changing the Zoom level is temporary and lasts only until you switch to a different message. The Zoom controls are available only for message content; they're unavailable when you preview an attachment in the Reading Pane.

> **SEE ALSO** For information about modifying Reading Pane functionality, see "Configure message options" in Chapter 13, "Customize Outlook options."

To display the content of a message

1. In the Mail module, do any of the following:

   - Open a message in its own window by double-clicking its header in the message list.

   - Read a message without opening it by clicking its header once in the message list to display the message in the Reading Pane.

   - Display the first three lines of each unread message under the message header by using the Preview feature.

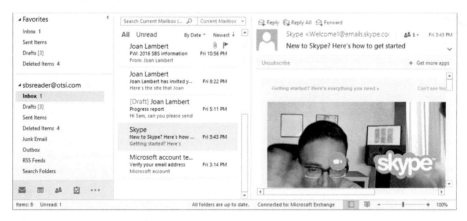

The message content is shown in the Reading Pane

To move through message content in the Reading Pane

1. In the Reading Pane, do any of the following:

   - Scroll at your own pace by dragging the vertical scroll bar that appears at the right side of the Reading Pane.

   - Move up or down one line at a time by clicking the scroll arrows.

   - Move up or down one page at a time by clicking above or below the scroll box.

   - Move up or down one page at a time by pressing the **Spacebar**. When you reach the end of a message by using this feature, called *Single Key Reading*, pressing the Spacebar again displays the first page of the next message. This option is very convenient if you want to read through several consecutive messages in the Reading Pane, or if you find it easier to press the Spacebar than to use the mouse.

Display attachment content

If a message has attachments, you can open or download them from the message window or Reading Pane. Outlook can also display interactive previews of many types of attachments, including Word documents, Excel workbooks, PowerPoint presentations, Visio diagrams, text files, XPS files, and image files.

If a preview app for a file type hasn't been installed, Outlook won't be able to preview a file of that type in the Reading Pane. You can display the apps that are used to preview files from the Attachment Handling page of the Trust Center window, which you open from the Outlook Options dialog box.

 SEE ALSO For information about Trust Center settings, see "Manage add-ins and security options" in Chapter 13, "Customize Outlook options."

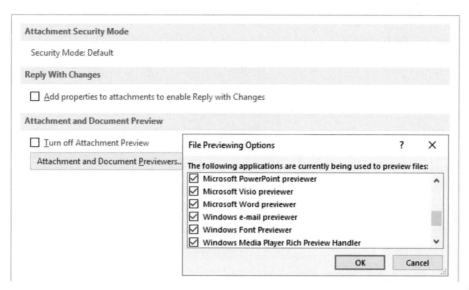

You can view which apps are used to preview files in the Reading Pane, or turn off the Attachment Preview feature

Clicking certain types of attachments displays a warning message asking you to confirm that the content comes from a trusted source. You can approve the content on a case-by-case basis or give Outlook permission to skip the warning message for files of this type.

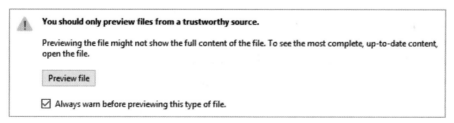

Consider whether it is safe to dismiss warnings for the file type

Previewing a file can save you a great deal of time. You can interact with the preview in many ways, to the point that you might not have to take the time to open the file at all.

If you suspect that an attachment might contain a virus, and you have a reputable anti-malware program installed, you might want to download the file and scan it for viruses before you open it.

To preview the content of a message attachment

1. In the open message window or **Reading Pane**, click the attachment once. The **Attachments** tool tab appears on the ribbon, and a preview of the attachment appears in the message content pane or Reading Pane.

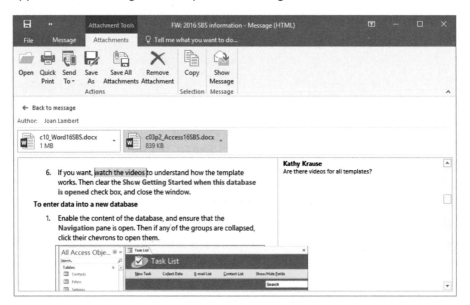

You use the same techniques to preview and open attachments in the message window and Reading Pane

To work with attachment content in the preview

1. Display the attachment preview, and then do any of the following:

   - Scroll vertically or horizontally through content.

   - Point to comment markup in a Word document to display the full comment.

   - Click worksheet tabs at the bottom of the preview area to switch between worksheets in an Excel workbook.

- Scroll vertically or click the **Next** button to move through slides in a Power-Point presentation. Transitions and animations function in the preview area.

- When previewing a PowerPoint presentation, click the slides in the preview area to advance through the presentation, including all transitions and animations; or click the **Next** button (the arrow) at the bottom of the vertical scroll bar to advance through the presentation without displaying the animated elements.

3

>  **SEE ALSO** For information about and tutorials for using PowerPoint 2016, refer to *Microsoft PowerPoint 2016 Step by Step*, by Joan Lambert (Microsoft Press, 2015).

- Click hyperlinks to open the target webpages or files, or click mailto links to create email messages.

To return from the attachment preview to the message content

1. Do either of the following:

   - In the upper-left corner of the message header, click **Back to message**.

   - On the **Attachments** tool tab, in the **Message** group, click the **Show Message** button. (The ScreenTip that appears when you point to the button says *Return to Message*.)

To open an attachment in the default app for that file type

1. In the message window or **Reading Pane**, do either of the following:

   - In the message header, double-click the attachment.

   - In the message header, click the attachment to display a preview. Then on the **Attachments** tool tab, in the **Actions** group, click **Open**.

To save an attachment to a storage drive

1. From the message window or **Reading Pane**, do either of the following:

   - Point to the attachment, click the arrow that appears, and then click **Save As**.

   - On the **Attachments** tool tab, in the **Actions** group, click the **Save As** button.

2. In the **Save As** dialog box, browse to the folder in which you want to save the file, and then click **Save**.

To save multiple attachments to a storage drive

1. From the message window or **Reading Pane**, do either of the following to display a list of all the files that are attached to the message:

    -   Point to any attachment, click the arrow that appears, and then click **Save All Attachments**.

    -   On the **Attachments** tool tab, in the **Actions** group, click the **Save All Attachments** button.

2. In the **Save All Attachments** list, all the attached files are selected by default. If you want to save only some of the files, click one file that you want to save, and then do either of the following:

    -   Press **Shift+click** to select contiguous files.

    -   Press **Ctrl+click** to select noncontiguous files.

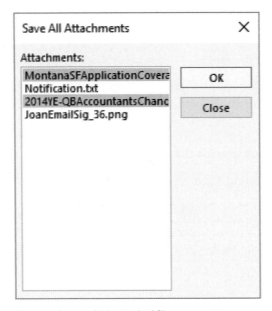

You can choose which attached files you want to save

3. When the files you want to save are selected in the list, click **OK**.

4. In the **Save All Attachments** dialog box, browse to the folder in which you want to save the files, and then click **OK**.

Display message participant information

After you receive a message (or after Outlook validates a recipient's name in a message that you're sending), you have access to contact information and a history of your communications with that person. There are three sources of information available in a message window: presence icons, contact cards, and the People Pane.

Outlook uses presence information provided by central administration server programs such as Office 365. If presence information is available, a square presence icon appears in the Reading Pane or message window to the left of each message participant's name, and a rectangular icon to the left of each contact picture, when shown in a message.

The presence icon (casually referred to as a *jelly bean* or *chiclet*) is color-coded to indicate the availability or online status of the message participant as follows:

- **Green** The person is online and available.

- **Red** The person is busy, in a conference call, or in a meeting.

- **Dark red with a white bar** The person does not want to be disturbed.

- **Yellow** The person is away or has not been active online for a certain length of time (usually five minutes).

- **Gray** The person is offline.

- **White** The person's presence information is not known.

> **TIP** This same set of presence icons is used in all Microsoft Office apps and on Microsoft SharePoint sites, to provide a consistent user experience. I don't display the presence icons in all the graphics in this book, but I do display some in this topic.

Pointing to a message participant's name displays an interactive contact card of information that includes options for contacting the person by email, instant message, or phone; for scheduling a meeting; and for working with the person's contact record.

Presence indicators   Communication options   Open Contact Card

You can initiate many types of communication from the contact card

Clicking the Open Contact Card button displays additional contact information and interaction options, and links to a more extensive range of information. From the expanded contact card, you can view the contact's position within the organization and which distribution lists he or she is a member of.

More information   Pin Contact Card

Pinning the contact card keeps it open even if you send or close the email message

3

> **TIP** A distribution list is a membership group created through Exchange and available from an organization's Global Address List. You can't create distribution lists, but you can create contact groups, which are membership groups saved in the Outlook Contacts module. For more information, see "Create contact groups" in Chapter 8, "Manage contact records."

Clicking any of the blue links initiates contact with the person through the stored phone number or email address, initiates a meeting request, or, if the person is in your address book, opens his or her contact record.

The Organization tab displays information about the person's manager and direct reports. The What's New tab displays social updates. The Membership tab displays information about distribution lists the contact is a member of. This information is available only for Exchange accounts.

The People Pane is an optional pane that displays information about conversation participants and your past communications with them, at the bottom of the message window or Reading Pane. In Outlook 2016, the People Pane is hidden by default; you can display it by clicking Normal or Minimized in the People Pane list on the View tab of any module.

In its minimized state, the People Pane displays small thumbnails that represent each message participant. If a person's contact record includes a photograph, the photo appears in the People Pane. If no photograph is available, a silhouette of one person represents an individual message participant, and a silhouette of three people represents a distribution list.

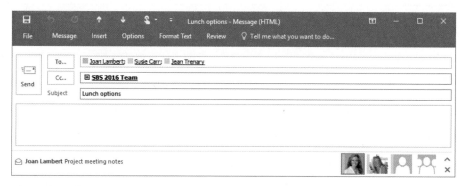

The minimized People Pane shows small thumbnails of the conversation participants

You can expand the People Pane to display either large thumbnails or a tabbed breakdown of communications for each message participant.

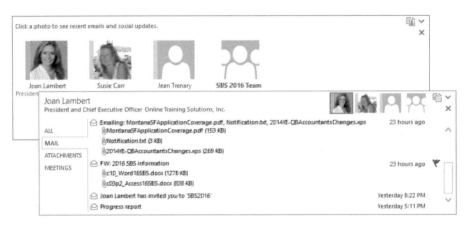

The expanded People Pane displays either participant images or a history of interactions with the selected participant

The All Items tab of the detailed view displays all your recent Outlook interactions with the selected person. If you're looking for a specific item, such as a meeting request or a document attached to a message, you can filter the item list.

The People Pane displays past interactions only when the Cached Exchange Mode feature is enabled. If the expanded People Pane doesn't display past information when you're viewing an Exchange account message, the likely problem is that Cached Exchange Mode is not enabled.

> **TIP** The detailed People Pane is available for all types of email accounts. The images in this book depict the People Pane for an Exchange account.

To display a message participant's contact information

1. Point to the person's name to display a simple contact card.

2. In the contact card, click the **Open Contact Card** button to display a more extensive range of information and interaction options.

To initiate contact from a contact card

1. In the basic contact card, do any of the following:

   - Click the **Instant Message** icon to initiate a Skype for Business message.

- Click the **Phone** icon to initiate a phone call through Skype for Business or your connected enterprise phone system.

- Click the **Video** icon to initiate a Skype for Business video chat.

- Click the **Email** icon to create a preaddressed email message form.

2. In the expanded contact card, click any blue link.

3

To expand the People Pane

1. Do any of the following:

- Click the **Expand** button at the right end of the pane.

- Drag the horizontal bar at the top of the pane.

- On the **View** tab of any module, in the **People Pane** list, click **Normal**.

> ✓ **TIP** The People Pane can occupy only a certain percentage of the message window, so the amount you can manually adjust the height of the People Pane to is dependent on the height of the message window.

To switch between detailed and simple views of the People Pane

1. Near the right end of the expanded People Pane header, click the **Toggle** button.

To filter the All Items list

1. Click the **Mail**, **Attachments**, or **Meetings** tab to display only interactions of that type.

To enable Cached Exchange Mode

1. On the **Info** page of the Backstage view of the Outlook program window, click **Account Settings**, and then in the list that appears, click **Account Settings**.

2. On the **E-mail** tab of the **Account Settings** dialog box, click your Exchange account, and then click **Change**.

3. On the **Server Settings** page of the **Change Account** wizard, select the **Use Cached Exchange Mode** check box, click **Next**, and then on the wizard's final page, click **Finish**.

4. Exit and restart Outlook to implement the change.

Respond to messages

You can respond to most email messages that you receive by clicking a response button either in the Reading Pane, in the message window, or in the Respond group on the Message tab. You can respond to a message by replying to the sender, replying to all the message participants, replying with a meeting request, replying with an instant message, or forwarding the message.

When you choose one of the following options, Outlook creates a new message based on the original message and fills in one or more of the address boxes for you:

- **Reply** Creates an email message, addressed to only the original message sender, that contains the original message text.

- **Reply All** Creates an email message, addressed to the message sender and all recipients listed in the To and Cc boxes, that contains the original message text. The message is not addressed to recipients of blind courtesy copies (Bcc recipients).

- **Reply with Meeting** Creates a meeting invitation addressed to all message recipients. The message text is included in the meeting window content pane. Outlook suggests the current date and an upcoming half-hour time slot for the meeting.

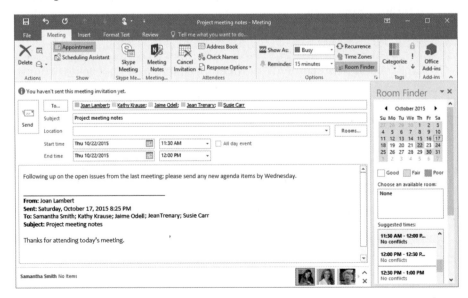

A meeting invitation created from a message

Message replies include the original message header and text, preceded by a space in which you can respond. Replies do not include any attachments from the original message.

You can add, change, and delete recipients from any reply email before sending it.

> **TIP** When responding to an email message, take care to use good email etiquette. For example, if your response is not pertinent to all the original recipients of a message, don't reply to the entire recipient list, especially if the message was addressed to a distribution list that might include hundreds of members. You can prevent other people from replying to all recipients of a message you send by addressing the message to yourself and entering other recipients in the Bcc box. Then the recipient list will not be visible to anyone.

You can forward a received message to any email address (regardless of whether the recipient uses Outlook) provided the message was not sent with restricted permissions. Outlook 2016 has the following message-forwarding options:

- **Forward** Creates a new message that contains the text of the original, and retains any attachments from the original message.

- **Forward As Attachment** Creates a blank message that contains no text but includes the original message as an attachment. The original message text and any attachments are available to the new recipient when he or she opens the attached message.

Both types of forwarded messages include the original message header and text, preceded by a space in which you can add information. Forwarded messages include attachments from the original message.

When you forward a message, Outlook does not fill in the recipient boxes for you.

If you reply to or forward a received message from within the message window, the original message remains open after you send your response. You can instruct Outlook to close original messages after you respond to them—you'll probably be finished working with the message at that point.

If your organization has the necessary unified communications infrastructure, you may also have these additional response options:

- **Call or Call All** Initiates a Voice over IP (VoIP) call from your computer to the phone number of the original message sender or sender and other message recipients.

- **Reply with IM or Reply All with IM** Opens an instant messaging window with the message sender or sender and other recipients as the chat participants. You must enter and send the first message to start the IM session.

> **TIP** The response options available in your Outlook installation might vary from those described here. The available response options for your installation are available from the Respond group that is on the Message tab of the message window and on the Home tab of the program window.

Nonstandard messages have alternative response options, such as the following:

- A meeting request includes options for responding to the request.

- A task assignment includes options for accepting or declining the assignment.

- If a message contains voting buttons, you can respond by opening the message, clicking the Vote button in the Respond group on the Message tab, and then clicking the response you want to send. Or you can click the InfoBar (labeled *Click here to vote*) in the Reading Pane and then click the response you want.

> **SEE ALSO** For information about polling other Outlook users in your organization, see "Change message settings and delivery options" in Chapter 4, "Enhance message content." For information about meeting requests, see "Respond to meeting requests" in Chapter 9, "Manage scheduling." For information about task assignments, see "Manage task assignments" in Chapter 11, "Track tasks."

To reply to an email message

1. At the top of the **Reading Pane** or in the **Respond** group on the **Message** tab, do either of the following:

   - Click the **Reply** button to create a response already addressed to the original sender. If the message had been sent to any other people, the reply would not include them.

   - Click the **Reply All** button to create a response already addressed to the original sender. If the message had been sent to any other people, the reply also includes them.

   The *RE:* prefix appears at the beginning of the message subject to indicate that this is a response to an earlier message. The original message, including its header information, appears in the content pane, separated from the new content by a horizontal line.

   > **TIP** Note that a Reply or Reply All response does not include attachments, even if there were attachments in the original message. (In fact, there is no indication that the original message had any.)

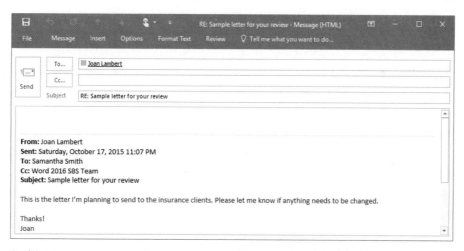

Replying to a message generates a new message addressed to the original sender

2. At the top of the content pane, enter the text of your reply.

3. In the response header, click the **Send** button to send the reply. The original message remains open on your screen.

Resending and recalling messages

If you want to send a new version of a message you've already sent—for example, a status report in which you update details each week—you can *resend* the message. Resending a message creates a new version of the message with none of the extra information that might be attached to a forwarded message. To resend a message, follow these steps:

1. From your **Sent Items** folder, open the message you want to resend. (Or, if you copied yourself on the message, you can open it from your **Inbox**.)

2. On the **Message** tab, in the **Move** group, click the **Actions** button (the ScreenTip that appears when you point to it says *More Move Actions*), and then in the list, click **Resend This Message**.

Outlook creates a new message form identical to the original. You can change the message recipients, subject, attachments, or content before sending the new version of the message.

If, after sending a message, you realize that you shouldn't have sent it—for example, if the message contained an error or was sent to the wrong people—you can *recall* it by instructing Outlook to delete or replace any unread copies of the message. If a recipient has already opened a message, it can't be recalled.

The message recall operation works only for recipients with Exchange accounts. Recipients with Internet email accounts or those who have already opened the original message will end up with both the original message and the recall notification or replacement message.

IMPORTANT You might want to test the message recall functionality within your organization before you have occasion to need it so that you can feel confident about the way it works.

To recall a message, follow these steps:

1. From your **Sent Items** folder, open the message you want to recall.

2. On the **Message** tab, in the **Move** group, click the **Actions** button, and then click **Recall This Message**. The Recall This Message dialog box offers options for handling the recalled message.

You can delete or replace a message you've sent if it hasn't been read yet

3. In the **Recall This Message** dialog box, click an option to indicate whether you want to delete or replace the sent message, and whether you want to receive an email notification of the success or failure of each recall. Then click **OK**.

4. If you choose to replace the message, a new message window opens. Enter the content that you want to include in the replacement message, and then send it.

To forward an email message

1. At the top of the **Reading Pane** or in the **Respond** group on the **Message** tab, click the **Forward** button to create a new version of the message that is not addressed to any recipient. The FW: prefix at the beginning of the message subject indicates that this is a forwarded message.

> **TIP** Any files that were attached to the original message appear in the Attached box. The message is otherwise identical to the earlier response. You address and send a forwarded message as you would any other.

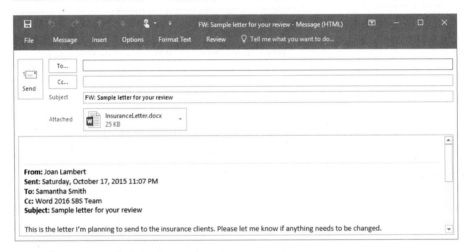

Forwarding a message includes the attachments

2. At the top of the content pane, enter the text of your reply.

3. In the response header, click the **Send** button to send the reply. The original message remains open on your screen.

To have Outlook close messages after responding

1. Open the **Outlook Options** dialog box, and then click the **Mail** tab.

2. On the **Mail** page, scroll to the **Replies and forwards** section.

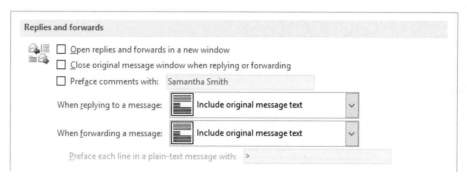

You can customize how Outlook opens, closes, and formats replies and forwards

3. Select the **Close original message window when replying or forwarding** check box.

4. Click **OK** to apply the changes and close the dialog box.

Skills review

In this chapter, you learned how to:

- Create and send messages
- Attach files and Outlook items to messages
- Display messages and message attachments
- Display message participant information
- Respond to messages

Practice tasks

The practice file for these tasks is located in the Outlook2016SBS\Ch03 folder. You can save the results of the tasks in the same folder.

> ⚠️ **IMPORTANT** As you work through the practice tasks in this book, you will create Outlook items that might be used as practice files for tasks in later chapters. If you haven't created specific items that are referenced in later chapters, you can substitute items of your own.

Create and send messages

Start Outlook, and then perform the following tasks:

1. Start a new email message. Begin entering your name or address in the **To** box, and notice the results that the Auto-Complete List provides. If you want to, remove one or more names or addresses from the list. (They'll be added to the list again the next time you send messages to them.)

2. Create a new email message, and do the following:

   • Address the message to yourself.

   • In the **Subject** box, enter **SBS Test**.

   • In the content pane, enter **Welcome to Outlook!**

   • Format the word *Welcome* in bold font and the word *Outlook* in blue font.

3. Close the message window, and have Outlook save a draft copy of the message.

4. Open the **Outlook Options** dialog box. Locate the Auto-Complete List, comma separator, and AutoSave settings discussed in this chapter and make any changes that you want to the standard configuration. Then close the dialog box.

5. Display the **Drafts** folder, and edit your draft in the **Reading Pane**. Append **Sincerely,** and your name on separate lines at the end of the message. Then send the message.

6. Display the Address Book and find out what contact lists are available to you. If you want to, follow the procedures described in this chapter to change the order in which Outlook searches the address books. Then close the Address Book.

7. Display the **Sent Items** folder and verify that the *SBS Test* message was sent.

Attach files and Outlook items to messages

Start File Explorer, browse to the practice file folder, and then perform the following tasks:

1. From the practice file folder, open the **AttachFiles** document in Word. Enter your name in the **Contact Information** section and save the file. Then save a copy of the file in the same folder with the name **AttachCopy**.

2. In the **AttachCopy** document, display the **Share** page of the Backstage view. Send a PDF copy of the document to yourself. Then close the document.

3. Display your Outlook Inbox. Create a new email message, and do the following:

   - Address the message to yourself.

   - In the **Subject** box, enter **SBS Attachment from Outlook**.

4. In the message window, display the **Attach File** menu. Notice that the two files you worked with in Word are at the top of the list. Attach the **AttachFiles** document to your message. Then send the message to yourself.

5. Display the contents of the practice file folder in File Explorer. Select the **Attach-Files** and **AttachCopy** messages. Right-click the selection, click **Send to**, and then click **Mail recipient** to create a new message.

6. Address the message to yourself, and enter **SBS Attachments from Explorer** as the message subject. Then send the message.

Display messages and message attachments

Display your Inbox, and then perform the following tasks:

1. In your Inbox, locate the **SBS Test** message that you sent to yourself in an earlier practice task.

2. Display the message content in the **Reading Pane**, and magnify the Reading Pane content.

3. In your Inbox, locate the **SBS Attachments from Explorer** message.

4. Click the **AttachFiles** attachment to preview its content in the **Reading Pane**. Scroll through the document by using the tools that are available in the **Reading Pane**, and by pressing keyboard keys.

5. Return from the attachment preview to the message content.

6. Save the **AttachFiles** attachment from the message to the practice files folder with the name **AttachCopy2**.

Display message participant information

Display your Inbox, and then perform the following tasks:

1. In your Inbox, locate an email message from another person (preferably some-one in your organization or who you have saved contact information for). Display the message in the **Reading Pane**.

2. In the **Reading Pane**, point to the sender's name or email address. Notice the information that is displayed in the contact card. Then expand the contact card to display more information.

3. From the contact card, initiate an email message to the person. Then close the message window without sending it.

4. If you want to, turn on the display of the **People Pane**. Then experiment with the display of the People Pane in the **Reading Pane** and in received and outgoing message windows.

Respond to messages

Display your Inbox, and then perform the following tasks:

1. In your Inbox, locate the **SBS Attachment from Outlook** message that you sent to yourself in an earlier set of practice tasks. Using this email message, do both of the following:

    - Reply to the message. Enter **Test of replying** in the message content, and then send it.

    - Forward the message to yourself. Enter **Test of forwarding** in the message content, and then send it.

2. Open each of the received messages from your Inbox. Notice the difference between the message subjects, and that only the forwarded message contains the original attachment.

3. If you want to, follow the procedures in this chapter to change the way that Outlook handles received messages after you respond to them.

Enhance message content

Messages composed in and sent from Microsoft Outlook 2016 don't have to consist only of plain text. They can contain diagrams and graphics, and can be visually enhanced by a judicious use of colors, fonts, and backgrounds. For more formal messages, you can attach a signature that includes your contact information, and perhaps a company logo.

You can add visual information to a message, contact record, or other Outlook item to bring it to your attention or to the attention of the recipient. For example, you can indicate that a message is of high importance or contains confidential information. You can also set options that notify you when a recipient reads a message or that prevent the recipient from forwarding or printing a message.

This chapter guides you through procedures related to personalizing default message formatting, applying thematic elements to individual messages, creating and using automatic signatures, incorporating imagery in messages, and changing message settings and delivery options.

In this chapter

- Personalize default message formatting
- Apply thematic elements to individual messages
- Create and use automatic signatures
- Incorporate images in messages
- Change message settings and delivery options

Practice files

For this chapter, use the practice file from the Outlook2016SBS\Ch04 folder. For practice file download instructions, see the introduction.

Personalize default message formatting

By default, the text content of an Outlook message is shown in black, 11-point Calibri (a font chosen for its readability), arranged in left-aligned paragraphs on a white background. You can change the appearance of the text in a message by applying either local formatting (character or paragraph attributes and styles that you apply directly to text) or global formatting (a theme or style set that you apply to the entire document) in the same way that you would when working in a Microsoft Word document or Microsoft PowerPoint presentation. However, if you prefer to use a specific font and color for all the messages you compose, you can save your preferences so that Outlook applies them to new messages and to message responses.

You set your default font and theme preferences from the Personal Stationery tab of the Signatures And Stationery dialog box. You specify font formatting for new messages and responses (replies and forwards) separately. (Even if you want to use the same font, you have to choose it twice.)

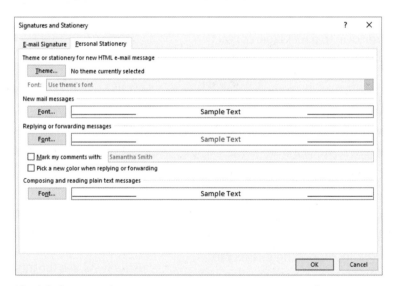

The default message fonts

The default settings use black Calibri for original messages and blue Calibri for responses. You can continue to use different colors to visually differentiate between original message content and your responses within a message trail. Or you might prefer to always use the same font regardless of whether a message is new—this simpler approach can help recipients to recognize message content from you.

When setting default fonts, you have access to the full range of options in the Font dialog box.

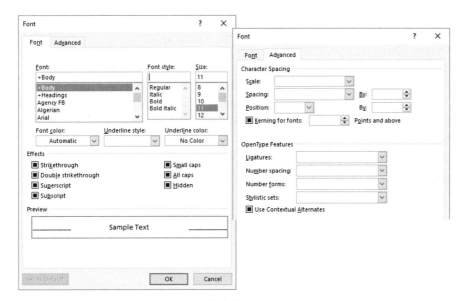

You have access to the full range of font options for email messages

The font effect check boxes contain squares to indicate that the effects are neither on nor off (which is basically the equivalent of being off). You can leave these as-is or choose to specifically turn on an effect.

It's best to choose a font face that is easy to read. Some aspects you might consider are:

- **Character width** Narrow fonts can be hard to read, and wide fonts can take up a lot of space.

- **Uppercase and lowercase letters** Some fonts display all letters uppercase.

- **Numbers that are easy to read** For example, some fonts display the number zero and the lowercase letter "o" almost identically. If you select one of these as your default font and then send someone a password that includes a zero, they might have difficulty reading it.

The Preview area of the Font dialog box displays the words *Sample Text* in the font that you select. That doesn't cover all the bases, so you might want to try out a few fonts in an email message before you make a selection.

Arial Narrow: AaBbCcDdEe 0123456789
Arial Rounded Bold: AaBbCcDdEe 0123456789
Bernard Condensed: AaBbCcDdEe 0123456789
Calibri: AaBbCcDdEe 0123456789
Candara: AaBbCcDdEe 0123456789
COPPERPLATE GOTHIC LIGHT: AABBCCDDEE 0123456789
Lucida Handwriting: AaBbCcDdEe 0123456789
Magneto: AaBbCcDdEe 0123456789
Tahoma: AaBbCcDdEe 0123456789
Times New Roman: AaBbCcDdEe 0123456789
Trebuchet: AaBbCcDdEe 0123456789

Some fonts aren't good choices for default message fonts

When you set a default message font in the Font dialog box, it becomes the Body font. The Set As Default button doesn't become active because, unlike when creating documents in Word or worksheets in Excel, there are no fonts to set other than the message font. You can't change the font that Outlook uses in information fields such as those in message headers, contact records, and appointments.

> **TIP** You can change the font of user interface elements such as the Folder Pane, message list, and rows and columns of table-style views. For more information, see "Customize user interface fonts" in Chapter 12, "Manage window elements."

Another font that you can set from this dialog box controls the way that plain-text messages you receive appear when you display them in Outlook. Many people send email messages from their smartphones, and they can configure messages to be sent as HTML or in plain text. (You can also choose one of these message types for messages that you subscribe to, such as package delivery notifications.) Plain text messages are simpler for software to render and to display consistently. If you don't set a different default, plain text messages will appear in Calibri.

In addition to the message fonts, you can specify an email message theme (a pre-selected set of fonts, colors, and graphic elements) that Outlook will use when you create messages. Most themes include a colored or illustrated graphic background that you can include or exclude by selecting or clearing the Background Image check box.

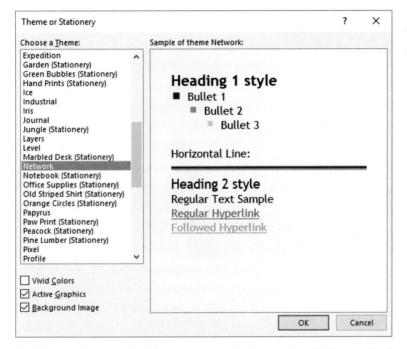

Email message themes include fonts, colors, page backgrounds, and inline graphic elements

Instead of choosing a complete theme, you can choose stationery (think of this as choosing a patterned paper on which to write letters). Some stationery options have quite pronounced graphic images (dozens of teddy bears parading across the page), whereas others are more subtle (green bubbles on a green background). Some stationery options have graphics across the entire page, whereas others confine the graphics to the left edge of the email "page" and leave a clear space for text and other email content.

Stationery options range from subtle to busy

Your choice of stationery does not control your default message font; you must set that separately, as previously discussed in this topic. If you choose to use stationery (and I'd caution you to make this choice judiciously), take care to choose a font color that is visible against the stationery background and also visible to recipients who choose to block graphic elements of email messages. For example, it might be tempting to use clean white lettering against the brown background of the Jungle stationery, but for recipients who block graphics, the message will display white lettering on a white background—in other words, the message will appear to be blank unless they select the message content.

To open the Signatures And Stationery dialog box

1. Click the **File** tab to display the Backstage view. In the left pane, click **Options** to display the Outlook Options dialog box.

2. In the left pane of the **Outlook Options** dialog box, click the **Mail** tab.

3. On the **Mail** page, in the **Compose messages** section, do either of the following:

   - To display the E-mail Signature tab, click the **Signatures** button.

   - To display the Personal Stationery tab, click the **Stationery and Fonts** button.

To change the default font for outgoing messages

1. Display the **Personal Stationery** tab of the **Signatures and Stationery** dialog box.

2. Do either of the following to open the Font dialog box:

   - To set the font for new messages, click the **Font** button in the **New mail messages** section.

   - To set the font for message responses, click the **Font** button in the **Replying or forwarding** section.

3. In the **Font** dialog box, configure the font that you want Outlook to use for the selected message type. Then click **OK**.

To change the default font for the display of plain-text messages

1. Display the **Personal Stationery** tab of the **Signatures and Stationery** dialog box.

2. In the **Composing and reading plain text messages** section, click the **Font** button.

3. In the **Font** dialog box, configure the font that you want Outlook to use when displaying plain-text messages. Then click **OK**.

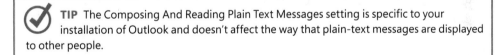 **TIP** The Composing And Reading Plain Text Messages setting is specific to your installation of Outlook and doesn't affect the way that plain-text messages are displayed to other people.

To open the Theme Or Stationery dialog box

1. On the **Personal Stationery** tab of the **Signatures and Stationery** dialog box, in the **Theme or Stationery for new HTML e-mail message** section, click the **Theme** button.

To specify a theme for outgoing messages

1. Open the **Theme or Stationery** dialog box.

2. In the **Choose a Theme** pane, click any entry that doesn't end with (Stationery) to display a preview in the right pane.

3. To display modified theme options, select or clear any of the following check boxes:

   - Vivid Colors

   - Active Graphics

   - Background Image

4. After selecting and configuring the theme you want, click **OK**.

5. If you want to use a font other than the theme font, do the following:

   a. In the **Theme or Stationery for new HTML e-mail message** section of the **Signatures and Stationery** dialog box, click the **Font** list to display the options.

You can override the theme font

   b. In the **Font** list, do either of the following:

      - To compose original messages with the theme font but use the font defined in the Replying Or Forwarding Messages section for responses, click **Use my font when replying and forwarding messages**.

      - To not use the theme font (but use the other theme elements), click **Always use my fonts**.

To specify a background stationery for outgoing messages

1. Open the **Theme or Stationery** dialog box.

2. In the **Choose a Theme** pane, click any entry that has **(Stationery)** appended to the name to display a preview in the right pane.

3. After selecting the background stationery you want, click **OK**.

Apply thematic elements to individual messages

If you prefer to apply thematic elements on an individual message basis, you can apply global formatting options—by using themes and style sets—with only a couple of clicks.

4

Apply and change themes

Nine of the standard Microsoft Office 2016 themes (which are not the same as the email message themes you can select in the Theme Or Stationery dialog box) are available from the Themes gallery on the Options tab in a message composition window. Each theme controls the colors, fonts, and graphic effects used in the message.

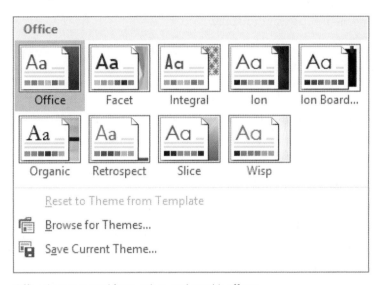

Office themes control fonts, colors, and graphic effects

The default theme for all email messages, Word documents, PowerPoint presentations, Microsoft Excel workbooks, and other Office 2016 documents is the Office theme. If you don't apply another theme to your message, the colors, fonts, and effects in your message are controlled by the Office theme.

You can modify the formatting applied by the current theme by changing the color scheme, font set, or effect style.

 TIP Office theme functionality is provided by Word 2016 and is available only when you have that app installed.

To change the theme of a message

1. On the **Options** tab of the message composition window, in the **Themes** group, click the **Themes** button, and then click the theme you want to apply.

To change the color scheme used in a message

1. Do either of the following:

   - On the **Options** tab of the message composition window, in the **Themes** group, click the **Colors** button (the ScreenTip says *Theme Colors*), and then click the color scheme you want to apply.

   - On the **Format Text** tab of the message composition window, in the **Styles** group, click the **Change Styles** button, click **Colors**, and then click the color scheme you want to apply.

To change the font set used in a message

1. Do either of the following:

   - On the **Options** tab of the message composition window, in the **Themes** group, click the **Fonts** button (the ScreenTip says *Theme Fonts*), and then click the font set you want to apply.

   - On the **Format Text** tab of the message composition window, in the **Styles** group, click the **Change Styles** button, click **Fonts**, and then click the font set you want to apply.

To change the effect style used in a message

1. On the **Options** tab of the message composition window, in the **Themes** group, click the **Effects** button (the ScreenTip says *Theme Effects*), and then click the effect you want to apply.

Apply and change styles

You can use *styles* to format text in email messages in the same way that you do in Word documents; however, most people won't compose email messages of the length and outline detail that would require those, so we'll discuss them only briefly in this book.

You can apply character and paragraph styles from the Styles gallery on the Format Text tab, or from the independent Styles pane. The benefit of the Styles pane is that it stays open and available while you work. You can dock the pane at the right side of the window or leave it floating anywhere on the screen.

> ✓ **TIP** If you create different types of Office documents (such as Word documents, PowerPoint presentations, and corporate email messages) for your organization, you can ensure the uniform appearance of all the documents by applying the same Office theme and style set to all the documents. For example, you might create a theme that incorporates your company's corporate fonts and logo colors.

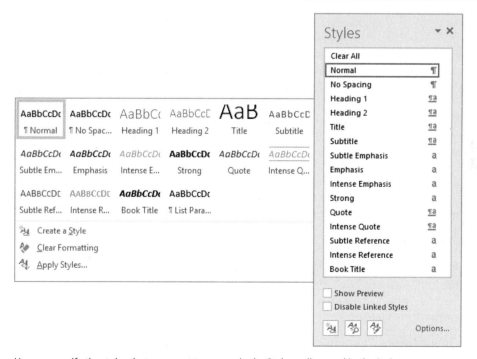

You can specify the styles that you want to appear in the Styles gallery and in the Styles pane

TIP You can preview the effect of a style on the currently selected text by pointing to the style in the Styles gallery, but not in the Styles pane.

A *style set* changes the colors, fonts, and paragraph formatting of individual styles. You can change the appearance of all the styles in a message by selecting any of the 17 available style sets (or by creating your own). Selecting a style set changes the appearance of all the text in the current message, and of the icons in the Styles gallery.

Effects of changing the style set

 SEE ALSO For more information about using themes, styles, and style sets to format content, refer to *Microsoft Word 2016 Step by Step* by Joan Lambert (Microsoft Press, 2015).

To display the full Styles gallery

1. On the **Format Text** tab, in the **Styles** group, click the **More** button to expand the Styles gallery.

To open the Styles pane

1. On the **Format Text** tab, click the **Styles** dialog box launcher.

To move the Styles pane

1. Point to the **Styles** pane header. When the pointer changes to a four-headed arrow, drag the pane.

2. Do any of the following:

   - Drag the pane to any location on the screen.

   - Drag the pane to the inside edge of the message composition window to dock it to the window.

   - Drag the pane away from the docking location to undock it.

To apply a style

1. Click anywhere in the word or paragraph you want to format, or select the specific text you want to format.

2. In the **Styles** gallery or **Styles** pane, click the style you want to apply.

To change the style set of a message

1. On the **Format Text** tab, in the **Styles** group, click the **Change Styles** button.

2. On the **Change Styles** menu, click **Style Set**, and then click the style set you want.

> **TIP** You can display the name of a style set and preview the effect of selecting it by pointing at its thumbnail in the Style Set gallery.

Create and use automatic signatures

When you send an email message to someone, you will most likely "sign" the message by entering your name at the end of the message text. You can have Outlook insert your signature text in outgoing messages by creating an email signature and assigning it to your email account. Your email signature can include additional information that you want to consistently provide to message recipients.

An email signature can include formatted text and graphics

A typical email signature would commonly include your name and contact information, but depending on your situation, you might also include information such as your company name, job title, a legal disclaimer, a corporate or personal slogan, a photo, and so on. You can even include your electronic business card as part or all of your email signature.

 SEE ALSO For more information about electronic business cards, see "Personalize electronic business cards" in Chapter 8, "Manage contact records."

You can create different signatures for use in different types of messages or for use when you're sending messages from different email accounts. For example, you might create a formal business signature for client correspondence, a casual business signature for interoffice correspondence, and a personal signature for messages sent from another account. Or you might create a signature that contains more information to send with original email messages, and a signature that contains less information to send with message replies.

You can format the text of your email signature in the same ways that you can format message text. If you want to apply formatting that's not available from the selection of buttons across the top of the signature content pane, you can create and format your signature in an email message composition window, copy the signature, and then paste it into the signature content pane.

A signature can include inline images, but the signature content pane doesn't support wrapping text around images, so if you want to do something fancier, create the signature look you want in an email message composition window, save a screen clipping of it as a graphic, and then insert the graphic into the signature content box.

> **TIP** All Office apps share the Microsoft Office Clipboard, so you can easily copy and move content between apps. You don't need to work from the Clipboard to paste the most recently cut or copied text into another location; it's stored in the shared Clipboard, so all Office apps have access to it. For example, you can cut or copy text or an image in a Word document and then paste it into an Outlook email message without ever directly accessing the Clipboard.

If you have Outlook configured to connect to multiple email accounts, you can assign the same email signature to multiple accounts, or assign a unique email signature to each email account. The signature you assign to the specific account will appear automatically in new messages you send from that account. You can also manually insert any email signature you've created in any message. Outlook inserts the email signature at the end of the message, replacing any existing email signature.

To display the E-mail Signature tab of the Signatures And Stationery dialog box

1. From any module, open the **Outlook Options** dialog box and display the **Mail** page.

2. In the **Compose messages** section, click the **Signatures** button.

Or

1. In a message composition window, display the **Message** tab or **Insert** tab.

2. In the **Include** group, click the **Signature** button and then click **Signatures**.

To create a simple signature

1. Display the **E-mail Signature** tab of the **Signatures and Stationery** dialog box. Any existing signatures are listed in the Select Signature To Edit box.

2. Below the **Select signature to edit** box, click the **New** button. Outlook prompts you to supply a name for the new signature before you can work with the signature content.

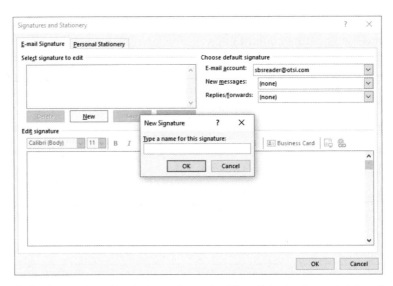

Assign a name that will make it easy for you to differentiate signatures when inserting them

3. In the **Type a name for this signature** box, enter a name that will help you differentiate the signature from others you create, such as *Work* or *Disclaimer*. Then click **OK** to create the signature and activate it for editing.

4. In the **Edit signature** box, enter the text that you want to include, and format the font if you want to.

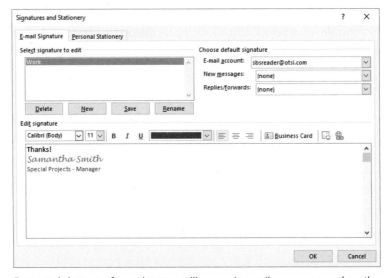

Formatted elements of your signature will appear in email messages exactly as they do here

5. When you're done with the simple signature, click **Save**.

To edit an existing email signature

1. Display the **E-mail Signature** tab of the **Signatures and Stationery** dialog box.

2. In the **Select signature to edit** box, click the signature you want to edit, to display it in the Edit Signature pane.

3. Make any changes you want, and then click the **Save** button.

To add an inline image to an email signature

1. Display the **E-mail Signature** tab of the **Signatures and Stationery** dialog box.

2. Create a new signature or choose a signature to edit.

3. In the **Edit signature pane**, click to position the cursor where you want to insert the picture.

4. On the toolbar above the pane, click the **Insert Picture** button (the second button from the right).

5. In the **Insert Picture** dialog box, browse to and select the image you want to insert, and then click **Insert**.

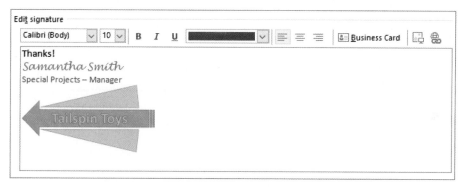

You can position an inline graphic anywhere within the text

6. Make any other changes you want, and then click the **Save** button.

To add fancy images to an email signature

1. In an email composition window, Word document, PowerPoint slide, or image editing app, create the signature you want and save it as an image file. Trim all empty space from the edges of the image.

2. Display the **E-mail Signature** tab of the **Signatures and Stationery** dialog box.

3. Create a new signature or choose a signature to edit.

4. In the **Edit signature pane**, select and delete any existing content that you don't want to include with the image.

5. Click to position the cursor where you want to insert the image.

6. On the toolbar above the pane, click the **Insert Picture** button (the second button from the right).

7. In the **Insert Picture** dialog box, browse to and select the image you want to insert, and then click **Insert**.

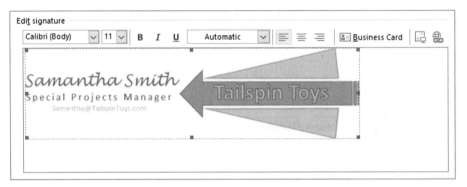

You can include text in addition to the graphic if you want

8. Make any other changes you want, and then click the **Save** button.

> 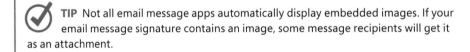 **TIP** Not all email message apps automatically display embedded images. If your email message signature contains an image, some message recipients will get it as an attachment.

To automatically add an email signature to outgoing messages

1. Display the **E-mail Signature** tab of the **Signatures and Stationery** dialog box.

2. In the **Choose default signature** section, do the following:

   - In the **E-mail account** list, click the account you want to assign the signature to.

   - In the **New messages** list, click the signature that you want Outlook to insert into all new email messages you send from the selected account.

   - In the **Replies/forwards** list, click the signature that you want Outlook to insert into all response message you send from the selected account.

3. In the **Signatures and Stationery** dialog box, click **OK**.

4. Create a new email message to verify that the signature appears.

 TIP If you have more than one email account set up in Outlook, you can configure different signatures for each account.

To manually insert an existing email signature in a message

1. In a message composition window, display the **Message** tab or the **Insert** tab.

2. In the **Include** group, click the **Signature** button.

3. In the **Signature** list, click the name of the email signature you want to insert.

 TIP If you have not previously set up a signature, clicking the Signature button displays a short list that includes a Signatures option; clicking this option opens the Signatures And Stationery dialog box in which you can create a signature.

To remove an email signature from a message

1. Select and delete the signature content as you would any other message content.

Incorporate images in messages

Email is a means of communicating information to other people, and, as the old saying goes, a picture is worth a thousand words. Using Outlook 2016, you can communicate visual information in the following ways:

- Share photographs with other people by attaching the photos to messages or embedding them in messages.

  🔍 **SEE ALSO** For information about attaching pictures to messages, see "Attach files and Outlook items to messages" in Chapter 3, "Send and receive email messages."

- Share information from websites, documents, and other visual presentations by capturing images of your screen directly from Outlook and then inserting those images in your message.

- Explain complicated processes and other business information by creating SmartArt graphics within messages or by embedding SmartArt graphics that you create in other Office 2016 apps.

- Communicate statistical information by creating a chart within a message.

You can insert all these types of images from the Illustrations group on the Insert tab into the content pane of an email message, calendar item, or task, or into the notes pane of a contact record. (One exception: you can't insert an image into a note.)

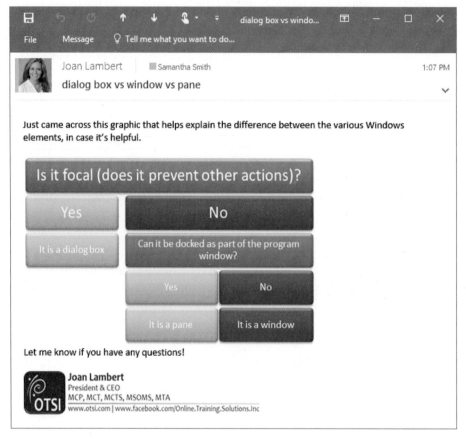

Two uses of images in an email message

Images can be especially valuable in business communications, when you need to clearly explain facts or concepts, particularly to a global audience. In Outlook 2016 (and other Office 2016 apps), you can depict processes, cycles, hierarchies, and other relationships by using SmartArt graphics, and you can depict graphical representations of numeric data by using charts.

TIP SmartArt graphic and charting functionality is provided by Word 2016 and is available only when you have that app installed.

SmartArt graphics are graphical representations of lists of information. You can create a SmartArt graphic directly in an email message by selecting the type of graphic you want to create and then entering the information to populate it. You can modify the SmartArt graphic to fit the information you want to present, change the graphic type if your original selection doesn't best represent the final information, and format the graphic with professionally themed color combinations and effects. When you send the message, Outlook converts the SmartArt graphic to a static graphic.

Charts are graphical representations of tables of data. Tables and charts are frequently created by using Excel. You can also create a chart directly in an Outlook email message. Charts you create in an email message look exactly like those you would create in an Excel workbook—because they are based on an Excel data source that is created from within Outlook.

When you send or receive a message that contains a chart or SmartArt graphic, the chart or graphic is converted to a static image (a picture) and resized to fit the message window. If you open the message from your Sent Items folder, you'll find that the same is true of the graphic in the sent message. You can copy and reuse the picture in other files, such as messages, documents, and presentations, but you can no longer edit it.

You work with all these types of images in an Outlook message just as you would in a Word document or on a PowerPoint slide. Because Outlook is about email, contact management, and calendaring, we're not going to get into a deep discussion of images and graphics in this book. If you would like more information you can find it in the *Microsoft Word 2016 Step by Step* or *Microsoft PowerPoint 2016 Step by Step* books (Microsoft Press, 2015).

Change message settings and delivery options

When you send a message, you can include visual indicators of the importance, sensitivity, or subject category of a message or other Outlook item, flag a message for follow-up, restrict other people from changing or forwarding message content, provide a simple feedback mechanism in the form of voting buttons, and specify message delivery options to fit your needs. Some of these options display icons in the message header that are visible to recipients directly in the Outlook message list.

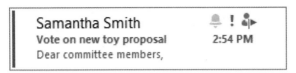

This message has a reminder, a status, and a follow-up flag. Voting buttons and Sensitivity don't display message header icons

In the message reading window, many of the options are represented by text rather than icons.

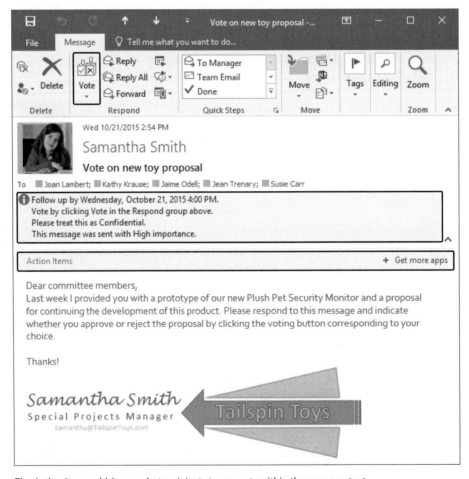

The Action Items add-in can alert recipients to requests within the message text

Common message settings and delivery options include the following:

- **Flags and reminders** You can place an outgoing message on your task list, add an informational reminder to it, or set a reminder to appear at a certain time and date, for yourself and for message recipients. The flag options are Call, Do not Forward, Follow up, For Your Information, Forward, No Response Necessary, Read, Reply, Reply to All, and Review.

- **Importance** You can indicate the urgency of a message by setting its importance to High or Low (the default importance is Normal). A corresponding banner appears in the message header and, if the Importance field is included in the view, an importance icon appears in the Inbox or other message folder.

- **Sensitivity** You can indicate that a message should be kept private by setting its sensitivity to Confidential, Personal, or Private. No indicator appears in the message folder, but a banner appears in the message header to indicate a sensitivity level other than Normal.

- **Security** If you have a digital ID, you can digitally sign the message; or you can encrypt the contents of the message.

- **Voting options** If you and your message recipients have Microsoft Exchange Server accounts, you can add voting buttons to your messages so that recipients can quickly select from multiple-choice response options.

- **Tracking options** You can track messages by requesting delivery receipts and read receipts. These receipts are messages automatically generated by the recipient's email server when it delivers the message to the recipient and when the recipient opens the message. Recipients might be prompted to approve the delivery of the receipts, so requesting them is no guarantee of receiving them.

- **Delivery options** You can have reply messages delivered to an email address other than yours, specify a date and time for the message to be delivered and to expire, and set advanced attachment format and encoding options.

 TIP You can assign a category to an outgoing message but it will not be visible to the recipient, only to the sender.

The most commonly used options are available directly in the message composition window, in the Tags group on the Message tab, and in the Tracking and More Options groups on the Options tab.

Some message options are available from the ribbon

Clicking the dialog box launcher in the lower-right corner of any of these groups opens the Properties dialog box, in which you can set all the options other than follow-up flags.

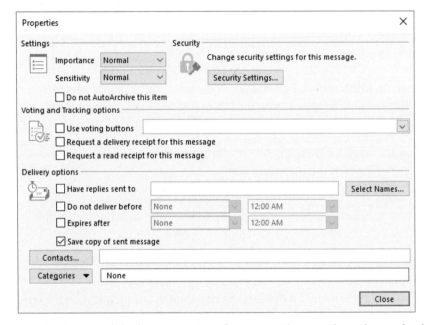

From the Properties dialog box, you can control message settings, security settings, and voting, tracking, and delivery options

You can limit the actions other people can take with messages they receive from you by restricting the message permissions. For example, you can prevent recipients from forwarding or printing the message, copying the message content, or changing the content when they forward or reply to the message. (Restrictions apply also to message attachments.) Within a message window, permission options are available both on the Info page of the Backstage view and in the Permission group on the Options tab.

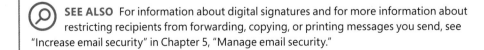

SEE ALSO For information about digital signatures and for more information about restricting recipients from forwarding, copying, or printing messages you send, see "Increase email security" in Chapter 5, "Manage email security."

To open the Properties dialog box

1. On the message composition window ribbon, click the dialog box launcher in any of the following groups:

   - The **Tags** group on the **Message** tab
   - The **Tracking** group on the **Options** tab
   - The **More Options** group on the **Options** tab

To indicate the importance of a message

1. Do either of the following:

   - On the **Message** tab, in the **Tags** group, click **High Importance** or **Low Importance**.
   - Open the **Properties** dialog box. In the **Settings** section, in the **Importance** list, click **Low**, **Normal**, or **High**.

To indicate the sensitivity of a message

1. Open the **Properties** dialog box.

2. In the **Settings** section, in the **Sensitivity** list, click **Normal**, **Personal**, **Private**, or **Confidential**.

To add standard voting buttons to a message

1. Do either of the following:

   - On the **Options** tab, in the **Tracking** group, click **Use Voting Buttons** to display the Use Voting Buttons list.
   - Open the **Properties** dialog box. In the **Voting and Tracking options** section, select the **Use voting buttons** check box. Then expand the adjacent list.

2. In the list, click one of the following:

   - Approve;Reject
   - Yes;No
   - Yes;No;Maybe

3. Close the **Properties** dialog box if you opened it in step 1.

   An information bar at the top of the message confirms that you've added voting buttons to the outgoing message.

Not all message options are flagged in the message, but voting buttons are

To add custom voting buttons to a message

1. Do either of the following:

   - On the **Options** tab, in the **Tracking** group, click **Use Voting Buttons** and then click **Custom**.

   - Open the **Properties** dialog box. In the **Voting and Tracking options** section, select the **Use voting buttons** check box.

2. In the **Use voting buttons** box, select and delete any current button labels. Then enter the custom button labels you want, separated by semicolons.

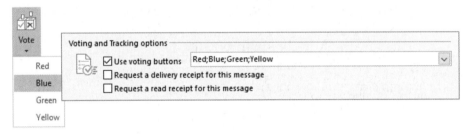

Custom voting buttons and the settings to create them

3. Close the **Properties** dialog box.

To request message receipts

1. In the **Tracking** group on the **Options** tab, or in the **Voting and Tracking options** section of the **Properties** dialog box, select one or both of the following check boxes:

   - Request a delivery receipt for this message

   - Request a read receipt for this message

2. Close the **Properties** dialog box if you opened it in step 1.

To direct message replies to a different email address

1. Do either of the following:

   - On the **Options** tab, in the **More Options** group, click **Direct Replies To**.

   - Open the **Properties** dialog box. In the **Delivery options** section, select the **Have replies sent to** check box.

2. In the **Have replies sent to** box, select and delete the current recipient. Then enter the email address or addresses (separated by semicolons) that you want replies to go to.

3. Close the **Properties** dialog box.

To delay the delivery of a message

1. Do either of the following:

   - On the **Options** tab, in the **More Options** group, click **Delay Delivery**.

   - Open the **Properties** dialog box. In the **Delivery options** section, select the **Do not deliver before** check box.

2. To the right of **Do not deliver before**, select or enter the date and time that you want to delay delivery until.

3. Close the **Properties** dialog box.

To set an expiration date for a message

1. Open the **Properties** dialog box.

2. In the **Delivery options** section, select the **Expires after** check box.

3. To the right of **Expires after** box, select or enter the date and time that you want the message to expire.

4. Close the **Properties** dialog box.

   The expiration of a message is indicated to the recipient in the message list and in the message header.

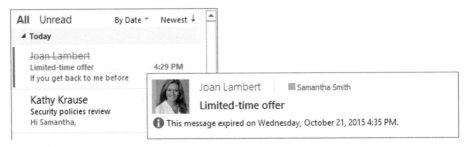

Expired messages are marked for both the recipient and the sender

To flag a message for follow-up by the recipient

1. On the **Message** tab, in the **Tags** group, click **Follow Up**, and then click **Add Reminder**. The Custom dialog box opens.

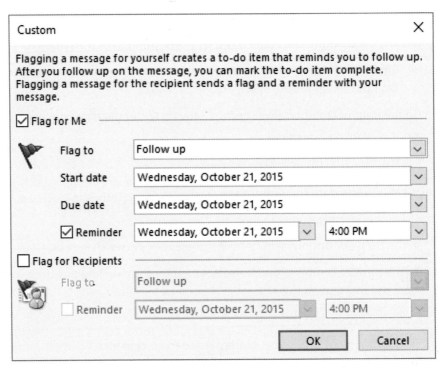

By default, the Custom dialog box is configured to set a reminder for the message sender and not the recipient

2. In the **Custom** dialog box, clear the **Flag for Me** check box and select the **Flag for Recipients** check box.

3. In the **Flag for Recipients** section, do the following:

- In the **Flag to** list, click **Follow up** (or one of the other available flags).

- If you want a reminder to appear to the recipient, select the **Reminder** check box and then specify a date and time for the reminder.

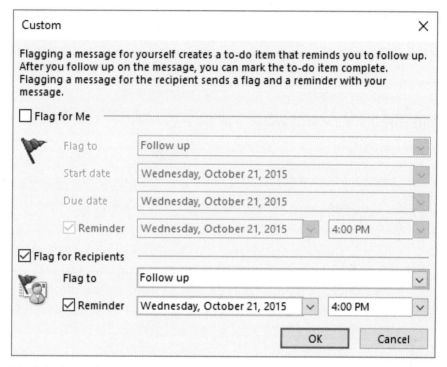

The dialog box configured to flag the message for the recipient to follow up

4. In the **Custom** dialog box, click **OK**.

Skills review

In this chapter, you learned how to:

- Personalize default message formatting
- Apply thematic elements to individual messages
- Create and use automatic signatures
- Incorporate images in messages
- Change message settings and delivery options

Practice tasks

The practice file for these tasks is located in the Outlook2016SBS\Ch04 folder.

> ⚠ **IMPORTANT** As you work through the practice tasks in this book, you will create Outlook items that might be used as practice files for tasks in later chapters. If you haven't created specific items that are referenced in later chapters, you can substitute items of your own.

Personalize default message formatting

Start Outlook, and then complete the following tasks:

1. Display the **Personal Stationery** tab of the **Signatures and Stationery** dialog box.

2. Set the default fonts for new messages and responses to the font, font size, and font color that you want to use.

3. Open the **Theme or Stationery** dialog box. Look through the available themes and stationery pages. Consider the effects of using one of these in your daily correspondence. If you identify a theme or stationery background that you feel would enhance your messages, select it and click **OK** to apply the setting. Otherwise, click **Cancel**.

4. If you chose a theme in step 3, review the **Font** options and select the font option you want to use. Then close the dialog box.

5. Display your Inbox, and do the following to test your settings:

   - Create a new email message and enter some text.

   - Respond to a received email message and enter some text.

   - If you don't like the results of your selections, close the unsent messages, repeat this set of tasks, and modify the settings.

6. When you're happy with the results, close the unsent messages and delete the message drafts, if prompted to do so.

Apply thematic elements to individual messages

Display your Inbox, and then complete the following tasks:

1. Create a new email message.

2. From the practice file folder, open the **ApplyThemes** document in Word and display it in Print Layout view.

3. In the **ApplyThemes** document, select the text starting with *Office Procedures* and continuing through the website URL. Then copy the text to the Clipboard.

4. Return to the message composition window that you opened in step 1, and paste the copied content into the message content pane. Notice that the text formatting changes immediately.

5. Adjust the size of the message composition window so you can see all the content. Then display the **Options** tab of the window.

6. In the **Themes** group, display the **Colors** menu. (Ensure that you can still see the headings of the message with the menu open.) Point to different color schemes to display a live preview of their effects on the message content. Then click a color scheme you like. In the message, notice the formatting that has changed.

7. In the **Themes** group, display the **Fonts** menu. Point to different font sets to preview them in the message, and then click a font set that you like. Notice the changes in the message content.

8. Display the **Format Text** tab of the message composition window.

9. From the **Styles** group, display the **Style Set** gallery. Point to different style sets to preview their effects on the message, and then click a style set you like. Notice the changes in the message content.

10. If you want to, enter **SBS style test** in the **Subject** box, and then send the message to yourself. Otherwise, close the message composition window without saving or sending the message.

Create and use automatic signatures

Display your Inbox, and then complete the following tasks:

1. Display the **E-mail Signature** tab of the **Signatures and Stationery** dialog box.

2. Create an email signature that is appropriate to your primary email account. It could be as simple as your name, or could also include contact information, a company slogan, a favorite saying, or other text. Assign an appropriate name to the email signature.

3. If Outlook doesn't automatically do so, assign the signature to new messages from the email account you created it for.

4. Close the dialog box, and display your Inbox.

5. Create a new email message from your primary account, and verify that the signature appears in the message.

6. From the message composition window, redisplay the **E-mail Signature** tab of the **Signatures and Stationery** dialog box.

7. Select the signature that you created in step 2, and make any changes that you want. For example, you might want to add information, apply formatting, insert fancy text from a Word document, or insert an image.

8. Close the dialog box and return to the message composition window you opened in step 5.

9. Delete the original email signature from the message, and then manually insert the updated signature.

10. Close the message window without sending or saving the message.

11. If you want to create other signatures or assign the signature you created in step 2 to responses or to other accounts, do so at this time.

Incorporate images in messages

There are no practice tasks for this topic.

Change message settings and delivery options

Display your Inbox, and then complete the following tasks:

1. Create a new email message, and do the following:

   - In the **To** box, enter your own email address.

   - In the **Subject** box, enter **Lunch preference**.

   - In the message content pane, enter **What do you want to eat for lunch?**

2. Using any of the procedures described in this chapter, do the following:

   - Set the message importance to **Low**.

   - Set the sensitivity to **Confidential**.

   - Add custom voting buttons to the message that allow you to vote for **Pizza**, **Salad**, or **Sandwiches**.

   - Request a delivery receipt and a read receipt.

   - Set the message to expire in about an hour.

   - Flag the message for follow-up by the recipient, and set a reminder for a time about a half hour away.

3. Send the message, and then do the following:

   - Watch for the message receipts.

   - When the message arrives, vote for your lunch preference.

   - When the reminder appears, dismiss it.

   - After the message expires, notice the changes in the message list and in the message window.

Manage
email security

5

To more easily manage the information you receive through email, you can specify how Outlook 2016 alerts you to and processes incoming messages. Chapter 14, "Manage email automatically," provides extensive information about creating rules to automatically deal with incoming messages of all types. This chapter focuses on dealing with unwanted messages, such as spam messages and phishing email. You can also take advantage of the many security features built into Outlook to keep your outgoing communications secure and to protect your computer system from spam, viruses, web beacons, and other modern electronic threats.

This chapter guides you through procedures related to blocking unwanted messages and increasing email security.

In this chapter

- Block unwanted messages
- Increase email security

Practice files

No practice files are necessary to complete the practice tasks in this chapter.

Block unwanted messages

Email has become a vital part of our business and personal communication systems, but there are certain types of messages you don't want to have to deal with—the unsolicited advertisements and messages, sometimes containing dangerous attachments, links, or offers, that can swamp your Inbox if your email address finds its way into the hands of unscrupulous mailing list vendors—or if you get a bit overzealous with your online shopping.

Most junk email messages (also called junk mail) fall into three general categories:

- **Spam messages** Unsolicited advertisements that are sent out to large groups of people, usually from a mailing list purchased from one of the many entrepreneurs who offer them—in spam messages of their own.

- **Phishing messages** Emails that contain requests for sensitive information such as your bank account or credit card number, have attachments that install malicious software on your computer, or contain links to webpages that masquerade as trusted, known entities and collect your user name, password, or other personal information that can be sold or otherwise used by scam artists for their own financial gain. In the past, you were in danger only if you submitted your information through the phishing site, but these sites are becoming increasingly sophisticated, and many now host malicious keystroke-logging software. You can infect your computer just by visiting such sites, which makes it vital that you protect yourself from these threats.

- **International financial scams** Originally a postal mail issue, these emails frequently take the form of advance-fee arrangements in which the message recipient is promised something of great value in exchange for a small fee. Advance-fee scams often involve notification of a vast inheritance or lottery jackpot, a large payment in exchange for your help getting money out of the sender's country or region, or promises of employment or romance. They can also take a more negative form of requests for help with medical bills or ransom payments. The messages might come from an email address that you recognize—for example, you might receive a request from a friend to urgently send money to him in a foreign country or region because he had his wallet stolen while on vacation. This might be a valid request, but it's also possible that your friend's email account security was breached and the message was sent to all the contacts in his address book by the person who would actually receive money that you transfer. If a request seems unusual, confirm it before you take action.

Phishing and financial scam messages are often filled with spelling errors, obviously incorrect information, webpage links unrelated to the purported sender, unidentifiable attachments, and absurd claims. It is highly improbable that you have inherited $45 million from a stranger in another country or region and will receive the money as soon as you transfer a $500 processing fee to the message sender's bank account. It would seem unlikely that these scams would find many willing victims, but in fact hundreds of millions of dollars have been lost to Internet fraud. According to the U.S. State Department Bureau of Consular Affairs, individuals of all ages and from all socio-economic backgrounds have lost considerable money on these scams, ranging from a few hundred dollars to hundreds of thousands of dollars. (One businessman reportedly paid over $5 million in a series of transactions.)

Most email providers include some form of filtering for malicious messages, but an amazing amount of junk mail is sent out into the world every day, and some of it will make it through your mail server's to your computer.

Outlook offers multiple levels of junk email filtering, and tools for guiding the delivery of messages that you do and don't want to receive. The Junk Email filter identifies messages that appear to be spam or of questionable origin, and either moves them to a special folder or deletes them. You can specify the level of filtering you want from the Junk Email filter, and specify email message senders or sending domains that you want to add to your Blocked Senders list, and hold messages from them in the Junk Email folder. You can also specify a list of email addresses or domains as Safe Senders whose messages should always be allowed through to your Inbox.

5

Trace message origins

The sender's name and email address that are shown in the message list don't always accurately represent the true message sender. Some (many) malicious message senders mask their email addresses with other email addresses, mask those with names that they think will look legitimate, and provide entirely different reply-to email addresses.

You can quickly check for additional information (and should do so before opening attachments or clicking links in a message of uncertain origin). For example, the message list might indicate that a message is from "Sister Mary Margaret," which could indicate that it is a genuine plea for aid from a charitable organization. In the Reading Pane, the message header might display "Sister Mary Margaret <johnsmith@humongousinsurance.com> as the sender. This could be an indication of false identification. If you're uncertain, you can display the message properties and review the Internet headers, which trace the message backward from your mail server to the sending mail server and provide the sender's email address as it is registered on the sending mail server. If the sender's email address in the Internet headers is something like zyxwvu@adatum.com or a strange foreign email address, it is likely to be a phishing message or an international financial scam.

To display the Internet headers of a received message, follow these steps:

1. Open the message and display the **Info** page of the Backstage view.

2. At the bottom of the **Info** page, click the **Properties** button to open the Properties dialog box for the message.

3. Scroll the **Internet headers** pane to display the message authentication and diagnostic information, or select and copy the text and paste it into a document or email message—there might be three or four pages of information.

This topic discusses three ways of managing junk email:

- Managing messages that Outlook delivers to the Junk Email folder

- Configuring Junk Email settings based on messages that Outlook delivers to your Inbox

- Independently configuring Junk Email filtering levels, safe and unsafe senders, and safe recipients

When managing messages in the Junk Email folder, Inbox, or other folder, you use commands on the Junk menu, which is available from the Home tab of the Mail module, the shortcut menu for a message in the message list, and the Message tab in the message window.

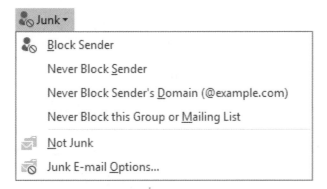

The Junk menu is available in all mail folders and received message windows

In each location, the Junk menu includes the following commands:

- **Block Sender** adds the sender's email address to your Blocked Senders list and moves the message to the Junk Email folder if it isn't already there.

> **SEE ALSO** See the sidebar "Trace message origins" earlier in this topic for information about locating the message sender's registered email address.

- **Never Block Sender** adds the sender's email address to your Safe Senders list. Future messages from the sender will not be routed to the Junk Email folder.

- **Never Block Sender's Domain (@example.com)** Adds the sender's email domain to your Safe Senders list. Future messages from any account on that domain will not be routed to your Junk Email folder. (For example, if the original message was from Sara@contoso.com, messages from anyone with an @contoso.com address will not be routed to the Junk Email folder.)

- **Never Block this Group or Mailing List** Adds the group or mailing list that the message was sent to, and that you are a member of, to your Safe Recipients list. Future messages sent to the group or mailing list will not be routed to your Junk Email folder.

- **Not Junk** Moves the message from the Junk Email folder to your Inbox and gives you the option of adding the sender or recipient (if the recipient is someone other than you) to the corresponding Safe list. This command is available only in the Junk Email folder.

- **Junk E-mail Options** Opens the Junk E-mail Options dialog box, in which you can configure the filtering level and manage your Safe Sender and Safe Recipient lists.

Manage messages in the Junk Email folder

By default, when Outlook receives a message that it deems to be either junk mail or a phishing message, it delivers that message to the Junk Email folder that is associated with your account rather than to your Inbox. (Each account you configure Outlook to connect to has its own Junk Email folder.) You might not be aware that one or more messages has been redirected to your Junk Email folder; if someone tells you that he or she has sent you a message but you haven't received it, it's a good idea to check whether it's in your Junk Email folder.

When the Junk Email folder contains messages, the number of unread messages in the folder is shown in brackets after the folder name in the Folder Pane.

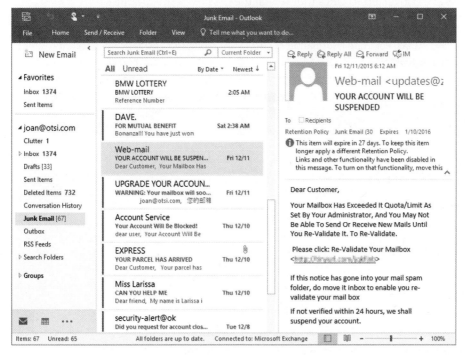

Many phishing messages have obviously incorrect information; others are vague enough to possibly fool you

Outlook converts message content in the Junk Email folder to plain text and disables any active links or content within the message. The InfoBar in the message header provides specific information about the message's status.

Any remote graphics (graphics that are displayed from Internet locations rather than embedded in the message—sometimes called *web beacons*) that were present in the message are converted to URLs that reveal the origins of the graphics.

 SEE ALSO For more information about web beacons, see "Increase email security" later in this chapter.

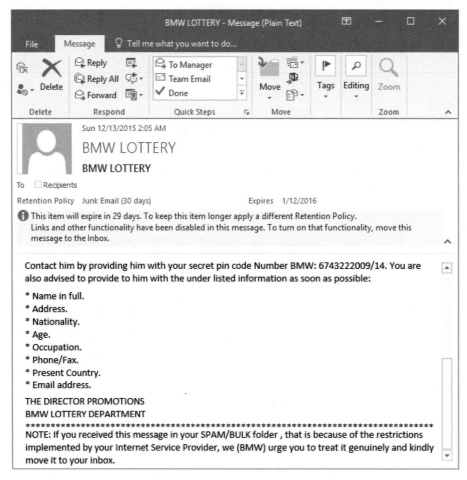

Outlook disables functionality in messages that it suspects to be junk email

Although the response options on the ribbon are active, you can't reply to a message from the Junk Email folder—you must first move it to the Inbox or another folder. You can forward a message from the Junk Email folder; for example, you might want to forward a message to someone else who can verify for you whether the message is valid. The forwarded message will be in plain-text format rather than in the original message format.

If you find a message in the Junk Email folder that isn't junk, you can indicate that to Outlook and alternatively approve the receipt of future messages sent from the message sender or to the message recipient. (For example, if you're a member of a mailing list or group and Outlook blocks a message that was sent to the group, you can approve the receipt of future message sent to that group from any sender.)

You can review the messages in the Junk Email folder and delete, move, or approve them individually, or you can periodically review the folder contents and then empty the entire folder at one time.

To display the Junk Email folder

1. In the **Folder Pane**, click **Junk Email**.

To move a valid message from the Junk Email folder without configuring related settings

1. In the **Junk Email** folder, select the message.

2. Do any of the following:

   - Drag the message to the destination folder in the **Folder Pane**.

   - Right-click the message, click **Move**, and then click the destination folder in the list.

   - On the **Home** tab, in the **Move** group, click the **Move** button, and then click the destination folder in the list.

> **TIP** You can move and manage individual messages from the message list in the Junk Email folder or from within an open message window. In the message window, on the Message tab, the Move menu is in the Move group and the Junk menu is in the Delete group.

To move a valid message from the Junk Email folder and configure related settings

1. In the **Junk Email** folder, select the message.

2. Do either of the following to display the Junk menu:

    - On the **Home** tab, in the **Delete** group, click the **Junk** button.

    - Right-click the message, and then click **Junk**.

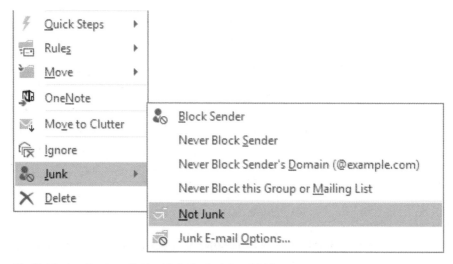

The Not Junk option is available only in the Junk Email folder

3. On the **Junk** menu, click **Not Junk** to open the Mark As Not Junk dialog box, which provides the option of trusting all future messages from the sender. Depending on the message header information, you might also have the option of trusting the message recipient.

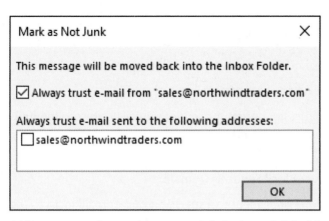

Add a message sender or recipient to your Safe Senders or Safe Recipients lists directly from a message

4. If you want to cancel the operation (leave the message in the Junk Email folder and not approve the sender or recipient), click the **Close** button (the **X**) in the upper-right corner of the dialog box.

   Or

   Do any of the following:

   - To add the message sender to your Safe Senders list, select the **Always trust e-mail from** check box.

   - If the **Mark as Not Junk** dialog box includes the **Always trust e-mail sent to the following addresses** box and you want to add the email address therein to the Safe Recipients list, select the check box.

   - Click **OK** to move the message to the Inbox.

To trust a message sender or recipient without moving a message from the Junk Email folder

1. Select the message, and then display the **Junk** menu.

2. On the **Junk** menu, do any of the following:

   - To stop routing messages from the sender's email address to the Junk Email folder, click **Never Block Sender**.

   - To stop routing messages from the sender's domain to the Junk Email folder, click **Never Block Sender's Domain**.

   - To stop routing messages sent to a specific group or mailing list to the Junk Email folder, click **Never Block this Group or Mailing List**.

3. In the confirmation message box, click **OK**.

To delete a message from the Junk Email folder

1. Select the message, and then do either of the following:

   - Press **Delete** to send the message to the Deleted Items folder.

   - Press **Shift+Delete** to bypass the Deleted Items folder and permanently delete the message.

To empty the Junk Email folder

1. In the **Folder Pane**, right-click the **Junk Email** folder, click **Empty Folder**, and then in the confirmation message box, click **Yes**.

Configure junk email settings in your Inbox

From any mail folder (most frequently your Inbox) you can send individual messages to the Junk Email folder and block or permit future messages from the message sender or sending domain. For example, if you receive messages from valid salespeople attempting to solicit business, you can file those as junk and save yourself from having to see follow-up messages from the same salesperson.

To move a message to the Junk Email folder and block future messages from the sender

1. Select the message, and then display the **Junk** menu.

2. On the **Junk** menu, click **Block Sender**.

SEE ALSO If you mistakenly block a sender, you can manually remove the email address from the Blocked Senders list in the Junk E-mail Options dialog box.

Configure junk email options

If you want to change the level of junk email filtering or manually populate the Safe Senders, Safe Recipients, and Blocked Senders lists, you can do so in the Junk E-mail Options dialog box.

TIP If Outlook is configured to connect to multiple email accounts, you configure the settings for each account separately. The Junk E-mail Options dialog box title bar indicates the account you're configuring options for.

The Junk E-mail Options dialog box has the following five tabs:

- On the Options tab, you can select a level of protection. If you don't have additional filters in place, such as those that might be supplied by your organization, you might prefer to click High. Otherwise, click Low.

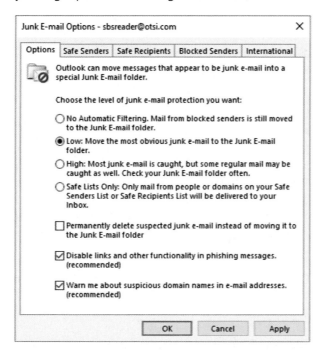

The Options tab of the Junk E-mail Options dialog box is a great starting place for configuring Outlook to filter out junk mail

If you want, you can have Outlook automatically delete suspected junk email instead of routing it to the Junk Email folder. This option should be used with caution, however, especially if you have applied one of the higher protection levels.

Note that the options to disable links and display warnings about suspicious domain names are unavailable to change. These settings are selected by default. Unless you are very confident that you have another protective system in place, leave these options selected.

■ On the Safe Senders tab, you manage the list of email addresses (for example, *tom@contoso.com*) or domains (in the form *@contoso.com*) from which messages will be routed directly to the Inbox.

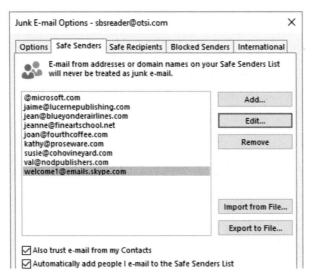

You can choose to trust all the email addresses in your Contacts folder or that you send email to

■ On the Safe Recipients tab, you can designate distribution lists or mailing lists that you belong to, so that messages sent to the lists by other members aren't treated as junk.

■ On the Blocked Senders tab, you can manage the list of email addresses and domains from which Outlook will automatically route messages to the Junk Email folder.

■ On the International tab, you have the option of blocking all messages from a top-level domain that is specific to a country or region, or all messages containing specific text encoding.

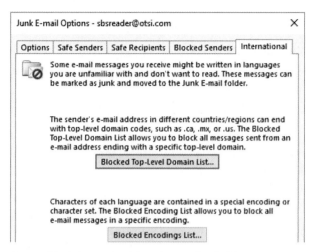

You can block the top-level domain associated with a country or region that you receive junk mail from

Outlook permits you to block only the top-level-domains (TLDs) that are specific to countries and regions. The encodings are primarily specific to languages, but also include some character sets.

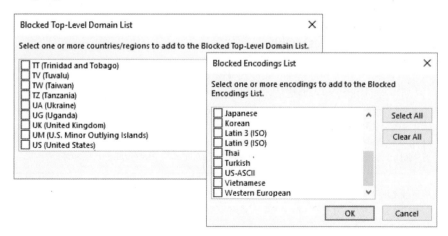

You can block all messages from specific locations or in specific character sets

> ✅ **TIP** The top-level domain (TLD), such as *.com*, is part of the domain name that is the base address of an email address or website. TLDs are governed by an international organization. Each TLD has a specific meaning: there are generic TLDs (such as .com and .net) that are available to anyone, sponsored TLDs (such as .edu, .gov, and .travel) that belong to private agencies or organizations, and two-letter country code TLDs that are intended to represent the country of origin or use of a site's content. Country code TLDs are frequently used for other purposes, however; for example, the TLD .am is assigned to Armenia, and .fm is assigned to the Federated States of Micronesia, but many radio stations have website addresses ending in these TLDs.

To open the Junk E-mail Options dialog box

1. In a mail module or received message window, display the **Junk** menu, and then click **Junk E-mail Options**.

To set the junk email protection level

1. In the **Junk E-mail Options** dialog box, on the **Options** tab, do any of the following:

   - To have Outlook block only email from senders on your Blocked Senders list, click **No Automatic Filtering**.

   - To have Outlook block the most obvious junk email, click **Low**.

   - To have Outlook apply stricter criteria to evaluate messages, click **High**.

   - To have Outlook block messages from any sender who isn't on your Safe lists, click **Safe Lists Only**.

2. If you want Outlook to bypass the Junk Email folder, select the **Permanently delete suspected junk e-mail** check box.

> ⚠ **IMPORTANT** If you set the protection level to High or to Safe Lists Only, don't select the option to permanently delete suspected junk email. With these settings, it is likely that the Junk Email filter will catch some valid messages.

3. Click **OK**.

To manage the Safe and Blocked lists

1. In the **Junk E-mail Options** dialog box, click the **Safe Senders**, **Safe Recipients**, or **Blocked Senders** tab.

2. Do any of the following:

   - To add an email address or domain to the list, click the **Add** button. Then in the **Add address or domain** dialog box, enter the address or domain you want to add, and click **OK**.

   - To modify an existing email address or domain in the list, click the address or domain, and then click the **Edit** button. In the **Edit address or domain** dialog box, make the changes you want, and then click **OK**.

   - To remove an email address or domain from the list, click the address or domain, and then click **Remove**.

3. Click **Apply** to apply the change and continue working in the dialog box, or click **OK** to apply the change and close the dialog box.

To automatically allow messages from known senders

1. In the **Junk E-mail Options** dialog box, on the **Safe Senders** tab, do either of the following:

   - To allow messages from any email address in your Contacts folder, select the **Also trust e-mail from my Contacts** check box.

   - To allow messages from anyone you've sent a message to, select the **Automatically add people I e-mail to the Safe Senders List** check box.

2. Click **Apply** or **OK**.

5

To block all messages from addresses within a specific top-level domain

1. In the **Junk E-mail Options** dialog box, on the **International** tab, click the **Blocked Encodings List** button.

2. In the **Blocked Encodings List** dialog box, select the check box of each character encoding that you want to block. Then click **OK**.

To block all messages in a specific character encoding

1. In the **Junk E-mail Options** dialog box, on the **International** tab, click the **Blocked Top-Level Domain List** button.

2. In the **Blocked Top-Level Domain List** dialog box, select the check box of each two-letter top-level domain that you want to block. Then click **OK**.

Increase email security

As discussed in the previous topic, messages that you receive can have attachments or contain links that expose your computer system to malicious software. Your outgoing messages can also be vulnerable to interception by malicious software that seeks to gather either personal information or email addresses. You can take security precautions with messages that you receive and send through Outlook to protect yourself and others.

In certain corporate environments, particularly those such as legal firms and accounting firms that handle sensitive data, specific email security procedures might be mandated and enforced at a server level. In the absence of such guidance, only you can decide whether any of these additional security measures are appropriate for your situation.

Apply security measures to incoming messages

Email is increasingly used to deliver marketing information to current and potential customers. Many companies include pictures in their marketing messages to help explain their products or to make the message more attractive and noticeable, but these pictures can make email messages large. To avoid this problem, some companies include links to pictures that are hosted on their server. When you preview or open the message, the pictures are displayed, but they aren't actually part of the message.

Some junk email senders use this same method to include *web beacons* in their messages. *Web beacons* are utilities that notify the sender when you read or preview the email message. The notification confirms that your email address is valid, and as a result, you might receive more junk email.

To help protect your privacy, Outlook includes features that block external content such as pictures and sounds. In addition to helping ensure your privacy, this blocking technique can save bandwidth resources, because you choose whether to download images and sounds, instead of Outlook downloading them automatically when you open a message.

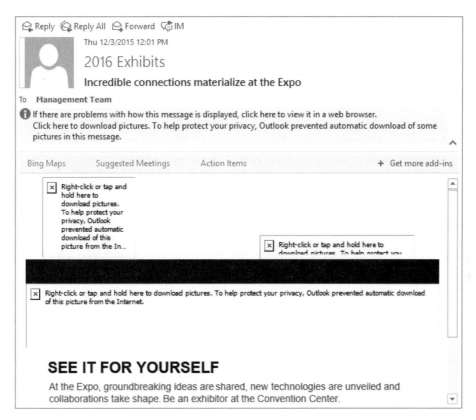

Placeholders indicate the locations of blocked images

By default, Outlook 2016 blocks external content to and from all sources other than those defined in the Safe Senders list and Safe Recipients list. When you open or preview a message that contains blocked content, an InfoBar in the message header provides options for handling the blocked content.

You can change the way Outlook handles external content. Under most circumstances, the security provided by the default settings far outweighs the slight inconvenience of manually downloading content. Many messages that contain blocked pictures are marketing messages that might not be of interest to you.

Viruses and other harmful software can easily be spread from computer to computer through active content embedded in or linked to from email messages. To ensure that you don't accidentally trigger active content in a received email message, you can display messages in plain text, rather than in Rich Text Format or HTML. Links, scripts, and other active content are disabled in plain text messages. (Unfortunately, so are formatting and graphics.)

To view the blocked content in an individual email message

1. Display a message that has blocked pictures.

2. At the top of the message window, click the **InfoBar**, and then click **Download Pictures**.

You can download pictures for one message or all messages from the sender

To display external content download settings

1. Display a message that has blocked pictures.

2. At the top of the message window, click the **InfoBar**, and then click **Change Automatic Download Settings** to display the Automatic Download page of the Trust Center.

Or

1. Click the **File** tab to display the Backstage view, and then click **Options**.

2. In the left pane of the **Outlook Options** dialog box, click **Trust Center**, and on the **Trust Center** page, click the **Trust Center Settings** button.

3. In the left pane of the **Trust Center** dialog box, click **Automatic Download**.

   The Automatic Download page of the Trust Center displays options that control whether Outlook automatically downloads and displays pictures in HTML email messages.

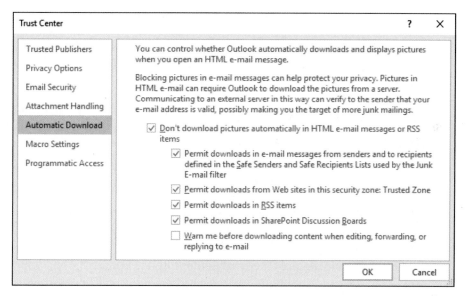

The default Automatic Download settings

 SEE ALSO For more information about configuring Outlook options and Trust Center settings, see Chapter 13, "Customize Outlook options."

To change the way Outlook handles external content

1. Display the **Automatic Download** page of the **Trust Center**.

2. If you want Outlook to download all externally stored pictures, clear the **Don't download pictures automatically** check box.

3. If you want Outlook to block externally stored pictures from senders or storage locations other than those that you define here, select the **Don't download pictures automatically** check box. Then select or clear the relevant **Permit downloads** check boxes to allow or block any of the following downloads:

   - Web content in messages from Safe Senders and Safe Recipients

   - Content stored on websites in your Trusted Zone

   - Web content in RSS feeds that you've subscribed to

   - Web content in posts to SharePoint Discussion Boards that you've subscribed to

4. If you permit specific downloads and want Outlook to alert you to web content in messages that you edit or respond to, select the **Warn me before downloading content** check box.

5. Click **OK** in the **Trust Center** dialog box and in the **Outlook Options** dialog box.

To display email security options

1. Click the **File** tab to display the Backstage view, and then click **Options**.

2. In the left pane of the **Outlook Options** dialog box, click **Trust Center**, and then on the **Trust Center** page, click the **Trust Center Settings** button.

3. In the left pane of the **Trust Center** dialog box, click **Email Security**.

   The Email Security page of the Trust Center displays options for encrypting email, obtaining and configuring digital IDs, reading email as plain text, and permitting scripts to run in shared or public folders.

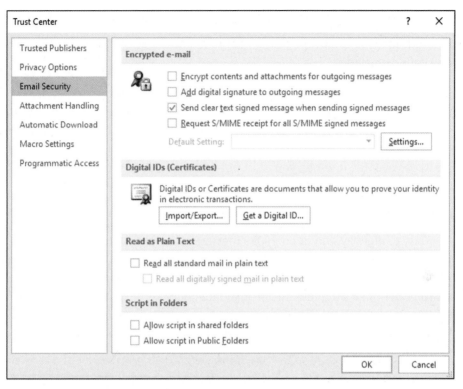

Options for protecting outgoing and received messages

To receive all messages in plain text format

1. Display the **Email Security** page of the **Trust Center** dialog box.

2. In the **Read as Plain Text** section, select the **Read all standard mail in plain text** check box. Then click **OK**.

Apply security measures to outgoing messages

Methods that you can use to protect outgoing messages include digitally signing and encrypting messages.

When sending messages, you can reassure message recipients that they are receiving valid messages from you by using a digital signature—a piece of code that validates the identity of a message sender (not the actual person, but the email account and computer from which the message originates). To send digitally signed or encrypted messages over the Internet, you must obtain a digital ID (a security certificate).

Configure Outlook to use a digital ID

If you try to digitally sign or encrypt a message without first installing a valid digital ID on your computer, Outlook prompts you to do so. If you prefer, you can obtain and install the digital ID before you need it, so you know that it will work when you need it to. You can obtain a digital ID from an independent certification authority. You might also be able to obtain one from your organization's IT department. Each certification level connotes a different level of trust; the highest is that of an independent certification authority.

Obtaining some types of digital IDs, such as those used to certify the source of software programs, involves a stringent application process that can take weeks to complete. However, applying for a commercial security certificate to certify documents and email messages is a relatively simple process. Many US and international certification companies offer digital IDs to certify email. You'll probably be most comfortable purchasing a certificate in your native currency. Regardless of the location of the certification authority, the digital ID is valid worldwide.

After you install the digital ID certificate on your computer, you must select it for message encryption in Outlook.

 TIP You can have more than one digital ID on your computer, and you can select which one to use for each document or message. For example, you might have one digital ID for business use and one for personal use.

To obtain a digital ID to sign or encrypt messages and documents

1. Display the **Email Security** page of the **Trust Center** dialog box.

2. In the **Digital IDs (Certificates)** section, click **Get a Digital ID** to display the Find Digital ID Services page of the Microsoft Office website in your default web browser. This webpage lists some of the providers from whom you can obtain a digital ID to certify email messages and documents.

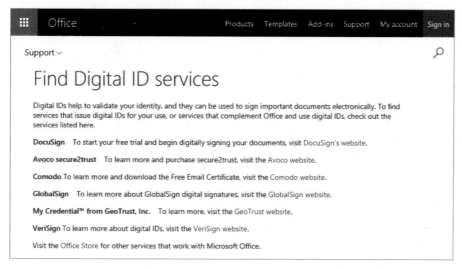

Some providers offer free certificates or free trial periods

3. Click the link at the end of a provider's description to display the provider's website.

4. Follow the instructions on the website to register for a digital ID and install the certificate on your computer. As part of the process, you'll likely be required to respond to an email message from your computer.

> **TIP** The commercial digital ID is associated with your email address; if you need to use it on another computer, you can reinstall it from the provider's site, or you can export the digital ID file from the original computer and import it on the other computer.

To configure Outlook to use an installed digital ID certificate

1. Display the **Email Security** page of the **Trust Center** dialog box. Then in the **Encrypted e-mail** section, click **Settings** to open the Change Security Settings dialog box.

2. In the **Security Settings Name** box, enter a name that identifies the digital ID certificate you're going to connect to. Then to the right of the **Signing Certificate** box, click the **Choose** button to display the available certificates.

The dialog box displays the digital signing certificates available on your computer

3. In the **Windows Security** dialog box, click the digital ID certificate you want to use to digitally sign outgoing messages, and then click **OK** to enter the certificate information in the Change Security Settings dialog box.

> 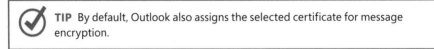 **TIP** By default, Outlook also assigns the selected certificate for message encryption.

4. Click **OK** in the **Change Security Settings** dialog box, in the **Trust Center** dialog box, and in the **Outlook Options** dialog box.

> **TIP** You can configure custom security settings for an outgoing message, but the route to the settings is somewhat convoluted. You open the Properties dialog box of the message, click Security Settings, and then in the Security Properties dialog box, click Change Settings.

To export a digital ID for storage or use on another computer

1. On the **Email Security** page of the **Trust Center** dialog box, in the **Digital IDs (Certificates)** section, click **Import/Export**.

2. In the **Import/Export Digital ID** dialog box, click **Export your Digital ID to a file**.

3. Click the **Select** button. In the **Windows Security** dialog box, click the digital ID certificate you want to export, and then click **OK**.

4. Browse to the location where you want to store the certificate file. In the **File name** box, enter a name for the certificate file. Then click **OK** to return to the Import/Export Digital ID dialog box.

5. In the dialog box, the Export option is no longer selected. Click **Export your Digital ID to a file** to reactivate the corresponding boxes.

6. In the **Password** and **Confirm** boxes, enter a password that will be required when importing the digital ID certificate on another computer.

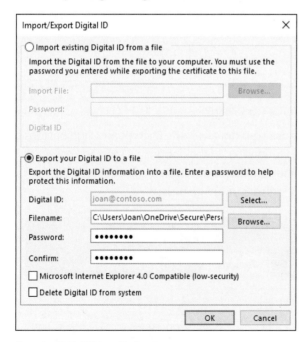

Export a digital ID to a file for storage or reuse

7. Click **OK**.

To import a digital ID from a file

1. On the **Email Security** page of the **Trust Center** dialog box, in the **Digital IDs (Certificates)** section, click **Import/Export**.

2. In the **Import/Export Digital ID** dialog box, click **Import existing Digital ID from a file**.

3. Browse to the file that contains the digital ID certificate.

4. Enter the password you assigned to the file when you created it.

Import/Export Digital ID	✕

◉ Import existing Digital ID from a file

Import the Digital ID from the file to your computer. You must use the password you entered while exporting the certificate to this file.

Import File: C:\Users\Joan\OneDrive\Secure\Pers· [Browse...]

Password: ••••••••

Digital ID

Import a digital ID from a file

5. Click **OK**.

Digitally sign or encrypt messages

After you configure Outlook to use your digital ID, the Encrypt and Sign buttons appear in the Permission group on the Options tab of the ribbon in a message composition window. You can digitally sign individual messages when you compose them, or you can instruct Outlook to digitally sign all outgoing messages.

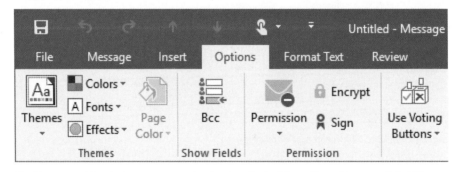

The Encrypt and Sign buttons are present only when Outlook is configured to use a digital ID

A digital signature validates the identity of the message sender, so other people know that the message came from you. A message with a valid digital signature has a red ribbon on its message icon and a digital signature icon (also a red ribbon) in its message header. When you receive a digitally signed message, you can click the digital signature icon to view information about the signature.

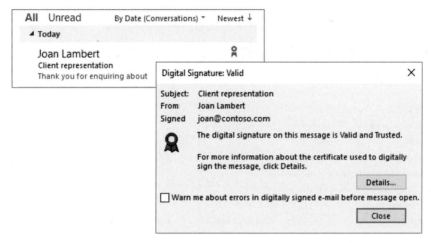

A digitally signed message and validation information

Encrypting a message scrambles the message content. For the message recipient to decrypt the encrypted message, the message sender and recipient must first exchange digitally signed messages and add the digital ID certificates to their contacts.

> **IMPORTANT** You must obtain and install a digital ID and configure Outlook to use the digital ID before you can perform the following procedures. For more information, see "Configure Outlook to use a digital ID" earlier in this topic.

To digitally sign an individual email message

1. In the message composition window, on the **Options** tab, in the **Permission** group, click the **Sign** button.

Or

1. In the message composition window, on the **Options** tab, click the **More Options** dialog box launcher to open the Properties dialog box.

2. In the **Properties** dialog box, click **Security Settings** to open the Security Properties dialog box.

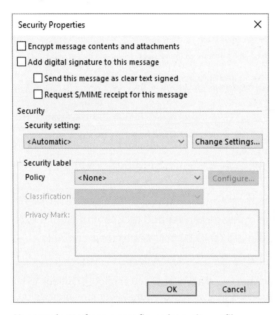

You can choose from preconfigured security profiles

3. In the **Security Properties** dialog box, select the **Add digital signature to this message** check box, and then click **OK**.

To digitally sign all outgoing messages

1. Display the **Email Security** page of the **Trust Center** dialog box.

2. In the **Encrypted e-mail** section, select the **Add digital signature to outgoing messages** check box.

3. If your message recipients might not have S/MIME (Secure Multipurpose Internet Mail Extensions) security (for instance, if you're sending messages to people who you know aren't using Outlook), ensure that the **Send clear text signed message when sending signed messages** check box is selected (this is the default setting).

4. Click **OK** in all the open dialog boxes.

To encrypt an individual message

1. In the message composition window, on the **Options** tab, in the **Permission** group, click the **Encrypt** button.

Or

1. From the message composition window, open the **Security Properties** dialog box.

2. In the **Security Properties** dialog box, select the **Encrypt message contents and attachments** check box, and then click **OK**.

To encrypt all outgoing messages

1. Display the **Email Security** page of the **Trust Center** dialog box.

2. In the **Encrypted e-mail** section, select the **Encrypt contents and attachments for outgoing messages** check box.

3. On the **Email Security** page of the **Trust Center** dialog box, in the **Encrypted e-mail** section, select the check box.

4. If you want to receive verification that a message recipient received an encrypted message in its encrypted format, select the **Request S/MIME receipt for all S/MIME signed messages** check box.

5. Click **OK**.

5

Restrict access by using rights management

If information rights management (IRM) is configured on your computer, you can restrict the actions that recipients can take with the messages that you send them.

If you don't want a message recipient to forward, copy, or print your message, you can send it with restricted permissions. When this protection is in place, other people cannot perform these tasks. If the restricted message includes an attachment, such as a Microsoft Word document, an Excel workbook, or a PowerPoint presentation, the recipient can't edit, copy, or print the attachment (unless you have set individual permissions to allow those actions within the document). The assigned permissions are indicated on the InfoBar of the message and apply no matter where the message is stored.

To restrict message permissions, you must have access to an IRM server. Your organization might have one. You must establish your credentials with the IRM licensing server and install a digital certificate associated with IRM to validate your identity.

After you configure your computer for IRM, the Permission list in the Permission group on the Options tab of the message composition window ribbon includes a list of restrictions.

Skills review

In this chapter, you learned how to:

- Block unwanted messages
- Increase email security

Practice tasks

No practice files are necessary to complete the practice tasks in this chapter.

Block unwanted messages

Perform the following tasks:

1. Display your **Junk Email** folder. If it contains messages, do the following:

   - Display a few messages in the **Reading Pane**. Identify any message content that has been disabled.

   - In the message list, scan the message senders and subjects to identify any messages that might be valid.

   - If you locate one or more valid messages, use the most appropriate option for each message to move it to your Inbox, allow future messages from the message sender or sender's domain, or allow future messages sent to the recipient address.

   - Locate a message that is definitely junk mail, and delete it from the Junk Email folder.

   - If you want to, empty the **Junk Email** folder.

2. Display your Inbox and scan the messages for any that you would like the junk mail filter to catch. If you locate a junk mail message, move it to the **Junk Email** folder and block future messages from the sender.

3. Open the **Junk E-mail Options** dialog box. Review the junk email protection levels, and select the one you want to use.

4. Review the **Safe** and **Blocked** lists, and add any domains or addresses that you want to the list.

5. Review the other available settings and configure them to suit your needs. Then close the **Junk E-mail Options** dialog box.

Increase email security

Display your Inbox, and then perform the following tasks:

1. Locate a message that contains blocked pictures (preferably from a company that you are familiar with). In the **Reading Pane** or message window, click the InfoBar and review the options. Consider the outcome of each option. If you want to, display the blocked pictures.

2. Display the **Automatic Download** page of the Trust Center. Review the available options and consider which of them you are comfortable with. Configure the options as you want them.

3. Display the **E-mail Security** page of the Trust Center. Review the available options and consider which of them you are comfortable with.

4. If you don't already have a digital ID for signing email messages, and want to practice working with one, do the following:

   • Follow the steps to display the digital ID vendors, and select a vendor. (At least one vendor offers a free email signing ID.)

   • Follow the digital ID vendor's instructions for acquiring the digital ID and installing the certificate on your computer.

   • Configure Outlook to use that certificate to digitally sign messages.

   • Send a digitally signed message to someone.

   • If you want to export the digital ID certificate for use on another computer or to store as a backup, do so.

Organize your Inbox

You can use Outlook 2016 to manage multiple email accounts, including multiple Microsoft Exchange Server accounts and their associated contacts, calendars, and other elements. Even if you use Outlook only for sending and receiving email messages, it can be challenging to keep track of them and to locate specific information that you're looking for. Fortunately, Outlook provides many simple yet useful features that you can use to organize messages and other Outlook items and to quickly find information you need.

By default, the message list displays the email messages you receive in order by time and date of receipt (from newest to oldest). You can arrange, group, and sort messages in Outlook to keep conversation threads together and to help you quickly determine which are the most important, decide which can be deleted, and locate any that need an immediate response.

You can simplify the process of organizing Outlook items of all kinds by assigning categories to related items. You can then arrange, sort, filter, and search for Outlook items by category.

This chapter guides you through procedures related to working with Conversation view, arranging messages by specific attributes, organizing items by using color categories, and organizing messages in folders.

In this chapter

- Display and manage conversations
- Arrange messages by specific attributes
- Categorize items
- Organize messages in folders

Practice files

No practice files are necessary to complete the practice tasks in this chapter.

Display and manage conversations

When a recipient replies to an email message, the exchange of multiple messages creates a *conversation*. Conversations that involve multiple recipients and responses can contain many messages. Conversation view is an alternative arrangement of messages grouped by subject. All the messages with the same subject appear together in your Inbox (or other message folder) under one conversation header.

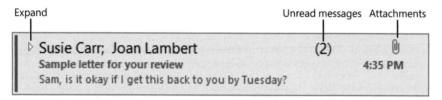

Until you expand the conversation header, the entire conversation takes up only as much space in your Inbox as a single message would

The conversation header provides information about the messages within the conversation, including the number of unread messages and whether one or more messages includes an attachment, is categorized, or is flagged for follow up.

You can display differing levels of messages within a conversation, as follows:

- Click the conversation header or the Expand button once to display the most recent message in the Reading Pane and to display all the unique messages in the conversation (the most recent message in each thread) in the message list. Reading only these messages will give you all the information that exists in the conversation.

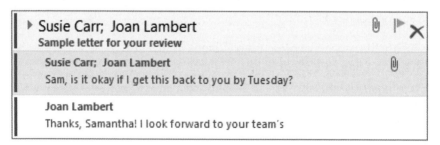

When a conversation is expanded to display unique messages, the conversation header displays recent participants and subjects

- Click the Expand button again to display all messages in the conversation, including messages from your Sent Items folder.

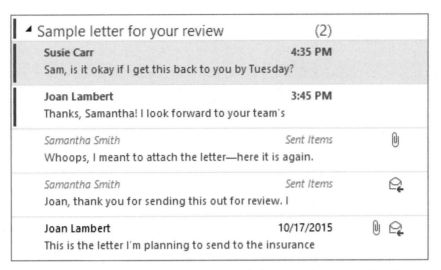

When the conversation is fully expanded, the conversation header displays only the subject

> **TIP** When an email conversation involves more than two people, particularly if the email was addressed to a large distribution list, often more than one person responds to the same message, and other people respond to each of those messages. Multiple conversations that emerge from the primary conversation are referred to as branches.

Benefits of displaying messages as conversations include the following:

- When you receive a message that is part of a conversation, the entire conversation moves to the top of your Inbox and the new message appears when you click the conversation header.

  A blue vertical line and bold blue subject indicate that a conversation includes unread messages. If there are multiple unread messages, the number is indicated in parentheses following the subject. The senders of the unread messages are listed below the subject.

- Sent messages are available from within the conversation. (They remain stored in the Sent Items folder, but you can read and open them from the Inbox.) This is particularly convenient when you need to access sent attachments that aren't available in the replies.

- You can manage all the messages that are part of a conversation as a group. Clicking the conversation headers selects all the messages in the conversation. You can move or categorize all the messages as a unit.

You can modify the way Conversation view displays messages to suit the way you work by turning the following display settings on or off:

- **Show Messages from Other Folders** By default, Conversation view displays messages stored in any folder, including sent messages that are stored in the Sent Items folder. (Within an expanded conversation, sent messages are indicated by an italic font.) You can turn off this setting to display only messages from the current folder.

- **Show Senders Above the Subject** By default, when a conversation is collapsed, the conversation header displays the names of all the conversation participants above the conversation subject; when the conversation is fully expanded, the conversation header displays only the subject. This setting reverses the order of the information in the conversation header; the names of the conversation participants are displayed above the conversation subject. In some cases, such as when Outlook displays a message on the second line, the subject might not be visible at all.

- **Always Expand Conversations** This setting causes Outlook to display all messages in a conversation when you click the Expand Conversation button or conversation header once.

- **Use Classic Indented View** This setting causes Outlook to indent older messages within individual message threads to show the progression of the thread. This setting is not as effective as the default setting for displaying split conversations, because a message might be at the root of multiple branches but can appear only once in the message list.

Outlook tracks conversations by subject regardless of whether you display the messages in Conversation view. You can use the following features to manage conversations:

- **Ignore Conversation** This command moves the selected conversation and any related messages you receive in the future directly to the Deleted Items folder.

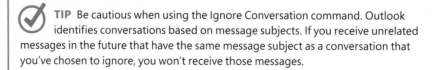

> **TIP** Be cautious when using the Ignore Conversation command. Outlook identifies conversations based on message subjects. If you receive unrelated messages in the future that have the same message subject as a conversation that you've chosen to ignore, you won't receive those messages.

- **Clean Up Conversation** This command deletes redundant messages—messages whose text is wholly contained within later messages—from a conversation or folder. By default, Outlook doesn't clean up categorized, flagged, or digitally signed messages. You can modify conversation clean-up settings when you clean up conversations, on the Mail page of the Outlook Options dialog box. For information about modifying mail settings, see "Configure message options" in Chapter 13, "Customize Outlook options."

 TIP Because Conversation view displays only unique messages until you fully expand the conversation, a specific message that you're looking for might not be immediately visible. If this happens, you can temporarily disable Conversation view by choosing a different message arrangement. For more information, see "Arrange messages by specific attributes" later in this chapter.

To turn Conversation view on or off for one or all folders

6

⚠ **IMPORTANT** Conversation view is available only when messages are arranged by date.

1. Do either of the following:

   - On the **View** tab, in the **Messages** group, select or clear the **Show as Conversations** check box.

   - Click the message list header, and then on the menu, click **Show as Conversations**.

Specify the scope of the change

2. In the **Microsoft Outlook** message box, indicate the scope of the change by clicking **All mailboxes** or **This folder**.

 TIP When you arrange a folder by an attribute other than date, Conversation view is temporarily disabled. For more information, see "Arrange messages by specific attributes" later in this chapter.

To display the messages within a conversation

1. Click the conversation header or the **Expand** button once to display the unique messages in the conversation.

2. Click the **Expand** button again to display all messages in the conversation.

To select all the messages in a conversation

1. Click the conversation header once.

To change the way conversations are displayed in the message list

1. On the **View** tab, in the **Messages** group, click **Conversation Settings**. On the Conversation Settings menu, a check mark indicates that an option is turned on.

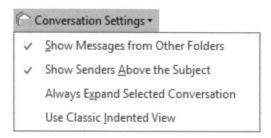

Change the default display settings

2. On the **Conversation Settings** menu, click a setting to turn it on or off.

To remove redundant messages from a conversation

1. Select any message in the conversation.

2. On the **Home** tab, in the **Delete** group, click **Clean Up**, and then on the menu, click **Clean Up Conversation**.

You can change the location to which Outlook moves messages when cleaning up

3. If the Clean Up Conversation message box opens, do the following:

    a. If you want to instruct Outlook to clean up conversations without requesting confirmation, select the **Don't show this message again** check box.

    b. If you want to change the conversation clean-up settings, click **Settings** to display the Mail page of the Outlook Options dialog box. Scroll to the **Conversation Clean Up** section, and change any of the settings you want to. Then click **OK**.

Conversation Clean Up
Cleaned-up items will go to this folder: [   ] Browse…
Messages moved by Clean Up will go to their account's Deleted Items.
☐ When cleaning sub-folders, recreate the folder hierarchy in the destination folder
☐ Don't move unread messages
☑ Don't move categorized messages
☑ Don't move flagged messages
☑ Don't move digitally-signed messages
☑ When a reply modifies a message, don't move the original

You can retain specific categories of messages

    c. Click **Clean Up**.

To remove redundant messages from a folder

1. Select any message in the folder.

2. On the **Home** tab, in the **Delete** group, click **Clean Up**, and then on the menu, click **Clean Up Folder** or **Clean Up Folder & Subfolders**.

3. If the Clean Up Folder message box opens, do the following:

    a. If you want to instruct Outlook to clean up folders without requesting confirmation, select the **Don't show this message again** check box.

    b. If you want to change the conversation clean-up settings, click **Settings** to display the Mail page of the Outlook Options dialog box. Scroll to the **Conversation Clean Up** section, and change any of the settings you want to. Then click **OK**.

    c. Click **Clean Up Folder**.

6

To ignore a conversation

1. Select any message in the conversation, and then do either of the following:

   - On the **Home** tab, in the **Delete** group, click **Ignore**.

   - Press **Ctrl+Del**.

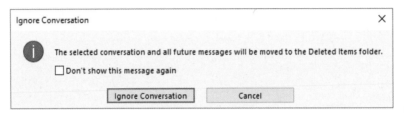

Automatically delete future messages in the conversation

1. If the Ignore Conversation message box opens, do the following:

   a. If you want to instruct Outlook to ignore conversations without requesting confirmation, select the **Don't show this message again** check box.

   b. Click **Ignore Conversation**.

To stop ignoring a conversation

1. Display the Deleted Items folder.

2. Locate and select any item in the ignored conversation.

3. On the **Home** tab, in the **Delete** group, the Ignore button is active for a conversation that is being ignored. Click the **Ignore** button to turn it off.

Arrange messages by specific attributes

By default, Outlook displays messages arranged by date, from newest to oldest. Alternatively, you can arrange items by any of the following attributes:

- **Account** Messages are grouped by the email account to which they were sent. This is useful if you receive messages for more than one email account in your Inbox (for example, if you receive messages sent to your POP3 account within your Exchange account mailbox).

- **Attachments** Messages are grouped by whether they have attachments and secondarily by date received.

- **Categories** Messages are arranged by the category you assign to them. Messages without a category appear first. Messages with multiple categories assigned to them appear in each of those category groups.

- **Flag: Start Date or Due Date** Unflagged messages and messages without specific schedules appear first. Messages that you've added to your task list with specific start or due dates are grouped by date.

- **From** Messages appear in alphabetical order by the message sender's display name. If you receive messages from a person who uses two different email accounts, or who sends messages from two different email clients (for example, from Outlook and from Windows Mail), the messages will not necessarily be grouped together.

- **Importance** Messages are grouped by priority: High (indicated by a red exclamation point), Normal (the default), or Low (indicated by a blue downward-pointing arrow).

- **To** Messages are grouped alphabetically by the primary recipients (the addresses or names on the To line). The group name exactly reflects the order in which addresses appear on the To line. Therefore, a message addressed to *Bart Duncan; Lukas Keller* is not grouped with a message addressed to *Lukas Keller; Bart Duncan*.

- **Size** Messages are grouped by size of the message, including any attachments. Groups include Huge (1–5 MB), Very Large (500 KB–1 MB), Large (100–500 KB), Medium (25–100 KB), Small (10–25 KB), and Tiny (less than 10 KB). This feature is useful if you work for an organization that limits the size of your Inbox, because you can easily locate large messages and delete them or move them to a personal folder.

- **Subject** Messages are arranged alphabetically by their subjects and then by date. This is similar to arranging by conversation except that the messages aren't threaded.

- **Type** Items in your Inbox (or other folder) are grouped by the type of item—for example, messages, encrypted messages, message receipts, meeting requests and meeting request responses, tasks, Microsoft InfoPath forms, and server notifications.

After arranging the items in your message list, you can change the sort order of the arrangement. The message list header displays the current sort order and arrangement of the message list.

Numbers come before letters when sorting from A to Z

By default, the messages within each arrangement are in groups specific to that category. For example, when messages are arranged by date, they are grouped by date: groups include each day of the current week, Last Week, Two Weeks Ago, Three Weeks Ago, Last Month, and Older. Each group has a header. You can collapse a group so that only the header is visible, or select and process messages by group.

Collapsing groups of messages displays only the group headers

In Single view or Preview view, you can sort messages by any visible column. If you want to sort by an attribute that isn't shown, you can add that column to the view.

To arrange messages by a specific attribute

1. Do any of the following:

   - In any view: On the **View** tab, in the **Arrangement** gallery, click the message attribute.

   - In Compact view: In the message list header, click the current arrangement, and then click the message attribute.

   - In Single view or Preview view: Right-click any column header, click **Arrange By**, and then click the message attribute.

To reverse the default sort order of the message list arrangement

1. Do any of the following:

   - In any view: On the **View** tab, in the **Arrangement** group, click **Reverse Sort**.

   - In Compact view: In the message list header, click the current sort order.

   - In Single view or Preview view: Right-click any column header, and then click **Reverse Sort**.

 TIP In a list view, you can sort by any column by clicking the column header, and reverse the sort order by clicking the column header again.

To group or ungroup messages

1. Do any of the following:

   - In any view: On the **View** tab, in the **Arrangement** gallery, click **Show in Groups**.

   - In Compact view: Click the message list header, and then on the menu, click **Show in Groups**.

   - In Single view or Preview view: Right-click the header of the column you want to group by, and then click **Group By This Field**.

To select a group of messages

1. Click the group header.

6

To expand the current message group

1. Do any of the following:

   - Click the arrow at the left end of the group header.

   - Press the **Right Arrow** key.

   - On the **View** tab, in the **Arrangement** group, click the **Expand/Collapse** button, and then click **Expand This Group**.

To collapse the current message group

1. Do any of the following:

   - Click the arrow at the left end of the group header.

   - Press the **Left Arrow** key.

   - On the **View** tab, in the **Arrangement** group, click the **Expand/Collapse** button, and then click **Collapse This Group**.

To expand or collapse all message groups

1. On the **View** tab, in the **Arrangement** group, click the **Expand/Collapse** button, and then click **Expand All Groups** or **Collapse All Groups**.

To reset the message arrangement (and other view settings)

1. On the **View** tab, in the **Current View** group, click the **Reset View** button.

2. In the **Microsoft Outlook** dialog box, click **Yes**.

Categorize items

To help you more easily locate Outlook items associated with a specific subject, project, person, or other common factor, you can create a category specific to that attribute and assign the category to any related items. You can assign a category to any type of Outlook item, such as a message, an appointment, or a contact record. For example, you might have categories for different people, clients, interest groups, or occasions.

Each category has an associated color, which provides a visual indicator in the item windows and in the module content views. More importantly, the category is a property that you can use to search, sort, and filter items within or across all the Outlook modules.

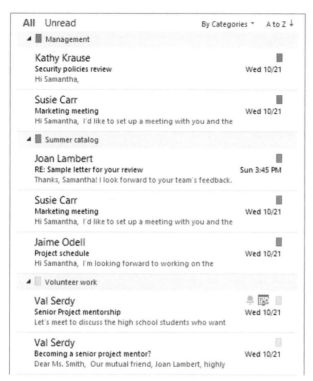

Messages that have multiple categories assigned appear in multiple category groups

Outlook 2016 comes with six starter categories named for their associated colors. You can rename these six categories to suit your needs. If you don't rename a standard color category before assigning it for the first time, Outlook gives you the option of renaming the category the first time you use it.

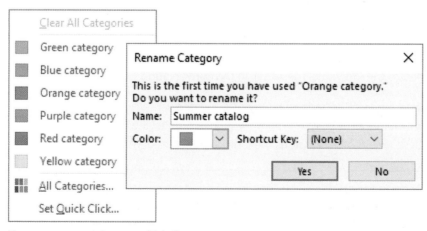

You can rename a category multiple times

You can create new categories as you need them. Each category can have the following elements:

- **Name** The category name can be one simple word or a long, descriptive phrase. The first 32 characters of the category name are visible in the Color Categories dialog box, but pointing to a truncated name displays the entire name in a ScreenTip.

- **Shortcut key** You can assign any of the 11 available keyboard shortcut combinations (Ctrl+F2 through Ctrl+F12) to the individual color categories.

- **Color** You can assign any of the 25 available colors to a category, or you can choose not to assign a color and to rely only on the name to distinguish between categories. When you assign a category that doesn't have an associated color to an Outlook item, the color block or color bar is shown as white. You can assign a color to multiple color categories.

Categories that you assign are represented by color blocks in a content list view, and by color bars in the open item window and in the Reading Pane.

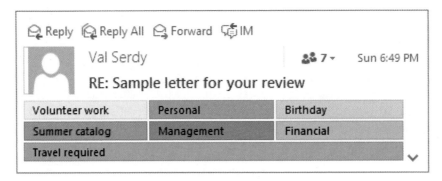

You can assign multiple categories to a message or other item

When Conversation view is on, the conversation header displays all the color category blocks assigned to the individual messages in the conversation.

You can designate one category as the Quick Click category. When displaying items in a view that includes a Categories column—such as Single view or Preview view—clicking the Categories column assigns the Quick Click category.

> **TIP** You can instruct Outlook to automatically assign a category to an incoming message that meets specific criteria by creating a rule. For more information, see "Create rules to process messages" in Chapter 14, "Manage email automatically."

You can apply a category with one click or by using a keyboard shortcut

To quickly view the items that have a specific category assigned to them, you can group items by category or include the category in a search. In a list view of any module, you can sort and filter by category. On the To-Do Bar, you can arrange flagged messages and tasks by category.

To display the Categorize menu

1. Do any of the following:

   • On the **Home** tab of any mail or contact folder, in the **Tags** group, click the **Categorize** button.

   • On the item tool tab (such as **Appointment** or **Meeting**) of any calendar item, in the **Tags** group, click the **Categorize** button.

   • Right-click an item or selection of items, and then click **Categorize**.

The Categorize menu displays recently assigned categories:

Store information in Outlook notes

You can store miscellaneous information such as reminders, passwords, account numbers, and processes by saving them in electronic notes. Because your notes are available to you from wherever you access Outlook, this can be a very convenient way of retaining information you might need later. And because you're less likely to accidentally delete a note than a message, it is safer than sending information to yourself in an email message.

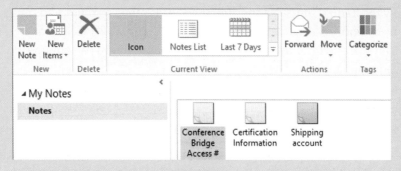

You can categorize notes to easily find them

You can enter only text into a note; you can't format the text or include graphic elements. Notes do support hyperlinks; if you enter a website address and then press Enter, the website address will change to blue underlined text to indicate that it is a hyperlink. You can click the hyperlink to open the website or page in your default web browser.

Although notes are a type of Outlook item, they don't appear in the same type of windows as messages, appointments, contact records, and tasks. Instead, they appear in the form of "sticky notes." By default, note icons and sticky note representations are a pale yellow color, like the color of standard paper sticky notes. When you assign a category to a note, the note color changes to the category color.

You can view, sort, and organize notes in the same way you do other Outlook items. The standard views include Icons, Notes List, and Last 7 Days.

As with other Outlook items, if you're looking for a specific piece of information in a note, you can quickly locate it by entering a search word or phrase in the Search Notes box at the top of the content area.

TIP The first time you access the Notes module, you must do so from the Folder List in the Folder Pane or by clicking Ctrl+5. Thereafter, you can also access it by clicking the ellipsis at the end of the Navigation Bar and then clicking Notes.

To store information in a note:

1. Display the **Notes** module.

2. On the **Home** tab, in the **New** group, click the **New Note** button to display a new note. The current date and time appear at the bottom.

3. Enter the subject or title of the note, press **Enter**, and then enter the information you want to store into the note. The first line of the note becomes its subject.

4. To save and close the note, click the **Close** button in the upper-right corner to display the note in the content area. Only the subject is visible. You can access the stored information by opening the note.

6

To open the Color Categories dialog box

1. Display the **Categorize** menu, and then click **All Categories**.

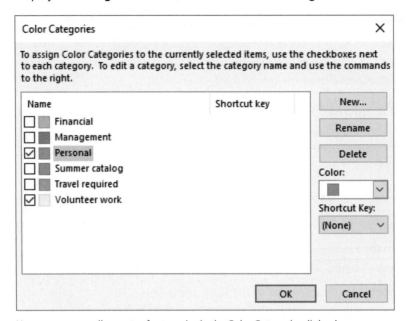

You can manage all aspects of categories in the Color Categories dialog box

To assign a category to a message or other item

1. Select the item or items that you want to categorize.

2. Display the **Categorize** menu, and then do either of the following:

    -   If the menu includes the category you want to assign, click the category.

    -   If the menu doesn't include the category you want to assign, click **All Categories**. In the **Color Categories** dialog box that opens, select the check box of the category you want to assign, and then click **OK**.

To assign or remove the Quick Click category

1. In any module content list view, click in the **Categories** column for the item.

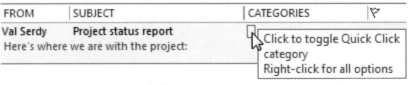

Clicking turns the category on and off

To remove a category from an item

1. Open the item, and then right-click the colored category bar.

2. On the shortcut menu, click **Clear** "*Category*", **Clear All Categories**, or the name of the category that you want to clear.

Or

1. Select or open the item, and then display the **Categorize** menu.

2. On the **Categorize** menu, click **Clear All Categories**, or click the category that you want to clear.

To create a category

1. Open the **Color Categories** dialog box, and then click **New**.

2. In the **Add New Category** dialog box, do the following, and then click **OK**:

   • In the **Name** box, enter the category name.

   • In the **Color** list, click the color you want to assign to the category.

   • If you want to assign a keyboard shortcut, click it in the **Shortcut Key** list.

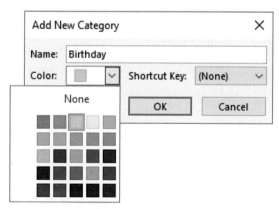

Choose from among 25 colors

To rename a category

1. Open the **Color Categories** dialog box.

2. Click the name or select the check box of the category, and then click **Rename** to activate the category name for editing.

3. Change or replace the category name, and then press **Enter** or click away from the active name box.

TIP The category order doesn't immediately change, but the next time you display the categories in a list or dialog box, they will be in alphabetical order.

To delete a category

1. Open the **Color Categories** dialog box.

2. Click the name or select the check box of the category, and then click **Delete** or press **Alt+D**.

3. In the **Microsoft Outlook** message box asking you to confirm the deletion, click **Yes**.

To set or change the Quick Click category

1. Display the **Categorize** menu, and then click **Set Quick Click**.

2. In the **Set Quick Click** dialog box, click the list, click the category that you want to set as the default, and then click **OK**.

Or

1. Open the **Outlook Options** dialog box, and display the **Advanced** page.

2. Scroll down on the Advanced page to display the **Other** section, and then click the **Quick Click** button.

3. In the **Set Quick Click** dialog box, click the list, click the category that you want to set as the default, and then click **OK**.

Organize messages in folders

After you read and respond to messages, you might want to keep some for future reference. You can certainly choose to retain them all in your Inbox if you want, but as the number of messages in your Inbox increases to the thousands and even tens of thousands, it might quickly become overwhelming. (Yes, faithful reader, it happens to the best of us!) To minimize your Inbox contents and avoid an accumulation of unrelated messages, you can organize messages into folders. For example, you can keep messages that require action on your part in your Inbox and move messages that you want to retain for future reference into other folders.

 TIP Because the Outlook search function provides the option of searching within all folders containing items of a particular type, you can easily locate a message that's been moved to a folder without having to remember which folder it's in.

Popular personal-organization experts advocate various folder structures (for paper folders and email message folders) as an important part of an organizational system. You can apply any of these ideas when you create folders in Outlook, or you can use any other structure that works for you. For example, you might create folders that designate the level of action required, create a folder for each project you're working on, or create a folder to store all messages from a specific person, such as your manager, regardless of the message subject.

Subfolders of the Inbox, in the Navigation pane of the Mail module and in the Folders list

When you create a folder, you specify the location of the folder within your existing Outlook folder structure and the type of items you want the folder to contain. You can create folders to contain the following types of items:

- Calendar items
- Contact items
- InfoPath Form items
- Journal items

- Mail and Post items
- Note items
- Task items

The selection you make governs the folder icon that precedes its name in the Folder Pane, the folder window layout, the ribbon tabs and commands available in the folder, and the content of the Folder Pane when displaying the folder.

You can move messages to folders manually, or if your organization is running Exchange, you can have the email system move them for you. You can automatically move messages to another folder by creating a rule—for example, you can automatically move all messages received from your manager to a separate folder. You can also set up different rules that go into effect when you're away from the office.

 SEE ALSO For information about automatically moving messages, see "Create rules to process messages" in Chapter 14, "Manage email automatically."

To create a message folder

1. Do either of the following to open the **Create New Folder** dialog box:

   - On the **Folder** tab, in the **New** group, click the **New Folder** button.

   - Press **Ctrl+Shift+E**.

The default settings in the Create New Folder dialog box match the module you open it from

2. In the **Name** box, enter a name for the new folder.

3. In the **Folder contains** list, click **Mail and Post Items**.

4. In the **Select where to place the folder** box, do one of the following:

    - Click your mailbox (at the top of the list) to create the folder at the same level as the Inbox.

    - Click your **Inbox** to create a subfolder of the Inbox.

5. Click **OK**.

To move a message to a folder

1. Drag the message from the message list to the destination folder in the **Folder Pane**.

Or

1. In the message list, select the message you want to move.

2. Do either of the following to display the **Move** menu:

    - On the **Home** tab, in the **Move** group, click the **Move** button.

    - Right-click the message, and then click **Move**.

Personal messages
Work messages
Parent-Teacher Association
Customers
Other Folder...
Copy to Folder...
Always Move Messages in This Conversation...
Move to Clutter

The Move menu automatically includes folders that you create

3. On the **Move** menu, do either of the following:

    - Click the folder you want to move the message to.

    - Click **Other Folder**. In the **Move Items** dialog box displaying the full Folders list, click the folder you want to move the message to, and then click **OK**.

 TIP When Conversation view is turned on, moving the last message of a conversation from a folder removes the conversation from that folder.

Print messages

Although electronic communications certainly have less of an environmental impact than paper-based communications, you might at times want or need to print an email message—for example, if you want to take a hard copy of it to a meeting for reference, or if you keep a physical file of important messages or complimentary feedback. You can print the message exactly as it appears in your Inbox or embellish it with page headers and footers. Outlook prints messages in Memo style, which prints your name, the message header information, and then the message content as shown on the screen, including font and paragraph formats.

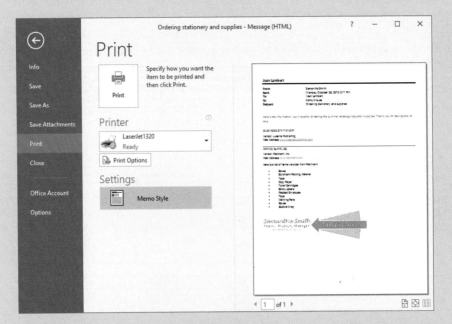

You can preview the message and modify the print settings

To preview and print a message, follow these steps:

4. In an open message window, display the **Print** page of the **Backstage** view. The right pane displays the message as it will appear when printed. In the **Printer** list, click the printer you want to use. Then do either of the following:

   - To print one copy of the message with the default settings, click the **Print** button.

   - To print only specific pages, print multiple copies, or print attachments, click the **Print Options** button, change the settings in the **Print** dialog box, and then click **Print**.

To print a message with the default settings, right-click the message in the message list, and then click Quick Print.

6

Skills review

In this chapter, you learned how to:

- Display and manage conversations

- Arrange messages by specific attributes

- Categorize items

- Organize messages in folders

Practice tasks

No practice files are necessary to complete the practice tasks in this chapter.

> ⚠ **IMPORTANT** As you work through the practice tasks in this book, you will create Outlook items that might be used as practice files for tasks in later chapters. If you haven't created specific items that are referenced in later chapters, you can substitute items of your own.

Display and manage conversations

Start Outlook, display your Inbox in Compact view, and complete the following tasks:

1. Display the messages in your Inbox as conversations. Notice the changes in the appearance and grouping of the messages in the message list.

2. Change the conversation settings so that the senders are shown below the subject in the message list instead of above it. Consider the benefits of the two options.

3. Select one conversation that has several messages, display the unique messages in the conversation, and then display all the messages in the conversation.

4. Remove redundant messages from the conversation.

5. Select any message in the conversation, and open the **Ignore Conversation** dialog box. Read the message in the dialog box, and then click **Cancel**.

6. Configure the conversation settings to suit your preferences.

Arrange messages by specific attributes

Display your Inbox in Preview view, and then complete the following tasks:

1. Use any method described in this chapter to arrange messages by sender (*From*).

2. Use any method described in this chapter to reverse the default sort order of the message list arrangement.

3. Switch to Compact view. Notice that the messages are no longer arranged by sender; the arrangement is only applied to the view in which you set it.

4. Use any method described in this chapter to group the messages in your Inbox.

5. Collapse a group of messages so that only the group header is displayed, and then expand the group again.

6. Collapse all message groups, and then expand them all.

7. Configure the view and arrangement settings to suit your preferences.

Categorize items

Display your Inbox in Compact view, and then complete the following tasks:

1. Create a new email message addressed to yourself. Enter Work with categories as the subject, and send the message.

2. When the message appears in your Inbox, select it.

3. Create a new color category, and do the following:

   - Name the category StepByStep.

   - Assign the **Dark Maroon** color to the category.

   - Assign the **Ctrl+F10** keyboard shortcut to the category.

4. Finish creating the category, and close any open dialog boxes. Notice that the selected message now has the StepByStep category assigned to it.

5. Set the **StepByStep** category as the Quick Click category.

6. Switch to Single view. In the message list, point to an unassigned category block in the **Categories** column to display the ScreenTip.

7. Click the block to assign the Quick Click category to the message. Then click again to remove the category.

Organize messages in folders

Display your Inbox, and complete the following tasks:

1. Create a new folder, and do the following:

   - Name the folder StepByStep.

   - Configure the folder to contain messages.

   - Save the folder as a subfolder of your Inbox.

2. Finish creating the folder. Then move the **Work with categories** message that you created in an earlier set of practice tasks to the **StepByStep** folder.

3. Retain the folder, message, and category for use in practice tasks in later chapters.

Part 3

Manage contacts

Store and access contact information

Having immediate access to current, accurate contact information for the people you need to interact with— by email, phone, mail, or otherwise—is important for timely and effective communication. You can easily build and maintain a detailed contact list (also called an *address book*) in the Outlook 2016 People module. From your address book, you can look up information, create messages, and share contact information with other people. You can also keep track of your interactions with people whose contact information you store in Outlook.

If you need to take contact information with you in a non-electronic format, you can print an address book or selected contact records in many different formats.

This chapter guides you through procedures related to saving and updating contact information, communicating with contacts, displaying different views of contact records, and printing contact records.

In this chapter

- Save and update contact information
- Communicate with contacts
- Display different views of contact records
- Print contact records

Practice files

No practice files are necessary to complete the practice tasks in this chapter.

Save and update contact information

You save contact information for a person or company by creating a contact record in an address book.

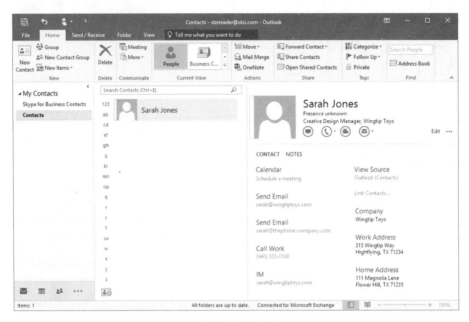

A contact record in the People card view of an address book

Contact records have four content pages: General, Details, Certificates, and All Fields. The General page stores the most common contact information, and is usually the only page you use. On the General page of a contact record, you can store the following types of contact information:

- Name, company name, and job title

- Business, home, and alternate addresses

- Business, home, mobile, pager, and other phone numbers

- Business, home, and alternate fax numbers

- Webpage address (URL), instant messaging (IM) address, and email addresses

- Photo, company logo, or other identifying image

- General notes, which can include text and illustrations such as photos, SmartArt diagrams, charts, and shapes

On the Details page of a contact record, you can store additional personal and organization-specific details, such as the following:

- Professional information, including department, office location, profession, manager's name, and assistant's name

- Personal information, including nickname, spouse or partner's name, birthday, anniversary, and the title (such as Miss, Mrs., or Ms.) and suffix (such as Jr. or Sr.) for use in correspondence

The Certificates page displays any digital ID certificates that you save for communications with that person, and the All Fields page displays all the fields in a specific category of information that you select.

Create and modify contact records

You can create a new contact record from scratch or from an email message that contains the contact's information. When you want to create a contact record from scratch, you can easily do so from any module or from an address book. After you save the contact record, it appears in the contact list.

You can create a contact record that contains only one piece of information (for example, a name or company name), or as much information as you want to include. You can quickly create contact records for several people who work for the same company by cloning the company information from an existing record to a new one.

> **TIP** In addition to creating individual contact records, you can create groups of contacts so that you can manage messaging to multiple people through one email address. For information, see "Create contact groups" in Chapter 8, "Manage contact records."

Contact record sources

Outlook stores contact information from different sources in separate address books. Some are created by Outlook, some by your email server administrator, and others by you.

Address books

The My Contacts list in the Folder Pane of the People module displays the address books that Outlook is connected to.

Address books can be created by apps, email accounts, or social networks, or by you

Address books in the My Contacts list can include the following:

- Outlook creates a Contacts address book for each account you connect to. The Contacts address book of your default email account is your main address book, and it is the address book that appears by default in the People module. The Contacts address book is empty until you add contact records to it.

- You can create custom address books that aren't associated with email accounts; for example, you might want to keep contact information for family and friends in an address book separate from client contact information, or you might maintain an address book for clients that meet specific criteria.

- If you connect Outlook to a social network or other external contact-management system, Outlook creates an address book that synchronizes with your contact list on the social network.

- If your organization stores contact information in a SharePoint contact list, you can import the contact list from SharePoint into Outlook as an address book.

To display the contents of an address book in the content area of the People module, click the address book in the My Contacts list.

SEE ALSO For information about creating address books, see "Create address books" in Chapter 8, "Manage contact records."

Global Address Lists

If you have a Microsoft Exchange Server account, you also have access to an official address book called the Global Address List (or *GAL*). Your organization's Exchange administrator maintains the GAL, which includes information about individuals within your organization, distribution lists, and resources (such as conference rooms and media equipment) that you can reserve when you schedule meetings. It can also include organizational information (each person's manager and direct subordinates) and group membership information (the distribution lists each person belongs to).

The Folder Pane of the People module doesn't include a link to the GAL. To display the GAL, click the Address Book button in the Find group on the Home tab of the People module or the Address Book button in the Names group on the Message tab of a message composition window. Outlook users can view the GAL, but not change its contents. Only an Exchange administrator can modify the GAL.

7

You can add to or change the information stored in a contact record at any time. If you need to change only basic information, such as the contact's email address or phone number, you can edit the entries in the contact's People card. This card format cleanly displays the available information exactly as it appears in the Reading Pane.

People cards have fewer editable fields than standard contact records

For the greatest level of detail, you can edit the information in the contact record window.

A typical contact record for a business contact

> ✅ **TIP** You can create a personalized electronic business card for yourself or for any of your contacts. For information, see "Personalize electronic business cards" in Chapter 8, "Manage contact records."

The contact record window organizes information on the General page in the following sections:

- **Name** In this section, you enter the name and basic information for the contact. The name can be the name of a person, company, or organization.

  After you enter a name in the Full Name box and move on to the next box, the contact's name appears on the contact record window title bar and in the business card representation.

The contact name is also copied to the File As box. The File As setting determines the order in which Outlook displays contact records in the contact list. By default, Outlook orders contacts by last name (Last, First order). If you prefer, you can change the order for new contacts to any of the following:

- First Last

- Company

- Last, First (Company)

- Company (Last, First)

■ **Internet** In this section, you can enter up to three email addresses, a webpage address, and an instant message (IM) address.

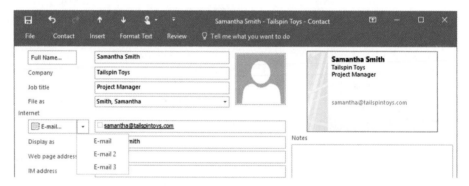

Click the arrow to the right of the field name to display additional instances of the field

After you enter an email address, Outlook formats the address as a hyperlink and enters the name and email address in the Display As box. This box indicates the way the contact will appear in the headers of email messages you exchange with this contact.

■ **Phone numbers** In this section, you can enter up to 19 different phone numbers for a contact, including Pager, Car, ISDN, and TTY/TDD. The contact record window displays only four phone numbers at a time. You can choose which numbers to display by clicking the arrow next to the Phone number box. You use the Check Phone Number dialog box to refine the number, by adding a country code or an extension, for example.

After you enter a 10-digit phone number in the appropriate box, and then press Tab, Outlook formats the string of numbers in standard telephone number format.

- **Addresses** In this section, you can add up to three addresses for the contact and note which address is the preferred mailing address. You can also display a map with the exact location of each address.

- **Notes** In this section, you can enter any notes you want. You can use the commands on the contact record window's Insert tab to insert files, pictures, shapes, tables, and much more in the Notes area, which expands to accommodate your content.

 SEE ALSO For information about adding an image to a contact record, see "Personalize electronic business cards" in Chapter 8, "Manage contact records."

Conform to name and address standards

7

After you enter information in a contact record, Outlook verifies that the information conforms to expected patterns. If Outlook detects possible irregularities, a Check dialog box opens, displaying the expected fields.

The Check dialog boxes fit contact information into standard patterns

The purpose of these dialog boxes is to verify that the contact information you save can be used for addressing correspondence or in a mail merge operation. You can insert, change, or delete information in these dialog boxes, or, if the information in the dialog box is correct as-is, you can close the dialog box without making changes by clicking Cancel.

To create a basic contact record in a list view

1. In Phone view or List view, under the **Full Name** header, click the **Click here to add a new contact** box, and then enter information in any of the fields displayed in the list.

> **TIP** The Click Here To Add A New Contact box is available only in address books that you can edit. It isn't available in synchronized address books from other sources such as LinkedIn.

To create a new contact record from a name in the header of an email message

1. In the **Reading Pane** or message window, in the email message header, right-click the underlined name or email address from which you want to create a contact record, and then click **Add to Outlook Contacts** to display a People card for the contact.

2. Insert or modify any information that you want to, and then click **Save** to save the contact record to your default address book.

> **TIP** If you want to add more details than you can in the People card, you can do so in the contact record window.

To open a new contact record window

1. Do any of the following:

    - In the Contacts module, on the **Home** tab, in the **New** group, click the **New Contact** button.

    - In any module, on the **Home** tab, in the **New** group, click the **New Items** button, and then click **Contact**.

    - Press **Ctrl+Shift+C**.

    - In any module, on the **Home** tab, click the **Address Book** button. Then, in the **Address Book** dialog box, click **New Entry**, and in the **New Entry** dialog box, click **New Contact**.

To enter the name and basic business information for a contact

1. In the contact record window, do either of the following:

   - Enter a name directly in the **Full Name** box.

   - Click the **Full Name** button to display the **Check Full Name** dialog box, and enter the information you want in the appropriate boxes.

2. Press the **Tab** key to move to the next box and continue adding the information you want.

3. When you finish, click the **Save & Close** button in the **Actions** group on the **Contact** tab.

To change the File As order for a contact record

1. In the contact record window, click the arrow at the right end of the **File as** box, and then click the order you want. The options are formed from the information in the contact record, and include the following:

   - Last, First

   - First last

   - Company

   - Last, First (Company)

   - Company (Last, First)

> **TIP** This procedure changes the File As order for the active contact only; to set the filing order for all your contacts, display the People page of the Outlook Options dialog box, expand the Default "File As" Order list, and then click the order you want.

To save one or more email addresses for a contact

1. In the **Internet** section of the contact record window, in the **Email** box, enter an email address.

   Or

To select an email address from an existing contact record, do the following:

a. Click the **Email** button to open the Select Name dialog box.

b. In the **Address Book** list, click the source you want to display contacts from.

c. Scroll the list to locate the contact email address you want to copy.

d. Click the contact, and then click **OK**.

2. In the **Display as** box, ensure that the display name is as you want it shown in the address field of a message.

3. If you want to add another email address, do the following:

a. Click the **E-mail** arrow (not the button), and then click **Email 2** or **Email 3**.

b. In the **Email 2** or **Email 3** field, enter or select an email address, and then press **Tab** to populate the **Display as** field.

c. In the **Display as** box, ensure that the display name is as you want it shown in the address field of a message.

To save a webpage or IM address for a contact

1. In the **Internet** section of the contact record window, do either or both of the following:

- In the **Web page address** box, enter a URL. Outlook formats the URL as a hyperlink.

- In the **IM address** box, enter an IM address for the contact.

To save one or more phone numbers for a contact

1. In the **Phone numbers** section of the contact record window, do any of the following:

- If the type of phone number you want to add is displayed on one of the phone number buttons, enter the phone number in the box next to that button.

- If the type of phone number you want to add is not displayed, click the arrow next to one of the buttons and select the type you want. Then enter the phone number in the box next to that button.

- Click a phone number button to display the **Check Phone Number** dialog box, and enter the information you want in the appropriate boxes. Then click **OK** to add the phone number to the phone number box.

To save one or more addresses for a contact

1. In the **Addresses** section of the contact record window, do any of the following:

   - Click the arrow to the right of the **Business**, **Home**, or **Other** button, and then click the type of address you want to save.

   - In the **Addresses** pane, enter the address, pressing **Enter** at the end of each address line.

   - Click the **Business**, **Home**, or **Other** button to display the Check Address dialog box. Enter the address information in the appropriate boxes, and then click **OK** to insert the address in the address box.

> **TIP** A selected check box to the left of the address field indicates that it is the default mailing address for the contact. If you enter multiple addresses for a contact and want to specify one as the default mailing address, display that address and then select the This Is The Mailing Address check box.

To enter notes for a contact

1. In the **Notes** section of the contact record window, click in the **Notes** pane, and then do any of the following:

   - Enter or paste content.

   - Use the commands on the **Insert** tab to insert an object.

   - Select text, and then use the commands on the **Format Text** tab to apply formatting.

To enter personal and professional details for a contact

1. In the contact record window, on the **Contact** tab, in the **Show** group, click the **Details** button.

2. On the **Details** page, enter the information you want to save with the contact record.

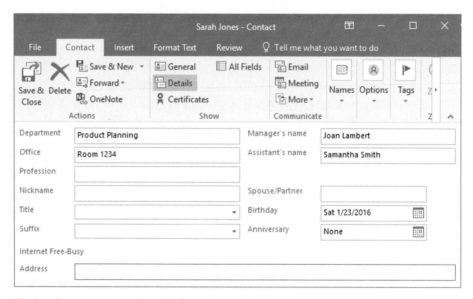

The Details page stores a variety of information

To edit contact information in a People card

1. Do either of the following to activate the content for editing:

   - To open the card, double-click an entry in the contact list.

   - To edit the content in the Reading Pane, click **Edit** in the contact record header area.

2. Change any of the available contact information.

3. In the lower-right corner of the People card or **Reading Pane**, click the **Save** button.

To edit contact information in a contact record window

1. Do any of the following to open the contact record window for the contact record that you want to edit:

    -   In People view, open the People card or display it in the **Reading Pane**, and then in the **View Source** area, click the link to the source contact record.

    -   In Business Card or Card view, double-click the card.

    -   In Phone or List view, double-click the list entry.

2. Change any of the contact information.

3. On the **Contact** tab, in the **Actions** group, click the **Save & Close** button.

To create a contact with the same company information as an existing contact

1. In the contact list, select the contact record for the contact whose company information you want to duplicate.

2. On the **Home** tab, in the **New** group, click the **New Items** button, and then click **Contact from the Same Company** to create a new contact record.

3. The new contact record contains whatever company information was in the original contact record, including the company name, webpage address, phone number, fax number, and mailing address. Because the contact record doesn't yet include a person's name, the **File as** name is set to the company name.

4. Enter the person's name, job title, and any other information you want to include in the new contact record.

5. Save and close the contact record window.

Communicate with contacts

Saving contact information for people in a physical or electronic address book is useful because it centralizes the information in one place so that you no longer have to remember the information or where to find it. The added benefit of saving contact information in an Outlook address book is that it makes the process of initiating communication with a contact much more efficient.

Create custom contact record fields

If you want to save information that doesn't match any of the built-in contact record fields, you can create a custom field. A custom field can contain information such as text, numbers, percentages, currency, Yes/No answers, dates, times, durations, keywords, and formulas.

To create a custom field, follow these steps:

1. Open a contact record window.

2. On the **Contact** tab, in the **Show** group, click **All Fields**.

3. In the lower-left corner of the **All Fields** page, click the **New** button.

4. In the **New Column** dialog box, enter the field name and select the field type and format.

New Column	✕
Name:	Hire Date
Type:	Date/Time
Format:	Thu 12/24/2015 3:26 PM
	OK Cancel

Custom fields can contain many specific types of information

5. Click **OK**.

Custom fields appear when you filter the All Fields page on User-Defined Fields In Folder. After you enter information in the custom field for a specific contact, it also appears in the User-Defined Fields In This Item list within that contact record.

Initiate actions from contact records

Contact records are useful not only for storing information; you can also initiate a number of actions that are specific to a selected contact. Commands for initiating communication are available in the Communicate group on the Contact tab of an open contact record or in the header of a People card.

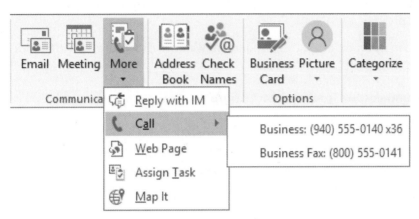

The Communicate options vary based on your environment and the information saved with the contact record

You can perform many actions from within a contact record window (but not in a People card) by using the commands in the Communicate group on the Contact tab. If you save the necessary information in a contact record, you can do the following:

- Initiate an email message or meeting request.

- In an environment that includes an instant messaging app such as Microsoft Skype for Business, you can start an IM session.

- In a unified communications environment that includes a Voice over IP (VoIP) phone system, you can call the contact.

- Display the webpage in your default Internet browser.

- Display a map of the active address in your default Internet browser.

- Assign an Outlook task.

After you install and configure Microsoft OneNote on your computer, you can create notes that are linked to the contact record.

To create Outlook items from a contact record window

1. On the **Contact** tab, in the **Communicate** group, do any of the following:

   - To open a preaddressed email message composition window, click the **Email** button.

   - To open a preaddressed meeting request window, click the **Meeting** button.

   - To open a preaddressed task assignment window, click **More**, and then click **Assign Task**.

To initiate communication from a contact record window

1. On the **Contact** tab, in the **Communicate** group, do either of the following:

   - To open a conversation window for the contact in your default instant messaging app, click **More**, and then click **Reply with IM**.

   - To start a VoIP call, click **More**, click **Call**, and then click the number you want to call.

To display information from a contact record window

1. On the **Contact** tab, in the **Communicate** group, click **More**, and then click either of the following:

   - To display the saved webpage in your default browser, click **Web Page**.

   - To display the current address on the Bing Maps webpage in your default browser, click the **Map It** button.

To create a OneNote notebook page linked to a contact record

1. On the **Contact** tab, in the **Actions** group, click the **OneNote** button.

2. In the **Select Location in OneNote** dialog box, select the OneNote section in which you want to create the linked note, and then click **OK**.

OneNote creates a new page in the selected section, prepopulated with information about the contact.

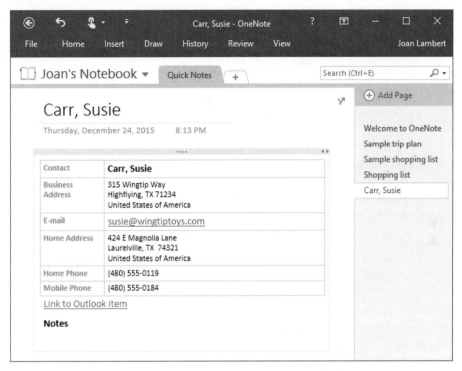

Clicking Link To Outlook Item opens the contact record window in Outlook

Select message recipients from address books

When you send an email message to a person whose contact information is stored in one of your address books, you can quickly address the message to that person by entering his or her name as it appears in the address book and letting Outlook validate the address. If you don't know the exact spelling of the name, you can open the address book from the email message composition window and look it up. You can also open the address book from any module and initiate the email from there.

To look up contacts from a message composition window

1. In the message composition window, on the **Message** tab, in the **Names** group, click the **Address Book** button to open the Select Name dialog box.

2. At the right end of the **Address Book** box, click the arrow, and then click the address book you want to search.

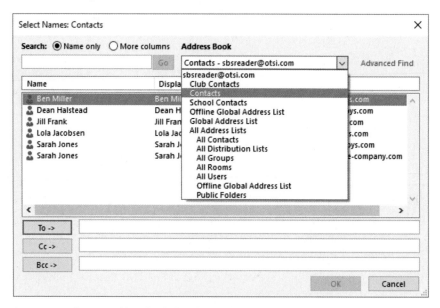

Insert names from an address book directly into the message composition window

3. Scroll through the **Name** list to locate the person's name. If you save multiple email addresses for that person, the name will appear once for each email address.

 TIP You can enter the first few letters of the person's name in the name box to scroll to entries beginning with those letters.

4. Double-click the name, or click it and then press **Enter** to add the email address to the To box as a primary message recipient.

5. If you want, do any of the following:

   - Click in the **Cc** box at the bottom of the dialog box, and then double-click another name, or click it and press **Enter**, to add the person as a secondary recipient.

   - Click in the **Bcc** box at the bottom of the dialog box, and then double-click another name, or click it and press **Enter**, to add the person as a private recipient.

> **TIP** If you click the To, Cc, or Bcc box in the message header before clicking the Address Book button, double-clicking the name adds the person to that box. You can also click the Cc or Bcc box and then click the adjacent button to open the Select Names dialog box with that box active.

6. After selecting all message recipients from the address book, click **OK** to close the **Select Names** dialog box and return to the message composition window.

To create an email message from an address book

1. In any module, on the **Home** tab, in the **Find** group, click the **Address Book** button to open the Address Book dialog box.

2. In the **Address Book** dialog box, select the name of the contact to whom you want to send an email message.

3. On the **File** menu, click **New Message**. A new message composition window opens with the name of the contact in the To box.

4. Compose the message and then send it.

Link contact records

You can link contact records to other contact records so that you can quickly locate other information related to a contact. For example, if you connect Outlook to a social media network such as Facebook or LinkedIn, you can link the Outlook, Facebook, and LinkedIn contact records for the same person, so that when you look up that person you have access to the contact information from all three sources. You link contact records from the People card.

To link a contact record with another contact record, follow these steps:

1. Display the address book in People view, and locate one of the contact records you want to link.

2. Display the People card of the contact in the **Reading Pane**, or open the People card.

3. Do either of the following to open the Linked Contacts window for the current contact record:

   - In the **Reading Pane**, under **View Source**, click **Link Contacts**.

   - In the People card header, click the **Options** button (...) and then click **Link Contacts**.

Display different views of contact records

You can view all your address books in the People module. You can also display a list of the contacts in an address book, including those in your organization's Global Address List.

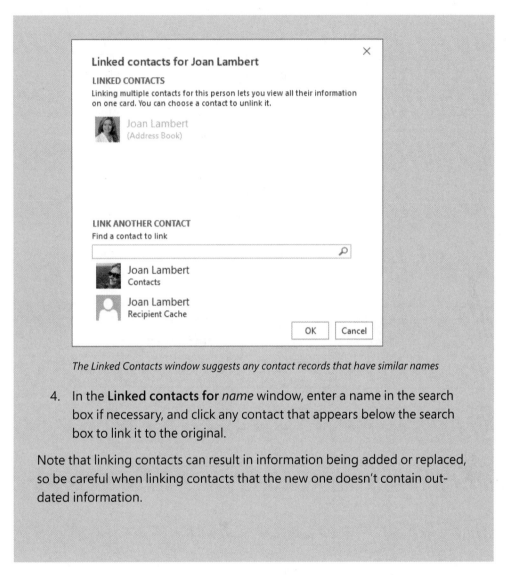

The Linked Contacts window suggests any contact records that have similar names

4. In the **Linked contacts for** *name* window, enter a name in the search box if necessary, and click any contact that appears below the search box to link it to the original.

Note that linking contacts can result in information being added or replaced, so be careful when linking contacts that the new one doesn't contain outdated information.

In the People module, you can display an address book in several different formats. Each view presents information from your contact records organized in different ways either on cards or in a list. If a standard view doesn't display precisely the information you want, you can modify it.

The standard views are:

- **People view** Displays only contact names and pictures in the contact list, and the available information for the selected contact on the People card and in the Reading Pane. Contact names are displayed in alphabetical order by first or last name, depending on the File As selection. This view displays information about the contact from multiple sources. For example, if you have an Outlook contact record for a person you network with on LinkedIn and Facebook, the People card displays a compilation of the information from all three locations. This view is the default view.

- **Business Card view** Displays the business card associated with each contact record—either the default card created by Outlook or a custom card if you have one. Business cards are displayed in the alphabetical order specified by the File As selection.

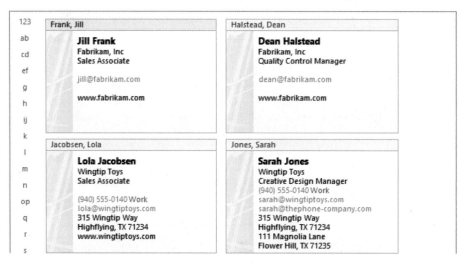

You can move quickly to groups of contact records by clicking the contact index

- **Card view** Displays contact information as truncated business cards that include limited information, such as job title and company name. Outlook displays the contact records in a compact card-like format that includes only text and no additional graphic elements.

123	**Frank, Jill**			**Jones, Sarah**	
ab	Full Name:	Jill Frank		Full Name:	Sarah Jones
cd	Job Title:	Sales Associate		Job Title:	Creative Design Manager
	Company:	Fabrikam, Inc		Company:	Wingtip Toys
ef	E-mail:	jill@fabrikam.com		Business:	315 Wingtip Way
gh	Business Home Page:	www.fabrikam.com			Highflying, TX 71234
ij				Home:	111 Magnolia Lane
	Halstead, Dean				Flower Hill, TX 71235
kl	Full Name:	Dean Halstead		Business:	(940) 555-0140
	Job Title:	Quality Control Manager		E-mail:	sarah@wingtiptoys.com
mn	Company:	Fabrikam, Inc		E-mail 2:	sarah@thephone-company.com
op	E-mail:	dean@fabrikam.com			
	Business Home Page:	www.fabrikam.com		**Miller, Ben**	
qr				Full Name:	Ben Miller
st	**Jacobsen, Lola**			Job Title:	Manufacturing Manager
	Full Name:	Lola Jacobsen		Company:	Fabrikam, Inc
uv	Job Title:	Sales Associate		E-mail:	ben@fabrikam.com
w	Company:	Wingtip Toys		Business Home Page:	www.fabrikam.com

Card view displays all the available primary contact information

- **Phone view** Displays a columnar list that includes each contact's name, company, and contact numbers. You can choose the grouping you want from the Arrangements gallery on the View tab.

- **List view** Displays a columnar list with contact records arranged in groups.

   In any list view, you can expand and collapse the groups or select and take action on an entire group of contacts. You can also enter information directly into any contact record field displayed in the list.

You can search and filter your contact records in any view by using the Instant Search feature from the search box at the top of the content area. You can sort contact records by any displayed column in a list view by clicking the column header.

 TIP Press Ctrl+E to move to the search box in the active module. For more information about keyboard shortcuts, see Appendix B, "Keyboard shortcuts."

You can change the fields displayed in each view; the way records are grouped, sorted, and filtered; the display font; the size of business cards; and other settings to suit your preferences. If you don't like your changes, you can reset the view to its default configuration.

7

To display contact records in an address book

1. In the People module, in the **Folder Pane**, click the address book that contains the contacts you want to display.

Or

1. Do any of the following:

   - In any module, on the **Home** tab, in the **Find** group, click the **Address Book** button to open the Address Book dialog box.

   - In a contact record window, on the **Contact** tab, in the **Names** group, click the **Address Book** button to open the Select Name dialog box.

   - In a message composition window, in the message header, click the **To**, **Cc**, or **Bcc** button to open the Select Names dialog box.

2. In the **Address Book** list, click the address book you want to display.

To display a different view of contact records in the People module

1. On the **Home** tab, in the **Current View** gallery, click **People**, **Business Card**, **Card**, **Phone**, or **List**.

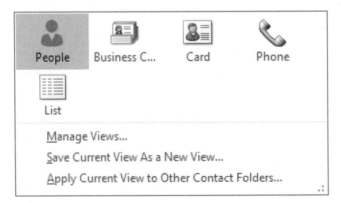

The standard view options for the People module

SEE ALSO For information about adding, moving, and removing fields in list views, see the "Content area views" section of "Work in the Mail module" in Chapter 2, "Explore Outlook modules."

Modify the settings of any view

You can make many interesting or useful changes to any view of any module in the Advanced View Settings dialog box. Explore the options on your own to identify settings that you could change to improve your Outlook experience.

To access the advanced view settings, do the following:

1. On the **View** tab, in the **Current View** group, click **View Settings** to open the Advanced View Settings dialog box for the current view.

The options vary depending on the currently displayed view

2. Do any of the following:

   - To change the displayed fields, field order, and height (in lines) in compact mode, click the **Columns** button.

   - To group entries by up to four fields, click the **Group By** button.

   - To sort entries by up to four fields, click the **Sort** button.

   - To filter entries by any field, click the **Filter** button.

   - To change the font of the column headings, list rows, or message previews, or to display grid lines, click the **Other Settings** button.

   - To set off entries that meet a specific condition by using a different font, style, size, color, or effect, click the **Conditional Formatting** button.

   - To set the format, label, width, or alignment of a field column, click the **Format Columns** button.

3. In the dialog box that opens, make the changes you want, and then click **OK**.

To sort contact records in a list view

1. In Phone view or List view, click any column header to sort the contact records based on that field. The sort arrow to the right of the column header indicates the sort order.

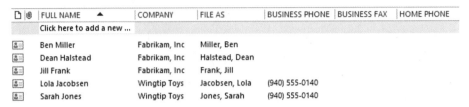

		FULL NAME ▲	COMPANY	FILE AS	BUSINESS PHONE	BUSINESS FAX	HOME PHONE
		Click here to add a new …					
		Ben Miller	Fabrikam, Inc	Miller, Ben			
		Dean Halstead	Fabrikam, Inc	Halstead, Dean			
		Jill Frank	Fabrikam, Inc	Frank, Jill			
		Lola Jacobsen	Wingtip Toys	Jacobsen, Lola	(940) 555-0140		
		Sarah Jones	Wingtip Toys	Jones, Sarah	(940) 555-0140		

Click any column header to sort by that column or to reverse the sort order

2. Reverse the sort order by clicking the active column header.

To group contact records in a list view

1. In Phone view or List view, on the **View** tab, on the **Arrangement** menu, click **Show in Groups** to select or clear the check mark.

2. In the **Arrangement** gallery, click the grouping you want.

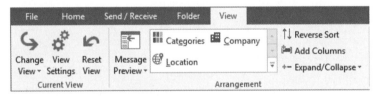

Arrangements are available only for list views

To resize columns in a list view

1. Point to the column separator between two columns. When the cursor changes to a double-headed arrow, double-click to change the column width to accommodate its contents, or drag the column separator to the right or left to widen or narrow the column width.

To specify the lines of information shown in a compact view

1. On the **View** tab, in the **Arrangement** group, click **Message Preview** and then click **Off**, **1 Line**, **2 Lines**, or **3 Lines**.

To reset the current view to its default settings

1. Do either of the following:

   - On the **View** tab, in the **Current View** group, click the **Reset View** button, and then click **Yes** in the message box that opens.

   - Open the **Advanced View Settings** dialog box, click the **Reset Current View** button, and then click **OK**.

Print contact records

You can print an address book or individual contact records, either on paper or to an electronic file (such as a PDF file or an XPS file), from the People module. As with printing any other Outlook item, you print contact records from the Print page of the Backstage view.

7

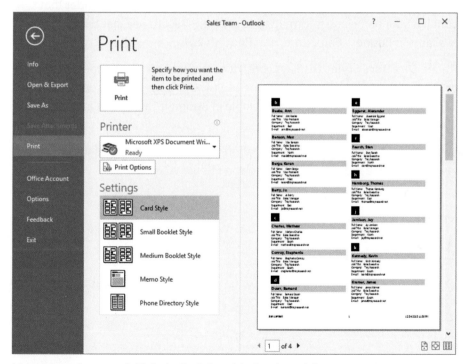

Many print styles are available in the Card view of the People module

> ⊘ **TIP** The Backstage view on your computer reflects your individual printer settings and might display other print options than those shown here.

Depending on the view, Outlook offers a variety of print styles:

- **Card Style** Displays contact information alphabetically in two columns. Letter graphics appear at the top of each page and the beginning of each letter group. The last page of the printout provides space for you to enter additional contact information. (Outlook refers to this as a *blank form*.) This style is available in Business Card, Card, and People views.

- **Small Booklet Style and Medium Booklet Style** Displays contact information alphabetically in one column and is formatted to print eight numbered pages (Small Booklet) or four numbered pages (Medium Booklet) per sheet. Letter graphics appear at the top of each page and the beginning of each letter group, and a contact index at the side of each page indicates the position of that page's entries in the alphabet. These styles are available in Business Card, Card, and People views.

- **Memo Style** Displays contact information under a memo-like header that contains your name and is formatted to print one record per sheet. This style is available in Business Card, Card, and People views.

- **Phone Directory Style** Displays contact names and phone numbers in two columns. Letter graphics appear at the top of each page and the beginning of each letter group. This style is available in Business Card, Card, and People views.

- **Table Style** Displays contact information in a table that matches the on-screen layout. This style is available in Phone and List views.

You can customize the layout of most of the default print styles, and save them as custom print styles.

On the Print page of the Backstage view, the preview pane depicts the appearance of the selected contact records when printed.

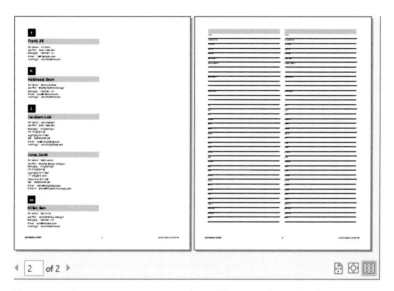

You can preview one or more pages as they will appear when printed

The page indicators in the lower-left corner of the preview pane indicate the number of pages required to print the selected contact records. You can move among the pages and change the display of the pages in the preview pane.

If the preview doesn't display the printout the way you want it to be printed, you can make adjustments in the Print dialog box. The options available in this dialog box vary depending on the view.

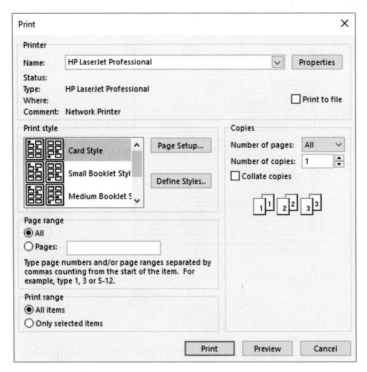

You can select specific contact records to be printed

Clicking the Page Setup button in the Print dialog box opens the Page Setup dialog box, where you can change settings on the Format, Paper, and Header/Footer tabs. For all print styles, you can change the fonts, paper size, page orientation and margins, header and footer, and other basic settings. For the Card Style layout, you can also change the layout of cards on the page, the number of blank forms to be printed, and how the alphabetical division of the cards is indicated.

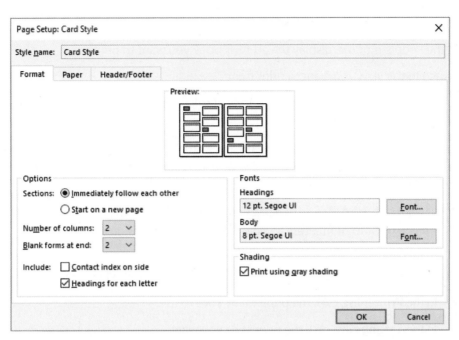

The Page Setup dialog box contents vary depending on the selected print style

Sometimes you might want to print only one or a few records from an address book. You can do this from either the List view or the Phone view of the address book. The default print style for individual contact records is Memo Style.

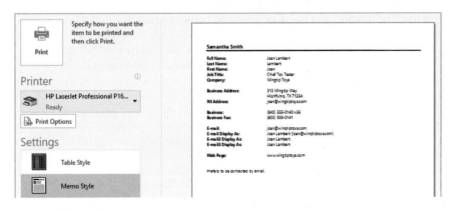

By default, Memo Style prints one contact record per page

To print contact records from an address book

1. In the People module, display the address book you want to print.

2. Switch to the view you want to print from:

   - To print contact records in Table Style, display the module in Phone view or List view.

   - To print the contact records in Card Style, Small Booklet Style, Medium Booklet Style, Memo Style, or Phone Directory Style, display the module in Business Card view, Card view, or People view.

3. If you want to print only one or a few contact records, click the first contact record you want to print. Press and hold the **Ctrl** key, and then click each other contact record you want to print to add it to the selection.

4. Display the **Print** page of the Backstage view, and then do the following:

   - In the **Printer** list, click the printer you want to use.

   - In the **Settings** list, click the print style you want.

5. Click the **Print** button.

   Or

   If you want to further configure the settings, click the **Print Options** button to open the **Print** dialog box, and make the changes you want. Then click the **Print** button to print the address book or selected contact records.

To move among pages in the Print preview pane

1. In the lower-left corner of the preview pane, do either of the following:

   - Click the left arrow or right arrow to move one page back or forward.

   - Enter a page number in the box to jump to a specific page.

To change the display of pages in the Print preview pane

1. In the lower-right corner of the preview pane, do any of the following:

   - To display the current page at 100% magnification, click the **Actual Size** button.

   - To display the current page at the largest size that fits the pane, click the **One Page** button.

   - To display multiple pages side-by-side, click the **Multiple Pages** button.

7

Skills review

In this chapter, you learned how to:

- Save and update contact information

- Communicate with contacts

- Display different views of contact records

- Print contact records

Practice tasks

No practice files are necessary to complete the practice tasks in this chapter.

Save and update contact information

Display the People module, and then do the following:

1. In your default address book, create a contact record that includes the following information:

    -   Full name: **Dante Durkin**

    -   Company: **Bellows College**

    -   Job title: **Professor**

    -   Email address: **dante@bellowscollege.com**

    Save and close the contact record.

2. Display your Inbox, and then do the following:

    a. Open a message from someone who isn't already in your address book.

    b. Create a contact record from the person's name in the message header.

    c. In the People card window, enter any additional information you have about that person.

    d. Save and close the contact record.

3. Display the People module. Use the contact index to locate the contact record you created in step 1, and then do the following:

    a. Open the contact record in a contact record window.

    b. Set the **File as** field to **Bellows College**.

    c. In the **Web page address** field, enter www.bellowscollege.com.

d. Add a second email address of dante@thephone-company.com.

e. Set the **Display as** text for the first email address to Dante Durkin (work), and for the second email address to Dante Durkin (home).

f. Display the **Home address** field, and enter your address. Then click the **Map It** button to display the location in Bing Maps. Verify that it's accurate, and then close the map window.

g. Save and close the contact record.

4. Create a new contact record that contains all the business contact information in the Dante Durkin contact record.

5. Enter the following additional information in the new contact record:

   - Full name: Abby Rodriguez

   - Title: Dean of Students

6. Notice that the **File as** order is already set to *Bellows College*, but the Address fields are blank. Then save and close the contact record.

Communicate with contacts

Display the People module, and then do the following:

1. Use the contact index to locate the contact records you created for **Bellows College** employees.

2. Open the contact record for **Abby Rodriguez**, and create an email message addressed to her.

3. In the open message composition window, click the **To** button. In the **Select Names** dialog box, display your default address book. Locate **Dante Durkin** in the address book, and add him as message recipient.

4. Close the message without saving or sending it.

Display different views of contact records

Display the People module, and then do the following:

1. Display each of the standard views of the People module. Note the information available in each view, and consider which would be most useful to you on a regular basis.

2. Display your default address book in List view.

3. Adjust the width of each column to fit its content.

4. Sort the contact records by **Full name**, then by **Company**, and then by **Email address**.

5. Reset the List view to its default settings.

Print contact records

Display the People module, and then do the following:

1. Preview your default address book as it would appear when printed as contact cards.

2. Preview the address book as it would appear when printed as a phone list.

3. If you want to, print the address book in the format that you prefer.

 TIP You can retain the contact records you create in this chapter, or delete them if you prefer to.

Manage contact records

8

You can simplify communications with specific groups of people by creating contact groups to which you can address messages as you would an individual contact. You can also create purpose-specific address books and organize contact records within the address books to make it easier to locate specific contact records. You can add contact records to a custom address book either by moving contact records that are already stored in Outlook, or by importing contact records from another app or file.

If you save contact information for business and personal contacts in Outlook, you can quickly accumulate a large collection of contact records. The search feature makes it easy to find a specific contact record based on any text within the contact record or any attribute, such as a color category, that you assign to it. Within each contact record, you can make preferred contact information easily discoverable by displaying it on the electronic business card version of the contact record. You can also display images—such as photographs or corporate logos—on business cards, to provide additional information when you view contacts in the default Business Card view.

This chapter guides you through procedures related to creating address books, importing and exporting contact records, creating contact groups, quickly locating contact information, and personalizing electronic business cards.

In this chapter

- Create address books
- Import and export contact records
- Create contact groups
- Quickly locate contact information
- Personalize electronic business cards

Practice files

For this chapter, use the practice files from the Outlook2016SBS\Ch08 folder. For practice file download instructions, see the introduction.

Create address books

When you open the People module, Outlook displays your default address book, which is the one created when you first configure Outlook to connect to an email account. The default address book stores contact records in a folder named *Contacts*. If you connect to a Microsoft Exchange Server account, the default address book is part of that account, and the information you store in the address book is available on all devices from which you connect to your account. Exchange Server also provides a Global Address List (GAL), which is an address book maintained centrally by your Exchange administrator.

You can track all your contacts—business and personal—within the address book of your default email account. However, you might find it useful to create a separate address book that contains contact records for only a specific group of people. For example, you might want to have an address book that contains only clients, relatives, club members, neighborhood contacts, parents and teachers from your child's school, or sports teammates.

TIP When searching for a specific contact record, you can search a single address book or search all address books within your Outlook configuration, including your organization's GAL. For more information, see "Quickly locate contact information" later in this chapter.

An address book is actually a folder that is designed to contain contact items. To create a new address book, you create a folder and select Contact Items as the folder contents. You can create a contact folder (an address book) from within any module and save it anywhere in the existing folder structure, but for organizational purposes you might want to create contact folders as subfolders of the original Contacts folder.

Address books are folders configured to contain contact items

 TIP In the Folders List shown in the Create New Folder dialog box, a contact card icon indicates each contact folder/address book.

The address books that you create appear in the My Contacts list in the People module. They aren't visually differentiated from the address books that Outlook creates.

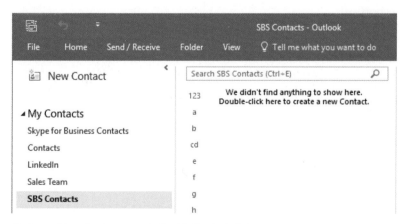

Custom address books appear in the My Contacts list

Unlike the Calendar module, in which you can display multiple calendars, the People module can display only one address book at a time. If you have multiple address books, you select the one that you want to display by clicking it in the Folder Pane.

> **TIP** You can't display your organization's GAL in the Folder Pane. To display it, click the Address Book button in the Find group on the Home tab of any module. In the Address Book dialog box that opens, in the Address Book list, click Global Address List.

You can populate an address book by creating new contact records in it, moving or copying existing contact records to it, or importing contact records from another file. You can share an address book with other Outlook users in your organization, or you can export it for distribution to other people.

> **SEE ALSO** For information about importing contact records from an external file, and exporting contact records to a file, see "Import and export contact records" later in this chapter. For information about sharing address books and other folders with coworkers, see "Share calendar information" in Chapter 10, "Manage your calendar."

To create an address book

1. Do either of the following to open the Create New Folder dialog box:

   - In the Mail, People, or Tasks module, on the **Folder** tab, in the **New** group, click the **New Folder** button.

   - In the Calendar module, on the **Folder** tab, in the **New** group, click the **New Calendar** button.

2. In the **Name** box, enter a name for the new address book.

3. In the **Folder contains** list, click **Contact items**. (If you create the folder from the People module, Contact Items is already selected.)

4. In the **Select where to place the folder** pane, do any of the following:

   - Click your email account address at the top of the folder structure to create the new folder at the same structural level as the module folders.

   - Click **Contacts** to create the address book as a subfolder of the default Contacts folder.

   - Click any other folder to create the address book as a subfolder of that folder.

> **TIP** The location you choose doesn't affect the way you access the address book from the People module or the functionality of the address book.

5. Click **OK** to create the new address book and add it to the My Contacts list in the Folder Pane of the People module.

To move contact records to another address book

1. In the People module, display the address book that contains the contact record or records you want to move.

2. In the contact list, click a contact record to select it. If you want to select additional contact records, hold down the **Ctrl** key and click each additional contact record.

3. Do any of the following:

   - Drag the selected records from the contact list to the destination address book in the Folder Pane.

   - Right-click and drag the selected records to the destination address book in the Folder Pane. When you release the mouse button, click **Move** on the shortcut menu.

   - On the **Home** tab, in the **Actions** group, display the **Move** list, and then click a folder in the list to move the selected records to that folder.

The Move list includes other address books that you can modify

 TIP If the folder you want to move the contacts to doesn't appear in your Move list, click Other Folder and then select the folder in the Move Items dialog box.

To copy contact records to another address book

1. In the People module, display the address book that contains the contact record or records you want to move.

2. In the contact list, click a record to select it. If you want to select additional contact records, hold down the **Ctrl** key and click each additional contact record.

3. Do any of the following:

   - Hold down the **Ctrl** key and drag the selected records from the contact list to the destination address book in the Folder Pane.

   - Right-click and drag the selected records to the destination address book in the Folder Pane. When you release the mouse button, click **Copy** on the shortcut menu.

   - On the **Home** tab, in the **Actions** group, display the **Move** list, and then click **Copy to Folder** to open the Copy Items dialog box displaying the full Folder List. Select the address book you want to copy the selected records to, and then click **OK**.

To delete an address book

1. Display the People module.

2. In the **My Contacts** list, right-click the address book you want to delete, and then click **Delete Folder**.

3. In the confirmation message box, click **Yes**.

Import and export contact records

If you have contact information for people saved in another file, you can import the information into an Outlook address book as contact records. You can import information from another Outlook data file (a .pst file) or from a comma-delimited plain-text file (a .csv file) into an address book. (You must create the address book first.) If you want to import information from another type of file, export the information into a .csv file first, and then import that .csv file.

Similarly, you can share contact records with other people who use Outlook or another contact-management app by exporting the contact records from Outlook into a .pst file or .csv file that other people can import.

You manage the import and export processes by using the Import And Export Wizard. The wizard provides a simple path through each process.

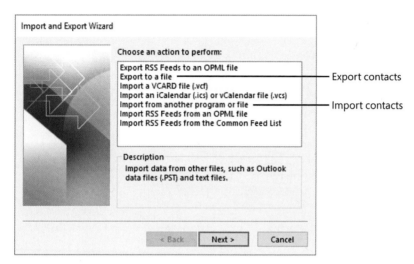

The correct wizard options for exporting and importing contact records

During the import process, you specify how Outlook should handle any contact records that exist in both the source file and the destination address book.

You can replace, duplicate, or block records that match those in the destination address book

If the information that you import wasn't originally created in Outlook, the fields might be identified by different names in the source file than the field names that Outlook uses. You can match the source fields to the standard Outlook field names by mapping the fields.

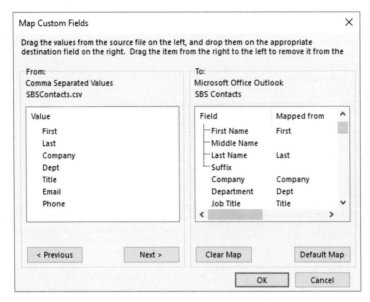

Match source file fields to Outlook address book fields before importing

When you export contact records from an Outlook address book to an Outlook data file (instead of a comma-delimited file), you have two additional options:

- You can export all the contact records in the address book, or filter the records during the export process to select only those that meet specific criteria.

- You can password-protect the exported file.

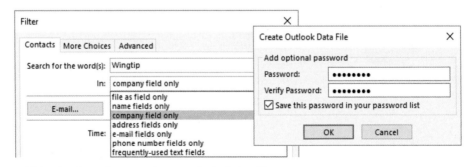

Additional options when exporting to an Outlook data file

To start the Import And Export Wizard

1. On the **Open & Export** page of the Backstage view, click **Import/Export**.

To import contact records from a .csv file

1. Start the Import And Export wizard.

2. In the **Choose an action to perform** list, click **Import from another program or file**. Then click **Next**. The name in the title bar changes to *Import a File* to indicate the path you're following in the wizard.

3. In the **Select file type to import from** pane, click **Comma Separated Values**. Then click **Next**.

4. Click the **Browse** button adjacent to the **File to import** box. In the **Browse** dialog box, navigate to the .csv file you want to import records from. Click the file, and then click **OK** to insert the file path in the File To Import box.

5. In the **Options** section below the file path, indicate how you want Outlook to handle contact records from the .csv file that match the names of existing contact records in the destination address book. Click **Next**, and then:

   - To overwrite duplicate items in the address book with those from the source file, click **Replace duplicates with items imported**.

   - To create additional versions of duplicate items, click **Allow duplicates to be created**.

   - To not import duplicate items, click **Do not import duplicate items**.

6. In the **Select destination folder** pane, locate the address book you want to import the contact records into. Click the address book, and then click **Next**.

8

The last page of the wizard displays a description of the import operation and provides additional configuration options.

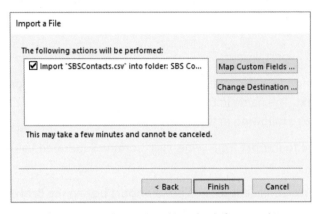

You can map fields or change the address book if you need to

7. If there is a possibility that the source file field names don't match the Outlook address book field names, click **Map Custom Fields** to open the Map Custom Fields dialog box, and then do the following:

   a. In the **From** pane, note the fields that are present in the source file.

   b. In the **To** pane, click the **Expand** button (+) to the left of any field group to display its fields.

   c. The Mapped From column displays the source file field that maps to each Outlook address book field. Review the mappings to ensure that they're correct.

   d. If you need to change a field mapping, drag the field from the **Value** list in the **From** pane and drop it on the **Field** list in the **To** pane. (Drag it from the left pane to the right pane.)

   > **TIP** Mapping a value to a field changes the mapping; you can't map one value to multiple fields.

   e. If you don't want to import a field, drag that field from the **Mapped from** list in the **To** pane to the **Value** list in the **From** pane. (Drag it from the right pane to the left pane.)

   f. When the mapping is correct, click **OK** to close the Map Custom Fields dialog box.

8. If you want to import the contact records to a different address book than you chose in step 6, click **Change Destination** to open the Select A Folder dialog box, click the address book you want to use, and then click **OK**. This doesn't affect the field mappings.

9. Click **Finish** to import the contact records into the selected address book.

To import contact records from an Outlook Data File (.pst file)

1. If you want to import contact records into an existing address book, display that address book in the People module.

2. Start the Import And Export wizard.

3. In the **Choose an action to perform** list, click **Import from another program or file**. Then click **Next**. The name in the title bar changes to *Import a File* to indicate the path you're following in the wizard.

4. In the **Select file type to import from** pane, click **Outlook Data File (.pst)**. Then click **Next**. The name in the title bar changes to *Import Outlook Data File*.

5. Click the **Browse** button adjacent to the **File to import** box. In the **Open Outlook Data Files** dialog box, navigate to the .pst file you want to import records from. Click the file, and then click **Open** to insert the file path in the File To Import box.

6. In the **Options** section below the file path, indicate how you want Outlook to handle contact records from the .pst file that match the names of existing contact records in the destination address book. Click **Next**, and then:

   - To overwrite duplicate items in the address book with those from the source file, click **Replace duplicates with items imported**.

   - To create additional versions of duplicate items, click **Allow duplicates to be created**.

   - To not import duplicate items, click **Do not import duplicate items**.

7. If the .pst file requires a password, the Outlook Data File Password dialog box opens. Enter the password in the **Password** box, and then click **OK**.

8

8. The wizard displays the contents of the selected .pst file. In the **Select the folder to import from** pane, expand the **Outlook Data File** folder, and click the address book you want to import records from.

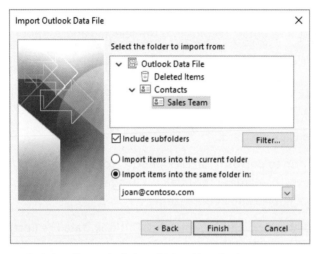

Outlook data files can include multiple address books

9. If you want to import only contact records that meet specific criteria, click the **Filter** button. In the **Filter** dialog box, specify one or more conditions that the contact records must meet. Then click **OK**.

10. Do either of the following:

    - If you want to import the contact records into the address book you displayed in step 1, click **Import items into the current folder**.

    - If you want to create a new address book containing the imported contact records, click **Import items into the same folder in**, and then in the list, click the account you want to create the address book in.

11. Click **Finish** to import the contact records into the selected address book or to create the address book.

To export contact records to a .csv file

1. Start the Import And Export wizard.

2. In the **Choose an action to perform** list, click **Export to a file**. Then click **Next**. The name in the title bar changes to *Export to a File* to indicate the path you're following in the wizard.

3. In the **Create a file of type** pane, click **Comma Separated Values**. Then click **Next**.

4. In the **Select the folder to export from** pane, locate and click the address book you want to export contact records from. Then click **Next**.

5. Click the **Browse** button adjacent to the **Save exported file as** box. In the **Browse** dialog box, navigate to the folder you want to create the .csv file in, and enter a name for the file in the **File name** box. Then click **OK** to insert the file path in the Save Exported File As box.

6. In the **Export to a File** dialog box, click **Next**.

   The last page of the wizard displays a description of the export operation and provides the option to map the Outlook address book fields to custom field names in the output file.

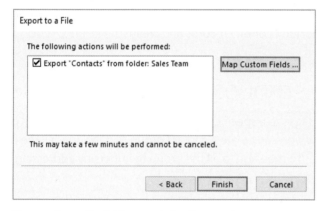

You can change the field names during the export process

7. Click **Finish** to export the contact records and create the .csv file.

To export contact records to an Outlook Data File (.pst file)

1. Start the Import And Export wizard.

2. In the **Choose an action to perform** list, click **Export to a file**. Then click **Next**. The name in the title bar changes to *Export to a File* to indicate the path you're following in the wizard.

3. In the **Create a file of type** pane, click **Outlook Data File (.pst)**. Then click **Next**. The name in the title bar changes to *Export Outlook Data File*.

8

4. In the **Select the folder to export from** pane, do the following, and then click **Next**:

   a. Locate and click the address book you want to export contact records from.

   b. If you want to export only contact records that meet specific criteria, click the **Filter** button. In the **Filter** dialog box, specify one or more conditions that the contact records must meet. Then click **OK**.

5. Click the **Browse** button adjacent to the **Save exported file as** box. In the **Open Outlook Data Files** dialog box, navigate to the folder you want to create the .pst file in, and enter a name for the file in the **File name** box. Then click **OK** to insert the file path in the Save Exported File As box.

6. In the **Export Outlook Data File** dialog box, click **Finish**.

7. The Create Outlook Data File dialog box opens. If you want to assign a password to the .pst file, enter the password in the **Password** and **Verify Password** boxes. Then click **OK** to export the contact records and create the .pst file.

Create contact groups

If you frequently send messages to a specific group of people, such as members of a project team, club, or family, you can create a contact group that includes all the group members. Then you can send a message to all the group members by addressing it to the contact group.

Contact groups have different icons and bold names to differentiate them from individual contact records

Contact groups are like personal versions of distribution lists. A distribution list is available to everyone on your Exchange Server network; a contact group is available only from the local address book you store it in. You can, however, send a contact group to other people for their own use.

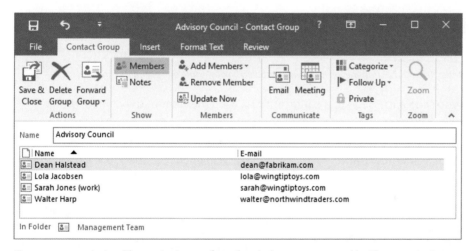

You can communicate with a contact group from the window or as you would with any contact

You can add individual people, resources, distribution lists, public folders, email-enabled Microsoft SharePoint site libraries, and other contact groups to a contact group.

You add a member to a contact group either by selecting an existing contact record from an address book or by providing a name and email address. When you use the latter method, you have the option to simultaneously create a contact record for the person.

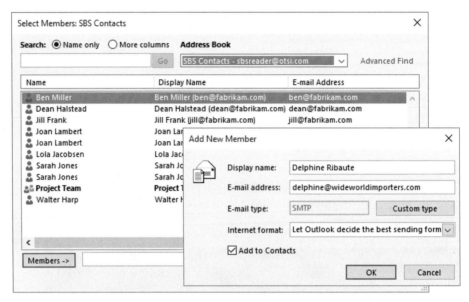

You can search for contacts in the Select Members dialog box by name or by other criteria

When you send a message to a contact group, each member of the contact group receives a copy of the message. If you want to send a message to most, but not all, members of a contact group, you can expand the contact group in the address field to a full list of its members, and remove individual recipients from the specific message before you send it.

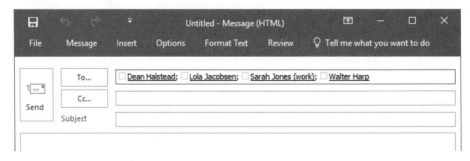

Expanding a contact group replaces the group name with the group members

To start creating a contact group

1. Do any of the following to open a new Contact Group window:

    -   In the People module, on the **Home** tab, in the **New** group, click the **New Contact Group** button.

    -   In the Mail, Calendar, or Tasks module, on the **Home** tab, in the **New** group, click **New Items**, click **More Items**, and then click **Contact Group**.

    -   In any module, press **Ctrl+Shift+L**.

2. In the **Name** box, enter a name for the group.

To add existing contacts to a contact group

1. Open the contact group window.

2. On the **Contact Group** tab, in the **Members** group, click the **Add Members** button.

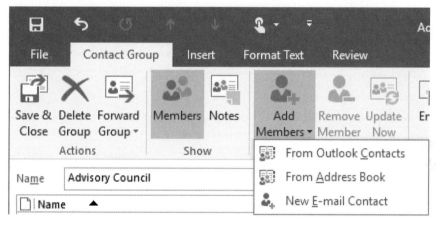

Add existing or new contacts to a group

3. In the **Add Members** list, do either of the following:

- Click **From Outlook Contacts** to open the Select Members dialog box displaying your default address book.

- Click **From Address Book** to open the Select Members dialog box displaying the address book designated as the first to check.

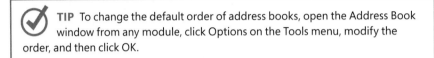 **TIP** To change the default order of address books, open the Address Book window from any module, click Options on the Tools menu, modify the order, and then click OK.

4. In the **Select Members** dialog box, if you want to choose contacts from a different address book, expand the **Address Book** list, and then click the address book you want to use.

5. In the **Select Members** dialog box, for each contact you want to add to the contact group, do either of the following to add the contact to the Members box:

- Click the contact, and then in the lower-left corner of the dialog box, click the **Members** button.

- Double-click the contact.

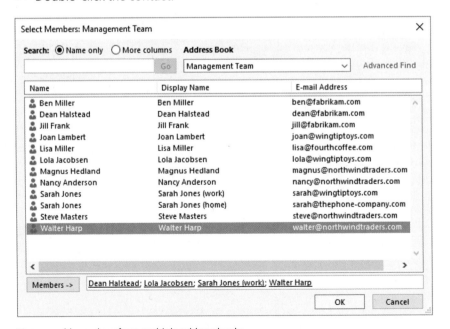

You can add members from multiple address books

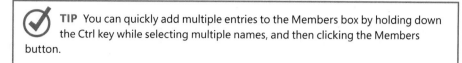

> ✓ **TIP** You can quickly add multiple entries to the Members box by holding down the Ctrl key while selecting multiple names, and then clicking the Members button.

6. When you are done adding contacts to the Members box, click **OK** to add the contacts to the contact group.

7. In the contact group window, on the **Contact Group** tab, click **Save & Close**.

To add new contacts to a contact group

1. Open the contact group window.

2. On the **Contact Group** tab, in the **Members** group, click the **Add Members** button, and then click **New E-mail Contact** to open the Add New Member dialog box.

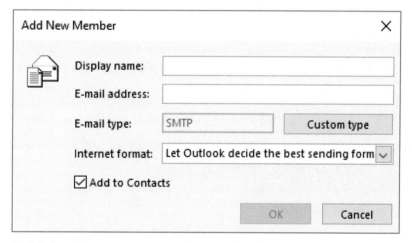

By default, adding a new email contact to a group also creates a contact record

3. In the **Display name** box, enter the name you want to display for the contact group member.

4. In the **E-mail address** box, enter the email address for the contact group member.

> ✓ **TIP** It's unlikely that you'd ever modify the E-mail Type or Internet Format setting. If you plan to create rich text messages for the contact group but want to send plain text versions to a specific recipient, you can select the plain text version in the Internet Format list.

8

5. If you don't want to create a contact record for the new contact group member in your default address book, clear the **Add to Contacts** check box.

6. Click **OK** to add the new contact to the contact group and create the contact record, if that option was selected.

To share a contact group with other people

1. Open the contact group window.

2. On the **Contact Group** tab, in the **Actions** group, click **Forward Group**.

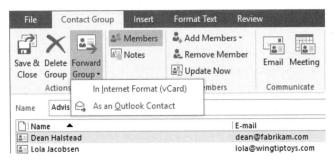

The best format depends on whether recipients run Outlook or another email app

3. Do either of the following to create an email message with the contact group attached:

    - To send an attachment that can be used by email apps other than Outlook, click **In Internet Format (vCard)**.

    - To send an attachment that can be saved in an Outlook address book, click **As an Outlook Contact**.

To update contact information for contact group members

1. Open the contact group window.

2. On the **Contact Group** tab, in the **Members** group, click the **Update Now** button. Outlook checks the group members against their contact records and updates the names and email addresses to reflect changes to the contact records.

To remove members from a contact group

1. Open the contact group window.

2. Select the member or members you want to remove from the group.

3. On the **Contact Group** tab, in the **Members** group, click the **Remove Member** button.

To expand a contact group in an email message address field

1. In the **To**, **Cc**, or **Bcc** field of the message composition window, click the **Expand** button (+) to the left of the contact group name. Outlook warns you that you can't contract the list after expanding it.

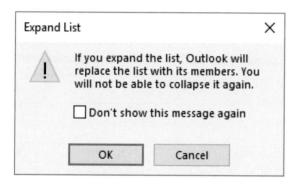

You can revert to the contact group by reentering it in the address box

2. In the **Expand List** message box, click **OK** to replace the contact group name with the individual names or display names of its members.

 TIP You can remove individual group members from the address field by clicking or dragging to select the group members and then pressing the Delete key.

Quickly locate contact information

You can use the Search feature in any Outlook module to immediately find a specific Outlook item within the current folder, an item of the same type in any folder, or an item of any type in any folder. Finding an item that contains, for example, a specific word is as simple as entering that word in the search box at the top of the content area. When you position the cursor in the search box, the Search tool tab appears on the ribbon. You can refine your search criteria or expand your search to include additional locations by using the commands available on the Search tab.

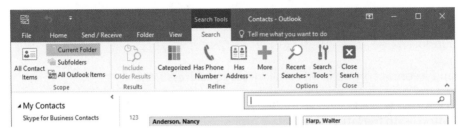

Filters on the Search tool tab of each module are specific to the items stored in each module

As you enter a search term in the Search box, Outlook filters the list to display only those contact records that contain the words that begin with the letters you've entered, and highlights the matches in the contact records. This highlighting appears in any view other than Business Card view.

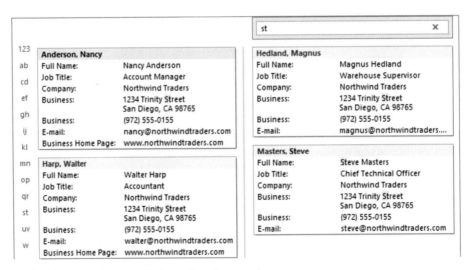

Outlook locates the letters at the beginning of any word

To search for contact records that contain specific text

1. In the People module, do either of the following to activate the search box and the Search tool tab:

   - Click in the search box at the top of the contact list.

   - Press **Ctrl+E**.

2. In the search box, enter the term that you want to search for. Outlook filters the list to display only those contact records that contain the letters you've entered, and highlights the matches in the contact records.

> **TIP** If Outlook doesn't automatically filter the contact records, press Enter or click the Search button after you enter the search term.

To change the scope of a search

1. On the **Search** tool tab, in the **Scope** group, do any of the following:

   - Click **All Contact Items** to display contact records from all address books.

   - Click **Current Folder** to display contact records from only the current address book.

   - Click **Subfolders** to display contact records from the current address book and any subfolders (address books stored below the current address book in the folder hierarchy).

   - Click **All Outlook Items** to display any Outlook items that meet the search criteria, including contact records, email messages, appointments, and tasks.

8

To search for contact records by a specific field

1. On the **Search** tool tab, In the **Refine** group, click any button to display a list of related options, and then click an option by which you want to refine the search.

    Outlook adds each refinement to the search box or displays it in a box below the search box.

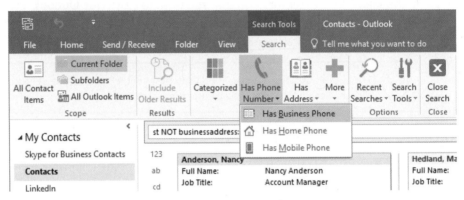

You can refine a search by multiple criteria

To clear search criteria

1. At the right end of the search box or any search field box below it, click the **Remove** button (**X**) to remove the corresponding criterion.

To repeat a previous search

1. On the **Search** tool tab, in the **Options** group, click the **Recent Searches** button, and then click the criteria of the previous search you want to repeat.

To end the search and return to the original address book

1. Do either of the following:

    *   On the **Search** tool tab, click the **Close Search** button.

    *   Clear all the search criteria.

Personalize electronic business cards

Within each contact record window, information appears not only in the fields of the contact record but also in the form of a graphic that resembles a business card. When you enter a person's contact information in a contact record, basic information appears in the business card shown in the upper-right corner of the contact window. This data includes the person's name, company, and job title; work, mobile, and home phone numbers; and email, postal, webpage, and instant messaging addresses. (Only the first 10 lines of information fit on the card.)

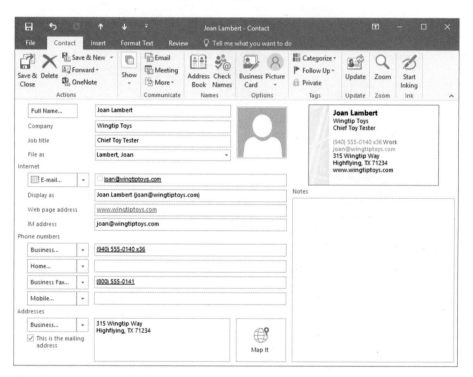

The default business card displays contact information and a gray placeholder image

If an image is associated with the person through Exchange, SharePoint, or a social network to which you've connected Outlook, the contact record includes the image. You can change the types of information that appear, rearrange the information fields, format the text and background, and add, change, or remove images, such as a logo or photograph.

Creating a business card for yourself provides you with an attractive way of presenting your contact information to people you correspond with in email. You can attach your business card to an outgoing email message or include it as part (or all) of your email signature. The recipient of your business card can easily create a contact record for you by saving the business card to his or her Outlook address book.

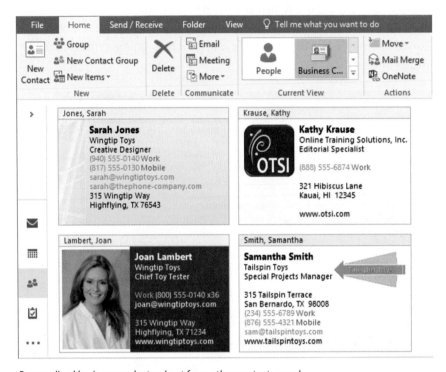

Personalized business cards stand out from other contact records

You can send entire contact records to other Outlook users to add to their address books or, if you prefer to share only the information shown on the associated business card, you can send the business card. You can include a business card as part or all of your email signature by clicking the Business Card button while creating or editing a signature.

 SEE ALSO For information about email signatures, see "Create and use automatic signatures" in Chapter 4, "Enhance message content."

To add a picture to an electronic business card

1. In the People module, open the contact record that you want to modify.

2. On the **Contact** tab, in the **Options** group, click the **Picture** button, and then click **Add Picture**. The Add Contact Picture dialog box opens, displaying the contents of your Pictures library.

3. In the **Add Contact Picture** dialog box, browse to the file folder that contains the picture you want to use, click the image, and then click **OK** to replace the placeholder image in the contact record window and business card with the photo you selected.

To modify the layout of an electronic business card

1. In the People module, open the contact record that you want to modify.

2. On the **Contact** tab, in the **Options** group, click the **Business Card** button to open the Edit Business Card dialog box.

Specify the order, color, and layout of the business card elements

3. In the **Card Design** section, do any of the following:

- To move the picture, expand the **Layout** list, and then click the location where you want to place the image.

- To change the background color, click the **Background Color** button, and then in the **Color** dialog box, select a color.

- To change the percentage of the card that is allocated to the picture, in the **Image Area** box, enter or select the percentage.

- To modify the alignment of the picture, in the **Image Align** list, click the alignment you want.

4. In the **Edit Business Card** dialog box, click **OK** to apply your changes.

To change the text shown on an electronic business card

1. Open the **Edit Business Card** dialog box for the contact record that you want to modify.

2. In the **Fields** section of the dialog box, do any of the following to modify the business card (but not the contact record):

- To remove a field from the business card, click the field name, and then click the **Remove** button.

- To add a field to the business card, click the **Add** button, click the field category, and then click the field you want to add.

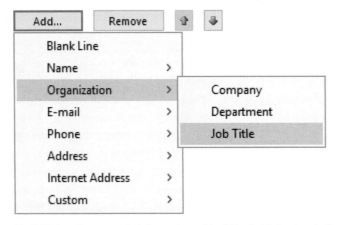

If a field doesn't yet contain information, a blank line holds its place in the card layout

- To change the text displayed for a field, in the **Edit** section of the dialog box, edit the displayed text.

- To reorder fields, click a field that you want to move, and then below the **Fields** pane, click the **Move Field Up** or **Move Field Down** button.

- To insert a blank line between fields, at the bottom of the **Fields** pane, click one of the **Blank Line** entries. Then below the **Fields** pane, click the **Move Field Up** button to position the blank line where you want it.

3. Repeat step 2 for each other field you want to modify.

4. In the **Edit Business Card** dialog box, click **OK** to apply your changes.

To modify the display of labels on an electronic business card

1. Open the **Edit Business Card** dialog box for the contact record that you want to modify.

2. To select the field label you want to modify, do either of the following:

   - On the business card preview, click the text.

   - In the **Fields** pane, click the field.

3. In the **Edit** section of the dialog box, do any of the following:

   - To remove the label from the field, in the **Label** list, click **No Label**.

   - To display a label adjacent to the field, in the **Label** list, click **Left** or **Right**.

   - To change the label text, select the label location, and then edit the text in the **Label** box.

   - To change the label color, select the label location, click the **Label Color** button, select a color, and then click **OK**.

4. Repeat steps 2 and 3 for each other field label you want to modify.

5. In the **Edit Business Card** dialog box, click **OK** to apply your changes.

8

To format the text of an electronic business card

1. Open the **Edit Business Card** dialog box for the contact record that you want to modify.

2. To select the text you want to format, do either of the following:

   - On the business card preview, click the text.

   - In the **Fields** pane, click the field.

3. In the **Edit** section of the dialog box, do any of the following:

   - In the text box below the formatting buttons, make any changes you want to the content of the field.

   - To change the text color, click the **Font Color** button, select a color, and then click **OK**.

   - To change the text size, click the **Increase Font Size** or **Decrease Font Size** button.

   - To apply a font effect, click the **Bold**, **Italic**, or **Underline** button.

   - To change the text alignment, click the **Align Left**, **Center**, or **Align Right** button.

4. Repeat steps 2 and 3 for each other field you want to format.

5. In the **Edit Business Card** dialog box, click **OK** to apply your changes.

To reset an electronic business card to the default settings

1. Open the **Edit Business Card** dialog box for the contact record that you want to modify.

2. Near the lower-right corner of the dialog box, click the **Reset Card** button.

To send an Outlook business card

1. In any view of the address book, click the contact record whose business card you want to send.

2. On the **Home** tab, in the **Share** group, click the **Forward Contact** button, and then click **As a Business Card** to create a new message that has the business card attached as a file and displayed in the content area.

3. Address and send the message.

Skills review

In this chapter, you learned how to:

- Create address books
- Import and export contact records
- Create contact groups
- Quickly locate contact information
- Personalize electronic business cards

8

Practice tasks

The practice files for these tasks are located in the Outlook2016SBS\Ch08 folder.

Create address books

Display the People module, and then perform the following tasks:

1. Create an address book named **My SBS Contacts** that is a subfolder of the primary Contacts address book.

2. Display the **Contacts** address book. Select any two contact records, and copy them to the **My SBS Contacts** address book.

Import and export contact records

Display the My SBS Contacts address book, and then perform the following tasks:

1. Import the contact records from the **SBSContacts.csv** file in the practice file folder into the **My SBS Contacts** address book you created in the preceding set of practice tasks.

2. During the import process, map the field headings from the .csv file to the corresponding address book headings.

3. If you want to, export the contact records from your **Contacts** address book to an Outlook Data File.

Create contact groups

Display the My SBS Contacts address book, and then perform the following tasks:

1. Create a contact group named **Team Leaders**.

2. Add the following people from the address book to the contact group:

   - **Alexander Eggerer**
   - **Stephanie Conroy**
   - **Ingelise Lang**
   - **Lee Oliver**

3. Add the following person to the contact group and to your address book:

   Name: Lisa Miller

   Email address: lisa@treyresearch.net

4. Save and close the contact group.

5. Verify that the Team Leaders contact group and Lisa Miller contact record were created in the My SBS Contacts address book.

6. Create an email message addressed to you and to the Team Leaders contact group, with the subject Test message to contact group.

7. In the **To** field, expand the **Team Leaders** contact group to display its members.

8. In the **To** field, replace the individual contact group members with the contact group, make sure you're still a message recipient, and then send the email message. (You'll receive the message, and undeliverable notifications for the Trey Research employees.)

9. Open the message when you receive it, and notice how the recipients are specified in the message header. Then close the message and delete the undeliverable message notifications.

10. In the **My SBS Contacts** address book, edit the contact record for **Lee Oliver**, and then change the email address from *lee@treyresearch.net* to lee.oliver@treyresearch.net. Save and close the contact record.

11. Open the **Team Leaders** contact group, and update the member information. Notice that Lee Oliver's email address changes.

12. Remove **Ingelise Lang** from the contact group. Then save and close the contact group.

Quickly locate contact information

Display the My SBS Contacts address book, and then perform the following tasks:

1. Use the search function to search the address book for contact records that contain the text **ma**. Notice that the search results include only contacts with names or email addresses that begin with the specified letters, but none that have the letters in another position.

2. Change the scope of a search to include all address books in your Outlook installation. Notice any changes in the search results.

3. Filter the search to include only contact records that contain **sales** in the **Title** field.

4. Clear all the search criteria to return to the original address book.

5. Repeat the search from the **Recent Searches** list.

6. Close the search to return to the original address book.

Personalize electronic business cards

Display the My SBS Contacts address book, and then perform the following tasks:

1. Open the contact record for **Jay Jamison**.

2. Add the **JJProfile** picture from the practice file folder to the electronic business card.

3. Experiment with modifying the content, layout, and formatting of the business card.

4. Save and close the contact record.

5. Email Jay Jamison's business card to yourself, and review the content of the message that you receive.

Part 4

Manage appointments and tasks

Manage scheduling

You can use the Outlook 2016 calendar to organize your daily activities and to remind you of important tasks and events. If you're a busy person and use the Outlook calendar to its fullest potential, it might at times seem as though the calendar runs your life—but that isn't necessarily a bad thing! Using the calendar effectively can help you stay organized, on time, and on task. You can schedule and track appointments, meetings, and events, and block time as a reminder to yourself to take care of tasks. And because you can also set up Outlook on your mobile device, you can be assured of having up-to-date schedule information available wherever and whenever you need it.

If you have a Microsoft Exchange Server account, a calendar is part of that account. Some Internet email accounts also have associated calendars. When you configure Outlook to connect to a different type of account, Outlook also connects to the associated calendar. If you don't have a calendar as part of your account, Outlook creates a blank calendar for you. You can easily schedule appointments, events, and meetings on any Outlook calendar.

This chapter guides you through procedures related to scheduling and changing appointments, events, and meetings; responding to meeting requests; and displaying different views of a calendar.

In this chapter

- Schedule appointments and events

- Convert calendar items

- Configure calendar item options

- Schedule and change meetings

- Respond to meeting requests

- Display different views of a calendar

Practice files

No practice files are necessary to complete the practice tasks in this chapter.

Schedule appointments and events

Appointments are blocks of time you schedule for only yourself (as opposed to meetings, to which you invite other Outlook users). An appointment has a specific start time and end time (as opposed to an event, which occurs for one or more full 24-hour periods).

Events are day-long blocks of time that you schedule on your Outlook calendar, such as birthdays, payroll days, or anything else occurring on a specific day but not at a specific time. In all other respects, creating an event is identical to creating an appointment, in that you can specify a location, indicate recurrence, indicate your availability, and attach additional information to the event item.

You can schedule an appointment by entering, at minimum, a subject and time in an appointment window or directly on the calendar. The basic appointment window also includes a field for the appointment location and a notes area in which you can store general information, including formatted text, website links, and even file attachments so that they are readily available to you at the time of the appointment.

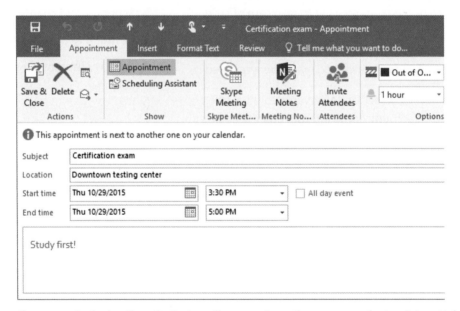

If your organization has Skype For Business, Skype meeting options appear on the Appointment tab

If you create an appointment that immediately follows or precedes another, the Info-Bar at the top of the window indicates that the appointment is adjacent to another on your calendar. If you create an appointment that has a time overlap with an existing appointment, the InfoBar indicates that the appointment conflicts with another.

To schedule an event, you need to provide only the date. You can schedule an event in an appointment window, or directly on the calendar.

> **TIP** You don't have to create appointments and events from scratch; you can also create them from email messages. For information, see "Convert calendar items" later in this chapter.

When the Calendar view is displayed, events are shown on the calendar in the date area; appointments are displayed in the time slots.

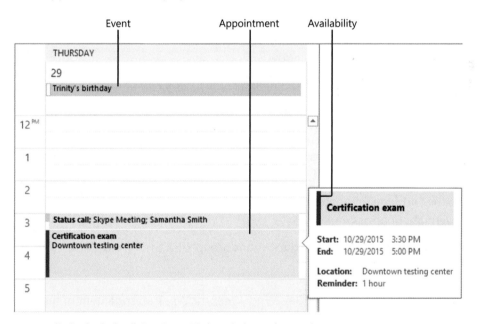

You can display basic details in a ScreenTip by pointing to the appointment or event

> **SEE ALSO** For information about setting availability, see "Configure calendar item options" later in this chapter.

> **IMPORTANT** The procedures in this chapter assume that you're working with an Exchange account. Some functionality might be unavailable if you're working with a calendar that's part of another type of account.

To open a new appointment window

1. In the Calendar module, do either of the following:

   - On the **Home** tab, in the **New** group, click **New Appointment**.

   - Press **Ctrl+N**.

Or

1. In any module, do either of the following:

   - On the **Home** tab, in the **New** group, click **New Items**, and then click **Appointment**.

   - Press **Ctrl+Shift+A**.

To schedule an appointment

1. Open a new appointment window.

2. In the **Subject** box, enter an identifying name for the appointment.

3. In the **Location** box, enter the appointment location, if it's pertinent, or any other information that you want to have available in the appointment header.

4. In the **Start time** row, enter or select a date and time. Outlook automatically sets the End Time to a half hour after the start time.

5. In the **End time** row, enter or select a date and time. An appointment can span overnight or across multiple days.

6. On the **Appointment** tab, in the **Actions** group, click the **Save & Close** button.

Or

1. Display the calendar in the Day, Work Week, or Week arrangement of the Calendar view.

2. Do either of the following in the calendar pane:

   - In the calendar, click the time slot at the appointment start time on the day of the appointment.

   - Drag from the appointment start time through to the appointment end time.

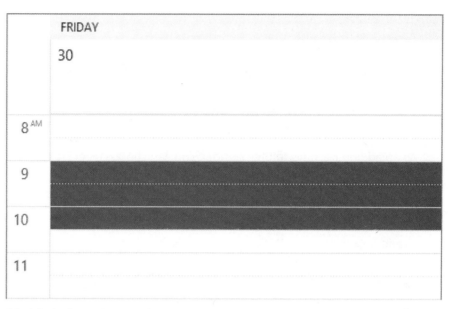

Schedule simple appointments directly on the calendar

When you release the mouse button, Outlook displays an editable bar that spans the selected time (or one time slot, as specified by the time scale of the calendar).

> **SEE ALSO** For information about setting the calendar time scale, see "Display different views of a calendar" later in this chapter.

3. In the editable bar, enter an identifying name for the appointment. When you begin typing, Outlook creates an appointment with the default availability and reminder time.

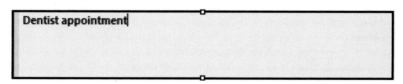

When an appointment is being edited on the calendar, it has sizing handles on the top and bottom

4. If you want to change the appointment time span, drag the top or bottom sizing handle.

5. Press **Enter** or click away from the bar to create the appointment.

Add holidays to your calendar

Holidays are a type of event, and it can be useful to have them on your calendar so you can plan around days that you might not be working or that businesses might be closed. Instead of creating events on your calendar for individual holidays, you can have Outlook add them for you.

When adding holidays to the calendar, you can choose from 111 countries or regions, and four religions. You can add multiple sets of holidays to your calendar, so if you work with clients or colleagues in another location, you can add those holidays to your calendar so you can anticipate scheduling issues.

To add holidays to your Outlook calendar, follow these steps:

1. Open the **Outlook Options** dialog box and display the **Calendar** page.

2. In the **Calendar options** section, click the **Add Holidays** button to open the **Add Holidays to Calendar** dialog box.

You can add holidays from a specific location or religion to your calendar

3. Select the check boxes of the locations or religions whose holidays you want to add to your calendar, and then click **OK**.

4. After Outlook adds the selected holidays to your calendar, click **OK** to close the **Outlook Options** dialog box.

TIP If you try to install the holidays of the same location or religion twice, Outlook notifies you of this and asks whether you want to import them again. If you inadvertently add the same set of holidays to the calendar twice, the easiest way to rectify the situation is to remove all occurrences of that location's holidays and then add them again.

Outlook adds the holiday occurrences from 2012 through 2022 to your calendar, and assigns a color category named *Holiday* to them.

SEE ALSO For information about categories, see "Categorize items" in Chapter 6, "Organize your Inbox."

To remove a set of holidays from your calendar, follow these steps:

1. Search the calendar for **category:holiday**. Narrow the search to a specific location or holiday by adding search criteria if necessary, to locate the holidays you want to remove.

Outlook highlights the search terms in the results

2. Select individual holidays you want to remove; or click any holiday in the list to activate the list, and then press **Ctrl+A** to select all the holidays in the search results. Then press the **Delete** key.

9

To schedule an event

1. Open a new appointment window.

2. In the **Subject** box, enter an identifying name for the event.

3. In the **Location** box, enter the event location, if it's pertinent, or any other information that you want to have available in the event header.

4. In the **Start time** row, enter or select the event date. Then at the right end of the row, select the **All day event** check box.

5. Enter any additional information as you would for an appointment. Then save and close the event.

Or

1. Display the Calendar view of the calendar.

2. Do either of the following:

   - In the Day, Work Week, or Week arrangement of the calendar, on the day that you want to create the event, click the space below the day and date, and above the time slots. This is the event slot.

   - In the Month arrangement of the calendar, click the day that you want to create the event.

3. Enter a title for the event, and then press **Enter**.

Convert calendar items

All Outlook calendar items are built from the same basic template. These two factors define a calendar item as an appointment, event, or meeting:

- Whether the item has specific start and end times or is all day

- Whether you invite other people through Outlook

You can easily convert an appointment into an event or meeting, or convert an event into an appointment or an invited event.

If you want to schedule an appointment, event, or meeting based on the information in an email message that you receive, you can easily do so by dragging the message to the calendar. For example, if a friend or co-worker sends you a message that contains the details of the grand opening for a local art gallery, you can add that information to your calendar. You can retain any or all of the message information as part of the calendar item so that you (or other meeting participants) have the information on hand when you need it. After creating the calendar item, you can delete the actual message from your Inbox.

To create an appointment from an email message

1. Display your Inbox.

2. Drag the message from the message list to the **Calendar** link or button on the **Navigation Bar**.

3. After the cursor changes to a plus sign, release the mouse button to create an appointment based on the message and open the appointment window for editing. The appointment has the subject and content of the original message. The start and end times are set to the next half-hour increment following the current time.

4. Set the date and times for the appointment, and do any of the following:

   - In the **Options** group, change the availability, reminder time, or recurrence.

   - In the **Tags** group, assign a category to the appointment, mark it as private, or change the priority.

   - In the content pane, edit the original message content to suit the requirements of the appointment.

5. In the appointment window, click the **Save & Close** button to save the appointment to your calendar.

 SEE ALSO For information about adding message content to your To-Do List, see "Create tasks" in Chapter 11, "Track tasks."

To convert an appointment to an event

1. Open the appointment window.

2. At the right end of the **Start time** row, select the **All day event** check box.

3. Change the event date, options, or tags, and then save and close the event window.

To convert an appointment to a meeting

1. Open the appointment window.

2. On the **Appointment** tab in the **Attendees** group, click the **Invite Attendees** button to add a To box to the header and display the meeting window features.

3. Enter contact information for the people you want to invite to the meeting.

4. Add a location if necessary, and then click the **Send Invitation** button.

To convert an event to an invited event

1. Open the event window.

2. On the **Event** tab, in the **Attendees** group, click the **Invite Attendees** button to add a To box to the header and display the meeting window features.

3. Enter contact information for the people you want to invite to the event.

4. Add a location if necessary, and then click the **Send Invitation** button.

To convert an event to an appointment

1. Open the event window.

2. At the right end of the **Start time** row, clear the **All day event** check box.

3. Set the appointment start and end times, and change the options as necessary. Then save and close the appointment window.

Configure calendar item options

Appointments, events, and meetings share many common elements, and you use the same techniques to work with those options in all types of calendar items. The five options that you can configure for all items are:

- **Time zones** You can specify the time zone in which an appointment, event, or meeting occurs. This helps to ensure that the start and end times are clearly defined when you're traveling or inviting people in multiple time zones to an online meeting. You have the option of specifying different time zones for the start time and the finish time. This is useful when your "appointment" is an airplane flight with departure and arrival cities located in different time zones, and you want the flight to show up correctly wherever you're currently located.

- **Availability** When creating an appointment or event, you indicate your availability (referred to as *Free/Busy time*) by marking it as Free, Working Elsewhere, Tentative, Busy, or Out Of Office. The appointment or event is color-coded on your calendar to match the availability you indicate. Your availability is visible to other Outlook users on your network and is also displayed when you share your calendar or send calendar information to other people.

  The default availability for new appointments and meetings is Busy, and for events is Free.

  > **SEE ALSO** For information about sharing your calendar with other Outlook users on your network and about sending your schedule information in an email message, see "Share calendar information" in Chapter 10, "Manage your calendar."

- **Reminder** By default, Outlook displays a reminder message 15 minutes before the start time of an appointment or meeting, or 12 hours before an event (at noon the preceding day). You can change the reminder to occur as far as two weeks in advance, or you can turn it off completely if you want to. If you synchronize your Outlook installation with a mobile device, reminders also appear on your mobile device. This is very convenient when you are away from your computer.

  > **TIP** Reminders can be indicated on the calendar by a bell icon. This option is turned off by default in Outlook 2016. You can turn it on in the Calendar Options section of the Calendar page of the Outlook Options dialog box.

- **Recurrence** If you have the same appointment, event, or meeting on a regular basis—for example, a weekly exercise class, a monthly team meeting, or an anniversary—you can set it up in your Outlook calendar as a recurring item. A recurring calendar item can happen at almost any regular interval, such as every Tuesday and Thursday, every other week, or the last weekday of every month.

  Configuring a recurrence creates multiple instances of the item on your calendar at the time interval you specify. You can set the item to recur until further notice, to end after a certain number of occurrences, or to end by a certain date. The individual occurrences of the recurring item are linked. When making

9

changes to a recurring item, you can choose to update all occurrences or only an individual occurrence of the appointment.

Recurring items are indicated on the calendar by circling arrows.

- **Privacy** You can tag a calendar item as Private if you want to ensure that the details aren't displayed when you share your calendar or send calendar information to other people.

    Private items are indicated on the calendar by a lock, and identified to other people as Private Appointment rather than by the subject.

You can specify time zones, your availability, the reminder time, and the recurrence, and mark an item as private, when you create the item. Alternatively, you can edit the item later and configure any of these options. The time zone can be specified only in the item window; the other options can be set on the item type–specific tab in the item window or the item type–specific tool tab that appears on the Outlook ribbon when you select an item on the calendar. In single-occurrence items, these tabs are labeled Appointment, Event, Meeting, or Invited Event. In recurring items, the tab names include Occurrence or Series to indicate whether you're editing one or all occurrences of the item.

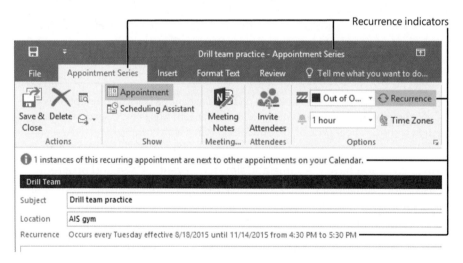

Outlook evaluates recurring items and provides information

You can assign categories and importance to appointments, events, and meetings in the same way that you do to messages and other Outlook items. In some ways, categories are more useful in the Calendar than in other modules.

Color categories provide information at a glance about your schedule.

To specify the time zone of an appointment or meeting

1. Open the item window.

2. On the **Appointment** or **Meeting** tab, in the **Options** group, click the **Time Zones** button to display the time zone controls in the Start Time and End Time rows. The time zone controls display the time zone your computer is currently set to.

3. Click the time zone control that you want to change, and then click the time zone.

Set the time zones to ensure that the time is accurate from any location

To hide the time zone controls

1. Select identical entries in the **Start time** and **End time** time zone controls.

2. On the **Appointment** or **Meeting** tab, in the **Options** group, click the **Time Zones** button to remove the controls.

9

To modify an appointment, event, or meeting

1. Display the calendar in the Day, Work Week, or Week arrangement of the Calendar view, with the appointment visible.

2. In the calendar pane, click the item once to select it. Then do any of the following:

    *   On the item type–specific tool tab, make any changes to the options or tags.

    *   Drag the item from the current time slot to a new time slot.

    *   Drag the top sizing handle to change an appointment start time.

    *   Drag the bottom sizing handle to change an appointment end time.

3. To open the item window, in which you can make other changes, do either of the following:

    *   Press **Enter**.

    *   On the item type–specific tool tab, in the **Actions** group, click **Open**.

To indicate your availability during an appointment, event, or meeting

1. Open the item window, or select the item on the calendar.

2. On the item-specific tab or tool tab, in the **Options** group, click the **Show As** list, and then click the availability.

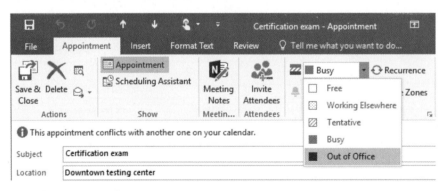

The default availability for appointments is Busy

To change the default reminder for an appointment, event, or meeting

1. Open the item window, or select the item on the calendar.

2. On the item-specific tab or tool tab, in the **Options** group, click the **Reminder** list, and then click the time (or click None to have no reminder).

To create recurrences of an appointment, event, or meeting

1. Open the item window, or select the item on the calendar.

2. On the item-specific tab or tool tab, in the **Options** group, click the **Recurrence** button to open the Recurrence dialog box. The default recurrence is weekly on the currently selected day of the week.

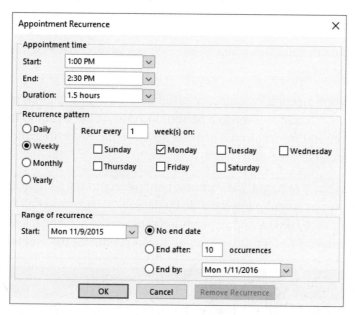

When configuring a recurrence, you can change the times, days, and frequency from the Appointment Recurrence dialog box

3. In the **Recurrence** dialog box, do any of the following:

   - In the **End** list, click the arrow and select an end time for the recurring meeting.

   - In the **Recurrence pattern** section, select how often you want the meeting to recur.

   - In the **Range of recurrence** section, select how many times you want to the meeting to occur, or select the last date you want the meeting to recur.

4. Click **OK** in the **Recurrence** dialog box to replace the Start Time and End Time fields in the appointment window with the recurrence details.

Schedule and change meetings

A primary difficulty when scheduling a meeting is finding a time that works for all the people who need to attend it. Scheduling meetings through Outlook is significantly simpler than other methods of scheduling meetings, particularly when you need to accommodate the schedules of several people. Outlook displays the individual and collective schedules of people within your own organization, and of people outside of your organization who have published their calendars to the Internet. You can review attendees' schedules to locate a time when everyone is available, or have Outlook find a convenient time for you.

You can send an Outlook meeting invitation (referred to as a *meeting request*) to anyone who has an email account—even to a person who doesn't use Outlook. You can send a meeting request from any type of email account (such as an Exchange account or an Internet email account).

The meeting window has two pages: the Appointment page and the Scheduling Assistant page. The Appointment page is visible by default. You can enter all the required information directly on the Appointment page, or use the additional features available on the Scheduling Assistant page to find the best time for the meeting.

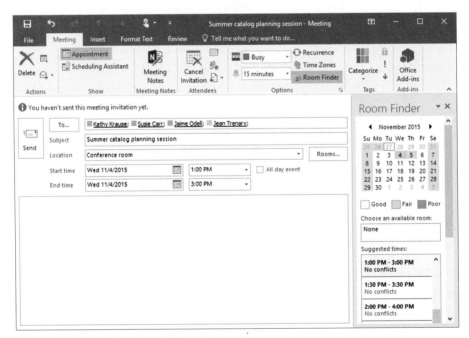

The Appointment page of a meeting window

The Room Finder is open by default on the right side of each page of the meeting window. This handy tool helps you to identify dates and times that work for the greatest number of attendees, in addition to available locations. The monthly calendar at the top of the Room Finder indicates the collective availability of the group on each day, as follows:

- Dates that occur in the past and nonworking days are unavailable (gray).

- Days when all attendees are available are Good (white).

- Days when most attendees are available are Fair (light blue).

- Days when most attendees are not available are Poor (medium blue).

> **TIP** All the capabilities of the Room Finder are available for Exchange accounts, but functionality is limited for other types of accounts. You can display or hide the Room Finder pane by clicking the Room Finder button in the Options group on the Meeting tab.

Managed conference rooms that are available at the indicated meeting time are shown in the center of the Room Finder. At the bottom of the Room Finder pane, the Suggested Times list displays attendee availability for appointments of the length of time you have specified for the meeting.

Selecting a date in the calendar displays the suggested meeting times for just that day. (Scheduling suggestions are not provided for past or nonworking days.) Clicking a meeting time in the Suggested Times list updates the calendar and the meeting request.

People you invite to meetings are referred to as *attendees*. By default, the attendance of each attendee is indicated as Required. You can inform noncritical attendees of the meeting by marking their attendance as Optional. You can invite entire groups of people by using a contact group or distribution list. You can also invite managed resources, such as conference rooms and audio/visual equipment, that have been set up by your organization's Exchange administrator.

A meeting request should have at least one attendee other than you, and it must have a start time and an end time. It should also include a subject and a location, but Outlook will send the meeting request without this information if you specifically allow it. The body of a meeting request can include text and web links, and you can also attach files. This is a convenient way to distribute meeting information to attendees ahead of time.

9

The secondary page of the meeting window is the Scheduling Assistant page, if your email account is part of an Exchange Server network. Otherwise, the secondary page is the Scheduling page, which doesn't include the Room Finder feature.

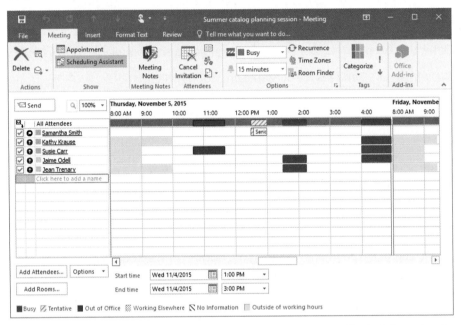

If you're organizing a meeting for a large number of people, you can view collective information about their schedules on the Scheduling or Scheduling Assistant page

The Scheduling and Scheduling Assistant pages include a group schedule that shows the status of each attendee's time throughout your working day. Outlook indicates your suggested meeting time on the group schedule. If free/busy information is available for meeting attendees, the status is indicated by the standard free/busy colors and patterns that match the legend at the bottom of the page. If no information is available (either because Outlook can't connect to an attendee's calendar or because the proposed meeting is further out than the scheduling information stored on the server), Outlook shows the time with gray diagonal stripes. The row at the top of the schedule, to the right of the All Attendees heading, indicates the collective schedule of all the attendees.

> **TIP** You can enter additional attendees in the To box on the Appointment page or in the All Attendees list on the Scheduling or Scheduling Assistant page. You can also add attendees by clicking the To button on the Appointment page or the Add Attendees button on the Scheduling or Scheduling Assistant page, and then selecting attendees from an address box.

You can change the time and duration of the meeting to work with the displayed schedules by selecting a different time in the Start Time and End Time lists, by dragging the vertical start time and end time bars in the group schedule, or by clicking the time you want in the Suggested Times list.

> **SEE ALSO** For information about creating a meeting request from an email message, see "Convert calendar items" earlier in this chapter.

Outlook tracks responses from attendees and those responsible for scheduling the resources you requested, so you always have an up-to-date report of how many people will attend your meeting. The number of attendees who have accepted, tentatively accepted, and declined the meeting request appears in the meeting header section when you open a meeting in its own window.

You might find it necessary to change the date, time, or location of a meeting after you send the meeting request, or to add or remove attendees. As the meeting organizer, you can change any information in a meeting request at any time, including adding or removing attendees, or canceling the meeting. Meeting attendees receive updates. Changes to meeting details are tracked so that attendees can quickly identify them.

To open a new meeting window

1. Do any of the following:

   - On the **Home** tab of the Calendar module, in the **New** group, click **New Meeting**.

   - On the **Home** tab of any module, in the **New** group, click **New Items**, and then click **Meeting**.

   - In any module, press **Ctrl+Shift+Q**.

9

To create a meeting request

1. Open a new meeting window.

2. In the **To** box, enter contact information for the attendees.

3. In the **Subject** box, enter an identifying name for the meeting.

4. In the **Location** box, enter the meeting location. If your organization uses Skype for Business, you can click the Skype Meeting button on the Meeting toolbar to enter Skype meeting information in the Location box and content pane.

5. In the **Start time** row, enter or select a date and time. Outlook automatically sets the End Time to a half hour after the start time.

6. In the **End time** row, enter or select a date and time. A meeting can span overnight or across multiple days.

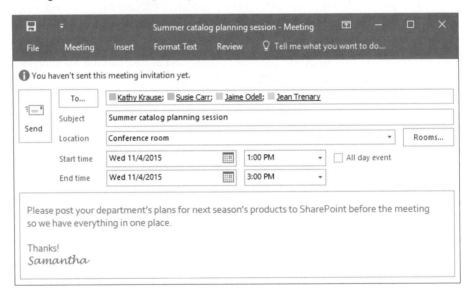

A basic meeting request

7. Verify the meeting details, and then click the **Send** button to add the meeting to your calendar and send the meeting request to the attendees.

To identify times that colleagues are available for meetings

> ⚠️ **IMPORTANT** This procedure is for Outlook users with Exchange email accounts. Free/busy time is available only for attendees in your organization or another connected organization, or attendees that share free/busy information through a web service.

1. On the **Meeting** tab, in the **Show** group, click the **Scheduling Assistant** button. The **All Attendees** list on the **Scheduling Assistant** page includes you and any attendees you entered in the **To** box. The icon next to your name, a magnifying glass in a black circle, indicates that you are the meeting organizer. The icon next to each attendee's name, an upward-pointing arrow in a red circle, indicates that he or she is a required attendee.

   > ✅ **TIP** If you're inviting someone as a courtesy, you can indicate that he or she does not need to attend by clicking the Required Attendee icon to the left of the attendee's name and then, in the list, clicking Optional Attendee.

2. If necessary, scroll to the bottom of the **Room Finder** to display the **Suggested times** list. The times shown are based on your schedule and the schedule information that is available for the attendees.

3. To add attendees, enter their email addresses in the **All Attendees** list, and then press **Tab** to update the Suggested Times list in the Room Finder.

4. If you need to change the meeting time or duration, you can do so by dragging the start time and end time bars on the group schedule or by entering times in the boxes below the group schedule.

5. Click the **Appointment** button in the **Show** group to return to the Appointment page, which reflects the current attendees and meeting times.

6. Verify the meeting details, and then click the **Send** button to add the meeting to your calendar and send the meeting request to the attendees.

9

To edit a meeting request

1. Open the meeting window for editing.

2. If the meeting is one of a series (a recurring meeting), Outlook prompts you to indicate whether you want to edit the meeting series or only the selected instance of the meeting. Click **Just this one** or **The entire series**.

3. Modify the date, time, notes, options, or attendees. Then click the **Send Update** button.

4. If you modified the attendees, Outlook prompts you to specify whether to send updates to all attendees or only to the changed attendees. Click one of the following to send the meeting updates:

   - Send updates only to added or deleted attendees

   - Send updates to all attendees

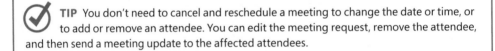 **TIP** You don't need to cancel and reschedule a meeting to change the date or time, or to add or remove an attendee. You can edit the meeting request, remove the attendee, and then send a meeting update to the affected attendees.

To cancel a meeting or a meeting occurrence

1. Select the meeting on your calendar, or open the meeting window.

2. Do either of the following:

   - On the **Meeting** tool tab, in the **Actions** group, click the **Cancel Meeting** button.

   - On the **Meeting Series** tool tab, in the **Actions** group, click the **Cancel Meeting** button, and then click **Cancel Occurrence** or **Cancel Series**.

 TIP The Cancel Meeting button is available only for meetings that you organize, not for meetings you're invited to.

A meeting window containing cancellation information opens.

Cancellation information

Cancelling a meeting removes it from attendees' calendars

3. Do either of the following:

- In the meeting header, click the **Send Cancellation** button. Outlook sends an updated meeting request to the attendees and removes the meeting from their calendars.

  If you change your mind about cancelling the meeting, click the **Close** button (**X**) at the right end of the message window title bar. Outlook reminds you that you haven't sent the cancellation and provides options. In the message box that appears, click **Don't cancel the meeting and close**, and then click **OK**.

You can't cancel a meeting without notifying the attendees

Respond to meeting requests

When you receive a meeting request from another Outlook user, the meeting appears on your calendar with your time scheduled as Tentative. Until you respond to the meeting request, the organizer doesn't know whether you plan to attend.

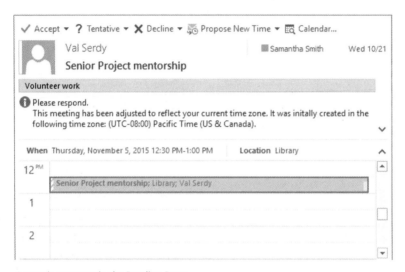

A meeting request in the Reading Pane

The meeting request displays your current calendar information at the time of the meeting, so you are aware of any schedule conflicts at that time. You can respond to a meeting request in one of these four ways:

- **Accept the request** Outlook deletes the meeting request and adds the meeting to your calendar.

- **Tentatively accept the request** This option indicates that you might be able to attend the meeting but are undecided. Outlook deletes the meeting request and shows the meeting on your calendar as tentatively scheduled.

- **Propose a new meeting time** Outlook sends your request to the meeting organizer for confirmation and shows the meeting with the original time on your calendar as tentatively scheduled.

- **Decline the request** Outlook deletes the meeting request and removes the meeting from your calendar.

If you don't respond to a meeting request, the meeting remains on your calendar with your time shown as tentatively scheduled and the meeting details in gray font rather than black.

When accepting or declining a meeting, you can choose whether to send a response to the meeting organizer. If you don't send a response, your acceptance will not be tallied, and the organizer will not know whether you are planning to attend the meeting. If you do send a response, you can add a message to the meeting organizer before sending it.

To respond to a meeting request

1. In the meeting window, in the **Reading Pane**, or on the shortcut menu that appears when you right-click the meeting request, click **Accept**, **Tentative**, or **Decline**.

2. Choose whether to send a standard response, a personalized response, or no response at all.

To propose a new time for a meeting

1. In the meeting window or in the **Reading Pane**, click **Propose New Time**, and then in the list, click **Tentative and Propose New Time** or **Decline and Propose New Time** to open the Propose New Time dialog box.

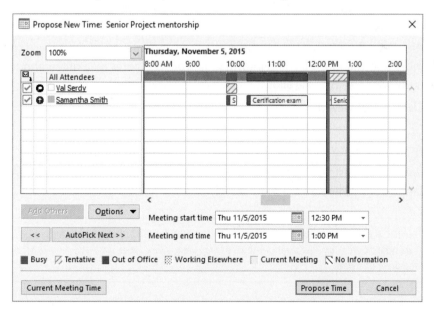

You can respond to a meeting request by proposing a different meeting time

2. In the **Propose New Time** dialog box, change the meeting start and end times to the times you want to propose, either by dragging the start time and end time bars or by changing the date and time in the lists, and then click the **Propose Time** button.

3. In the meeting response window that opens, enter a message to the meeting organizer if you want to, and then click **Send** to send your response and add the meeting to your calendar as tentatively scheduled for the original meeting time. If the meeting organizer approves the meeting time change, you and other attendees will receive updated meeting requests showing the new meeting time.

Display different views of a calendar

Just as you can with other Outlook modules, you can specify the way that Outlook displays calendar information (the view) and the attribute by which that information is arranged (the arrangement).

The Calendar module has these four content views:

- **Calendar** This is the standard view in which you display your Outlook calendar. In the Day, Work Week, or Week arrangement, Calendar view displays the subject, location, and organizer (if space allows) of each appointment, meeting, or event, in addition to the availability bar and any special icons, such as Private or Recurrence.

- **Preview** In the Day, Work Week, or Week arrangement, Preview view displays more information, including information from the notes area of the appointment window, as space allows.

- **List** This list view displays all appointments, meetings, and events on your calendar.

- **Active** This list view displays only future appointments, meetings, and events.

When working in a list view, you can group calendar items by selecting a field from the Arrangement gallery on the View tab.

> ⚠ **IMPORTANT** In this book, we assume you are working in Calendar view, and refer to the standard Calendar view arrangements as *Day view*, *Work Week view*, *Week view*, *Month view*, and *Schedule view*.

The available arrangements vary based on the view. In Calendar view and Preview view, the arrangements are based on the time span, and include the following:

- **Day** Displays one day at a time separated into half-hour increments.

- **Work Week** Displays only the days of your work week. The default work week is Monday through Friday from 8:00 A.M. to 5:00 P.M. Time slots that fall within the work week are white on the calendar; time slots outside of the work week are colored.

> 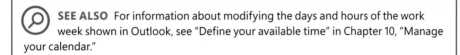 **SEE ALSO** For information about modifying the days and hours of the work week shown in Outlook, see "Define your available time" in Chapter 10, "Manage your calendar."

- **Week** Displays one calendar week (Sunday through Saturday) at a time.

- **Month** Displays one calendar month at a time, in addition to any preceding or following days that fall into the displayed weeks.

- **Schedule view** Displays a horizontal view of the calendar for the selected time period. You can add other people's calendars as rows in this view, so that you can easily compare multiple calendars for specific time periods.

9

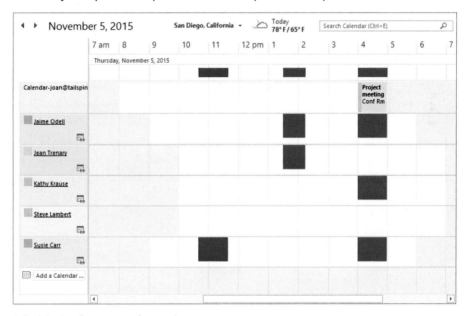

Schedule view for a group of co-workers

This arrangement is very useful for comparing limited time periods for multiple calendars, such as those of the members of a calendar group.

> **SEE ALSO** For information about calendar groups, see "Share calendar information" in Chapter 10, "Manage your calendar."

You switch among arrangements by clicking the buttons in the Arrangement group on the View tab of the Calendar module ribbon.

> ✓ **TIP** If you've made changes to any view (such as the order in which information appears) and want to return to the default settings, click the Reset View button in the Current View group on the View tab. If the Reset View button is unavailable, the view already displays the default settings.

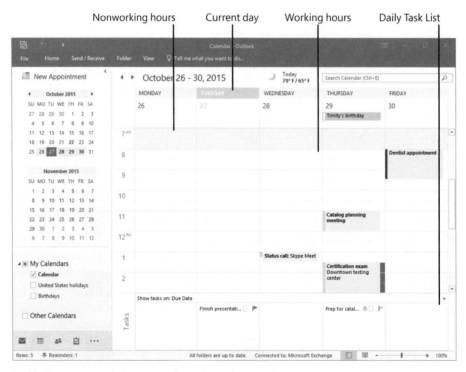

In this view, you can display your entire work week at one time

You can use these additional tools to change the time period shown in the calendar:

- Display the previous or next time period by clicking the Back button or the Forward button next to the date or date range in the calendar header.

- Display the current day by clicking the Today button in the Go To group on the Home tab.

- Display a seven-day period starting with the current day by clicking the Next 7 Days button in the Go To group on the Home tab.

- Display week numbers to the left of each week in Month view and in the Date Navigator. If you implement this option, you can click the week tab to display that week.

> **TIP** Specific weeks are referred to in some countries or regions by number to simplify the communication of dates. (For example, you can say you'll be out of the office "Week 24" rather than "June 7–11.") Week 1 is the calendar week in which January 1 falls, Week 2 is the following week, and so on through to the end of the year. Because of the way the weeks are numbered, a year can end in Week 52 or (more commonly) in Week 53. To display week numbers in the Date Navigator and in the Month view of the calendar, select the Show Week Numbers... check box on the Calendar page of the Outlook Options dialog box.

To display your calendar for a month

1. Do either of the following:

   - On the **Home** tab, in the **Arrange** group, click the **Month** button to display your calendar for the month.

   - Press **Ctrl+Alt+4**.

To navigate in Month view

1. Do either of the following:

   - To the left of the date range in the calendar header, click the **Forward** button to move the calendar forward one month, or the **Back** button to move the calendar back one month.

   - On the **View** tab, in the **Current View** group, click the **Change View** button and then, in the gallery, click **Preview** to display additional details on the monthly calendar.

9

Use the Date Navigator

By default, the Outlook 2016 Calendar module displays the current month and next month in the Date Navigator at the top of the Folder Pane. These compact monthly calendars provide quick indicators of the current date, the time period that is displayed in the content pane, days that you are free, and days that you are busy.

The Date Navigator is a convenient and useful tool

The current date is indicated by a blue square. The date or dates currently displayed in the calendar are indicated by light blue highlighting. Bold dates indicate days with scheduled appointments, meetings, or events. Days of the preceding and following months appear on the two default calendars in gray.

You can display more or fewer months by changing the width or height of the area allocated to the Date Navigator. To change the size of the Date Navigator area, do either of the following:

- Drag the right edge of the Folder Pane to the right to increase the width, or to the left to decrease the width.

- Drag the horizontal border below the Date Navigator calendars down to increase the height, or up to decrease the height.

The Date Navigator displays each month in seven-day weeks. The first day of the week shown in the Date Navigator is controlled by the First Day Of Week setting on the Calendar page of the Outlook Options dialog box. When the Date Navigator displays more than one month, each month shows either five or six weeks at a time—whichever is necessary to show all the days of the currently selected month.

You can display a specific day, week, month or range of days in the calendar by selecting it in the Date Navigator. When you're displaying the Calendar in the Week arrangement, selecting a day displays the week that contains it. Otherwise, the Calendar arrangement changes to show the time period that you select.

Use these techniques to work with the Date Navigator:

- To display a day, click that date.

- To display a week, point to the left edge of the week; when the pointer direction changes from left to right, click to select the week. (You can configure the Calendar Options to display week numbers in the Date Navigator and Calendar. If you do, clicking the week number displays the week.)

- To display a range of days (from two days to a maximum of six weeks), point to the first date you want to display and then drag across the Date Navigator to the last date.

- To change the period of time displayed in the calendar one month at a time, click the Previous or Next arrow on either side of the month name, at the top of the Date Navigator.

- To move multiple months back or forward, press the month name, and then drag up or down on the list that appears.

9

To display a seven-day week in the calendar

1. In the **Date Navigator** at the top of the **Folder Pane**, point to the left edge of a calendar row that contains one or more bold dates.

2. When the cursor changes to point toward the calendar, click once to display the selected seven-day week in the calendar.

To display your work week schedule

1. Do either of the following:

   - On the **Home** tab, in the **Arrange** group, click the **Work Week** button.

   - Press **Ctrl+Alt+2**.

   The first time slot of your defined work day appears at the top of the pane. Time slots within your work day are white; time slots outside of your work day are shaded.

To display your calendar for a day

1. On the **View** tab, in the **Arrangement** group, click the **Day** button to display only the selected day's schedule.

To display today's schedule

1. On the **Home** tab, in the **Go To** group, click the **Today** button. If the calendar wasn't previously displaying the current week, it does so now. The times displayed remain the same. The current day and the current time slot are highlighted.

To display your task list on the Calendar

1. On the **View** tab, in the **Layout** group, click the **Daily Task List** button and then do any of the following:

   - Click **Normal** to display the task list area below the calendar.

   - Click **Minimized** to display a single row below the calendar. The minimized Daily Task List displays a count of your total, active, and completed tasks for the day.

   - Click **Off** to hide the task list.

 TIP The Daily Task List is available in the Day, Work Week, or Week arrangement of the Calendar. It is not available in Month view or Schedule view.

To return the calendar to its default settings

1. In the **Change View** gallery, click **Calendar** to return the calendar to its default settings.

2. Then in the **Current View** group, click **Reset View** to return to the default calendar state.

Skills review

In this chapter, you learned how to:

- Schedule appointments and events
- Convert calendar items
- Configure calendar item options
- Schedule and change meetings
- Respond to meeting requests
- Display different views of a calendar

9

Practice tasks

No practice files are necessary to complete the practice tasks in this chapter.

> ⚠ **IMPORTANT** As you work through the practice tasks in this book, you will create Outlook items that might be used as practice files for tasks in later chapters. If you haven't created specific items that are referenced in later chapters, you can substitute items of your own.

Schedule appointments and events

Start Outlook, display your Calendar, and then perform the following tasks:

1. Create a new appointment with the subject **SBS Study Session**, and configure it as follows:

   - Set the date to one week from today.
   - Set the time from **11:30 A.M.** to **12:30 P.M.**
   - Specify the location as **Library Meeting Room**.
   - Keep all other default settings, and save and close the appointment.

2. Create a new all-day event named **National Dessert Day**, and configure it as follows:

   - Set the date to the next occurrence of **October 14**.
   - Keep all other default settings, and save and close the event.

Convert calendar items

Display your Inbox, and then perform the following tasks:

1. Locate the **SBS Test** message that you sent to yourself in Chapter 3, "Send and receive email messages."

2. Create an appointment based on the message, and configure it as follows:

   - Change the subject from *SBS Test* to **SBS Rafting Trip**.
   - Set the date to next Saturday, and the time from **11:00 A.M.** to **2:00 P.M.**
   - Specify the location as **To Be Determined**.
   - Keep all other default settings, and save and close the appointment.

3. Display your Calendar.

4. Locate the **SBS Rafting Trip** appointment, and then do the following:

   - Convert the appointment to an all-day event.

   - Keep all other default settings, and save and close the event.

5. Locate the **SBS Rafting Trip** event, and then do the following:

   - Invite a friend to the event.

   - In the content pane, enter **I'm practicing my Outlook scheduling skills. Please accept this invitation.**

   - Send the event invitation.

Configure calendar item options

Display your Calendar, and then perform the following tasks:

1. Locate the **SBS Study Session** appointment that you created in the first set of practice tasks for this chapter.

2. Open the appointment window, and display the time zone controls.

3. Change the **Start time** and **End time** to occur in a time zone that is one hour earlier than your own.

4. Set your availability during the appointment to **Out of Office**.

5. Set a reminder for **1 hour** before the appointment.

6. Configure the appointment to recur **Monthly**, on the **first Monday** of each month, and to end after **3** occurrences.

7. Save and close the appointment series.

Schedule and change meetings

This practice task is designed for Outlook users in Exchange environments.

Display your Calendar, and then perform the following tasks:

1. Create a new meeting with the subject **SBS Project Review**, and configure it as follows:

   - Invite a colleague from your Exchange network.

   - Specify the location as **My Office**.

   - Set the date to next Thursday.

2. In the **Room Finder**, look at the **Date Navigator** and scroll the **Suggested Times** list for information about availability. In the **Suggested times** list, click a half-hour time slot that shows *No conflicts*.

3. Display the **Scheduling Assistant** page of the meeting invitation, and do the following:

   - Wait for the group calendar to display your colleague's availability. Notice the color blocks that identify the working hours and availability of each person and of the group.

   - Verify that the selected time is shown as available for both of you. If it isn't, change the time by dragging the start and end time markers.

4. Return to the **Appointment** page of the meeting invitation and verify the meeting information. In the content pane, enter I'm practicing scheduling meetings. Please accept this meeting request. Then send the meeting invitation.

5. On your calendar, locate the **SBS Project Review** meeting, and open the meeting window.

6. Display the **Scheduling Assistant** page of the meeting window, and do the following:

   - Add another colleague to the attendee list, and wait for the group calendar to display his or her availability.

   - Scroll the group calendar backward and forward a few days to identify times that you and your colleagues are busy or out of the office.

   - If necessary, change the meeting time and date by selecting them in the area below the group calendar.

7. Return to the **Appointment** page of the meeting invitation and verify the meeting information. Then send the meeting update to all attendees.

Respond to meeting requests

This practice task is designed for Outlook users in Exchange environments.

Display your Inbox, and then perform the following tasks:

1. Ask a colleague to send you a meeting request.

2. When you receive the meeting request, review the information in the Reading Pane, and then open the meeting request.

3. From the meeting request window, display your calendar. Notice the colors and patterns that represent the unaccepted meeting request and your availability during that time.

4. Return to the meeting request. Respond as **Tentative**, and propose a new time for the meeting.

Display different views of a calendar

Display your Calendar in Calendar view, and then perform the following tasks:

1. Display your calendar for the current month.

2. In the **Date Navigator**, notice the shading that identifies the current day. Click a different day that shows no appointments, to display your calendar for only that day. Then click the **Next Appointment** bar on the right side of the day to display the day of the next appointment on your calendar.

3. Switch to the **Work Week** calendar arrangement, and turn on the display of the **Daily Task List** below the calendar.

4. Change to the **Active** view of your calendar to display only your future appointments, events, and meetings.

5. If you want to, add the holidays from your country or region to the calendar. Notice the change in the calendar content displayed in the Active view.

6. Configure the Calendar to display the view and arrangement that you like best.

Manage your calendar

10

The Outlook calendar has many features that can help you to efficiently manage your schedule. You can configure the Outlook calendar to make specific times available for co-workers to schedule meetings, to track your schedule in two time zones, and to smoothly switch between time zones when you travel.

In addition to the default calendar that's linked to your primary email account, you can create, import, link to, subscribe to, and manage other calendars within the Calendar module. In the Calendar module, you can view either separate or composite views of information stored in multiple calendars. Each calendar and the appointments on it are color-coded to make it easier to discern the source.

You can share your calendar information with other people in several ways; for example, you can share an entire calendar or only selected information with people inside or outside of your organization.

If you want to work with a paper copy of your calendar, you can print out the information for specific date ranges. Outlook offers many different formats for printed calendars; you can choose the print style and level of detail that fit your needs.

This chapter guides you through procedures related to defining your available time, configuring time zones, working with multiple calendars, sharing calendar information, and printing a calendar.

In this chapter

- Define your available time
- Configure time zones
- Work with multiple calendars
- Share calendar information
- Print a calendar

Practice files

No practice files are necessary to complete the practice tasks in this chapter.

Define your available time

The Outlook calendar differentiates between working time and nonworking time. The calendar timeslots within the time you indicate as your work time are colored differently from those outside of your work time, and are the only timeslots made available to your co-workers when they schedule meetings with you through Outlook.

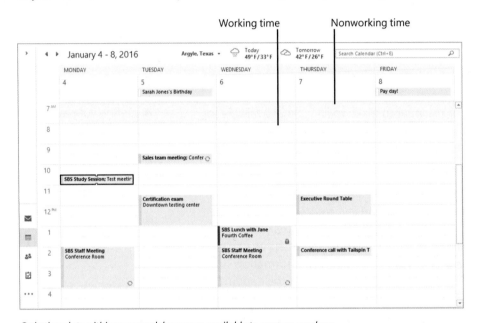

Only timeslots within your work hours are available to your co-workers

By default, the Outlook work week is defined as from 8:00 A.M. to 5:00 P.M. (in your local time zone), Monday through Friday. You can change this to match your individual work schedule. You can specify a start time and end time for your standard work day, specify the days of the week that you work, and specify the day of the week that you'd like to appear first when you display only the work week in your calendar.

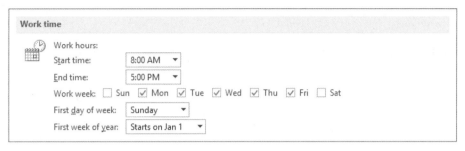

The default work week settings

To display your work week

1. On the **Home** tab, in the **Arrange** group, click the **Work Week** button.

 SEE ALSO For information about displaying daily task lists for each day of your work week, see "Display different views of tasks" in Chapter 11, "Track tasks."

To modify your work week settings

1. On the **Home** tab, click the **Arrange** dialog box launcher to display the Calendar page of the Outlook Options dialog box. The Work Time section at the top of the page displays the work week settings.

2. Do any of the following:

    *   In the **Start time** list, select your work day starting time.

    *   In the **End time** list, select your work day ending time.

    *   In the **Work week** section, select the check boxes for the days you work, and clear the check boxes for the days you don't.

    *   In the **First day of week** list, select the first day of your work week.

 TIP Outlook doesn't allow you to define a work day that crosses midnight or to define different start and end times for different days.

10

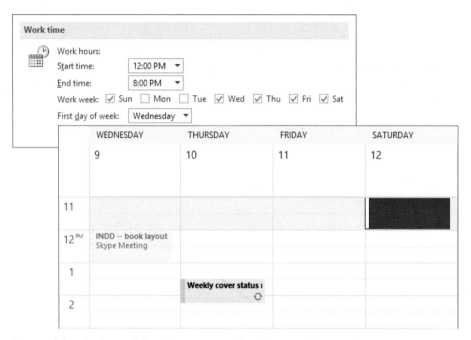

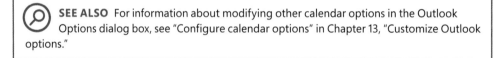

You can define the days and times that you are available to meet with co-workers

3. In the **Outlook Options** dialog box, click **OK**.

> 🔍 **SEE ALSO** For information about modifying other calendar options in the Outlook Options dialog box, see "Configure calendar options" in Chapter 13, "Customize Outlook options."

Configure time zones

When you travel with your portable computer to locations in other time zones, you'll probably change the time zone on your computer to match the time zone you're in. When you change the time zone, the times shown in the Outlook window—such as appointment times and email message receipt times—change to match the new time zone.

> ✓ **TIP** If your computer is running Windows 10 and has GPS functionality, you can choose to have Windows change the computer time zone automatically to match your location. To do so, display the Date & Time page of the Settings window, and then set the Set Time Zone Automatically toggle button to On.

In Day view, Work Week view, and Week view, the Calendar module displays the time next to each time slot. You can configure Outlook to display any time zone you want, or to display two time zones, and you can label the time zones. If you have co-workers or clients in another time zone, or are making plans to travel, displaying multiple time zones can assist with scheduling meetings or simply keeping track of the time in the other location.

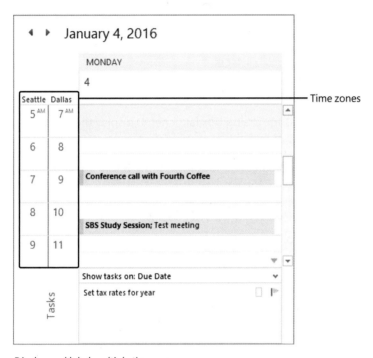

Display and label multiple time zones

When you display two time zones, the primary time zone is the one immediately to the left of the calendar time slots.

To specify the time zone shown on the calendar

1. On the **Home** tab, click the **Arrange** dialog box launcher to display the Calendar page of the Outlook Options dialog box.

2. In the **Time zones** section of the Calendar page, in the first **Time zone** list, click the time zone you want Outlook to display.

3. If you want to label the time column, enter the label in the first **Label** box.

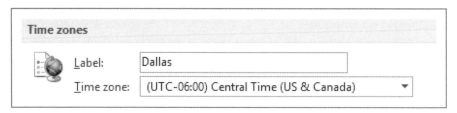

Use any labeling convention; the column displays up to seven characters

4. In the **Outlook Options** dialog box, click **OK**.

To display two time zones on the calendar

1. On the **Home** tab, click the **Arrange** dialog box launcher to display the Calendar page of the Outlook Options dialog box.

2. In the **Time zones** section of the Calendar page, select the **Show a second time zone** check box.

3. In the second **Time zone** list, click the time zone you want to display.

4. If you want to label the time columns, enter the labels in the first and second **Label** boxes.

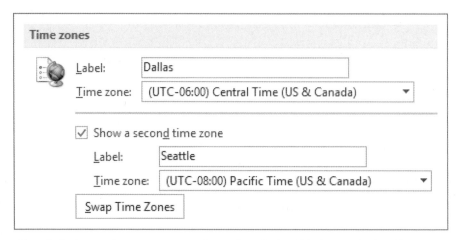

When displaying two time zones, you can change the order in which they are displayed by swapping them

5. In the **Outlook Options** dialog box, click **OK**.

To switch the primary and secondary time zones

1. Display the **Calendar** page of the **Outlook Options** dialog box.

2. In the **Time zones** section of the Calendar page, click the **Swap Time Zones** button.

3. In the **Outlook Options** dialog box, click **OK**.

Specify appointment time zones

When you schedule an appointment or meeting, you have the option of specifying the time zone—for both the start time and the end time of the appointment or meeting. If you travel frequently, you might find that it is worth your time to do this. Here's an example of why you would want to do this:

Imagine that you live in Dallas, Texas (in the Central Time Zone). You have a meeting that occurs every Wednesday at noon. You travel to Seattle, Washington (in the Pacific Time Zone, two hours earlier than Central Time) for one week. When you arrive in Seattle, you change the time zone of your computer to Pacific Time. The appointments on your calendar shift to accommodate the time zone change. Your Wednesday meeting now appears on the calendar at 10:00 A.M. You call in to the meeting at the appropriate time.

During the meeting, you learn of a client presentation that will occur at 2:00 P.M. the following Tuesday. You enter the presentation as an appointment on your calendar at 2:00 P.M. Tuesday, but you do not specify the time zone of the presentation.

When you return to Dallas, you change the time zone of your computer to Central Time. On Wednesday morning, you look at your calendar and find out that you need to attend the client presentation. The presentation is on your calendar for 4:00 P.M. When you arrive at the client site, the presentation has already ended. Because you didn't specify the time zone of the appointment, the appointment time shifted by two hours when you returned to Dallas.

SEE ALSO For more information about specifying appointment time zones, see "Configure calendar item options" in Chapter 9, "Manage scheduling."

10

Work with multiple calendars

The Calendar button or link on the Navigation Bar connects to the calendar of your default email account. You can also display the following types of calendars in the Calendar module:

- **Calendars of other Exchange email accounts** Outlook displays a calendar named Calendar for each Exchange account you connect to. When you connect to multiple accounts, Outlook appends the associated email address to the calendar name in the Folder Pane so you can differentiate between them.

- **Custom calendars** You create a calendar as a folder that contains calendar items, in the same way that you create mail folders, address books, or task lists.

- **Calendars of people within your organization** Within an organization that uses Exchange, you can display the availability of your co-workers, individually or in a group, without special permission.

- **Shared calendars** Other Outlook users can share their calendars with you.

- **SharePoint site calendars** You can connect a Microsoft SharePoint calendar to Outlook.

- **Internet calendars** You can subscribe to or import calendars from the Internet.

 SEE ALSO For information about Internet calendars, see "Connect to other calendars" later in this topic.

In the Calendar module, the Folder Pane displays a list of the available calendars. You can save multiple calendars in a calendar group to simultaneously display or hide all the calendars in the group. Each calendar has an assigned color. When multiple calendars are displayed, the calendar colors are shown in the Folder Pane and also in the content pane.

Display calendars side by side to discern individual schedules

Connect to other calendars

Co-workers within an organization that uses Exchange can share full or partial details of their calendars with each other. Even if they don't, you can display a co-worker's availability by opening his or her calendar in Outlook. The default settings permit co-workers to view the availability (such as Free, Busy, Out Of Office, or Working Elsewhere) of other members of their Exchange organization without displaying specific details of appointments. This information, which is also used by the Scheduling Assistant, permits you to locate times that are suitable for meeting with co-workers.

> **SEE ALSO** For information about sharing your calendar with co-workers and requesting that they share theirs with you, see "Share calendar information" later in this chapter.

A variety of specialized calendars, such as those that track professional sports schedules, holidays, entertainment, and scientific data, are available online. (For example, your local school district or sports team might offer an Internet calendar on its website that you can import or subscribe to.)

Internet calendars are files that have the extension .ics. You can locate Internet calendars by searching from a web browser, by locating links on the websites of specific organizations, or by visiting a calendar-sharing website such as iCalShare (located at *www.icalshare.com*).

You can work with an Internet calendar in one of two ways:

- **Subscribe to the calendar** You receive updates from the calendar publisher as they occur, but you can't change the calendar data.

- **Import the calendar** You can interact with a local copy of the calendar in Outlook. You can change the calendar data, but you won't receive any updates provided by the calendar publisher.

Many Internet calendars have a link or button that you can click to start the subscription or import process. If the Internet calendar you want to connect to doesn't provide a simple method, you can manually connect to it.

To display a co-worker's calendar in your Outlook Calendar module

1. Display the Calendar module.

2. On the **Home** tab, in the **Manage Calendars** group, click **Open Calendar**.

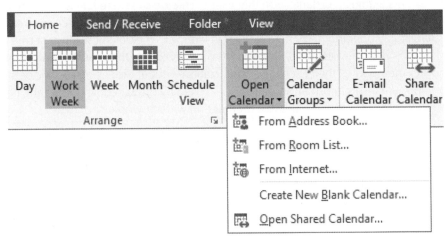

Calendar sources you can connect to

3. On the **Open Calendar** menu, click **From Address Book** to open the Select Name dialog box.

4. In the **Address Book** list, click **Global Address List** to display the members of your Exchange organization.

5. Locate the person whose calendar you want to display, and double-click the name to insert it in the Calendar box.

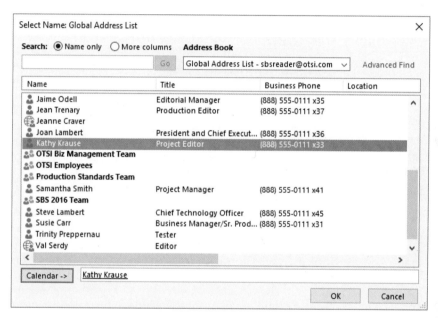

You can display a calendar for anyone who has a mailbox on your Exchange server

6. Click **OK** to open the selected calendar in the Calendar module content area and add it to the Shared Calendars list in the Folder Pane (even though its owner hasn't officially shared it with you).

 TIP If you close the calendar, it remains in the Shared Calendars list so you can easily redisplay it.

To create a calendar group of co-workers

1. On the **Home** tab, in the **Manage Calendars** group, click **Calendar Groups**.

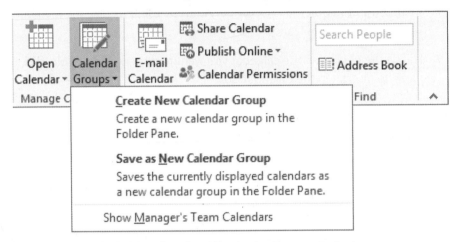

You can create a calendar group from the address book or the current calendars

2. On the **Calendar Groups** menu, click **Create New Calendar Group**.

3. In the **Create New Calendar Group** dialog box, enter a name for the calendar group, and then click **OK** to open the Select Name dialog box.

4. In the **Address Book** list, click **Global Address List** to display the members of your Exchange organization.

5. For each person whose calendar you want to include in the calendar group, locate and double-click the person's name to insert it in the Calendar box.

6. Click **OK** to create the calendar group, add it to the Folder Pane, and open the calendar in the Calendar module content area.

To manage a calendar group

1. In the **Folder Pane**, click the calendar group name to activate it.

2. Right-click the calendar group name, and then do any of the following:

    -   To add a calendar to the group, click **Add Calendar**, click the calendar source, and then select the calendar.

    -   To rename the group, click **Rename Group**, enter the new name, and then press **Enter**.

- To delete the calendar group, click **Delete Group**, and then in the **Microsoft Outlook** message box, click **Yes** to confirm the deletion.

- To remove a calendar from the group, right-click the calendar name, and then click **Delete Calendar**.

To connect to a SharePoint calendar

1. Display the SharePoint calendar you want to connect to.

2. On the SharePoint list ribbon, click the **Calendar** tab, and then in the **Connect & Export** group, click the **Connect to Outlook** button.

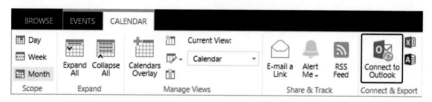

Connect Outlook to a SharePoint calendar from SharePoint

3. Do the following to permit the connection from SharePoint to Outlook and add the SharePoint calendar to the Other Calendars list in the Folder Pane:

- In the browser dialog box that opens, click **Allow**.

- In the **Microsoft Outlook** message box, click **Yes**.

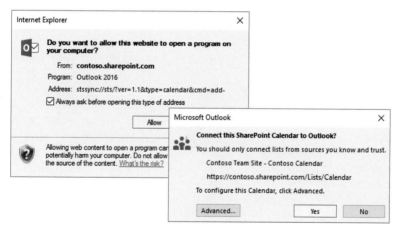

You should only connect to calendars you know and trust

To manually import or subscribe to an Internet calendar

1. On the Internet, locate the calendar you want to connect to and copy the address of its .ics file.

2. In Outlook, display the Calendar module.

3. On the **Home** tab, in the **Manage Calendars** group, on the **Open Calendar** menu, click **From Internet**.

4. In the **New Internet Calendar Subscription** dialog box, paste the address of the .ics file, and click **OK**. Then in the **Microsoft Outlook** message box, click **Yes** to add the calendar to Outlook and subscribe to updates. The Internet calendar appears in the Other Calendars list in the Folder Pane.

Manage the display of multiple calendars

You can display calendars individually, or you can display more than one calendar at a time. For example, you might have separate business and personal calendars and want to view them together. By default, Outlook displays multiple calendars in Side-By-Side mode. In this mode, each calendar tab has a Close button (an X) near its right edge, and each calendar tab other than your default calendar has a View In Overlay Mode button (a left-pointing arrow) near its left edge.

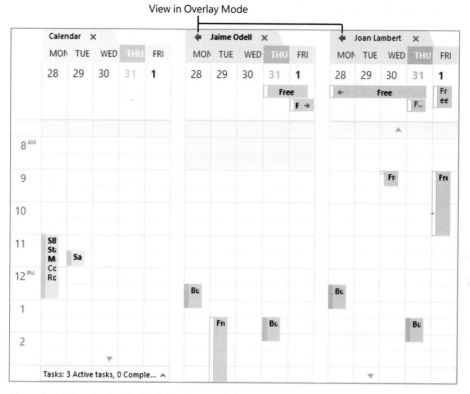

The order of the calendars in the Folder Pane and the content area is the same; your default calendar always appears first

You can view multiple calendars next to each other, or you can overlay them to display a composite view of the separate calendars. When you view and scroll through multiple calendars, they all display the same date or time period.

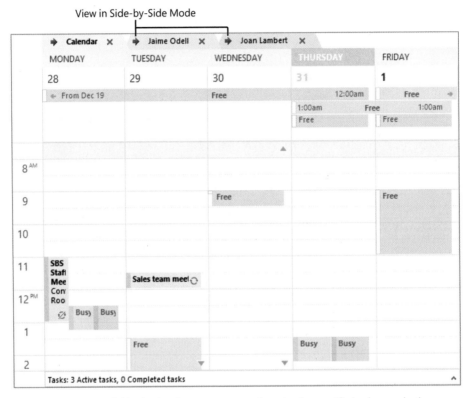

Appointments on overlaid calendars have gray text on the calendar-specific background color

When displaying three or more calendars, you can combine the side-by-side and overlay views.

> ✓ **TIP** When displaying multiple calendars, you can copy items from one time, date, or calendar to another, by holding down the Ctrl key and dragging the original item to the location to which you want to copy it.

To display a calendar

1. In the **Folder Pane**, select the check box to the left of the calendar name.

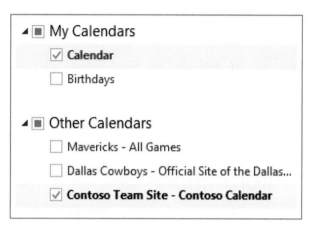

The calendar colors highlight the active calendar names

You must display at least one calendar at all times; Outlook does not permit you to clear all the check boxes.

To make a calendar active

1. Do either of the following:

   - Click the calendar tab.

   - Click any calendar item.

To overlay calendars

1. On the tab of each of the secondary calendars, click the **View in Overlay Mode** button. The calendars stack in the order that you overlay them, with the last on top.

 TIP When calendars are overlaid, the Search box indicates the active calendar. The active calendar items have black text and the others gray.

10

To display calendars side by side

1. On the tab of each of the secondary calendars, click the **View in Side-By-Side Mode** button.

To close a calendar

1. Do either of the following:

   - On the calendar tab, click the **Close Calendar** button.

   - In the **Folder Pane**, clear the check box to the left of the calendar name.

Share calendar information

Co-workers can view your available working time when they schedule meetings with you or view your calendar through Outlook. If you want to share more information with co-workers or with people outside of your organization, you have several options for doing so:

- You can allow selected co-workers to view calendar item details by sharing your calendar with them.

- You can allow selected co-workers to view your entire calendar and to make appointments and respond to meeting requests on your behalf by delegating control of the calendar to them.

- You can publish your calendar to the Office.com website or to a corporate web server and then share the published calendar with any person who has access to the Internet.

- You can send a professional graphic representation of your appointments during a selected date range by email to any person who uses an HTML-capable email program (not only people who use Outlook), including colleagues, friends, and family members.

The options for sending, sharing, and publishing calendar information are available from the Share group on the Home tab of the Calendar module.

Share calendars with co-workers

If your email address is part of an Exchange network, your co-workers can display your availability from your default calendar for the purpose of scheduling meetings with you. You can share a calendar (or any other Outlook folder) with other people on your network and give them permission to display, modify, or create items. You can share your default calendar or a secondary calendar that you create, import, or subscribe to. The level of access each co-worker has is governed by the permissions you assign to him or her.

You can also change the default permission level to permit co-workers to display additional information without specifically sharing the calendar.

When you share a calendar, you give the person permission to see a specific amount of detail about each appointment, meeting, or event on the calendar. The detail options are:

- **Availability only** Displays time blocks marked as Free, Busy, Tentative, Working Elsewhere, or Out Of Office. This is the default detail level.

- **Limited details** Displays time blocks labeled with the appointment, meeting, or event subject and the availability.

- **Full details** Displays time blocks labeled with the appointment, meeting, or event subject, the location, the availability, and all meeting details.

After you share a calendar, you can specify the actions each person with whom you share the calendar can perform. You can either select a role, which assigns specific Read, Write, Delete, and other permission settings, or you can select individual settings in each category. There are a wide variety of roles, including Owner, Editor, Author, Reviewer, and Contributor.

10

The following table describes the specific permissions conferred by each level.

Role	Read	Create	Edit	Delete	Folder role
Owner	Full details	Items and subfolders	All items	All items	Owner and contact
Publishing Editor	Full details	Items and subfolders	All items	All items	None
Editor	Full details	Items	All items	All items	None
Publishing Author	Full details	Items and subfolders	Own items	Own items	None
Author	Full details	Items	Own items	Own items	None
Nonediting Author	Full details	Items	None	Own items	None
Reviewer	Full details	None	None	None	None
Contributor	Free/Busy time	Items	None	None	None

You can delegate control of your calendar (and other Outlook modules) so that a co-worker or assistant can receive, create, and respond to meeting requests on your behalf. You receive copies of the meeting requests and copies of your delegate's responses, but you don't have to respond.

To share a calendar with a co-worker

1. Do either of the following to create a sharing invitation message:

   - Display the calendar you want to share. On the **Home** tab, in the **Share** group, click the **Share Calendar** button.

   - In the **Folder Pane**, right-click the calendar you want to share, click **Share**, and then click **Share Calendar**.

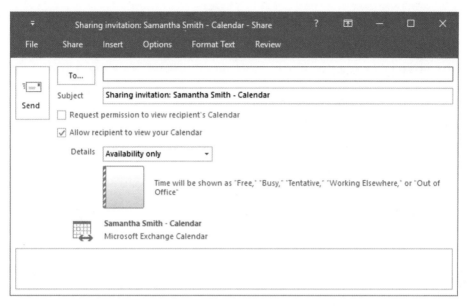

You can request reciprocal sharing of the other person's calendar

> **TIP** If you're sharing an Exchange calendar, the message is an invitation to share the calendar. If you're sharing an imported calendar, the message includes the calendar as an attachment.

10

2. In the **To** box, enter the name or email address of the person you want to share your calendar with.

3. If you'd like to request that the person reciprocate by sharing his or her calendar with you, select the **Request permission to view recipient's Calendar** check box.

4. In the **Details** list, click the level of detail you want to share: **Availability only**, **Limited details**, or **Full details**.

5. Add any notes you want to in the content pane, and then click the **Send** button.

6. In the **Microsoft Outlook** message box, click **Yes** to confirm that you want to share the calendar with the specified permissions.

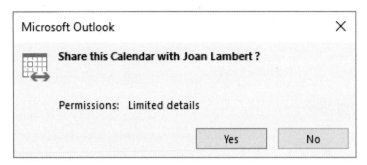

Confirm the detail level before approving the sharing operation

Outlook sends the message.

To open or share a calendar from a sharing request

1. Display the sharing request in a message window or in the **Reading Pane**.

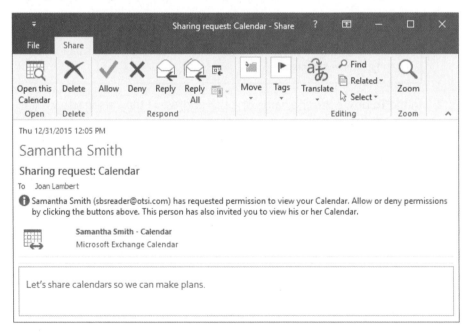

You can deny the sharing of your calendar

2. To add the shared calendar to the list of calendars available in your Calendar module, on the **Share** tab of the ribbon, in the **Open** group, click **Open this Calendar**.

3. If the sender requested reciprocal sharing, respond to the request by doing either of the following in the **Respond** group:

   - To share your calendar with the person, click **Allow**. This creates a new sharing message. In the **Details** list, click **Availability only**, **Limited details**, or **Full details** to indicate the amount of information you want to share. Add a note if you want, and then click **Send**. Then in the **Microsoft Outlook** message box, click **Yes** to confirm that you want to share the calendar with the specified permissions.

   - To not share your calendar, click **Deny**. In the **Microsoft Outlook** message box that opens, click **Edit the response before sending**, **Send the response now**, or **Don't send a response** to indicate how you want to respond to the person who requested sharing. Then click **OK**. If you choose to edit the response, add your comments to the email message that opens, and then click **Send**.

To set permissions for a shared calendar

1. Do either of the following:

   - Display the calendar you want to set permissions for. On the **Home** tab, in the **Share** group, click the **Calendar Permissions** button to display the Permissions tab of the Calendar Properties dialog box.

   - In the **Folder Pane**, right-click the calendar you want to set permissions for, click **Properties**, and then in the **Calendar Properties** dialog box, click the **Permissions** tab.

10

2. In the pane at the top of the **Permissions** tab of the **Calendar Properties** dialog box, click the name of the person whose permissions you want to modify.

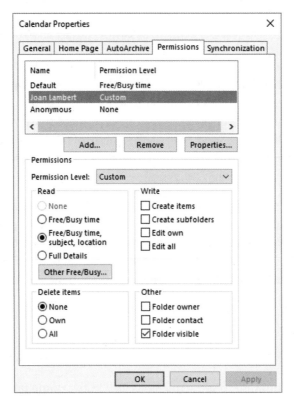

You can give people permission to display information or modify your calendar without first sharing it

3. In the **Permissions** section, do any of the following:

- In the **Permission Level** list, click a role to assign the default permissions associated with that role.

- In the **Read** section, click the level of detail you want to permit the person to display.

- In the **Write** section, select the check box of each type of item you want to permit the person to change.

- In the **Delete Items** section, click the type of items you want to permit the person to delete.

- In the **Other** section, select the **Folder owner** or **Folder contact** check box if you want to assign the person to that role. Leave the **Folder visible** check box selected for anyone you share the calendar with.

4. In the **Calendar Properties** dialog box, click **OK**.

To change the default level of information visible to co-workers

1. Display the **Permissions** tab of the **Calendar Properties** dialog box.

2. In the pane at the top of the tab, click **Default**.

3. In the **Read** section, click **Free/Busy time, subject, location** or **Full details**.

4. In the **Calendar Properties** dialog box, click **OK**.

To delegate control of your calendar to another Outlook user

1. On the **Info** page of the **Backstage** view, click **Account Settings**, and then click **Delegate Access**.

2. In the **Delegates** dialog box, click **Add** to open the Add Users dialog box. In the **Address Book** list, click **Global Address List**.

10

3. In the **Add Users** dialog box, click the person you want to delegate control to, click **Add**, and then click **OK** to close the Add Users dialog box and open the Delegate Permissions dialog box.

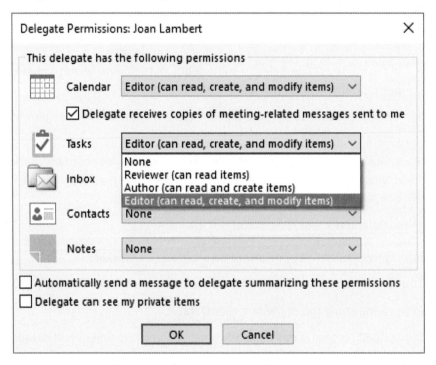

You can delegate permissions for each module from this dialog box

4. In the **Delegate Permissions** dialog box, in the **Calendar** list, click the role you want to assign to the person. The default role, *Editor*, delegates full management of calendar items.

5. Repeat step 4 for any other module you want to permit the person to manage.

6. Select the **Automatically send a message...** check box to inform the person of the permissions you're delegating to him or her.

7. If you want to allow the person to view details of items that you mark as Private, select the **Delegate can see my private items** check box.

8. In the **Delegate Permissions** dialog box, click **OK** to add the person to the list in the Delegates dialog box.

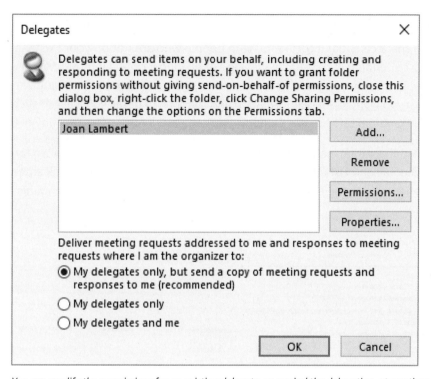

You can modify the permissions for an existing delegate, or rescind the delegation, at any time

9. At the bottom of the **Delegates** dialog box, select one of the following delivery options for meeting requests and responses:

   - If you want to receive copies of meeting communications, click **My delegates only, but send a copy of meeting requests and responses to me**.

   - If you don't want to receive meeting communications, click **My delegates only**.

   - If you want to receive original meeting communications, click **My delegates and me**.

10. In the **Delegates** dialog box, click **OK** to implement the delegation and send the summary message, if you chose that option.

Share calendar information outside of your organization

You can share calendar information with people who are not on your Exchange network by sending it in an email message or posting it on the Internet. When you share a calendar by using one of these methods, you can choose the period of time for which you want to share information and the level of detail you want to share. If you have multiple calendars in Outlook, you can send information from any of them.

When you share information in an email message, you can choose from two formats: Daily Schedule and List Of Events. Whichever format you choose, Outlook embeds the information that you select into the email message and attaches it as an .ics file to the message.

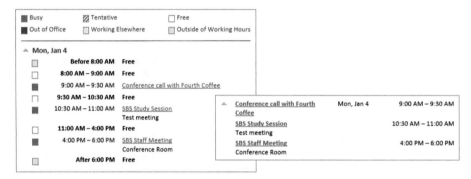

The same day shown as a Daily Schedule and a List Of Events

To send a calendar by email

1. Do either of the following to open a new message window and the Send A Calendar Via E-mail dialog box:

    - Display the calendar that you want to share. On the **Home** tab, in the **Share** group, click the **E-mail Calendar** button.

    - In the **Folder Pane**, right-click the calendar you want to share, click **Share**, and then click **E-mail Calendar**.

2. In the **Send a Calendar via E-mail** dialog box, in the **Calendar** list, click the calendar you want to share.

3. In the **Date Range** list, do either of the following:

- To share a fixed time period, click **Today, Tomorrow, Next 7 Days, Next 30 Days**, or **Whole Calendar**.

- To share a custom date range, click **Specify dates**. Then in the **Start** and **End** boxes that appear, enter or select the first and last dates of the date range you want to share.

4. In the **Detail** list, click **Availability only**, **Limited details**, or **Full details**.

5. In the **Advanced** section of the dialog box, click the **Show** button to display additional sharing options.

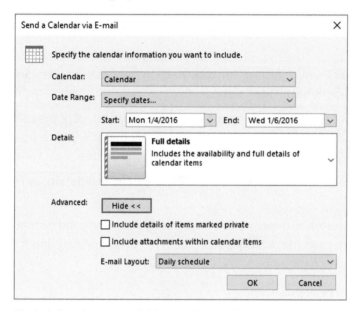

The Include options are available only when you share calendar details

6. In the **Advanced** section of the dialog box, do either or both of the following to refine the details that you share:

- If you chose the Limited Details option and want to share Private items, select the **Include details of items marked private** check box.

- If you chose the Full Details option and want to share files or items that are attached to appointments, select the **Include attachments within calendar items** check box.

7. In the **E-mail Layout** list, click **Daily schedule** or **List of events** to specify the format of the message content.

8. Click **OK** to embed the selected calendar information in the email message window and attach the same information as an .ics file. You can send the email message to any recipient. A recipient using Outlook or another email program that supports .ics files can view your calendar in that program.

To publish a calendar online

1. Do either of the following to display the Publish Calendar page of Outlook Online in your default web browser (sign in if you are prompted to do so):

   • Display the calendar that you want to share. On the **Home** tab, in the **Share** group, click the **Publish Online** button, and then click **Publish This Calendar**.

   • In the **Folder Pane**, right-click the calendar you want to share, click **Share**, and then click **Publish This Calendar**.

2. On the **Publish calendar** page, in the **Select a calendar** list, click the calendar you want to publish. You can publish only calendars that you created, not calendars that you opened or subscribed to from elsewhere.

3. In the **Select permissions** list, click **Availability only**, **Limited details**, or **Full details**.

4. Click the **Save** button to generate two links that you can copy and distribute: the HTML link displays the published calendar in a browser window, and the ICS link allows people to subscribe to the calendar.

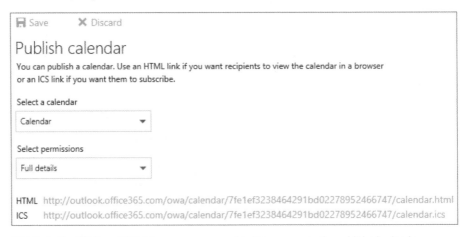

Distribute the HTML or ICS link to anyone you want to have access to the published calendar

Print a calendar

Sometimes, you might find it convenient to print a day, week, month, or other period of your calendar—for instance, if you're traveling without a laptop or want to have your weekly schedule quickly available in your briefcase. You can easily print any time period of your calendar.

The amount of detail that appears depends on the period you print and the print style you choose

Outlook offers several built-in print styles, and you can create others if you want. The available print styles vary based on what view you're in when you choose the Print command.

The default print styles include the following:

- **Daily Style** Prints the selected date range with one day per page. Printed elements include the date, day, TaskPad, reference calendars for the current and upcoming months, a breakdown of working hours in 30-minute blocks, and an area for notes. From the Page Setup dialog box, you can choose whether to print the TaskPad and notes areas.

- **Weekly Agenda Style** Prints the selected date range with one calendar week per page, including reference calendars for the selected and following month. From the Page Setup dialog box, you can specify how to arrange the days and whether to print the TaskPad and Notes areas.

> **SEE ALSO** For information about setting the first day of the week, see "Define your available time" earlier in this chapter.

- **Weekly Calendar Style** Prints the selected date range with one calendar week per page. Each page includes date range and time increments for working hours, and reference calendars for the selected and following month. From the Page Setup dialog box, you can choose a vertical or horizontal layout, split the week across two pages, include a task list, add an area for handwritten notes, specify the range of hours to print, and print only your designated work week rather than a standard seven-day week.

- **Monthly Style** Prints a page for each month in the selected date range. Each page includes the selected month with a few days showing from the previous and subsequent months, along with reference calendars for the selected and following month. From the Page Setup dialog box, you can specify to print a single month across two printer pages, and whether to display the TaskPad and Note areas.

- **Tri-fold Style** Prints a page for each day in the selected date range. Each page includes the daily schedule, weekly schedule, and TaskPad. From the Page Setup dialog box, you can choose which calendar element appears in each section.

- **Calendar Details Style** Lists your appointments for the selected date range, in addition to the accompanying appointment details.

To preview and print a calendar

1. In the Calendar module, display part or all of the time period you want to print.

2. Display the Backstage view. In the left pane, click **Print** to display the available printing options and a preview of the current period's calendar as it would appear when printed. Outlook selects a print style that suits the currently displayed period.

3. On the **Print** page, do any of the following:

   - In the **Printer** list, click the printer you want to use.

   - In the **Settings** list, click the print style you want.

   - Click the **Print** button to print the current date range and print configuration.

4. To change the preview display, do any of the following:

   - To display a different page of a multipage calendar, enter the page number in the **Page Navigator**, or click the **Previous** or **Next** arrow.

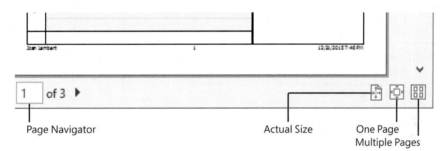

Preview controls

   - To magnify the calendar page entries, click the **Actual Size** button.

   - To display one page at the maximum size that fits the preview area, click the **One Page** button.

   - To display more than one page (if printing a multipage calendar), click the **Multiple Pages** button.

   - If the vertical scroll bar is active, scroll up or down through the content.

   - If the horizontal scroll bar is active, scroll left or right across the page.

10

MONDAY	Daily Task List
	Arrange by: Due Date
4	**Tue 1/5/2016**
7AM	☐ SBS Tradeshow Schedule
	☐ SBS Make dinner reservations
	☐ SBS Order Brochures
8	☐ Progress report
9 Conference call with Fourth Coffee	
10	
SBS Study Session	
Test meeting	
11	
12PM	
1	
2 **SBS Staff Meeting**	Notes
Conference Room	
3	
4	
5	

Display the preview at actual size to confirm that it includes the content you want to print

5. To make additional changes, click the **Print Options** button to open the Print dialog box.

6. In the **Print** dialog box, do any of the following:

   • To change the calendar being printed, expand the **Print this calendar** list, and then click the calendar you want to print.

   • To print only specific pages of a multipage calendar, in the **Page range** section, click **Pages**, and then enter the pages you want to print.

- To specify a date range to print, in the **Print range** section, select or enter the **Start** and **End** dates.

- To display only availability for items that are marked as Private, select the **Hide details of private appointments** check box.

- Click **Print** to print the calendar with the current settings, **Preview** to save the settings and return to the Print page of the Backstage view, or **Cancel** to return to the Print page without saving the settings.

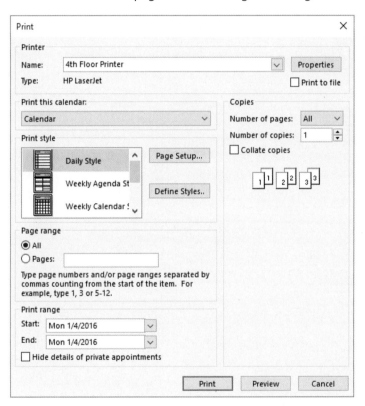

Change the printer, calendar, print style, or date range before printing

10

Skills review

In this chapter, you learned how to:

- Define your available time
- Configure time zones
- Work with multiple calendars
- Share calendar information
- Print a calendar

Practice tasks

No practice files are necessary to complete the practice tasks in this chapter.

Define your available time

Display the Calendar module, and then perform the following tasks:

1. Display the Work Week view of your calendar. Note the working days and times that are shown in Work Week view, and notice the color difference between working time and nonworking time.

2. In the **Outlook Options** dialog box, on the **Calendar** page, display the **Work time** section, and then do the following:

   a. Review the settings, and notice the correlation to the Work Week view of your calendar.

   b. Set your work hours to start at **12:00 PM** and end at **9:00 PM**.

   c. Set your work week to include only **Monday**, **Tuesday**, and **Friday**.

   d. Set the first day of the week to **Thursday**.

   e. Click **OK** to close the dialog box and implement your changes.

3. Notice the change in the Work Week view of the calendar. Scroll forward to the next work week, and notice the working days and times.

4. Display the Week view of your calendar. In the Date Navigator and on the calendar, notice the order of the days of the week.

5. Return to the **Work time** section of the **Calendar** page of the **Outlook Options** dialog box. Match the **Work time** settings to your actual work week (or a close approximation). Then click **OK** to close the dialog box and implement your changes.

Configure time zones

Display the Calendar module, and then perform the following tasks:

1. Display the Day view of your calendar, and navigate to a day that includes multiple appointments, meetings, or events.

2. In the **Outlook Options** dialog box, on the **Calendar** page, display the the **Time zones** section, and then do the following:

   a. Select the option to display a second time zone, and choose a time zone that is different from your own.

   b. Enter a label for each time zone.

   c. Click **OK** to close the dialog box and implement your changes.

3. Notice the two time zones shown to the left of the daily calendar. Consider the circumstances under which this might be of use to you.

4. Switch the primary and secondary time zones, and notice the change in the times of your appointments.

5. Display the Work Week view of the calendar and notice any changes in your appointments and events due to the time zone change.

6. Switch back to the original time zones, and then configure the **Time zones** settings as you want them.

Work with multiple calendars

Display the Calendar module, and then perform the following tasks:

1. Display the Week view of your calendar, and navigate to a week that includes multiple appointments, meetings, or events.

2. If your organization uses Microsoft Exchange, do the following:

   a. Display a co-worker's calendar in your Outlook Calendar module.

   b. Notice the colors assigned to the calendars.

   c. Overlay the calendars, and then change the active calendar and notice the change in the font and color of the calendar items.

   d. Create a calendar group that includes three co-workers, and display it on your calendar. Hide the calendar group, and then display only one calendar from the group.

3. If you have access to a SharePoint site that includes a calendar, do the following:

   a. Display the SharePoint calendar.

   b. Connect the SharePoint calendar to Outlook, and provide the permission necessary to display the SharePoint calendar in your Calendar module.

4. Open your default web browser, and then locate an Internet calendar that you can subscribe to. This might be on the website of a sports team, school, company, or community organization, or on a calendar-sharing website such as iCalShare (located at *www.icalshare.com*).

5. Import or subscribe to the Internet calendar and ensure that it appears in your Calendars module.

6. Overlay all the active calendars, and then display them side by side.

7. Close all the calendars other than your default calendar.

8. In the **Folder Pane**, delete the calendar group and each calendar that you don't want to retain. (You can't delete your default calendar.)

Share calendar information

Display the Calendar module, and then perform the following tasks:

1. If you have a calendar associated with an Exchange account, display that calendar, and then do the following:

   a. Inform a colleague that you want to practice sharing calendars.

   b. Share your calendar with your colleague, with the level of detail that you are comfortable with. In the sharing request, ask your colleague to share his or her calendar with you, with Limited Details or Full Details.

   c. When your colleague responds, open his or her calendar from the sharing request and note the level of detail that is visible.

2. Open the **Properties** dialog box for any calendar, and then do the following:

   a. Review the available permission settings.

   b. If you want to change the default level of information visible to your co-workers, do so.

   c. If you want to give specific permissions to another person, do so.

   d. Close the **Properties** dialog box.

3. Display the calendar delegation controls, and then do the following:

   - Consider the circumstances under which someone would want to delegate access to a calendar or other module to someone else within the organization.

   - If you want to delegate control of your calendar to someone else, do so (remember to send a delegation notification). Then test whether your delegate can control the calendar as expected.

4. Send limited details of your calendar for the next 10 days to yourself by email, using the email layout that you prefer. Review the email message when you receive it, and notice the information that is available. Experiment with clicking links in the message and expanding and collapsing calendar sections.

5. Publish the current week of your calendar online. Send the HTML and ICS links to yourself in an email message. Click each link and note the results.

Print a calendar

Display the Calendar module, and then perform the following tasks:

1. Display the Work Week view of your calendar, and navigate to a week that includes multiple appointments, meetings, or events.

2. Display the **Print** page of the Backstage view, and notice the print layout that Outlook selects for the current time period.

3. Magnify the preview area to display the calendar content at its actual size. Notice the details and types of information that are available in the printed calendar.

4. Click each of the other print layouts, and notice the available information.

5. Display the print layout that you find most useful.

6. Open the **Print Options** dialog box, and change the date range to be printed so that it includes more days than are shown by the selected print layout.

7. Return to the preview, and scroll through the pages of the calendar as it will appear when printed.

8. If you have an available printer and want to test printing the calendar, print the first page of the current calendar configuration.

Track tasks

Many people keep one or more task lists going at all times, listing things to do, things to buy, people to call, and other tasks. You might write these task lists on pieces of paper, use a smartphone app to keep the list on your phone, or have a cool device such as an Amazon Echo that keeps a list of the things you tell it you need to buy, and makes the list available through an app.

But paper lists can get lost, and apps have to be kept up to date. You might find it easier to use the built-in task-tracking functionality in Outlook 2016. You can add tasks, flag messages for follow-up, assign due dates, receive reminders, and mark tasks as complete when you finish them. You can even assign tasks to other people, and if those people use Outlook, you can view their progress on assigned tasks as they track progress milestones.

You can display your tasks and flagged items in several locations within Outlook, so you stay aware of them. You can keep multiple task lists, or categorize tasks so you can filter the list for tasks that are related to a specific topic.

This chapter guides you through procedures related to creating tasks, managing tasks, managing task assignments, and displaying different views of tasks.

In this chapter

- Create tasks
- Manage tasks
- Manage task assignments
- Display different views of tasks

Practice files

No practice files are necessary to complete the practice tasks in this chapter.

Create tasks

If you use your Outlook task list to its fullest potential, you frequently add tasks to it. You can create one-time or recurring tasks in different ways, accept a task assignment from someone else, or add an existing Outlook item (such as a message) to your task list by "flagging" the item. Regardless of how or where you create a task, all tasks and flagged messages are moderated by the Tasks module and displayed in various views, including the To-Do List and Tasks folders in the Tasks module, the Tasks peek available in any module, and the Daily Task List available in the Calendar module.

> **SEE ALSO** For information about the To-Do List and Tasks views, see "Display different views of tasks" later in this chapter. For information about the Daily Task List, see "Display different views of a calendar" in Chapter 9, "Manage scheduling." For information about the Tasks peek, see "Personalize the Outlook app window" in Chapter 12, "Manage window elements."

Although you probably won't need to use any of these features, you can attach files to task items, and you can include text, tables, charts, illustrations, hyperlinks, and other content in the task window content pane by using the same commands you use in other Outlook item windows and in other Microsoft Office apps, such as Word. You can also set standard Outlook item options such as recurrence, color categories, reminders, and privacy.

Create task items

You can create a task item by entering the task information in a task window or in the entry box (labeled either *Type a new Task* or *Click here to add a new Task*, depending on the view) that is at the top of any of the task lists (in the Tasks module, in the Tasks peek, or in the Daily Tasks List). The amount of information you can enter when creating the task item varies based on the location in which you create it.

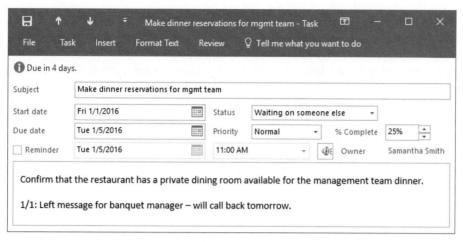

A task can contain many types of information

To create a task item, the only information you need is the subject, which in the case of a task would be the thing you need to get done, such as "Write this chapter" or "Process payroll." As with many other types of Outlook items, you can set several options for tasks to make it easier to organize and identify them:

- **Start date and due date** You can display tasks on the various Outlook task lists on either the start date or the due date. The color of the task flag indicates the due date.

- **Status** You can track the status of a task to remind yourself of your progress. Specific status options include Not Started, In Progress, Completed, Waiting On Someone Else, or Deferred. You also have the option of indicating what percentage of the task is complete. Setting the percentage complete to 25%, 50%, or 75% sets the task status to In Progress. Setting it to 100% sets the task status to Complete.

11

- **Priority** You can set the priority to add a visual indicator of a task's importance. Unless you indicate otherwise, a task is created with a Normal priority level. Low priority displays a blue downward-pointing arrow, and High priority displays a red exclamation point. You can sort and filter tasks based on their priority.

- **Recurrence** Many tasks need to be done every week or month. Instead of creating a unique task for each occurrence, you can set a task to recur on a regular basis; for example, you might create a *Process payroll* task that recurs every month. Only the current instance of a recurring task appears in your task list. When you mark the current task as complete, Outlook creates the next instance of the task.

- **Category** Tasks use the same category list as other Outlook items. You can assign a task to a category to associate it with related items such as messages and appointments.

- **Reminder** You can set a reminder for a task in the same way you do for an appointment. The reminder appears until you dismiss it or mark the task as complete.

> **TIP** From the Outlook Options dialog box, you can configure Outlook to set reminders for all new tasks. For more information, see "Configure contact and task options" in Chapter 13, "Customize Outlook options."

- **Privacy** Marking a task as private ensures that other Outlook users to whom you delegate account access can't see the task details.

From any view of the task list, you can assign the task to a category, change the due date, add a reminder, mark the task as complete, or delete the task entirely. To access these commands, right-click the task name, category, or flag, and then click the option you want. None of the options are required, but they can be helpful to you when sorting, filtering, and prioritizing your tasks.

> **TIP** The fields available in the Tasks List vary based on the list view you're displaying. For information about the available views, see "Display different views of tasks" later in this chapter.

To create a simple task that is due today

1. Do either of the following to activate the task entry box:

   - On the Navigation Bar, point to the **Tasks** button. At the top of the Tasks peek, click **Type a new task**.

   - On the To-Do Bar, at the top of the Tasks peek, click **Type a new task**.

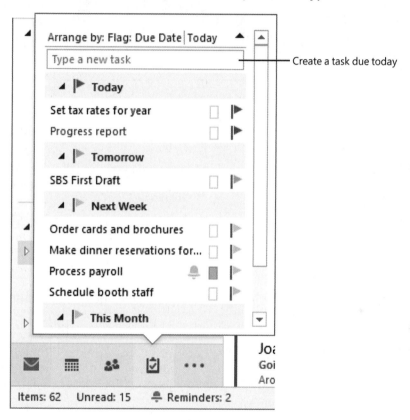

You can change the due date by dragging the task to a different section

2. Enter the task title, and then press **Enter** to create the task with a due date of *Today*.

To create a simple task without a due date

1. In the Tasks module, near the top of the content pane, click **Type a new Task** or **Click here to add a new Task** (depending on the current view).

Create a task without a due date

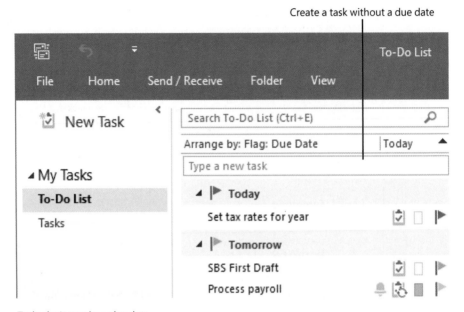

Tasks don't require a due date

2. Enter the task title, and then press **Enter** to create the task with a due date of *None*.

To create a detailed task

1. Do any of the following to open a new task window:

   - In the Tasks module with the ribbon open, on the **Home** tab, in the **New** group, click the **New Task** button.

   - In the Tasks module with the ribbon hidden, at the top of the **Folder Pane**, click the **New Task** button.

     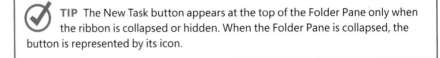 **TIP** The New Task button appears at the top of the Folder Pane only when the ribbon is collapsed or hidden. When the Folder Pane is collapsed, the button is represented by its icon.

- In any module, on the **Home** tab, in the **New** group, in the **New Items** list, click **Task**.

- In any module, press **Ctrl+Shift+K**.

 SEE ALSO For more information about keyboard shortcuts, see Appendix B, "Keyboard shortcuts."

2. In the task header, in the **Subject** box, enter a name for the task. This is the only information that is required.

3. Do any of the following in the task header:

   - To assign a start date or due date, select or enter dates in the **Start date** and **Due date** boxes.

   - To set the task priority, in the **Priority** list, click **Low**, **Normal**, or **High**.

4. To add notes, click in the text pane, and then enter text or use the commands on the **Insert** tab to insert images and other content.

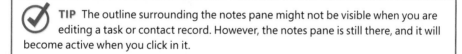 **TIP** The outline surrounding the notes pane might not be visible when you are editing a task or contact record. However, the notes pane is still there, and it will become active when you click in it.

5. If you want to hide details of the task from co-workers, on the **Task** tab, in the **Tags** group, click the **Private** button.

6. On the **Home** tab, in the **Actions** group, click the **Save & Close** button to add the task to your task list.

 SEE ALSO For information about the Tasks peek and pinning peeks to the To-Do Bar, see "Personalize the Outlook app window" in Chapter 12, "Manage window elements."

11

To create a recurring task

1. Create a task item by using any method, and then open the task in a task window.

2. On the **Task** tab, in the **Recurrence** group, click the **Recurrence** button to open the Task Recurrence dialog box.

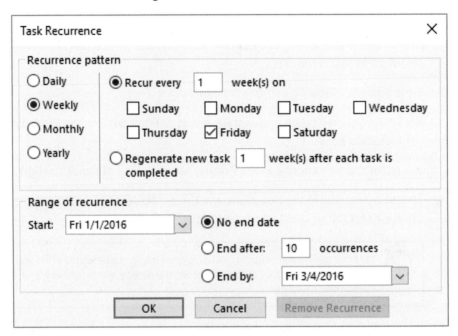

Tasks can recur on a specific schedule or a specific length of time after you complete each occurrence

3. In the **Recurrence pattern** section, do any of the following to set the recurrence:

    *   Click **Daily**, and then enter the number of days between occurrences or click **Every weekday**.

    *   Click **Weekly**, and then enter the number of weeks between occurrences and select the check boxes of the days on which the task is due in those weeks.

    *   Click **Monthly**, and then specify the day of the month and the number of months between occurrences.

- Click **Yearly**, and then specify the date or the day of the month on which the task is due.

4. In the **Range of recurrence** section, do the following:

   - If the first occurrence of the task isn't immediate, enter or select a date in the **Start** box.

   - If the task occurs a specific number of times, click **End after**, and then enter the number of occurrences.

   - If the task has a specific end date, click **End by** and then enter or select a date in the adjacent box.

5. Click **OK** to save the recurrence configuration.

To flag a task for follow-up or another action

1. Do either of the following:

   - Open the task in a task window. On the **Task** tab, in the **Tags** group, click the **Follow Up** button.

   - Display any view of the task list. Right-click the task name, and then click **Follow Up**.

2. To flag the task for follow up, in the **Follow Up** list, click **Today**, **Tomorrow**, **This Week**, **Next Week**, or **No Date**.

   > **TIP** Flagging an item for follow up This Week or Next Week sets the start date to the first working day of the specified week and the due date to the last working day of the week. (Therefore, changing a due date from Today to This Week has no effect if today is the last day of the work week.) The default work week is Monday through Friday, but the start and due dates reflect your own work week configuration. For information about changing the days and times of your work week, see "Define your available time" in Chapter 10, "Manage your calendar."

3. To flag the task for a different action, do the following:

   a. In the **Follow Up** list, click **Custom** to open the Custom dialog box.

11

b. In the **Custom** dialog box, click the **Flag to** arrow, and then click **Call**, **For Your Information**, or **Review**.

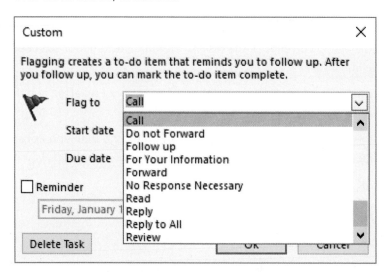

Some conditions pertain to messages rather than to tasks

c. Click **OK** to save the flag.

To set a reminder for a task

1. Do either of the following:

    -   In the task header, select the **Reminder** check box to set a reminder for the default time on the task due date.

    -   On the **Task** tab, in the **Tags** group, click the **Follow Up** button, and then click **Add Reminder** to open the Custom dialog box.

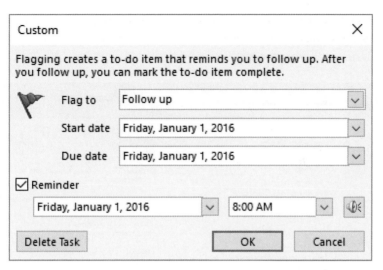

You can set the default reminder time in the Outlook Options dialog box

2. To customize the reminder, in the task header or **Custom** dialog box, select or enter a date and time for the reminder.

Create tasks from Outlook items

You frequently need to take action based on information you receive in Outlook—for example, information in a message or in a meeting request. You might want to add information from another Outlook item to your task list, to ensure that you complete any necessary follow-up work.

Depending on the method you use, you can either create a new task from an existing item or add the existing item to your To-Do List by flagging it. Flagging a message (or other Outlook item) for follow-up adds the item to the default To-Do List view of your task list. However, it does not create a separate task item, so to retain the task, you must retain the message; you can move the message between mail folders, but deleting the message also deletes it from the task list.

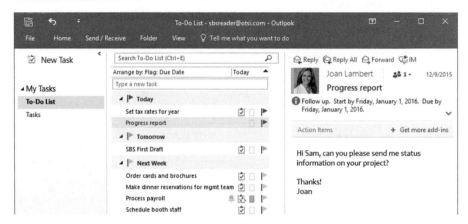

Flagging a message for follow up adds it to your To-Do List

To add a message to your To-Do List by flagging it

1. In the Mail module, do any of the following:

   - Point to the message in the message list, and then click the flag icon that appears.

   > **TIP** Flagged messages appear on your task list under the default due date header. You can change the default due date by configuring the Quick Click flag either from the Tasks page of the Outlook Options dialog box or from the shortcut menu that appears when you right-click a message flag.

   - Point to the message in the message list, right-click the flag icon that appears, and then click a specific due date: **Today**, **Tomorrow**, **This Week**, **Next Week**, **No Date**, or **Custom** (which you can use to set specific start and end dates).

   - Drag the message to the Tasks peek on the To-Do Bar and drop it under the heading for the due date you want to assign to it. (If the due date you want doesn't already have a heading in the task list, drop the message under another heading and then assign the due date you want.)

The flag remains visible in the message list, follow-up information appears below the message header in the Reading Pane, and the subject of the message appears in the Today category in the Tasks peek.

To create a new task from an existing Outlook item

1. Display the module that contains the item you want to create the new task from.

2. Do either of the following:

    - Drag the item to the **Tasks** button on the Navigation Bar, and when a plus sign appears next to the cursor, release the mouse button.

      This method opens a task window that already has information filled in from the original item. You can change settings, add information and attachments, assign the task to other people, and make other changes.

    - Drag the item to the Tasks peek on the To-Do Bar, and release the mouse button when the red horizontal insertion line indicates that the item will be inserted in the position you want. If the item is an email message, the flag icon is now visible on the message in the message list.

Manage tasks

By default, tasks appear in the Task List and To-Do List sorted by date. Flagged messages are included in the To-Do list view of tasks, but some of the methods for updating them are different than the methods used to update task items. For example, you cannot track the status of a flagged message.

> **TIP** Outlook stores your tasks in the Tasks folder. If you want to track different types of tasks separately, you can also create additional task lists by creating folders that contain task items. For example, you might want to keep a business-related task list and a personal task list, or an individual task list and a shared task list.

11

Update tasks

You can display a task in a task window, or in the Reading Pane; you can also preview details on the To-Do bar. You can change the details or dates of a task and track the progress you've made on it in the task window. You can change most task details directly from a task list.

To display the Reading Pane in the Tasks module

1. In the Tasks module, on the **View** tab, in the **Layout** group, click the **Reading Pane** button.

2. In the **Reading Pane** list, click **Right** or **Bottom** to display the Reading Pane.

To display a task in the Reading Pane

1. In the task list, click the task to display the task's contents in the Reading Pane.

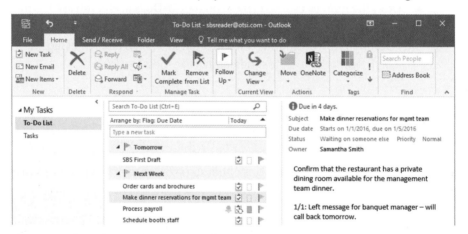

The commands available on the Home tab differ for tasks and flagged items

To preview task details in the Tasks peek

1. In any module, display the Tasks peek on the Navigation Bar or the To-Do Bar.

2. In the Tasks peek, point to a task or flagged message to display a ScreenTip that contains the start date, the reminder time, the due date, the folder in which the message appears, any categories assigned to the message, and other information.

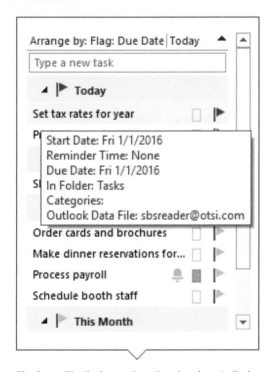

The ScreenTip displays task settings but doesn't display notes

To open a task in a task window

1. In any view of the task list, double-click the task.

To open a flagged message from the Tasks peek

1. In any module, display the Tasks peek on the Navigation Bar or the To-Do Bar.

2. In the Tasks peek, double-click the message to open it in a message window.

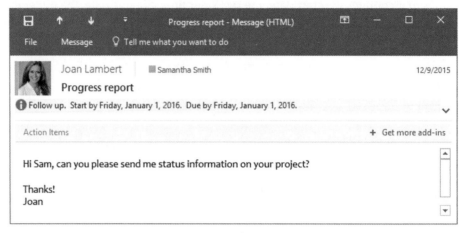

The message header provides information about the follow-up date

To change the follow-up date of a flagged message

1. In the message list or Tasks peek, right-click (don't click) the flag to display the list of due date options.

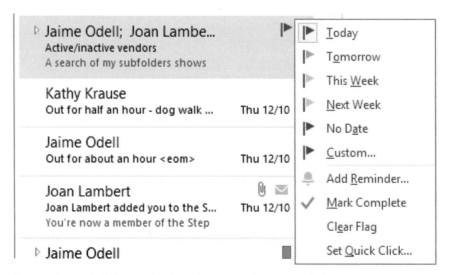

You can change the follow-up date from the message list or any task view

IMPORTANT Clicking an active flag marks the item as complete in the Inbox, and removes it from the Tasks peek. For more information, see "Remove items from your task list" later in this topic.

2. In the list, click the date you want.

To rename a task

1. Display any view of the task list.

2. Right-click the task name, and then click **Rename Task** to activate the task subject for editing.

3. Enter the new task subject, and then press **Enter** to save your changes.

To update the status of a task

1. Open the task window.

2. In the task header, do either of the following:

   - In the **Status** list, click **Not Started**, **In Progress**, **Completed**, **Waiting On Someone Else**, or **Deferred**.

   - In the **% Complete** list, enter or select (by clicking the arrows) the percentage of the project you estimate as complete to change the status to reflect your selection.

     Tasks that are 0% complete are Not Started, tasks that are from 1% to 99% complete are In Progress, and tasks that are 100% complete are Completed.

 TIP You can track the status of task items and assigned tasks, but not of messages or other items that have been flagged for follow up.

Remove items from your task list

When you complete a task or follow up on a flagged item, you have three options for managing its presence on your task list: marking the task or flagged item as complete, removing the flag from a flagged item, or deleting the task or flagged item entirely.

Marking a task or flagged item as complete retains a record of the item on your task list. Completed tasks are visible only in certain task list views.

There are several ways to mark a task or flagged item as complete. Whichever method you use, when you display an unfiltered view of your task list, the completed task is crossed through, the Complete check box is selected, and the flag is changed to a check mark. In the task window for the completed task, Status is set to Completed and % Complete is set to 100%. (In other words, doing any one thing accomplishes all the others.)

□	✔	SUBJECT	DUE DATE	▲	✓
		Click here to add a new Task			
↕	✔	~~Atomi invoicing for Deco~~	~~Wed 11/25/2015~~		✓
↕	✔	~~Restyle PowerPoint RTFs~~	~~Mon 12/7/2015~~		✓
↕	✔	~~Email to Susie regarding indexing standards~~	~~Mon 12/7/2015~~		✓
↕	☐	Create author SP accounts	Wed 12/16/2015		▶
↕	☐	Call Haverty's re broken recliner handles	Wed 12/16/2015		▶
👥	☐	Review editorial test results	Fri 12/18/2015		▷
🔁	☐	Atomi invoicing for Deco	Fri 12/25/2015		▷

Completed tasks are hidden in many views, but you can display them

After you mark an instance of a recurring task as complete, Outlook generates a new instance of the task at whatever interval you specified when creating the task.

Removing the flag from a flagged item such as a message or contact record retains the item in its original location but removes it from your task list entirely.

Deleting a task or flagged item moves the task or the original item to the Deleted Items folder; it is permanently deleted when you empty that folder. No record of it remains on your task list or in its original location (such as your Inbox).

To mark a task or flagged item as complete

1. Do any of the following:

   - Display any view of the task list, right-click the task, and then click **Mark Complete**.

   - In the Tasks peek, point to the flag at the right end of the item, and when the flag turns bright red, click it to mark the task as complete.

   - In the Tasks module, click the task or item to make it active, and then on the **Home** tab, in the **Manage Task** group, click the **Mark Complete** button.

- In the task window, change the **Status** to **Completed** or the **% Complete** setting to **100%**.

- In views that include a check box preceding the task subject (most list views), select the check box.

- In views that include a colored flag, click the flag once.

To remove the flag from a flagged message or other item

1. Do any of the following:

   - In the Tasks peek, right-click the flag at the right end of the item, and then click **Clear Flag**.

   - In the Tasks module, click the flagged item to select it, and on the **Home** tab, in the **Manage Task** group, click the **Remove from List** button.

   - In any module, right-click the flagged item, click **Follow-up**, and then click **Clear Flag**.

To delete a task item

1. Do either of the following:

   - In the Tasks module, click the task to make it active, and then on the **Home** tab, in the **Delete** group, click the **Delete** button.

   - In any view, right-click the task, and then click **Delete**.

11

Manage task assignments

You can assign tasks from your Outlook task list to other people within and outside of your organization (and other people can assign tasks to you). Outlook indicates assigned tasks in your task list by adding a blue arrow pointing to a person on the task icon, similar to that of a shared folder in File Explorer.

Assign tasks to other people

You can assign tasks to other people. When you assign a task to someone who is part of your Microsoft Exchange Server network, Outlook sends a task request, similar to a meeting request, to the person you designated. The assignee can accept or decline the task assignment by clicking the corresponding button in the Reading Pane or in the task window header. If the assignee accepts the task, it appears on his or her task list, and Outlook shows the task status in your task list as Assigned.

You can assign a task to someone outside of your network, but he or she will receive it as a message attached to a message and it won't have task item functionality or maintain a link to the task on your list. If you do this, Outlook shows the task status as Waiting For Response From Recipient until you change it yourself.

When you assign a task, you can choose whether to keep a copy of the task on your own task list or transfer it entirely to the assignee's task list. Either way, the task remains on your own task list until accepted, so you won't lose track of it. (If the recipient declines the task, you can return it to your task list or reassign it.)

 TIP You can assign only actual task items; you can't assign flagged messages that appear in your task list. The items you've assigned are visible only when you choose to include them in your view of the task list.

After you assign a task to someone else, ownership of the task transfers to that person, and you can no longer update the information in the task window. (The assignee becomes the task owner, and you become the task originator.) If you keep a copy of the task on your task list, you can follow the progress as the assignee updates the task status and details, and you can communicate information about the task to the owner by sending status reports. Unless you choose otherwise, Outlook automatically sends you a status report on an assigned task when the assignee marks the task as complete.

You can view the status of tasks you have assigned to other people by displaying your task list in Assignment view.

 SEE ALSO For information about task list views, see "Display different views of tasks" later in this chapter.

The assignee receives a task request that he or she can accept or decline. Either action generates a response message to you. As with meeting requests, the task request recipient has the option of sending a message with the response.

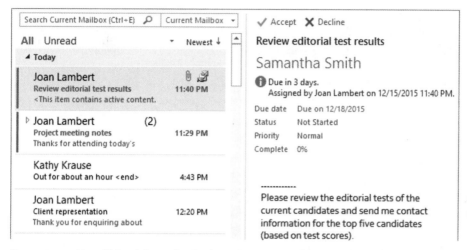

Be sure to provide sufficient information for the assignee to complete the task successfully

 TIP Only Exchange users have the Accept and Decline options in the task request message; Internet email account users do not.

If you assign a task and the assignee declines the assignment, the task doesn't automatically return to your task list; you need to either reclaim the task (return it to your own task list) or reassign it.

To assign a task to someone else

1. With the task window open, on the **Task** tab, in the **Manage Task** group, click the **Assign Task** button to display a **To** box and **Send** button in the task header.

2. In the **To** box, enter the name or email address of the person you want to assign the task to.

11

3. Note that the **Keep an updated copy of this task on my task list** and **Send me a status report when this task is complete** check boxes are selected by default. You can clear the check boxes if you don't want Outlook to perform those actions.

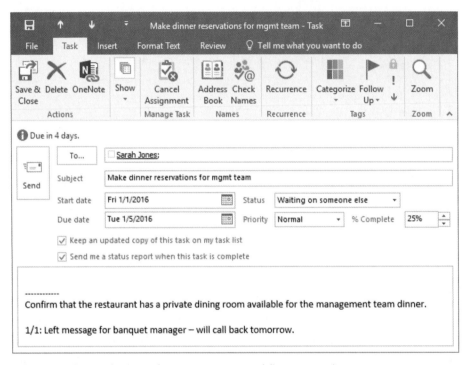

When you assign a task, you can keep a copy on your task list or remove it

4. Review the task subject, dates, status, priority, and completion settings and ensure that they are as you want them—after you assign the task, you will no longer be able to change the task details.

5. In the task header, click the **Send** button. A message box notifies you that the task reminder previously set for this task will be turned off when you assign it to another person.

Assigning a task cancels any reminder that you've set for yourself

6. In the **Microsoft Outlook** message box, click **OK** to send the task request. Outlook will notify you when the assignee accepts or declines the task.

To reclaim or reassign a declined task

1. Open the declined task assignment. The Manage Task group on the Task tab of the task window ribbon includes commands specific to managing the declined task.

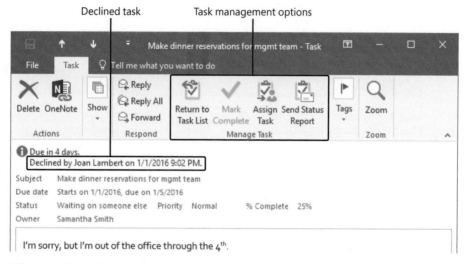

When an assignee declines a task, you can reclaim or reassign it

2. In the **Manage Task** group, do either of the following:

- Click the **Return to Task List** button to reclaim the task.

- Click the **Assign Task** button to reassign the task.

Respond to task assignments

When another person assigns a task to you, you receive a task request.

You can update the details of a task assigned to you by someone else in the same way that you do tasks that you create.

To accept or decline a task request

1. Do any of the following:

- In the **Reading Pane**, at the top of the task request, click **Accept** to accept the task.

- In the **Reading Pane**, click **Decline** to decline the task.

- With the task request selected in the message list, press **Alt+C** to accept the task.

- Press **Alt+D** to decline the task.

Or

1. Open the task request. The Task tab of the task window ribbon includes additional options for managing the task request.

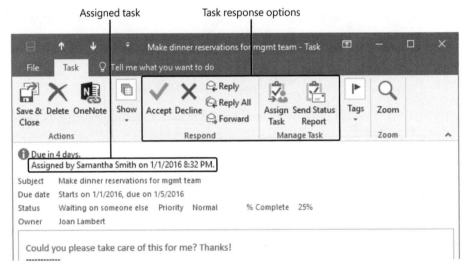

You can respond in several ways to a task assignment

2. Do either of the following:

- In the **Respond** group, click the **Accept** button to accept the task or the **Decline** button to decline the task, and to send the associated response to the task owner. You have the option of editing the response before it is sent.

- In the **Respond** group, click **Reply** to send a message to the task owner without accepting or declining the task, or the **Forward** button to forward the task content to another person without reassigning the task.

To reassign a task that was assigned to you

1. Open the task request.

2. On the **Task** tab, in the **Manage Task** group, click the **Assign Task** button, and follow the procedure described earlier in this topic to assign the task to another person.

To send a status report about a task that was assigned to you

1. Open the task window.

2. On the **Task** tab, in the **Manage Task** group, click the **Send Status Report** button to generate an email message that has the task information in the **Subject** field and message body.

3. Address the message to the people you want to send the report to, and then send the message. In the Styles list, you can choose from five page layouts and color schemes.

Display different views of tasks

Outlook 2016 makes it simple to keep your task list at your fingertips. You can view tasks in several different locations. The primary task management location is the Tasks module, but you have easy access to your current tasks from the Daily Task List in the Calendar module or the Tasks peek in any module.

Display tasks in the Tasks module

The Folder Pane of the Tasks module displays two virtual folders:

- **To-Do List** Displays tasks and flagged messages in To-Do List view, with the Reading Pane open on the right.

    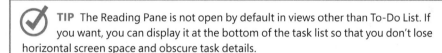

    TIP The Reading Pane is not open by default in views other than To-Do List. If you want, you can display it at the bottom of the task list so that you don't lose horizontal screen space and obscure task details.

- **Tasks** Displays only task items in Simple List view. This view displays the subject, due date, categories, and flags for each folder item and a check box that you can select to indicate that an item has been completed.

In either folder, you can change the view and the arrangement of the folder content. The view filters the content, and the arrangement orders the filtered content.

The other built-in views are Active, Assigned, Completed, Detailed, Next 7 Days, Overdue, Prioritized, Server Tasks, and Today. Detailed view displays all active and completed items in list format; most of the other views display only the items

11

corresponding to the view name (for example, Active view displays only the active items in the folder and Completed view displays only the completed items).

You can search and filter your tasks in any view by using the Instant Search feature from the search box at the top of the content area. You can sort tasks by any displayed column in a list view by clicking the column header.

 TIP Press Ctrl+E to move to the search box in the active module. For more information about keyboard shortcuts, see Appendix B, "Keyboard shortcuts."

You can change the fields displayed in each view; the way tasks are grouped, sorted, and filtered; the display font; and other settings to suit your preferences. If you don't like your changes, you can reset the view to its default configuration. You perform all these procedures in the Tasks module in the same way that you do in other modules.

Completed tasks remain in the Tasks folder until you delete them, so they are available there if you want to view them.

To display tasks and flagged items in the Tasks module

1. In the Tasks module, in the **Folder Pane**, do one of the following:

   - To display active task items and flagged items, click **To-Do List**.

   - To display active and completed tasks, click **Tasks**.

To display a different view of the Tasks module

1. Do either of the following:

   - On the **Home** tab, in the **Current View** group, click **Change View**.

   - On the **View** tab, in the **Current View** group, click **Change View**.

2. In the **Change View** gallery, click **Detailed**, **Simple List**, **To-Do List**, **Prioritized**, **Active**, **Completed**, **Today**, **Next 7 Days**, **Overdue**, **Assigned**, or **Server Tasks**.

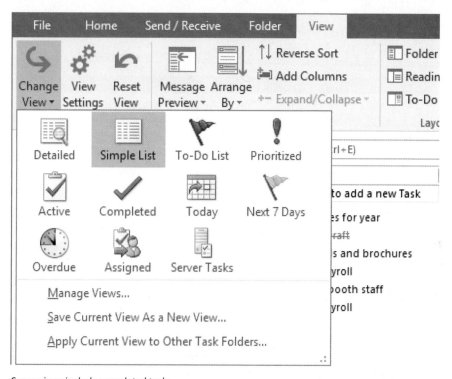

Some views include completed tasks

If the view you select filters the task list, the words *Filter Applied* appear at the left end of the status bar to indicate that the folder is displaying a filtered view of the available items (for example, the To-Do List displays only active items).

The status bar alerts you to a filtered view

Outlook Today

The Outlook Today page, which was at one time the Outlook home page, displays your upcoming appointments and tasks.

You can get a quick overview on the Outlook Today page

You can display the Outlook Today page at any time by clicking your email account at the top of the Folder Pane (your email account is visible in the Mail module and Folder List).

Clicking Customize Outlook Today in the upper-right corner of the Outlook Today page displays options for specifying the page content and setting it as your home page, so that it displays the information that is most helpful to you when you first start Outlook.

Customize Outlook Today   Save Changes   Cancel

Startup   ☐ When starting, go directly to Outlook Today

Messages   Show me these folders: [Choose Folders...]

Calendar   Show this number of days in my calendar [5 ▼]

Tasks   In my task list, show me: ◉ All tasks
                                            ○ Today's tasks
                                               ☑ Include tasks with no due date

                  Sort my task list by: [Due Date ▼] then by: [(none) ▼]
                                   ○ Ascending   ○ Ascending
                                   ◉ Descending   ◉ Descending

Styles   Show Outlook Today in this style: [Standard ▼]

Specify the messages, calendar items, and tasks shown on the Outlook Today page

In the Styles list, you can choose from five page layouts and color schemes.

Variations of the Standard style, and the Summer and Winter styles

11

To sort tasks in a list view

1. In any view other than To-Do view, click any column header to sort the tasks based on that field. The sort arrow to the right of the column header indicates the sort order.

2. Reverse the sort order by clicking the active column header.

To group tasks

1. On the **View** tab, in the **Arrangement** group, on the **Arrange By** menu, click **Show in Groups** to select or clear the check mark.

2. In the **Arrange By** gallery, click the grouping you want.

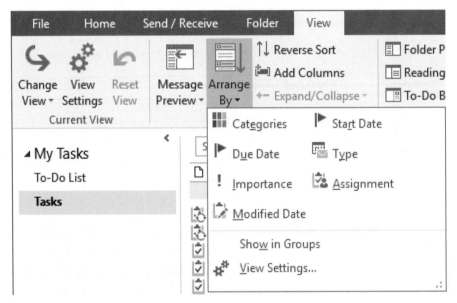

Control the order of tasks by choosing an arrangement or sorting a field

> **SEE ALSO** For information about adding, moving, and removing fields in list views, see the "Content area views" section of "Work in the Mail module" in Chapter 2, "Explore Outlook modules." For information about modifying advanced view settings, see the sidebar "Modify the settings of any view" in Chapter 7, "Store and access contact information."

To reset the current view to its default settings

1. Do either of the following:

   - On the **View** tab, in the **Current View** group, click the **Reset View** button, and then click **Yes** in the message box that opens.

   - Open the **Advanced View Settings** dialog box, click the **Reset Current View** button, and then click **OK**.

Display tasks in other modules

In any module, you can display the Tasks peek on the To-Do Bar. The Tasks peek displays a task list in which tasks are grouped and sorted by due date. (You can also sort this list by category, start date, folder, type, or importance, or you can create a custom arrangement.) You can scroll through the list to display all your tasks or collapse the groups you don't want to view. To increase the space available for your task list, you can close or reduce the height of other To-Do Bar elements.

> **SEE ALSO** For information about the To-Do Bar, including changing the type and amount of content displayed, see "Personalize the Outlook app window" in Chapter 12, "Manage window elements."

11

In the Calendar module, you can display the Daily Task List below the calendar in Day, Work Week, or Week view. The Daily Task List displays the tasks due, including the category and task type, on each day of the displayed time period. In Day view, the start date, due date, and reminder time also appear.

Daily Task List

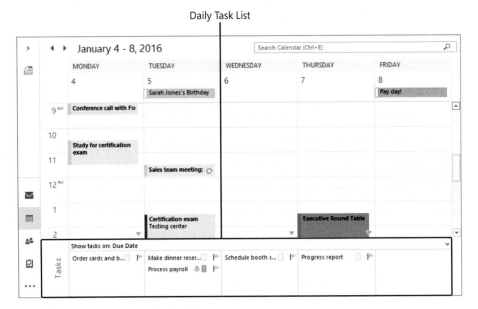

Track and schedule your tasks for each day

As with the Folder Pane and the People Pane, you can minimize the Daily Task List so that it displays only the number of active and completed tasks and provides more space for you to work.

To display the Daily Task List

1. Display the Day, Work Week, or Week view of your primary calendar.

2. On the **View** tab, in the **Layout** group, click the **Daily Task List** button, and then click **Normal**.

To schedule a task from the Daily Task List on your calendar

1. Drag the task from the **Daily Task List** pane to the timeslot on your calendar.

To minimize the Daily Task List

1. Do either of the following:

   - At the right end of the **Daily Task List** pane header, click the **Minimize** button.

   - On the **View** tab, in the **Layout** group, click the **Daily Task List** button, and then click **Minimized**.

To expand the minimized Daily Task List

1. Do either of the following:

   - At the right end of the **Daily Task List** pane header, click the **Minimize** button.

   - On the **View** tab, in the **Layout** group, click the **Daily Task List** button, and then click **Normal**.

To close the Daily Task List

1. On the **View** tab, in the **Layout** group, click the **Daily Task List** button, and then click **Off**.

Skills review

In this chapter, you learned how to:

- Create tasks

- Manage tasks

- Manage task assignments

- Display different views of tasks

11

Practice tasks

No practice files are necessary to complete the practice tasks in this chapter.

Create tasks

Display the Tasks module, and then perform the following tasks:

1. In the **Folder Pane**, click **To-Do List** to display tasks grouped by due date.

2. From the **Type a new task** box at the top of the content pane, create the task Complete Chapter 11 practice tasks. Notice that the task is created without a due date.

3. Open a new task window and create a task that has the following properties:

   Subject: Read Chapter 12

   Due date: Tomorrow

   Priority: Low

4. Set a reminder to appear at **9:00 AM** tomorrow morning. Then save and close the task.

5. Select the task in the task list, and then change the **Follow Up** date to **This Week**.

6. Open a new task window and create a task that has the following properties:

   Subject: My Birthday

   Start date and **Due date**: Enter or select the date of your next birthday

   Recurrence: Yearly, on your birthday, with no end date

7. Set a reminder to appear one month before your birthday, so you have time to plan a celebration. Then save and close the task.

8. Display the Mail module, and then do the following:

   a. Point to the **Tasks** button on the Navigation Bar to display the Tasks peek. Notice that the tasks you created in steps 2, 3, and 6 are in their respective due date groups.

   b. From the **Type a new task** box at the top of the Tasks peek, create the task *Have a great day!* Notice that the task is added to the Tasks peek with a due date of *Today*.

9. Choose a message from your message list, and flag it for follow up.

10. Choose a message from your message list, and create a new task from the message.

Manage tasks

Display the To-Do List in the Tasks module, and then perform the following tasks:

1. If the **Reading Pane** isn't open, display it on the right side of the window.

2. In the task list, click the message that you flagged in the previous set of practice tasks, and review the content in the **Reading Pane**.

3. Change the follow-up date of the flagged message to **Next Week**.

4. Open the **Complete Chapter 11 practice tasks** item in a task window.

5. Set the **% Complete** to **30%**. Notice that the Status changes from *Not Started* to *In Process*.

6. Rename all occurrences of the **My Birthday** task with your name as the subject.

7. Mark the **Have a great day!** task as complete.

8. Delete the task item that you created from a message in the previous set of practice tasks.

9. Display the Mail module. From the Tasks peek, display the details of the **Complete Chapter 11 practice tasks** item in a ScreenTip. Note any information that the ScreenTip doesn't include.

10. From the Tasks peek, open the message that you worked with in steps 2 and 3. Clear the flag from the message, and then close the message window.

Manage task assignments

Display the Tasks module, and then perform the following tasks:

1. Create a task named **Practice assigning tasks**.

2. Assign the task to someone else, and ask him or her to decline the assignment.

3. From the response message, reassign the task to another person and ask him or her to accept the assignment.

4. After the assignment is accepted, open the task from your task list and notice what changes you can make, and what actions you can perform, with the assigned task.

Display different views of tasks

Display the To-Do List in the Tasks module, and then perform the following tasks:

1. Notice the items that are available in the To-Do List, and how they are organized.

2. In the **Folder Pane**, click **Tasks**. Notice the difference in the items shown in this view.

3. Sort the **Tasks** list in another order.

4. Display three other views of the Tasks module. Consider which of the views is most useful to you, and end with that view.

5. Change the arrangement of the tasks in the view that you chose in step 4.

6. Reset the current view to its default settings.

7. Display the Calendar module in Work Week view.

8. Display the **Daily Task List** below the calendar pane.

9. Locate a day that has a task in the **Daily Task List**. Drag the task from the **Daily Task List** to the **12:00 PM** slot on the calendar to allocate that time for completing the task.

10. Minimize the **Daily Task List**, and notice the information available on it.

11. If you want to use the **Daily Task List**, expand it; otherwise, close it.

Part 5

Maximize efficiency

Manage window elements

The Outlook user interface has a default configuration that is suitable for the way that most people interact with it, but you have many options for configuring the appearance and arrangement of the app window elements to suit your preferences.

You can modify window elements to free up screen space or to gain efficiencies based on the specific functions you perform when working in Outlook. You can change the size of the Folder Pane, put frequently used commands at your fingertips by adding them to the Quick Access Toolbar, hide ribbon tabs that you don't use, or centralize the commands that you do use on a custom tab.

You can take things a step further and customize the fonts that are used in the module panes. You can change the basic font for all the content in a specific module view, or specify a font treatment for items that meet specific conditions.

This chapter guides you through procedures related to personalizing the Outlook app window, customizing the Quick Access Toolbar, customizing the ribbon, and customizing the user interface fonts.

In this chapter

- Personalize the Outlook app window
- Customize the Quick Access Toolbar
- Customize the ribbon
- Customize user interface fonts

Practice files

No practice files are necessary to complete the practice tasks in this chapter.

Personalize the Outlook app window

In Chapter 1, "Outlook 2016 basics," I discussed the four primary areas of the Outlook 2016 app window in which you work with Outlook items: the Folder Pane, content area, Reading Pane, and To-Do Bar. Throughout this book you've worked with email messages, appointments, contact records, and tasks in each of these areas and experienced some of the ways in which you can modify the display of the window elements.

You might find that the default arrangement of these areas is ideal for the way you work. But if you view the app window on a low-resolution screen, don't need all the available tools, or would like more space for the main work area, you can easily change the appearance and layout of the workspace of each of the app window elements.

You manage the display of most window elements from the View tab of the ribbon. Your preferences are preserved from session to session. When you restart Outlook, the app window elements will appear the same way they did when you last exited the app.

 SEE ALSO For information about managing the People pane, see "Display message participant information" in Chapter 3, "Send and receive email messages."

You can configure the layout of the Folder Pane, Navigation Bar, Reading Pane, and To-Do Bar by using commands in the Layout group of the View tab of the ribbon. You can also work directly from each element.

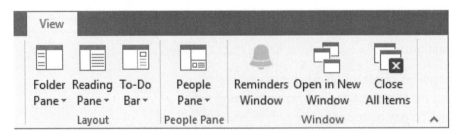

Layout commands are the same on the View tab of any module

Configure the Folder Pane

You can increase the space available for the content pane by hiding or minimizing the Folder Pane. The minimized Folder Pane is a vertical bar on the left side of the app window. It displays buttons for the folders that you designate as favorites, and you can pop it out temporarily to access other folders. When the Folder Pane is open, a section at the top of the Navigation Pane displays links to the favorite folders.

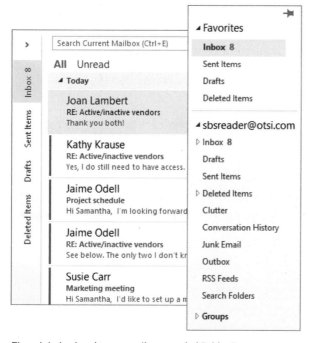

The minimized and temporarily expanded Folder Panes

By default, the Favorites section contains links to the Inbox, Sent Items, Drafts, and Deleted Items folders of your primary email account. You can add and remove folders from the section, or you can hide the section.

To hide or display the Folder Pane

1. On the **View** tab, in the **Layout** group, click the **Folder Pane** button, and then do either of the following:

   - To hide the Folder Pane, click **Off**.

   - To display the Folder Pane at its standard width, click **Normal**.

12

To change the Folder Pane width

1. Point to the right border of the **Folder Pane**.

2. When the cursor changes to a double-headed arrow, drag the border to the left or right.

To work from a minimized Folder Pane

1. To display the Folder Pane as a vertical bar on the left side of the app window, do either of the following:

   - At the top of the **Folder Pane**, click the **Minimize the Folder Pane** button.

   - On the **View** tab, in the **Layout** group, click the **Folder Pane** button, and then click **Minimized**.

   Buttons on the minimized Folder Pane give you one-click access to the folders included in your Favorites list.

2. To temporarily display the Folder Pane content, at the top of the minimized **Folder Pane**, click the **Expand the Folder Pane** button.

3. To return to the standard Folder Pane width, click the **Expand the Folder Pane** button, and then in the upper-right corner of the temporary pane, click the thumbtack.

To work with favorite folders

1. Do any of the following:

   - To display or hide the Favorites section of the Folder Pane, click **Favorites** in the **Layout** group on the **View** tab.

   - To add a folder shortcut to the Favorites section, right-click the folder in the **Navigation Pane**, and then click **Show in Favorites**.

   - To move a folder shortcut within the Favorites section, drag the folder name.

   - To remove a folder from the Favorites section, right-click the folder, and then click **Remove from Favorites**.

Configure the Navigation Bar

The default Navigation Bar is at the bottom of the Folder Pane. It displays buttons that link to the four primary Outlook modules, and an Options button that gives you access to other modules. Alternatively, you can display the Navigation Bar across the bottom of the app window, just above the status bar, with text labels instead of buttons. In either format, you can display from one to eight module links, and specify their order.

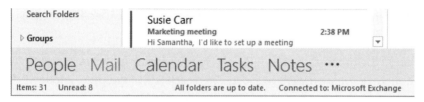

The full Navigation Bar displaying five reordered links

To configure the Navigation Bar

1. To open the Navigation Options dialog box, do either of the following:

   - On the Navigation Bar, click the **Options** button (...), and then click **Navigation Options**.

   - On the **View** tab, in the **Layout** group, click the **Folder Pane** button, and then click **Options**.

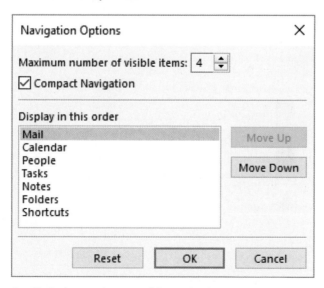

Specify the form and content of the Navigation Bar

2. In the **Navigation Options** dialog box, do any of the following:

- To configure the Navigation Bar to span the app window above the status bar and display module links as names, clear the **Compact Navigation** check box.

- To configure the Navigation Bar as part of the Folder Pane and display module links as buttons, select the **Compact Navigation** check box.

- To display more or fewer module links, enter or select a number (from 1 to 8) in the **Maximum number of visible items** box.

- To change the order of the module links, in the **Display in this order** pane, click a module that you want to move. Then click the **Move Up** or **Move Down** button. The Navigation Bar displays the module links from left to right in the order they appear in the pane from top to bottom.

3. Click **OK** to apply your changes, or click **Reset** to return the Navigation Bar to its default settings.

Display module peeks

In either Navigation Bar configuration, you can "peek" at the current content of the Calendar, People, or Tasks module by pointing to the module link or button. The Calendar peek displays this month's Date Navigator and today's appointments, the People peek displays the contacts you've saved as favorites and a search box, and the Tasks peek displays your upcoming tasks and a new task entry box.

Peeks give you a look at current info without changing modules

If you want to have the information available all the time, you can dock one or more peeks to the right side of the app window in a pane called the To-Do Bar. You can display and configure the To-Do Bar for each individual module.

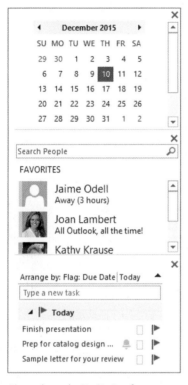

Pin peeks to the To-Do Bar for easy access

12

To display peeks

1. On the Navigation Bar, point to (don't click) the **Calendar**, **People**, or **Tasks** button or link.

To pin peeks to the To-Do Bar

1. Do either of the following:

    • Display the peek that you want to add to the To-Do Bar. In the upper-right corner of the peek, click the **Dock the peek** button.

    • On the **View** tab, in the **Layout** group, click the **To-Do Bar** button, and then click any inactive peek to pin it to the To-Do Bar. (A check mark indicates a pinned peek.)

TIP If the To-Do Bar isn't already open, pinning a peek displays it. Peeks are displayed on the To-Do Bar in the order that you add them. To change the order, remove all peeks other than the one you want on top, and then select other peeks in the order you want them.

To remove peeks from the To-Do Bar

1. Do either of the following:

   - On the To-Do Bar, in the upper-right corner of the peek, click the **Remove the peek** button (the **X**).

   - On the **View** tab, in the **Layout** group, click the **To-Do Bar** button, and then click any active peek to remove it from the To-Do Bar.

⚠ **IMPORTANT** Changes you implement might make your Outlook window appear different from those shown in this book. I depict the Outlook window with the Folder Pane open, the compact Navigation Bar, the Reading Pane displayed on the right side of the window, and the To-Do Bar off except when they are used in a procedure.

To hide the To-Do Bar in the active module

1. On the **View** tab, in the **Layout** group, click the **To-Do Bar** button, and then click **Off**.

✓ **TIP** You configure the To-Do Bar content and presence for each individual module.

To resize the To-Do Bar or its content

1. Do either of the following:

   - To change the width of the To-Do Bar, point to the left edge of the To-Do Bar, and when the pointer turns into a double-headed arrow, drag to the left or right.

   - To change the height of a peek, point to the separator between two peeks, and when the pointer changes to a double-headed arrow, drag up or down.

Configure the Reading Pane

The Reading Pane displays the content of the currently selected item. You can display the Reading Pane on the right side or bottom of the content area, or close it entirely. It is most often used in the Mail module, but you can configure it as you like individually in any module.

To display or hide the Reading Pane

1. On the **View** tab, in the **Layout** group, click the **Reading Pane** button, and then do one of the following:

   - To display the Reading Pane to the right of the content area, click **Right**.

   - To display the Reading Pane below the content area, click **Bottom**.

   - To hide the Reading Pane, click **Off**.

To resize the Reading Pane

1. Do either of the following:

   - When the **Reading Pane** is open on the right side of the app window, point to its left edge.

   - When the **Reading Pane** is open at the bottom of the app window, point to its top edge.

2. When the pointer changes to a double-headed arrow, drag the left edge left or right, or the top edge up or down.

To configure Reading Pane functionality

1. On the **View** tab, in the **Layout** group, click the **Reading Pane** button, and then click **Options** to open the Reading Pane dialog box.

Single key reading advances the content of the Reading Pane

2. In the **Reading Pane** dialog box, select or clear the check boxes to configure the reading functionality the way you want it.

12

Customize the Quick Access Toolbar

The commands you use to control Outlook are available from the ribbon, located at the top of the app window and in each Outlook item window. As you use Outlook, you will become familiar with the locations of the commands you use most frequently. To save time, you can place frequently used commands on the Quick Access Toolbar, which is located, by default, in the upper-left corner of the app window. To save even more time, you can move the Quick Access Toolbar from its default position above the ribbon to below the ribbon, to lessen the distance from the content you're working with to the command you want to invoke.

Outlook has separate Quick Access Toolbars for the app window and each item type window. In the app window, the default Quick Access Toolbar displays the Send/Receive button and the Undo button. In the individual item windows, the default Quick Access Toolbar displays the Save, Undo, Redo, Previous, and Next buttons.

You can add commands to the Quick Access Toolbar directly from the ribbon, or from the Quick Access Toolbar page of the Outlook Options dialog box.

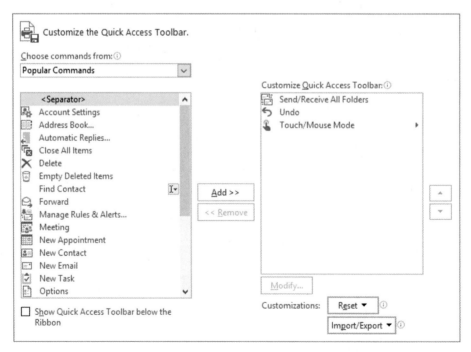

The Quick Access Toolbar page of the Outlook Options dialog box

TIP You can display a list of commands that do not appear on the ribbon by clicking Commands Not In The Ribbon in the Choose Commands From list on the Quick Access Toolbar or Customize Ribbon page of the Outlook Options dialog box.

You can customize the Quick Access Toolbar in the following ways:

- You can add any command from any group of any tab, including any tool tab, to the toolbar.

- After you add commands to the Quick Access Toolbar, you can reorganize them and divide them into groups to simplify the process of locating the command you want.

- If you want to start over, you can reset the Quick Access Toolbar to its default configuration.

 TIP The settings on the Quick Access Toolbar page of the Outlook Options dialog box apply to the app window or to the item window, depending on where you were working when you displayed the page.

As you add commands to the Quick Access Toolbar, it expands to accommodate them. If you add a lot of commands, it might become difficult to view the text in the title bar, or all the commands on the Quick Access Toolbar might not be visible, defeating the purpose of adding them. To resolve this problem and also position the Quick Access Toolbar closer to the file content, you can move the Quick Access Toolbar below the ribbon.

12

 TIP Even though most commands are now available on the ribbon, you can still invoke many commands by using keyboard shortcuts. For more information, see Appendix B, "Keyboard shortcuts."

To add a command to the Quick Access Toolbar from the ribbon

1. Do either of the following:

   - Right-click a command on the ribbon, and then click **Add to Quick Access Toolbar**. You can add any type of command this way; you can even add a drop-down list of options or gallery of thumbnails.

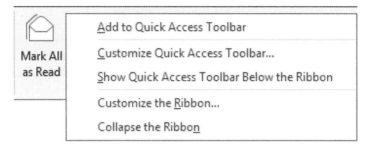

Add any button to the Quick Access Toolbar directly from the ribbon

- At the right end of the Quick Access Toolbar, click the **Customize Quick Access Toolbar** button. On the menu of commonly used commands, click a command you want to add.

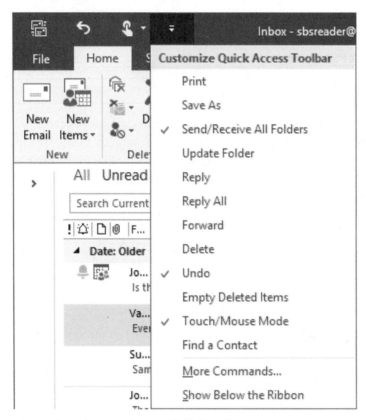

Commonly used commands are available from the menu

To display the Quick Access Toolbar page of the Outlook Options dialog box

1. Do any of the following:

   - At the right end of the Quick Access Toolbar, click the **Customize Quick Access Toolbar** button, and then click **More Commands**.

   - Click the **File** tab and then, in the left pane of the Backstage view, click **Options**. In the left pane of the **Outlook Options** dialog box, click **Quick Access Toolbar**.

   - Right-click any ribbon tab or empty area of the ribbon, and then click **Customize Quick Access Toolbar**.

To add a command to the Quick Access Toolbar from the Outlook Options dialog box

1. Display the **Quick Access Toolbar** page of the **Outlook Options** dialog box.

2. In the **Choose commands from** list, click the tab the command appears on, or click **Popular Commands**, **Commands Not in the Ribbon**, **All Commands**, or **Macros**.

3. In the **Choose commands from** pane, locate and click the command you want to add to the Quick Access Toolbar. Then click the **Add** button.

To display a separator on the Quick Access Toolbar

1. Display the **Quick Access Toolbar** page of the **Outlook Options** dialog box.

2. In the right pane, click the command after which you want to insert the separator.

3. Do either of the following:

   - In the left pane, double-click **<Separator>**.

   - Click **<Separator>** in the left pane, and then click the **Add** button.

To move buttons on the Quick Access Toolbar

1. Display the **Quick Access Toolbar** page of the **Outlook Options** dialog box.

2. In the right pane, click the button you want to move. Then click the **Move Up** or **Move Down** arrow until the button reaches the position you want.

12

To move the Quick Access Toolbar

1. Do either of the following:

   - At the right end of the Quick Access Toolbar, click the **Customize Quick Access Toolbar** button, and then click **Show Below the Ribbon** or **Show Above the Ribbon**.

   - Display the **Quick Access Toolbar** page of the **Outlook Options** dialog box. In the area below the **Choose commands from** list, select or clear the **Show Quick Access Toolbar below the Ribbon** check box.

To reset the Quick Access Toolbar to its default configuration

1. Display the **Quick Access Toolbar** page of the **Outlook Options** dialog box.

2. In the lower-right corner, click **Reset**, and then click either of the following:

   - **Reset only Quick Access Toolbar**

   - **Reset all customizations**

3. In the **Microsoft Office** message box verifying the change, click **Yes**.

> ⚠ **IMPORTANT** Resetting the Quick Access Toolbar does not change its location. You must manually move the Quick Access Toolbar by using either of the procedures described earlier.

Customize the ribbon

Even if Outlook 2016 is the first version of the app you've worked with, by now you'll be accustomed to working with commands represented as buttons or lists on the ribbon. The ribbon was designed to make all the commonly used commands visible so that people can more easily discover the full potential of the app. But many people perform the same set of tasks all the time, and for them, buttons (or groups of buttons) that they never use might be considered just another form of clutter.

If you don't want to entirely hide the ribbon, you can modify its content. From the Customize Ribbon page of the Outlook Options dialog box, you can control the tabs that appear on the ribbon, and the groups that appear on the tabs.

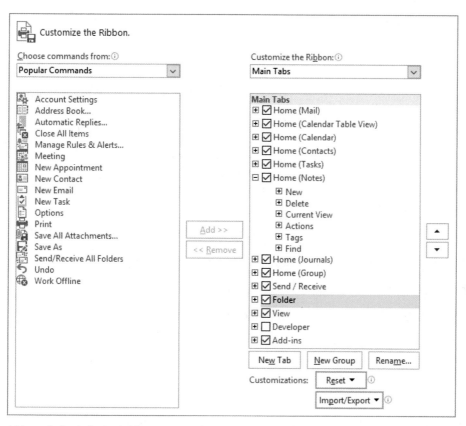

Hide or display individual ribbon tabs

On this page, you can customize the ribbon in the following ways:

- You can hide an entire tab.

- You can remove a group of commands from a tab. (The group is not removed from the app, only from the tab.)

- You can move or copy a group of commands to another tab.

- You can create a custom group on any tab and then add commands to it. (You cannot add commands to a predefined group.)

- You can create a custom tab. For example, you might want to do this if you use only a few commands from each tab and you find it inefficient to flip between them.

12

If you make changes to the ribbon configuration and don't like them, you can easily reset everything back to the default configuration.

> ⚠ **IMPORTANT** Although customizing the default ribbon content might seem like a great way of making the app yours, I don't recommend doing so. A great deal of research has been done about the way that people use the commands in each app, and the ribbon has been organized to reflect the results of that research. If you modify the default ribbon settings, you might end up inadvertently hiding or moving commands that you need. Instead, consider the Quick Access Toolbar to be the command area that you customize and make your own. If you add all the commands you use frequently to the Quick Access Toolbar, you can hide the ribbon and have extra vertical space for document display. (This is very convenient when working on a smaller device.) Or, if you really want to customize the ribbon, do so by gathering your most frequently used commands on a custom tab, and leave the others alone.

To display the Customize Ribbon page of the Outlook Options dialog box

1. Do either of the following:

   - Display the **Outlook Options** dialog box. In the left pane, click **Customize Ribbon**.

   - Right-click any ribbon tab or empty area of the ribbon, and then click **Customize the Ribbon**.

To permit or prevent the display of a tab

1. Display the **Customize Ribbon** page of the **Outlook Options** dialog box.

2. In the **Customize the Ribbon** list, click the tab set you want to manage:

   - All Tabs

   - Main Tabs

   - Tool Tabs

3. In the **Customize the Ribbon** pane, select or clear the check box of any tab. (The File tab isn't included in the tab list, because you can't hide it.)

To remove a group of commands from a tab

1. Display the **Customize Ribbon** page of the **Outlook Options** dialog box.

2. In the **Customize the Ribbon** list, click the tab set you want to manage.

3. In the **Customize the Ribbon** pane, click the **Expand** button (+) to the left of the tab you want to modify.

4. Click the group you want to remove, and then in the center pane, click the **Remove** button.

To create a custom tab

1. Display the **Customize Ribbon** page of the **Outlook Options** dialog box.

2. Click the tab after which you want to insert the new tab.

3. On the **Customize Ribbon** page, click the **New Tab** button to insert a new custom tab below the active tab in the Customize The Ribbon pane. The new tab includes an empty custom group.

```
Main Tabs
⊞ ☑ Home (Mail)
⊟ ☑ New Tab (Custom)
         New Group (Custom)
⊞ ☑ Home (Calendar Table View)
⊞ ☑ Home (Calendar)
```

Creating a new tab and group

To rename a custom tab

1. Display the **Customize Ribbon** page of the **Outlook Options** dialog box.

2. In the **Customize the Ribbon** pane, click the custom tab. Then click the **Rename** button.

3. In the **Rename** dialog box, replace the existing tab name with the tab name you want, and then click **OK**.

To create a custom group

1. Display the **Customize Ribbon** page of the **Outlook Options** dialog box.

2. On the **Customize Ribbon** page, in the right pane, click the tab you want to add the group to. Then click the **New Group** button to add an empty custom group.

12

To rename a custom group

1. Click the custom group, and then click the **Rename** button to open the Rename dialog box in which you can specify an icon and display name for the group.

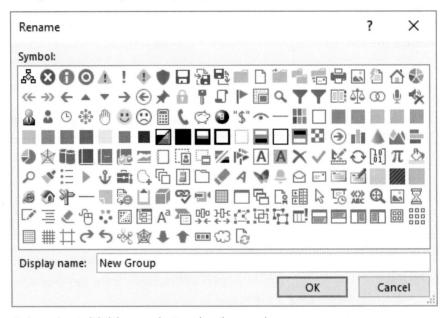

Assign an icon to label the group button when the group is narrow

2. In the **Rename** dialog box, do the following, and then click **OK**:

   - In the **Display name** box, replace the current name with the group name that you want to display.

   - In the **Symbol** pane, click an icon that you want to display when the ribbon is too narrow to display the group's commands.

To add commands to a custom group

1. Display the **Customize Ribbon** page of the **Outlook Options** dialog box.

2. In the **Customize the Ribbon** list, expand the tab set you want to manage, and then click the group you want to add the commands to.

3. In the **Choose commands from** list, click the tab the command appears on, or click **Popular Commands**, **Commands Not in the Ribbon**, **All Commands**, or **Macros**.

4. In the left list, locate and click the command you want to add to the group. Then click the **Add** button.

To reset the ribbon to its default configuration

1. Display the **Customize Ribbon** page of the **Outlook Options** dialog box.

2. In the lower-right corner, click **Reset**, and then click either of the following:

   • **Reset only selected Ribbon Tab**

   • **Reset all customizations**

Customize user interface fonts

As screen resolutions increase and screen sizes decrease, it gets harder to read on-screen content. It hadn't occurred to me to do anything about it until a Canadian colleague showed me that he had increased the size of his Folder Pane font. You can't modify the Folder Pane font anymore, but you can modify the font of the module content, and of items that meet specific criteria. This has been a great favorite of my onsite training clients, and you might like it too.

You can change the font used in the message list of the Mail module. You can set the fonts for all items, or for items that meet specific criteria.

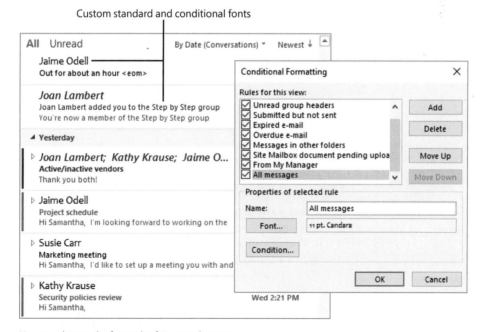

You can change the font color for unread messages

You can also change the fonts of the row and column headings in table-style views.

A custom column heading font

You change the fonts of each module view independently, from the Advanced View Settings dialog box for that view.

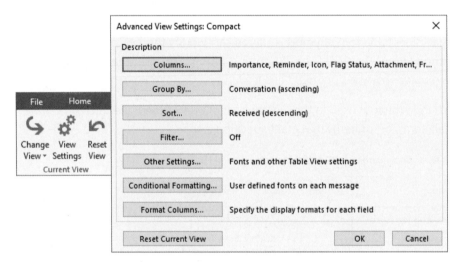

You can change the default fonts for messages and column headings

To change the heading and body fonts for a table view

1. Display the module view that you want to customize.

2. On the **View** tab, in the **Current View** group, click **View Settings** to open the Advanced View Settings dialog box for the current module view.

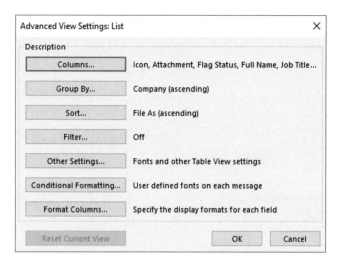

The descriptions give examples for the current module view

3. Click the **Other Settings** button to open the Other Settings dialog box.

The default settings

4. Do either of the following to open the Font dialog box:

    - To change the heading font, click the **Column Font** button.

    - To change the body font, click the **Row Font** button.

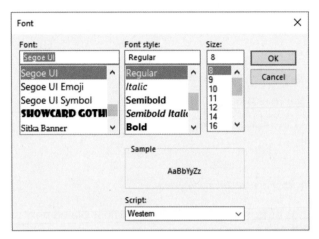

The Font Style and Size options might differ from those in the standard Font dialog box

5. In the **Font** dialog box, set the font, font style, and font size that you want to use for the heading or body text in the current module view. Then click **OK** in each of the three open dialog boxes.

To change the font of all items or items that meet a specific condition

1. Open the **Advanced View Settings** dialog box for the module view you want to modify.

2. Click the **Conditional Formatting** button to open the Conditional Formatting dialog box.

3. Click the **Add** button to create a new rule, named *Untitled*, and activate the **Condition** button.

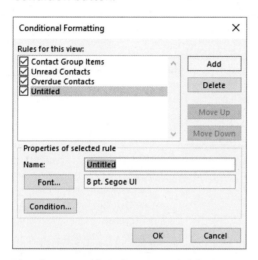

The rules are specific to the current module view

4. Replace the rule name with a descriptive name for your own reference, and then click the **Font** button.

5. In the **Font** dialog box, set the font, font style, and font size that you want to use, and then click **OK.**

6. If you want to apply the font to all items, click **OK** in each of the open dialog boxes and in the message box requesting confirmation that you want to apply the font to all items.

12

7. If you want Outlook to use the font only for items that meet specific criteria, click the **Condition** button to open the Filter dialog box.

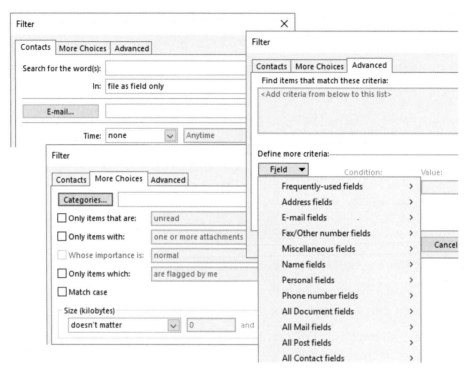

Define the conditions that invoke the formatting rule

8. On the **Contacts**, **More Choices**, and **Advanced** tabs of the dialog box, define the conditions of the rule that applies the selected font formatting. Then click **OK**.

To reset a view to its default settings

1. Open the **Advanced View Settings** dialog box for the module view you want to reset.

2. Click the **Reset Current View** button, click **Yes** in the confirmation message box, and then click **OK** to close the Advanced View Settings dialog box.

Skills review

In this chapter, you learned how to:

- Personalize the Outlook app window
- Customize the Quick Access Toolbar
- Customize the ribbon
- Customize user interface fonts

12

Practice tasks

No practice files are necessary to complete the practice tasks in this chapter.

Personalize the Outlook app window

Start Outlook, display your Inbox, and then perform the following tasks:

1. Configure the Navigation Bar options to display the full-width Navigation Bar with the maximum number of module links, organized in the order that you're most likely to use them.

2. Display the Calendar peek, and pin it to the To-Do Bar. On the **Date Navigator**, click a day next week to display that day's schedule in the peek.

3. Display the People peek, click in the search box, and enter the name of someone you know is in your contact list. When the contact information appears in the peek, right-click it, and then click **Add to Favorites** to add the contact to the People peek.

4. Add the People peek to the To-Do Bar, and then click the name of the person you added in step 3 to display his or her contact information.

5. If necessary, resize the peeks on the To-Do Bar so there is sufficient space for the content of each.

6. Minimize the **Folder Pane**.

7. Temporarily expand the **Folder Pane**, and add a folder to the **Favorites** section at the top of the pane.

8. From the minimized **Folder Pane**, open the folder that you added to the **Favorites** section in step 7.

9. Display the **Reading Pane** on the right side of the window, and then on the bottom. Consider circumstances under which each location might be a good choice.

10. Configure the Navigation Bar, To-Do Bar, **Folder Pane**, favorite folders, and **Reading Pane** to suit the way you work.

Customize the Quick Access Toolbar

Display your Outlook Inbox, and then perform the following tasks:

1. Move the Quick Access Toolbar below the ribbon. Consider the merits of this location versus the original location.

2. From the **Customize Quick Access Toolbar** menu, add the **Empty Deleted Items** command to the Quick Access Toolbar.

3. Display the Calendar module. Notice that the Quick Access Toolbar is the same as in the Mail module because you're still in the app window.

4. From the **Home** tab of the ribbon, add the following commands to the Quick Access Toolbar:

   - From the **New** group, add the **New Meeting** command.

   - From the **Options** group, add the **Show As** command.

   Notice that the New Meeting command is presented on the Quick Access Toolbar as a button, and the Show As command as a list, just as they are on the ribbon.

5. Point to the commands you added to the Quick Access Toolbar and then to the same commands on the **Home** tab. Notice that ScreenTips for commands on the Quick Access Toolbar are identical to those for commands on the ribbon.

6. Display the People module. From the **New** group on the **Home** tab, add the **New Contact** command to the Quick Access Toolbar.

7. Display the **Quick Access Toolbar** page of the **Outlook Options** dialog box, and then do the following:

   - In the **Choose commands from** list, click **Commands Not in the Ribbon**.

   - From the **Choose commands from** pane, add the **Options** button to the Quick Access Toolbar.

   - In the **Customize Quick Access Toolbar** pane, move the **New Contact** command above the New Meeting command.

   - Insert separators before and after the **New** commands.

   - Insert two separators before the **Empty Deleted Items** command (the first command you added to the default toolbar).

8. Close the **Outlook Options** dialog box and observe your customized Quick Access Toolbar. Note the way that a single separator sets off commands, and the way that a double separator sets off commands.

9. Redisplay the **Quick Access Toolbar** page of the **Outlook Options** dialog box.

10. Reset the Quick Access Toolbar to its default configuration, and then close the dialog box. Notice that resetting the Quick Access Toolbar does not change its location.

Customize the ribbon

Display any Outlook module, and then perform the following tasks:

1. Display the **Customize Ribbon** page of the **Outlook Options** dialog box.

2. Remove the **Send/Receive** tab from the ribbon, and add the **Developer** tab (if it isn't already shown).

3. Create a custom tab and name it MyShortcuts.

4. Move the **MyShortcuts** tab to the top of the right pane so that it will be the leftmost optional ribbon tab (immediately to the right of the File tab).

5. Change the name of the custom group on the **MyShortcuts** tab to Backstage, and select an icon to represent the group.

6. Create another custom group on the **MyShortcuts** tab. Name the group New Items, and select an icon to represent the group.

7. In the **Choose commands from** pane, display the commands from the File tab, and add the **Account Settings** and **Automatic Replies** commands from the pane to the **Backstage** group. Then display commands that aren't in the ribbon, and add the **New Office Document** and **New Recurring Appointment** commands from the pane to the **New Items** group.

8. Close the **Outlook Options** dialog box and display your custom tab. Click each of the commands to observe what it does. Notice that you can now access all these areas of the app with one click.

9. Change the width of the app window to collapse at least one custom group, and verify that the group button displays the icon you selected.

10. Restore the app window to its original width and redisplay the **Customize Ribbon** page of the **Outlook Options** dialog box.

11. Reset the ribbon to its default configuration, and then close the dialog box.

Customize user interface fonts

Display the Tasks module in Detail view, and then perform the following tasks:

1. Change the column heading and body fonts to fonts of your choice, and observe the effect.

2. Switch to To-Do List view, and notice that the fonts in this view of the module were not affected.

3. Display the Mail module in Compact view.

4. Change the default font for all items to a font of your choice.

5. Create a conditional formatting rule to format the message list font of messages that were sent only to you in a different color. Save the changes and observe the effects.

6. Locate a message that has the conditional formatting you created in step 6. Open the message and notice that the module view rule doesn't affect the font in the message window.

7. Reset the Compact view of the Mail module and the Detail view of the Tasks module to their default settings.

Customize Outlook options

Outlook 2016 is a high-powered information management system. Microsoft has set up the app to function in a way that will be of the most use to the most people, but the fact is that each of us has different working styles and different needs for our working environment.

You can configure Outlook functionality to make it the most efficient platform for the way you work. You can modify many aspects of the way Outlook handles messages, calendar items, contact records, and general operations. You make these changes from the Outlook Options dialog box. Many of the options available in the Outlook Options dialog box are discussed in context in other chapters in this book. This chapter includes information about all the available options, including a few that power users of Outlook might find particularly useful to modify.

This chapter guides you through procedures related to configuring general Office and Outlook options; configuring options for the Mail, Calendar, People, and Tasks modules; configuring search, language, and advanced options; and managing add-ins and security options.

In this chapter

- Configure general Office and Outlook options
- Configure message options
- Configure calendar options
- Configure contact and task options
- Configure search and language options
- Configure advanced options
- Manage add-ins and security options

Practice files

No practice files are necessary to complete the practice tasks in this chapter.

About the Outlook Options dialog box

The options discussed in this chapter are available in the Outlook Options dialog box, which you open from the Backstage view. Each Office app has its own Options dialog box. Because so many options are available for each app and for Office, they are divided among pages (and in some cases, additional dialog boxes that you open from the pages). The pages are represented by page tabs in the left pane of the Outlook Options dialog box.

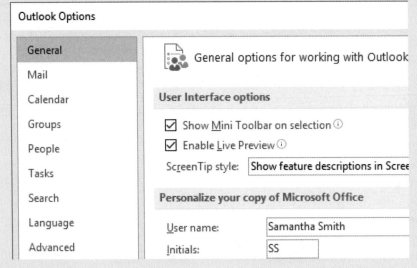

Shading indicates the active page tab

The left pane of the Outlook Options dialog box is divided into three sections:

- The first section contains the General, Mail, Calendar, Groups, People, Tasks, Search, Language, and Advanced page tabs. These are the pages of options that Outlook users will most commonly make changes to when customizing the app functionality.

- The second section contains the Customize Ribbon and Quick Access Toolbar page tabs. These are the pages on which you customize the presentation of commands in the user interface.

- The third section contains the Add-ins and Trust Center page tabs. These pages are access points for higher-level customizations that can affect the security of your computer, and are not often necessary to modify.

SEE ALSO This chapter discusses the options on the pages in the first and third sections of the Outlook Options dialog box. For information about customizing the ribbon and Quick Access Toolbar, see Chapter 12, "Manage window elements."

A brief description of the page content appears at the top of each page. Each page is further divided into sections of related options. The General page contains information that is shared among the Office apps. Other pages contain options that are specific to the app or to the file you're working in.

The images in this chapter depict the default selections for each option. Many options have only on/off settings as indicated by a selected or cleared check box. Options that have settings other than on or off are described in the content that precedes or follows the image.

13

Configure general Office and Outlook options

Options that affect the user interface and startup behavior of Outlook are available from the General page of the Outlook Options dialog box.

General options for working with Outlook

The options in the User Interface Options and Personalize sections of the General page are shared among all the Office apps that are installed on the computer you're working on, and include the following:

- You can turn off the Mini Toolbar, which hosts common formatting commands and appears by default when you select content.

- You can turn off the Live Preview feature if you find it distracting to have content formatting change when the pointer passes over a formatting command.

- You can minimize or turn off the display of ScreenTips when you point to buttons.

- You can specify the user name and initials you want to accompany your comments and tracked changes, and override the display of information from the account that is associated with your installation of Office.

- You can choose the background graphics and color scheme (Office theme) that you want to use for all the Office apps. You can also set these on the Account page of the Backstage view.

> **TIP** You can't set individual user information, backgrounds, or themes for individual Office apps running under the same user profile. For information about Office backgrounds and themes, see "Manage Office and Outlook settings" in Chapter 1, "Outlook 2016 basics."

In addition to these shared options, you can set Outlook as the default app for managing your email, calendar, and contacts. This overrides the Mail and Calendar apps that are built in to Windows.

To open the Outlook Options dialog box

1. Click the **File** tab to display the Backstage view.
2. In the left pane, click **Options**.

To display a specific page of the Outlook Options dialog box

1. Open the **Outlook Options** dialog box.
2. In the left pane, click the tab of the page that you want to display.

To close the Outlook Options dialog box

1. Do either of the following:
   - To commit to any changes, click **OK**.
   - To cancel any changes, click **Cancel** or click the **Close** button (**X**) in the upper-right corner of the dialog box.

To enable or disable the Mini Toolbar

1. Open the **Outlook Options** dialog box, and display the **General** page.
2. In the **User Interface options** section, select or clear the **Show Mini Toolbar on selection** check box.

13

To enable or disable the Live Preview feature

1. Display the **General** page of the **Outlook Options** dialog box.

2. In the **User Interface options** section, select or clear the **Enable Live Preview** check box.

To control the display of ScreenTips

1. Display the **General** page of the **Outlook Options** dialog box.

2. In the **User Interface options** section, display the **ScreenTip style** list, and then click any of the following:

   - **Show feature descriptions in ScreenTips**
   - **Don't show feature descriptions in ScreenTips**
   - **Don't show ScreenTips**

To change the user identification that appears in comments and tracked changes

 IMPORTANT The User Name and Initials settings are shared by all the Office apps, so changing them in any one app immediately changes them in all the apps.

1. Display the **General** page of the **Outlook Options** dialog box.

2. In the **Personalize your copy of Microsoft Office** section, do the following:

   - In the **User name** and **Initials** boxes, enter the information you want to use.
   - Select the **Always use these values regardless of sign in to Office** check box.

Configure message options

Many of the settings that users commonly modify are available on the Mail page of the Outlook Options dialog box. These include settings for composing original messages and responses; receiving and reading messages; cleaning up conversations; saving, sending, and tracking messages; and default message format options.

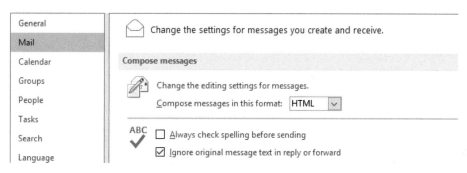

Most of the useful options are on the Mail page

Outlook includes several options you can use to manage your email most effectively. To avoid losing your work, you can choose to have Outlook save messages you have created but not yet sent. When new messages arrive, you can choose to have Outlook alert you by playing a sound, briefly changing the pointer to an envelope icon, showing an envelope icon in the notification area, or any combination of these effects. You can also set default options for sending a message. For example, if you are concerned about privacy, you might choose to set the sensitivity of all new messages to Private.

The options on the Mail page are divided into 11 sections. Because this is where you're likely to make most of your changes, we'll take a look at each section.

13

Compose messages

The Compose Messages section of the Mail page includes options for changing the behavior of Outlook while you're creating a new message. These options control the way Outlook composes and proofs text; your email signatures; and your default fonts, stationery, and email themes.

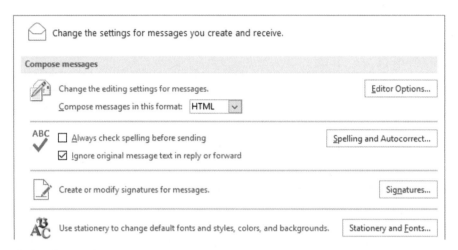

Options for outgoing messages

Clicking either Editor Options or Spelling And Autocorrect in the Compose Messages section displays the Proofing page of the Editor Options dialog box. From the Proofing page, you can set AutoCorrect options to specify how Outlook will correct and format the content of your messages as you type them, and customize the settings for checking spelling and grammar. Because Outlook uses Word as its text editor, these options are the same as those in Word.

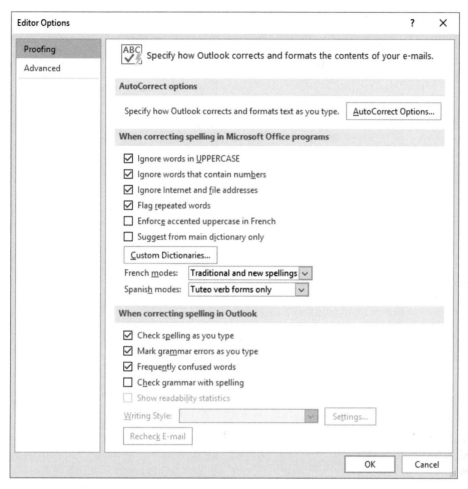

The proofing options are similar to those in Word

More extensive editing options are available on the Advanced page of the Editor Options dialog box.

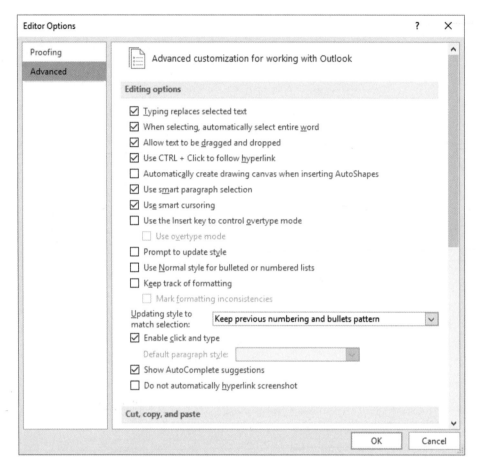

Options that control default formatting

The Advanced page of the Editor Options dialog box is divided into multiple sections in which you can very specifically control the way Outlook works with text:

- In the Editing Options section of this page, you can turn on or off advanced editing features, such as how Outlook selects and moves text, whether to track formatting changes, and whether Overtype mode is available.

- In the Cut, Copy, And Paste section, you can specify whether Outlook will apply source or destination formatting to text copied within a message, between messages, and from other apps. You can also set options for smart cut and paste (whether to automatically add and remove spaces as needed) and the Paste Options button (whether it appears after a paste operation).

- In the Display section, you can set whether measurements are shown in inches, centimeters, millimeters, points, or picas; whether pixels are shown for HTML features; whether ScreenTips display keyboard shortcuts; and whether character positioning is optimized for layout rather than readability.

To change the default message format

1. Display the **Mail** page of the **Outlook Options** dialog box.

2. In the **Compose messages** section, expand the **Compose messages in this format** list, and then click **HTML**, **Rich Text**, or **Plain Text**.

> **SEE ALSO** For information about email signatures, stationery, and fonts, see "Personalize default message formatting" in Chapter 4, "Enhance message content." For information about editing options, see *Microsoft Word 2016 Step by Step*, by Joan Lambert (Microsoft Press, 2015).

Outlook panes

The Outlook Panes section of the Mail page includes only the Reading Pane button, which opens the Reading Pane dialog box. (This same dialog box is available with the Navigation Pane dialog box in the Outlook Panes section of the Advanced page of the Outlook Options dialog box.)

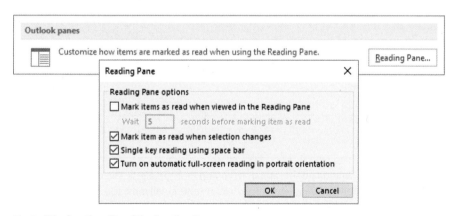

Control the functionality of the Reading Pane

You can display the Reading Pane in any Outlook module. It is most useful in the Mail module, of course, but can also come in handy in certain views of other modules.

By default, Outlook does not mark a message as read when you preview it in the Reading Pane, but does so when you select another message. You can change these default settings by selecting or clearing the Mark Items As Read When Viewed In The Reading Pane and Mark Item As Read When Selection Changes check boxes in the Reading Pane dialog box.

With the Single Key Reading feature, which is turned on by default, you can move up or down in the Reading Pane one page at a time by pressing the Spacebar. When you reach the end of a message, pressing the Spacebar again displays the first page of the next message. If you find it distracting, you can turn it off by clearing the Single Key Reading Using Space Bar check box in the Reading Pane dialog box.

 SEE ALSO For information about working in the Reading Pane, see "Display messages and message attachments" in Chapter 3, "Send and receive email messages."

Message arrival

The Message Arrival section of the Mail page includes options for controlling the way Outlook notifies you of an incoming message.

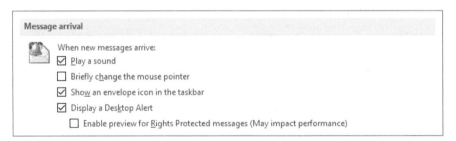

Message arrival options

 SEE ALSO For information about taskbar icons and desktop alerts, see the sidebar "New mail notifications" in Chapter 3, "Send and receive email messages."

Conversation Clean Up

The Conversation Clean Up section of the Mail page includes options for the Clean Up command. If you don't want the command to delete redundant messages, you can specify a folder in which the command will place the redundant messages. (You could then review the contents of the folder and delete the redundant messages after verifying that they are, in fact, redundant.) You can also specify the types of messages that the Clean Up Conversation command moves and keeps.

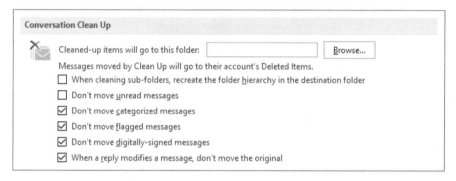

Conversation Clean Up options

> 🔍 **SEE ALSO** For information about managing conversations, see "Display and manage conversations" in Chapter 6, "Organize your Inbox."

Replies and forwards

The Replies And Forwards section of the Mail page includes options for managing the content of response messages. You can choose to close the original message window when you respond to a message, to insert your name or some other identifier before your response text, and whether and how to include original message text in a response.

13

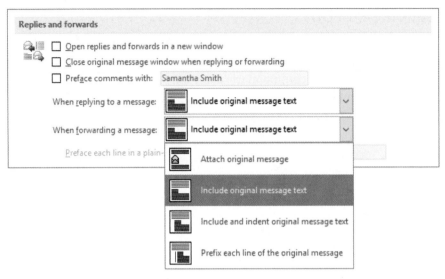

Options for replying to and forwarding messages

When forwarding a message, you can attach the original message (as a separate message) or include the original message text in your response and optionally indent it or indent it and insert a vertical line to the left of the original message text block. When replying to a message, you have all the same options and additionally can choose to not include the original message text in your response.

 SEE ALSO For information about replying to and forwarding messages, see "Respond to messages" in Chapter 3, "Send and receive email messages."

To configure the inclusion of original message content in a message reply

1. Display the **Mail** page of the **Outlook Options** dialog box.

2. In the **Replies and forwards** section, expand the **When replying to a message** list, and then click any of the following:

   - **Do not include original message**

   - **Attach original message**

   - **Include original message text**

   - **Include and indent original message text**

   - **Prefix each line of the original message**

3. If you choose Prefix Each Line Of The Original Message, the Preface Each Line In A Plain-Text Message With box becomes active. Enter the character or characters you want to prepend to each line of the original message (include a space after the character for readability).

To configure the inclusion of original message content in a forwarded message

1. Display the **Mail** page of the **Outlook Options** dialog box.

2. In the **Replies and forwards** section, expand the **When forwarding a message** list, and then click any of the following:

   - **Attach original message**

   - **Include original message text**

   - **Include and indent original message text**

   - **Prefix each line of the original message**

3. If you choose Prefix Each Line Of The Original Message, the Preface Each Line In A Plain-Text Message with box becomes active. Enter the character or characters you want to prepend to each line of the original message (include a space after the character for readability).

Save messages

The Save Messages section of the Mail page includes options for saving temporary copies of messages that have not yet been sent, message replies from a location other than the Inbox, the original versions of messages you have forwarded, and messages you have sent.

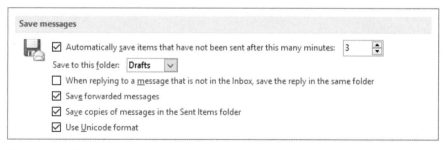

Options for saving messages

By default, Outlook saves the first draft of a message three minutes after you begin composing the message, and resaves the message every three minutes thereafter. You can choose to save message drafts as frequently as once per minute or as infrequently as every 99 minutes, or choose to turn off the message draft saving feature.

The default location for saved message drafts is the Drafts folder, which is a top-level mailbox folder that appears in the Folder Pane at the same level as your Inbox. You can alternatively save message drafts in your Inbox, in the Sent Items folder, or in the Outbox.

To change how frequently Outlook saves message drafts

1. Display the **Mail** page of the **Outlook Options** dialog box.

2. In the **Save messages** section, do either of the following:

   - To save drafts more or less often, in the **Automatically save items that have not been sent** box, enter or select the number of minutes.

   - To turn off the automatic saving of message drafts, clear the **Automatically save items that have not been sent** check box.

To change the folder in which Outlook saves message drafts

1. Display the **Mail** page of the **Outlook Options** dialog box.

2. In the **Save messages** section, expand the **Save to this folder** list, and then click any of the following:

   - **Drafts**

   - **Inbox**

   - **Sent Mail**

   - **Outbox**

 SEE ALSO For more information about message drafts, see "Create and send messages" in Chapter 3, "Send and receive email messages."

Send messages

The Send Messages section of the Mail page includes options for composing and sending messages, in addition to options for resolving names against known email addresses, handling meeting requests after you respond, and managing the Auto-Complete List.

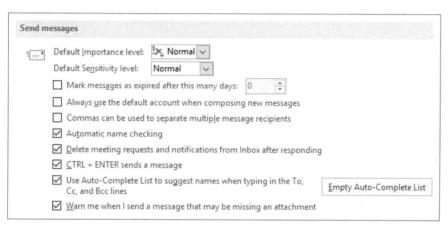

Message sending options

An important option to note in this section is the Commas Can Be Used To Separate Multiple Message Recipients option. Until you select this check box, you must separate email addresses in the To, Cc, and Bcc boxes by using semicolons.

> **SEE ALSO** For information about importance and sensitivity level settings, see "Change message settings and delivery options" in Chapter 4, "Enhance message content."

To send messages to multiple recipient addresses separated by commas

1. Display the **Mail** page of the **Outlook Options** dialog box.

2. In the **Send messages** section, select the **Commas can be used to separate multiple message recipients** check box.

To modify the display of matching recipients

1. Display the **Mail** page of the **Outlook Options** dialog box.

2. In the **Send messages** section, do either of the following:

   - To reset the list of suggestions, click the **Empty Auto-Complete List** button.

   - To stop Outlook from suggesting recipients, clear the **Use Auto-Complete List to suggest names when typing in the To, Cc, and Bcc lines** check box.

MailTips

From the MailTips section of the Mail page, you can control the display of MailTips, which are server-generated messages that appear in the header of a message composition window to notify you of various conditions that apply to an outgoing message. (MailTips are available only for Microsoft Exchange Server accounts.)

MailTips are an extremely useful feature that are designed to alert you to situations that might affect whether you want to send a message. For example, MailTips can warn you when you're composing a message to a sender who is currently out of the office, has a full mailbox, or is external to your organization. MailTips can also alert you when you're composing a message to a large distribution group, when a message is too large for you to send or for the recipient to receive, and when you reply to all recipients of a message that you were Bcc'd on.

MailTips options

Your Exchange administrator can turn specific MailTips on and off, and can also configure custom MailTips for your organization. MailTips are displayed for your information only; they don't stop you from sending an email message, but they do let you know if the message might not reach the intended recipient (or might reach more recipients than you intend).

> **TIP** Policy Tips are an Exchange Server feature designed to prevent you from sending messages that violate your company's security policies. For example, Policy Tips can prevent you from forwarding messages that contain bank account numbers, credit card numbers, driver's license numbers, or taxpayer identification numbers to external recipients. Your Exchange administrator can configure Policy Tips that notify you of potentially sensitive information in an outgoing message, require you to provide a business justification for sending the message, or prevent you from sending the message. Policy Tips are managed by your Exchange administrator and can't be configured from within Outlook.

MailTips settings are specific to each Exchange account that you have configured Outlook to connect to. You set your MailTips preferences for each account by selecting that account in the Apply To This Account list at the top of the dialog box.

Tracking

The Tracking section of the Mail page includes options for requesting notifications when a message that you send is delivered to a recipient and when a message is marked by the recipient as read; and options for processing notification requests attached to messages that you receive. This section also includes options for processing responses you receive to meeting requests and voting requests that you send.

Tracking

Delivery and read receipts help provide confirmation that messages were successfully received. Not all e-mail servers and applications support sending receipts.

For all messages sent, request:

☐ Delivery receipt confirming the message was delivered to the recipient's e-mail server

☐ Read receipt confirming the recipient viewed the message

For any message received that includes a read receipt request:

○ Always send a read receipt

○ Never send a read receipt

◉ Ask each time whether to send a read receipt

☑ Automatically process meeting requests and responses to meeting requests and polls

☑ Automatically update original sent item with receipt information

☐ Update tracking information, and then delete responses that don't contain comments

☐ After updating tracking information, move receipt to:　[🗑 Deleted Items]　[Browse...]

Message tracking options

13

Delivery receipts can be a useful tool when you send an important message and need to know whether it's reached its intended recipient. (However, not all types of email accounts support all types of receipts.) When you receive a message that has a read receipt request attached, Outlook prompts you to confirm whether you want to send a read receipt. You can make this choice for each individual message or select the Never Send A Read Receipt option to refuse all read receipt requests.

 TIP Be cautious when approving read receipt requests, because some mass-mailing companies use these to determine whether an email address is active.

Message format

The Message Format section of the Mail page includes options for specifying how Outlook displays your message content on the screen and the format in which Outlook sends messages outside of your organization.

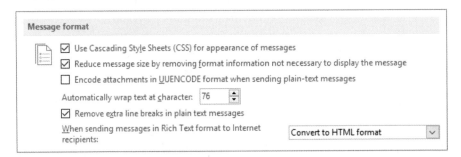

Message format options

It's unlikely that you'll need to change any of these options, but they are available in the event that you want to.

Other

The Other section of the Mail page includes options for displaying the Paste Options button, moving among open messages, and expanding conversations when navigating through the Inbox by using the keyboard. You can also specify what occurs when you move or delete an open item. Options include opening the previous or next item in the folder, or returning to the folder without opening another item.

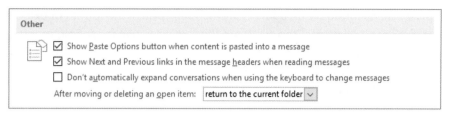

Options in the Other section

Configure calendar options

Options on the Calendar page control settings for displaying and managing Outlook calendars, and for scheduling appointments and resources.

Many Outlook users will want to configure the days and times that constitute the work week. You do this in the Work Time section of the Calendar page. The times you specify as work hours (on the days you specify as work days) are available in Outlook for other users to schedule meetings with you. Specifying the first day of your work week controls the Work Week view of the calendar.

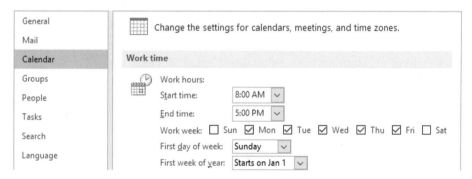

You can select all seven days as work days if necessary

SEE ALSO For information about specifying your work days and first day of the work week, see "Define your available time" in Chapter 10, "Manage your calendar."

In the Calendar Options section, you can set the default reminder time for new appointments and meetings, control the Propose New Times settings, add the holidays of many countries or regions and religions to your calendar, specify the level of calendar detail available to co-workers (as a group and individually) when they check your free/busy status, configure an additional calendar, control the format of external meeting requests, and control the display of the reminder icon for appointments and meetings.

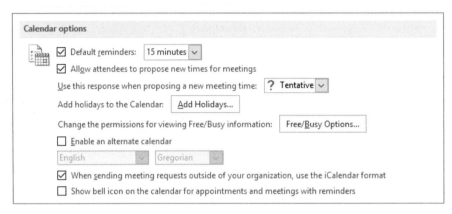

Options for Calendar content and items

> **SEE ALSO** For information about managing holidays on the calendar, see the sidebar "Add holidays to your calendar" in Chapter 9, "Manage scheduling."

The Display Options section includes options for configuring the appearance and functionality of calendars. Of note in this section are the limits for the minimum and maximum number of calendars that can be displayed in Schedule view.

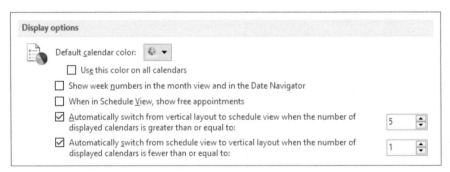

Calendar display options

The Time Zone section includes options for displaying a label at the top of the time column in Day view, Work Week view, and Week view, and for managing a second time zone.

Calendar time zone options

 SEE ALSO For information about adding and swapping time zones, see "Configure time zones" in Chapter 10, "Manage your calendar."

The Scheduling Assistant section of the Calendar page includes options for managing the display of information on the Scheduling Assistant page of a meeting window. (The Scheduling Assistant is available only for Exchange accounts.)

In the Automatic Accept Or Decline section, you can click the Auto Accept/Decline button, which opens a dialog box in which you can configure Outlook to process meeting requests without your input.

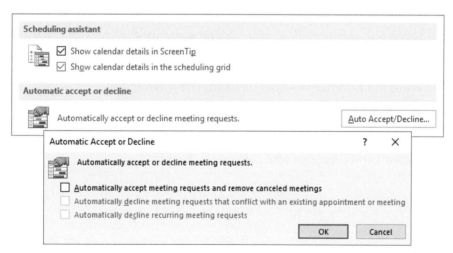

When you choose to automatically accept meeting requests, you can also choose the types of meeting requests to decline

 SEE ALSO For information about using the Scheduling Assistant, see "Schedule and change meetings" in Chapter 9, "Manage scheduling."

13

In the Weather section, you can control whether the calendar header displays the Weather Bar, and whether it shows temperatures in Celsius or in Fahrenheit.

You configure the Weather Bar location from the Calendar module

To modify the default display of reminders

1. Display the **Calendar** page of the **Outlook Options** dialog box.

2. In the **Calendar options** section, do either of the following:

    - To change the default reminder time, expand the **Default reminders** list, and then click an option from **0 minutes** to **2 weeks**.

    - To have reminders off by default, clear the **Default reminders** check box.

To remove the Propose New Time option from meeting requests

1. Display the **Calendar** page of the **Outlook Options** dialog box.

2. In the **Calendar options** section, clear the **Allow attendees to propose new times for meetings** check box.

To display a visual indicator for calendar items that have reminders

1. Display the **Calendar** page of the **Outlook Options** dialog box.

2. In the **Calendar options** section, select the **Show bell icon on the calendar for appointments and meetings with reminders** check box.

Configure contact and task options

The Groups, People, and Tasks pages of the Outlook Options dialog box each have only a few simple options.

Group options

Outlook 2016 supports Office 365 Groups, which are shared workspaces that contain community mailboxes, calendars, document libraries, and notebooks. If your organization uses Office 365, administrators can set up public or private Office 365 Groups. Group members can subscribe to receive individual copies of messages sent to the group, or keep their inboxes tidy by monitoring the messages received by the group in a separate node of the Folder Pane.

From the Groups page of the Outlook Options dialog box, you can control the display of group headers in Outlook.

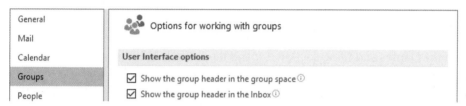

Options for the display of Office 365 Groups

Contact options

Options on the People page control settings for creating and organizing contact records, displaying a second contact index (in Arabic, Cyrillic, Greek, Thai, or Vietnamese), and displaying pictures in Outlook items and in the People peek.

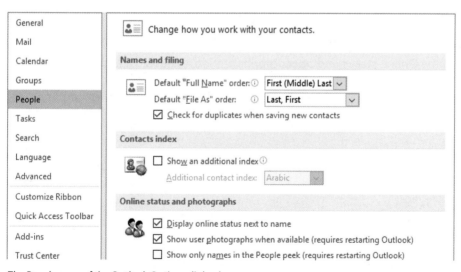

The People page of the Outlook Options dialog box

13

To specify the format of full names in contact records

1. Display the **People** page of the **Outlook Options** dialog box.

2. In the **Names and filing** section, expand the **Default "Full Name" order** list, and then click one of the following:

   - **First (Middle) Last**

   - **Last First**

   - **First Last1 Last2**

To specify the format of the filing order of contact records

1. Display the **People** page of the **Outlook Options** dialog box.

2. In the **Names and filing** section, expand the **Default "File As" order** list, and then click one of the following:

   - **Last, First**

   - **First Last**

   - **Company**

   - **Last, First (Company)**

   - **Company (Last, First)**

To control the display of social network photos in messages and contact records

1. Display the **People** page of the **Outlook Options** dialog box.

2. In the **Online status and photographs** section, select or clear the **Show user photographs when available** check box.

3. After you close the Outlook Options dialog box, restart Outlook to effect the change.

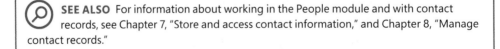

SEE ALSO For information about working in the People module and with contact records, see Chapter 7, "Store and access contact information," and Chapter 8, "Manage contact records."

Task options

Options on the Tasks page control settings for setting a task reminder time, managing assigned tasks, displaying overdue and completed tasks, and setting the default due date for flagged items. In addition, you can allocate a specific number of hours per day and per week that are available for working on tasks.

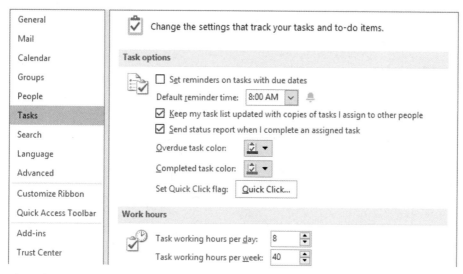

The Tasks page of the Outlook Options dialog box

 SEE ALSO For information about managing task items, see Chapter 11, "Track tasks."

Configure search and language options

13

Options on the Search page control the scope of standard searches and the way Outlook displays search results.

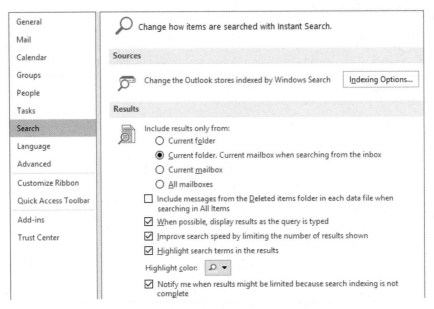

The Search page of the Outlook Options dialog box

Clicking the Indexing Options button in the Sources section of the Search page displays options for controlling the indexing scope.

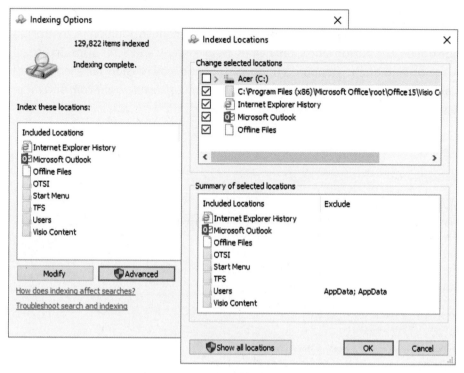

You can modify the scope of the index to exclude specific folders and apps

 TIP If you experience significant trouble with the Outlook search feature, you might find that you need to rebuild the index. You can do so from the Advanced Options dialog box, which requires administrator permission.

 SEE ALSO For information about Outlook search, see "Quickly locate contact information" in Chapter 8, "Manage contact records."

13

Options on the Language page control the dictionaries that are used by Outlook when it checks the spelling and grammar of message content, in addition to controlling language options for button labels, tab names, Help content, and ScreenTips. To use a language other than the standard Windows language, you must install a language pack. Language packs are available for download from *office.microsoft.com* and might also be supplied to you through Windows Update.

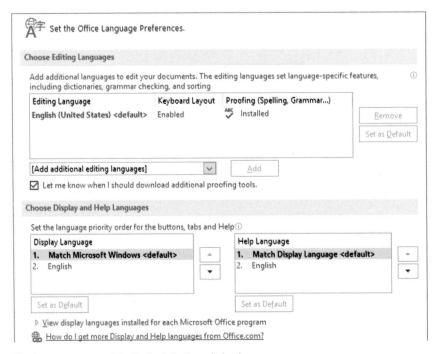

The Language page of the Outlook Options dialog box

 SEE ALSO For information about installing language packs, see *Microsoft Word 2016 Step by Step*, by Joan Lambert (Microsoft Press, 2015).

Configure advanced options

Options on the Advanced page control settings for customizing a wide variety of standard Outlook actions and responses. All the settings that didn't fit into another category are available on this page, and that includes many of the settings that you will likely want to configure.

The Outlook Panes section of the Advanced page includes options for customizing the Navigation Bar and Reading Pane. The same Reading Pane dialog box is available in the Outlook Panes section of the Mail page of the Outlook Options dialog box.

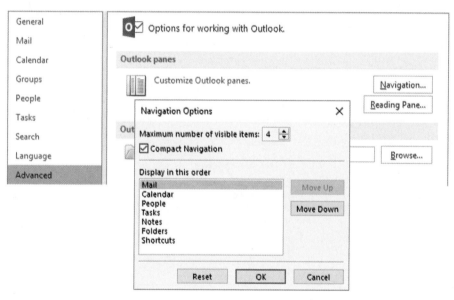

Customize the appearance and content of the Navigation Bar

13

The Outlook Start And Exit section includes options for setting the default folder (the folder you first view when you start Outlook) and for emptying the Deleted Items folders (of all configured accounts) when you exit Outlook. Note that this option is not turned on by default. If you need to manage the size of your mailbox, selecting this option is a good starting point.

From the AutoArchive section, you can open the AutoArchive dialog box. In this dialog box, you can configure automatic archival operations separate from those that might be managed by your organization's Exchange administrator. The AutoArchive feature is turned off by default.

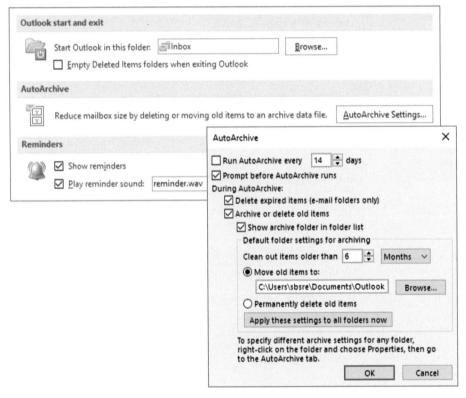

You can specify item archiving options and upcoming appointment reminder options

From the Reminders section, you can configure the display of task reminders and the accompanying audio signal.

From the Export section of the Advanced page, you can start the Import And Export wizard that you can use to move information between Outlook and other apps.

 SEE ALSO For information about the Import And Export wizard, see "Import and export contact records" in Chapter 8, "Manage contact records."

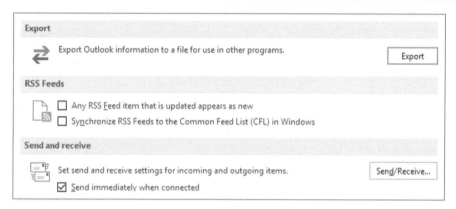

Options for exporting, receiving, and sending information

You can use Outlook 2016 as an RSS feed reader; feeds that you subscribe to appear in the RSS Feeds folder. In the RSS Feeds section of the Advanced page, you can configure settings for the display and synchronization of RSS feeds.

From the Send And Receive section of the Advanced page, you can configure options for synchronizing Outlook with email servers when online and offline.

The Developers, International Options, and Display sections of the Advanced page include options that will probably be used only by advanced Outlook users. The International Options section includes options for using English message flags and headers when working in another language, setting encoding for outgoing messages

13

and business cards, managing international domain names in email addresses, and combining non-Latin and English characters in email messages and addresses.

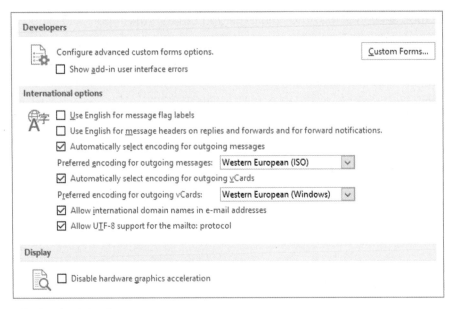

Infrequently used options

The Other section of the Advanced page includes useful options for setting the default color category and confirming the permanent deletion of items. From this section, you can also import group schedules that you created in a previous version of Outlook.

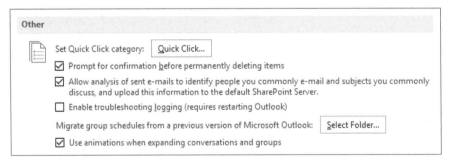

Options that don't fit into other categories

To automatically empty your Deleted Items folders

1. Display the **Advanced** page of the **Outlook Options** dialog box.

2. In the **Outlook start and exit** section, select the **Empty Deleted Items folders when exiting Outlook** check box.

To automatically archive items

1. Display the **Advanced** page of the **Outlook Options** dialog box.

2. In the **AutoArchive** section, click the **AutoArchive Settings** button.

3. In the **AutoArchive** dialog box, select the **Run AutoArchive every** check box, and then in the adjacent box, enter or select the frequency.

4. In the **During AutoArchive** section, review the options and configure the settings to meet your needs. Then click **OK**.

Manage add-ins and security options

The final section of pages in the Outlook Options dialog box contains the settings that you should definitely think carefully about before changing, because they can affect the security of your system.

Manage add-ins

Add-ins are utilities that add specialized functionality to an app but aren't full-fledged apps themselves. Outlook uses only COM add-ins (which use the Component Object Model).

There are several sources of add-ins:

- You can purchase add-ins from third-party vendors; for example, you can purchase an add-in that allows you to assign keyboard shortcuts to Outlook commands that don't already have them.

- You can download free add-ins from the Microsoft website or other websites.

- When installing a third-party app, it might install an add-in that allows it to interact with Microsoft Office 2016 apps.

> **TIP** Be careful when downloading add-ins from websites other than those you know and trust. Add-ins are executable files that can easily be used to spread viruses and otherwise wreak havoc on your computer. For this reason, default settings in the Trust Center intervene when you attempt to download or run add-ins.

13

Information about the add-ins that are installed on your computer, and access to manage them, is available from the Add-ins page of the Outlook Options dialog box.

The Add-ins page displays installed and disabled add-ins

Each type of add-in has its own management interface. You can add and remove add-ins, turn off installed add-ins, and enable add-ins that have been disabled.

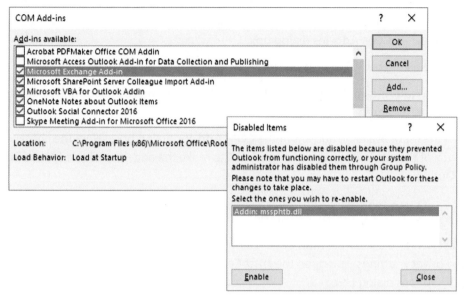

Display and manage active and disabled add-ins

Many add-ins install themselves, but to use some add-ins, you must first install them on your computer and then load them into your computer's memory.

To managed installed COM add-ins

1. Display the **Add-Ins** page of the **Outlook Options** dialog box.

2. In the **Manage** list at the bottom of the page, click **COM Add-ins**. Then click the adjacent **Go** button.

3. In the **COM Add-ins** dialog box, do any of the following, and then click **OK**:

   - To enable an add-in, select its check box.

   - To disable an add-in, clear its check box.

   - To remove an add-in, click the add-in name, and then click **Remove**.

To install a COM add-in

1. Display the **COM Add-ins** dialog box.

2. In the dialog box, click **Add** or **Add New**.

3. In the **Add Add-in** dialog box, navigate to the folder where the add-in you want to install is stored, and double-click its name.

4. In the list of available add-ins in the **COM Add-ins** dialog box, select the check box of the new add-in, and then click **OK** to make the add-in available for use in Outlook.

Configure Trust Center options

The Trust Center is a separate multipage dialog box in which you can configure security and privacy settings. You open the Trust Center from the Trust Center page of the Outlook Options dialog box.

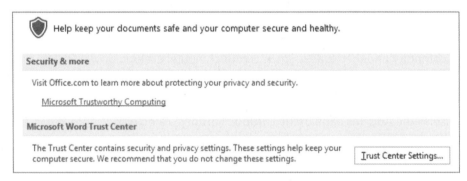

Continue at your own risk

The Trust Center settings aren't exposed directly on the page; you must click a button next to a warning informing you that you shouldn't change any of the settings. It's certainly true that if you don't take care when modifying the Trust Center settings, you could expose Outlook, your computer, and your network to malicious software. It's more common to modify these settings in Word than in Outlook, but review the available settings so you can evaluate whether any of them would be appropriate to change in your specific situation.

The Trust Center has the following seven pages of options that you can configure:

- Trusted Publishers

- Privacy Options

- Email Security

- Attachment Handling

- Automatic Download

- Macro Settings

- Programmatic Access

When you first open the Trust Center, the Automatic Download page is active. As in the Outlook Options dialog box, you click a page tab name in the left pane to display that page in the right pane.

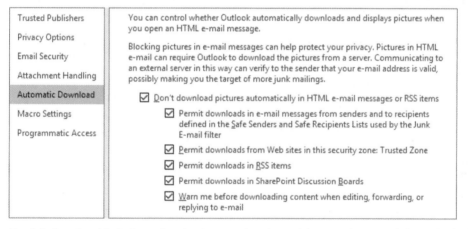

The default settings block picture downloads to guard against web beacons that report information back to the sender

Most pages display options that are very specific to the page name. When you're working in Outlook, some circumstances will send you directly to this dialog box—for example, if you open a file that contains macros, and then click the info bar to enable them, Outlook takes you to the Macro Settings page.

13

Some, but not all, of the Trust Center pages include buttons that you can click to reset that set of options to the defaults, so take care when making changes; if you're uncertain whether you should invoke a change, click Cancel to close the Trust Center without committing to the changes.

As with options in the Outlook Options dialog box, you should take the time to familiarize yourself with the Trust Center settings so you know what changes it is possible to make, in the event that it is appropriate to do so in your computing environment.

To open the Trust Center

1. In the left pane of the **Outlook Options** dialog box, click the **Trust Center** page tab.

2. On the **Trust Center** page, click the **Trust Center Settings** button.

Skills review

In this chapter, you learned how to:

- Configure general Office and Outlook options

- Configure message options

- Configure calendar options

- Configure contact and task options

- Configure search and language options

- Configure advanced options

- Manage add-ins and security options

Practice tasks

No practice files are necessary to complete the practice tasks in this chapter.

Configure Outlook options (all topics)

Start Outlook, and then perform the following tasks:

1. Open the **Outlook Options** dialog box.

2. Explore each page of the dialog box.

3. On the **General**, **Mail**, **Calendar**, **Groups**, **People**, **Tasks**, **Search**, **Language**, and **Advanced** pages, do the following:

   - Notice the sections and the options in each section.

   - Note the options that apply only to the current file.

   - Modify the options on the page as necessary to fit the way you work.

4. Close the **Outlook Options** dialog box.

Manage add-ins and security options

Start Outlook, and then perform the following tasks:

1. Open the **Outlook Options** dialog box.

2. Display the **Add-ins** page, and then do the following:

   - Review the add-ins that are installed on your computer.

   - Notice the types of add-ins that are active, and display the dialog box for that type of add-in.

   - Notice add-ins that are turned on or off, and modify the setting if you want to.

   - Close the dialog box.

3. Display the **Trust Center** page, and then do the following:

   - Open the Trust Center.

   - Review the settings on each page of the Trust Center, but don't make any changes.

   - Close the Trust Center.

4. Close the **Outlook Options** dialog box.

Manage email automatically

To more easily manage information you receive through email, you can specify how Outlook 2016 alerts you to and processes incoming messages. When you travel or will be unavailable to respond to incoming email messages for a period of time, you can use the Automatic Replies feature to inform message senders of your status and to set expectations for message response times.

You can create rules to process messages that arrive while you're out of the office, to ensure that information gets to the people who need it. You can also create rules that evaluate all your incoming or outgoing messages and perform actions with the messages that meet specific conditions.

If you frequently perform a specific set of actions on messages that you receive, you can save time by saving the action series as a Quick Step. You can then perform the series of actions on items in your Inbox by clicking one button (or using a keyboard shortcut). Outlook comes with five built-in Quick Steps to get you started, and you can easily create your own.

This chapter guides you through procedures related to automatically replying to messages, creating rules to process messages, and managing messages by using Quick Steps.

In this chapter

- Automatically reply to messages
- Create rules to process messages
- Manage messages by using Quick Steps

Practice files

No practice files are necessary to complete the practice tasks in this chapter.

Automatically reply to messages

If your organization is running Microsoft Exchange, you can use the Automatic Replies feature (previously called the Out Of Office Assistant) to inform people who send you email messages of your availability. When you turn on the Automatic Replies feature, Outlook replies automatically to messages received from other people (but only to the first message from each person). You provide whatever textual information you want within the body of the automatic reply message (commonly referred to as an *out-of-office message*, or *OOF message*).

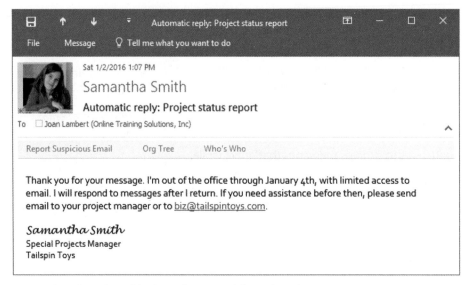

Automatic replies can provide alternative contact information when you're away

The purpose of the Automatic Replies feature is to provide standard information to message senders and co-workers. When you're away from your computer, an automatic reply can set expectations for when a correspondent can expect a personal response from you. You don't have to be physically out of the office to use this feature; some people use it to let other people know when responses will be delayed for other reasons, such as when they are working on a project that will prevent them from responding promptly to messages, or to inform customers who might be in different time zones of their standard working hours.

You can provide different messages to people within your organization and people external to your organization. The out-of-office functionality in Outlook is provided by Exchange Server. The specific automatic reply features might differ depending on the features that are turned on for your organization. If your organization has MailTips turned on, your automatic reply message is displayed to co-workers in a MailTip at the top of messages they address to you.

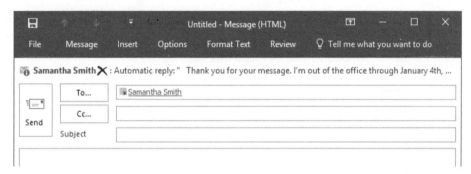

Automatic replies provide valuable information to co-workers

When you are using an Exchange account, automatic replies include the following features:

- You can create two automatic reply messages—one that Outlook sends only to people in your organization (on the same domain) and another it sends either to everyone else or only to the people in your primary address book.

  When you have separate internal and external messages, you can distinguish the information made available to co-workers, to friends and business contacts, and to the general public (including senders of spam). For example, you might include your itinerary and mobile phone number only in replies to internal contacts. For contacts not within your organization, you might include only your return date in your reply. For the general public, you might not send any reply at all.

- You can specify the font, size, and color of automatic reply message text and apply bold, italic, or underline formatting.

- You can format paragraphs as bulleted or numbered lists, and control the indent level.

- You can specify start and end dates and times for your automatic reply messages so that you don't have to remember to turn off automatic replies, or you can turn them on and off manually.

14

> **TIP** To set up automatic replies when you'll be out of the office for a week, set the start time to the end of the day on the last day you'll be in the office, and the end time to the end of the last day you'll be out of the office. This ensures that anyone who sends a message that you won't be able to respond to within a normal business response time period will receive an automatic reply.

The Automatic Replies feature is off until you explicitly turn it on; it does not coordinate with your free/busy information in the Calendar module.

You manage automatic replies from the Info page of the Backstage view.

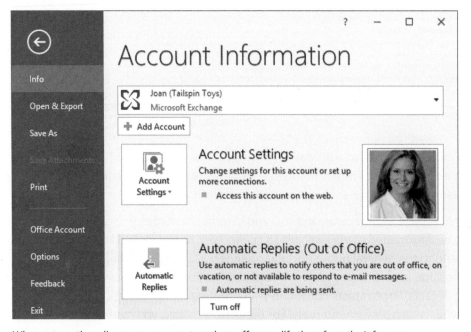

When automatic replies are on, you can turn them off or modify them from the Info page

You configure and turn on automatic replies from the Automatic Replies dialog box. This dialog box includes two tabs: Inside My Organization and Outside My Organization. If automatic replies are turned off, the content pane and commands are unavailable on both tabs. When you turn on automatic replies, the commands become available and you can set the date range, enter a message in the content pane, and format the text much as you would any message text.

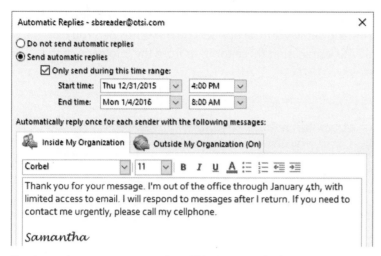

Your internal message goes to senders within your organization

The Outside My Organization tab includes options for sending automatic replies to all people outside of your organization, only to people with email addresses that are present in your primary Outlook address book, or not at all.

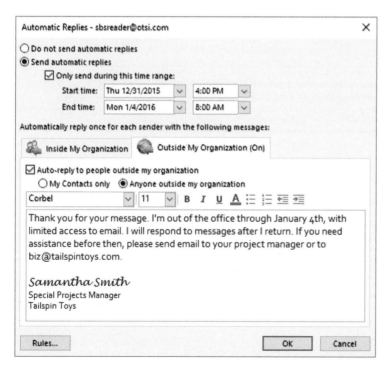

You can specify types of external message senders who will receive your automatic reply

14

When automatic replies are turned on, an InfoBar appears in the app window below the ribbon, and an Automatic Replies button appears on the status bar. You can manage your automatic replies by using these tools, or from the Info page of the Backstage view.

Automatic reply management tools

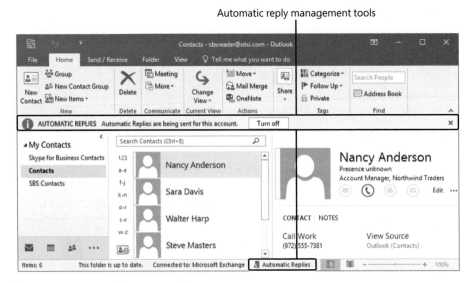

The InfoBar is displayed in every module

> **SEE ALSO** For information about using rules to automatically forward, reply to, delete, alert you to, or otherwise process incoming messages, see "Create rules to process messages" later in this chapter.

To turn on automatic replies

1. Display the **Info** page of the Backstage view. In the account list at the top of the page, select the Exchange account for which you want to configure automatic replies. Then click the **Automatic Replies** button.

> ⚠ **IMPORTANT** The functionality in this procedure is available only for Exchange accounts. If you select another account type, the Automatic Replies button is not available on the Info page.

2. In the **Automatic Replies** dialog box, click **Send automatic replies** to activate the time range check box, content pane, and formatting commands.

3. If you want Outlook to turn automatic replies on and off for you, do the following:

   a. Select the **Only send during this time range** check box.

   b. In the **Start time** area, enter or select the date and time you want Outlook to start sending replies.

   c. In the **End time** area, enter or select the date and time you want Outlook to stop sending replies.

   If you don't select the check box, Outlook will send automatic replies from the time you turn them on until you turn them off manually.

4. On the **Inside My Organization** tab, in the content pane, enter a message you want Outlook to send to message senders within your organization. Use the tools above the content pane to format the message text.

14

5. Display the **Outside My Organization** tab.

6. If you want Outlook to send automatic replies only to people within your organization, clear the **Auto-reply to people outside my organization** check box, and then skip to step 9.

7. If you want Outlook to send automatic replies to both internal and external message senders, select the **Auto-reply to people outside my organization** check box, if necessary, and then do either of the following:

   - To send external replies only to message senders whose email addresses are saved in your primary address book, click **My Contacts only**.

   - To send external replies to any message senders outside of your organization, click **Anyone outside my organization**.

8. On the **Outside My Organization** tab, in the content pane, enter a message you want Outlook to send to the external message senders you selected in step 7. Use the tools above the content pane to format the message text.

9. On either tab, click **OK** to turn on automatic replies and return to the Info page.

> **TIP** If you make changes to either the internal or the external reply message, but not to both, when you close the Automatic Replies dialog box, Outlook displays a message box that asks whether you want to change the other reply message. This useful reminder helps ensure that you keep both versions up to date.

To turn off automatic replies

1. Do any of the following:

   - On the information bar, click **Turn off**.

   - On the **Info** page of the Backstage view, in the **Automatic Replies** area, click **Turn off**.

   - On the status bar or on the **Info** page of the Backstage view, click the **Automatic Replies** button. In the **Automatic Replies** dialog box, click **Do not send automatic replies**, and then click **OK**.

Manage messages while you're away

You can have Outlook process messages that arrive while you are out of the office by using rules that are in effect only when the Automatic Replies feature is on. For example, if you will be out of the office but are expecting an important message from a particular sender, you can have Outlook send you an alert when a message from that sender arrives.

To set up automatic reply rules, follow these steps:

1. In the **Automatic Replies** dialog box, click **Rules** to open the Automatic Reply Rules dialog box. Then click **Add Rule** to open the Edit Rule dialog box.

Create simple rules that Outlook applies only when automatic replies are turned on

2. In the **Edit Rule** dialog box, enter or select the conditions that will trigger the rule, select the check boxes of the actions you want Outlook to perform, and provide any additional information that is necessary.

3. Click **OK** in each of the open dialog boxes to create the rule. Outlook will apply the rule when automatic replies are turned on.

14

Create rules to process messages

You can have Outlook evaluate your incoming or outgoing email messages and take various actions with them based on sets of instructions you set up, called *rules*. You can create rules based on different message criteria, such as the message sender, message recipients, message content, attachments, and importance. By using rules, you can have Outlook move, copy, delete, forward, redirect, reply to, or otherwise process messages based on the criteria you specify. You can choose from a collection of standard rules or create your own.

If you have an Exchange Server account, you can set up rules that are applied to messages as they are received or processed by your Exchange server, and rules that go into effect only when you indicate that you are unavailable, by setting up an automatic reply. For any type of email account, you can set up rules that are applied to messages stored on your computer.

 SEE ALSO For information about configuring Outlook to respond to and process messages for you, see "Automatically reply to messages" earlier in this chapter.

Outlook provides a wizard to walk you through the process of creating rules. You can base a rule on a template provided by Outlook, or you can start from a blank rule for incoming or outgoing messages.

When you start from a rule template, the wizard displays placeholders for the specific conditions and actions associated with the rule, and you replace the placeholders with values to create the rule. For example, if you choose the *Move messages with specific words in the subject to a folder* template, the description includes placeholders for the words that will be in the subject of the incoming messages you want to move, and for the name of the folder you want to move the messages to.

Rule templates provide structure, and you provide details

When you create a rule based on a blank rule, you specify whether to apply the rule to messages that you send or that you receive, select conditions and actions to define the rule, and provide the values for the conditions and actions.

Which condition(s) do you want to check?
Step 1: Select condition(s)

- [ ] with specific words in the subject
- [ ] through the specified account
- [ ] marked as importance
- [ ] marked as sensitivity
- [ ] sent to people or public group
- [ ] with specific words in the body
- [ ] with specific words in the subject or body
- [ ] with specific words in the recipient's address
- [ ] assigned to category category
- [ ] assigned to any category
- [ ] which has an attachment
- [ ] with a size in a specific range
- [ ] uses the form name form
- [ ] with selected properties of documents or forms
- [ ] which is a meeting invitation or update
- [ ] from RSS Feeds with specified text in the title
- [ ] from any RSS Feed
- [ ] of the specific form type

What do you want to do with the message?
Step 1: Select action(s)

- [ ] assign it to the category category
- [ ] move a copy to the specified folder
- [ ] flag message for action in a number of days
- [ ] clear message's categories
- [ ] mark it as importance
- [ ] stop processing more rules
- [ ] mark it as sensitivity
- [ ] notify me when it is read
- [ ] notify me when it is delivered
- [ ] Cc the message to people or public group
- [ ] defer delivery by a number of minutes
- [ ] apply retention policy: retention policy

You can specify multiple conditions and multiple actions

You can add conditions and actions to any rule, regardless of whether you create it from a template or from a blank rule. You can also set exceptions to the rules.

Are there any exceptions?
Step 1: Select exception(s) (if necessary)

- [ ] except if the subject contains specific words
- [ ] except through the specified account
- [ ] except if it is marked as importance
- [ ] except if it is marked as sensitivity
- [ ] except if sent to people or public group
- [ ] except if the body contains specific words
- [ ] except if the subject or body contains specific words
- [ ] except with specific words in the recipient's address
- [ ] except if assigned to category category
- [ ] except if assigned to any category
- [ ] except if it has an attachment
- [ ] except with a size in a specific range
- [ ] except if it uses the form name form
- [ ] except with selected properties of documents or forms
- [ ] except if it is a meeting invitation or update
- [ ] except if it is from RSS Feeds with specified text in the title
- [ ] except if from any RSS Feed
- [ ] except if it is of the specific form type

Conditions, actions, and exceptions vary for incoming and outgoing message rules

To create a rule from a rule template

1. On the **Info** page of the Backstage view, click the **Manage Rules & Alerts** button to display the Email Rules tab of the Rules And Alerts dialog box.

2. On the **E-mail Rules** tab, click **New Rule** to start the Rules Wizard.

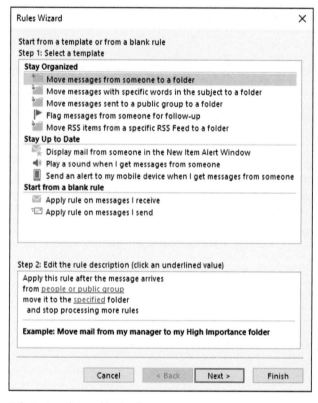

Select a template or blank rule to start

3. In the **Step 1: Select a template** pane, click any rule template (those in the Stay Organized and Stay Up To Date sections). The conditions and actions associated with the template appear in the Step 2 pane.

4. In the **Step 2: Edit the rule description** pane, click each of the underlined place-holders, and supply the value.

5. Click **Next** to display the list of conditions Outlook can evaluate for messages of the type that are managed by the selected template. The conditions that are already in effect are selected.

14

6. If you want Outlook to evaluate more conditions, do the following for each additional condition:

   a. In the **Step 1** pane, select the check box for the condition you want to add.

   b. In the **Step 2** pane, click the placeholder and provide the specific value.

7. Click **Next** to display the list of actions Outlook can perform with messages of the type that are managed by the selected template. The actions that are already in effect are selected.

8. If you want Outlook to perform more actions, do the following for each additional action:

   a. In the **Step 1** pane, select the check box for the action you want to add.

   b. In the **Step 2** pane, click the placeholder and provide the specific value.

9. Click **Next** to display the list of exceptions Outlook can evaluate for messages of the type that are managed by the selected template. If you want Outlook to process exceptions, do the following for each exception:

   a. In the **Step 1** pane, select the check box for the exception you want to add.

   b. In the **Step 2** pane, click the placeholder and provide the specific value.

10. Click **Next** to display the final page of the Rules Wizard.

You can run the rule on existing messages

11. In the **Step 1** section of the summary page, in the **Specify a name for this rule** box, edit the suggested name as necessary to provide a clear description.

12. In the **Step 2** section of the summary page, do any of the following:

    a. If you want to run the rule on messages you've already received, select the **Run this rule now on messages already in Inbox** check box.

    b. If you want to run the rule on messages that you receive in the future, select the **Turn on this rule** check box.

    c. If you want the rule to apply to all the email accounts you use in Outlook, select the **Create this rule on all accounts** check box.

13. In the **Step 3** section of the summary page, review the rule conditions, actions, and exceptions. Make any changes that you want.

14. Click **Finish** to save the rule. In the Rules And Alerts dialog box, a selected check box to the left of the rule name indicates that the rule is active.

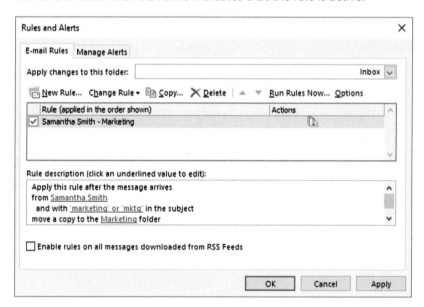

You can review all existing rules from this dialog box

15. In the **Rules and Alerts** dialog box, click **OK**.

To create a rule from a blank template

1. On the **Info** page of the Backstage view, click the **Manage Rules & Alerts** button to display the Email Rules tab of the Rules And Alerts dialog box.

2. On the **E-mail Rules** tab, click **New Rule** to start the Rules Wizard.

3. In the **Step 1: Select a template** pane, click **Apply rule on messages I receive** or **Apply rule on messages I send**.

4. Click **Next** to display the list of conditions Outlook can evaluate for messages of the selected type. For each condition you want Outlook to evaluate, do the following:

   a. In the **Step 1** pane, select the check box for the condition you want to evaluate.

   b. In the **Step 2** pane, click the placeholder and provide the specific value.

   If you don't select any conditions, Outlook will evaluate all incoming or outgoing messages. This is a valid option.

5. Click **Next** to display the list of actions Outlook can perform with messages of the selected type. For each action you want Outlook to perform with messages that meet the specified conditions, do the following:

   a. In the **Step 1** pane, select the check box for the action you want to perform.

   b. In the **Step 2** pane, click the placeholder and provide the specific value.

6. Click **Next** to display the list of exceptions Outlook can evaluate for messages of the selected type. If you want Outlook to process exceptions, do the following for each exception:

   a. In the **Step 1** pane, select the check box for the exception you want to add.

   b. In the **Step 2** pane, click the placeholder and provide the specific value.

7. Click **Next** to display the final page of the Rules Wizard.

8. In the **Step 1** section of the summary page, in the **Specify a name for this rule** box, edit the suggested name as necessary to provide a clear description.

9. In the **Step 2** section of the summary page, do any of the following:

   a. If you want to run the rule on messages you've already received, select the **Run this rule now on messages already in Inbox** check box.

   b. If you want to run the rule on messages that you receive in the future, select the **Turn on this rule** check box.

   c. If you want the rule to apply to all the email accounts you use in Outlook, select the **Create this rule on all accounts** check box.

10. In the **Step 3** section of the summary page, review the rule conditions, actions, and exceptions. Make any changes that you want.

11. Click **Finish** to save the rule. In the Rules And Alerts dialog box, a selected check box to the left of the rule name indicates that the rule is active.

12. In the **Rules and Alerts** dialog box, click **OK**.

To manage rules

1. On the **Info** page of the Backstage view, click the **Manage Rules & Alerts** button to display the Email Rules tab of the Rules And Alerts dialog box.

2. Do any of the following:

   - To turn off a rule, clear the check box to the left of the rule name.

   - To modify a rule, click the rule name (not the check box), click the **Change Rule** button, and then click **Edit Rule Settings** to display the rule in the Rules Wizard. Modify the conditions, actions, or exceptions of the rule, and then click **Finish** to save your changes.

   - To delete a rule, click the rule name (not the check box), click the **Delete** button, and then in the **Microsoft Outlook** dialog box that opens, click **Yes** to confirm that you want to delete the rule.

3. In the **Rules and Alerts** dialog box, click **OK**.

14

Manage messages by using Quick Steps

Quick Steps are sets of processes that you can perform on an email message in your Inbox (only) by clicking a button. If you frequently perform multiple tasks with a single message, you might find that you can save time by creating a Quick Step. For example, you can reply to an email message and delete the original message, or you can flag a message for follow-up and move it to a specific folder.

Quick Steps are available from the Quick Steps gallery on the Home tab of the Mail module, and from the shortcut menu that appears when you right-click a message or group of messages. If you use Quick Steps frequently, you can save even more time by assigning keyboard shortcuts to up to nine of them.

A new installation of Outlook includes these five built-in Quick Steps:

- **Move To** Moves the selected message to a folder that you specify the first time you use the Quick Step and marks the message as read. After you specify the folder, the Quick Step name changes to include the folder name.

- **To Manager** Forwards the selected message to a person or people you specify the first time you use the Quick Step. You can edit the Quick Step to include Cc and Bcc recipients, a specific message subject, a follow-up flag, a level of importance, and specific message text, and to send the message one minute after you click the Quick Step command.

- **Team Email** Creates a message to a person or people you specify the first time you use the Quick Step. You can edit the Quick Step to include Cc and Bcc recipients, a specific message subject, a follow-up flag, a level of importance, and specific message text, and to send the message one minute after you click the Quick Step command.

- **Done** Moves the selected message to a folder that you specify the first time you use the Quick Step, marks the message as read, and marks the message as complete so that a check mark is displayed in the follow-up flag location.

- **Reply & Delete** Creates a response to the original message sender and immediately deletes the original message.

> ⚠ **IMPORTANT** The Reply & Delete Quick Step deletes the original message before you send the reply. If you close the response message composition window without sending it, the original message will no longer be in your Inbox. If you want to respond to the original message, you first need to retrieve it from your Deleted Items folder.

A Quick Step can perform up to 12 actions. You can modify the actions performed by existing Quick Steps, or you can create your own. You can choose from 25 actions in six categories: Filing; Change Status; Categories, Tasks and Flags; Respond; Appointment; and Conversations.

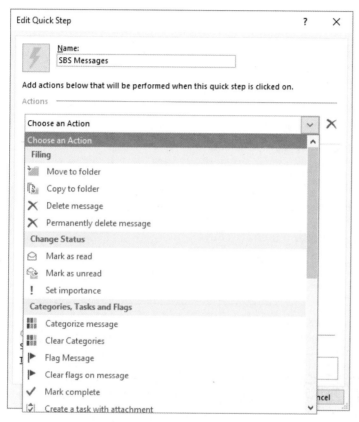

Quick Steps can perform many types of actions

> ✓ **TIP** If you connect to multiple accounts, the Quick Steps in each Mail module are specific to that account. Only the Quick Steps that can be performed on the selected message or messages will be shown as available.

14

To configure a built-in Quick Step for use

1. On the **Home** tab, in the **Quick Steps** gallery, click the Quick Step to open the First Time Setup dialog box.

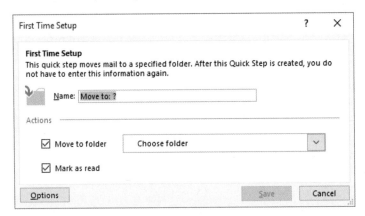

Some generic Quick Steps require that you supply information the first time you use them

2. Do either of the following, and then click **Save**:

   - For the *Move To* or *Done* Quick Step, specify a destination folder by clicking it in the **Move to folder** list.

   >  **TIP** If the Move To Folder list doesn't include the folder you want to use, click Other Folder and then, in the Select Folder dialog box, browse to the folder.

   - For the *To Manager* or *Team Email* Quick Step, specify one or more message recipients in the **To** box.

To use a Quick Step

1. In the Inbox, select one or more messages.

2. In the **Quick Steps** gallery, click the Quick Step that you want to run.

To edit a Quick Step

1. In the **Quick Steps** gallery, right-click the Quick Step, and then click **Edit** to open the Edit Quick Step dialog box.

You can add, change, or remove actions

2. Do any of the following, and then click **Save**:

   - In the **Name** box, enter a new name for the Quick Step.

   - In the **Actions** section, modify the actions the Quick Step performs.

   - In the **Shortcut key** list, click a key combination.

   - In the **Tooltip text** box, enter the text that you want to appear when you point to the Quick Step in the gallery.

14

To create a custom Quick Step

1. On the **Home** tab, in the **Quick Steps** group, click the **More** button to expand the menu, and then click **Create New** to open the Edit Quick Step dialog box.

2. In the **Name** box, replace **My Quick Step** with the name you want.

3. In the **Actions** section, click the **Choose an action** arrow, and then click the first action you want the Quick Step to perform.

4. Depending on the action you select, you might be prompted to provide specific information such as a recipient, folder, or category. Provide the requested information.

5. For each additional action that you want to Quick Step to perform, click **Add Action**, select the action, and provide any necessary specifics.

> **TIP** Some actions might not be available in subsequent action lists, if they can't be performed after the preceding actions.

6. If you want to assign a keyboard shortcut to the Quick Step, expand the **Short-cut key** list, and then click the keyboard shortcut you want to use. (Options are Ctrl+F1 through Ctrl+F9.)

7. If you want Outlook to display information when you point to the Quick Step in the gallery, enter that text in the **Tooltip text** box.

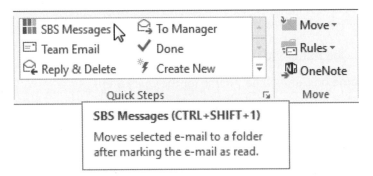

Tooltips can help you remember the purpose of each Quick Step

8. In the **Edit Quick Step** dialog box, click **Finish** to add the new Quick Step to the Quick Steps gallery.

To reorder the Quick Steps in the Quick Step gallery

1. On the **Home** tab, in the **Quick Steps** group, click the **More** button to display the gallery and menu, and then click **Manage Quick Steps** to open the Manage Quick Steps dialog box.

2. In the **Quick step** list on the left, click the Quick Step you want to move. Then click the **Up** or **Down** button to change the position of the Quick Step in the list and gallery.

3. Click **OK** to save the change and close the dialog box.

Skills review

In this chapter, you learned how to:

- Automatically reply to messages
- Create rules to process messages
- Manage messages by using Quick Steps

14

Practice tasks

No practice files are necessary to complete the practice tasks in this chapter.

Automatically reply to messages

Perform the following tasks:

1. Create an automatic reply message to senders within your organization.

2. Turn on automatic replies, and notice the indicators that appear in the Backstage view and in the app window.

3. Send a message to yourself, and review the automatic reply message that you receive.

4. Consider the different circumstances in which you could benefit from the use of automatic replies.

5. Turn off automatic replies.

Create rules to process messages

Perform the following tasks:

1. Create a rule that displays an alert when you receive a message from yourself. While working in the Rules Wizard, consider the types of incoming or outgoing message rules that might be useful to you.

2. Save the rule with the name **Alert Me**, and turn on the rule.

3. Send a message to yourself, and notice the result.

4. Turn off the rule, and then delete it.

5. If you want to create any rules to process incoming or outgoing messages, do so.

Manage messages by using Quick Steps

Display your Inbox, and then perform the following tasks:

1. Investigate the existing Quick Steps and consider which of them might be useful to you.

2. If you want to configure a built-in Quick Step for a specific purpose, do so.

3. Create a custom Quick Step that performs a process or multiple processes that you perform manually on email messages that you receive. Give the Quick Step a meaningful name and provide explanatory tooltip text. Then save the Quick Step.

4. On the **Home** tab, in the **Quick Steps** group, point to your custom Quick Step and confirm that the tooltip text appears.

5. Select one or more messages in your Inbox and run the custom Quick Step. Evaluate the results.

6. Create any additional Quick Steps that you want. Assign a keyboard shortcut to any Quick Steps that you anticipate you will use often.

Appendix A

Get connected

By using Outlook 2016, you can easily manage one or more email accounts. You can configure Outlook to connect to many different types of business and personal email accounts. If your organization uses Microsoft Exchange Server or Exchange Online, you can use Outlook to work with all the features of your Exchange account, including email, calendaring, contact tracking, task tracking, and notes. If your organization also uses Microsoft Skype for Business, you can initiate audio and video calls, instant messaging sessions, online meetings, and more from Outlook 2016.

A default installation of Outlook 2016 supports the following types of email accounts:

- **Exchange** You can configure Outlook 2016 to connect to an Exchange account hosted on Exchange Online, Exchange Server 2016, Exchange Server 2013, and Exchange Server 2010. If your organization uses any of these versions of Exchange Server, you can send mail within or outside of your organization's network. Messages are stored centrally on the Exchange server. They are also stored locally in a data file on your computer. Outlook synchronizes with the server when you're connected to it either over a corporate network or over the Internet, so you can work with existing Outlook items and create new items while working offline.

  Using Outlook 2016, you can connect to a corporate Exchange account without connecting your computer directly to the corporate network. Recent versions of Exchange automatically route all Outlook client access through protocols that bypass the requirement for a direct corporate network connection.

- **Exchange ActiveSync–compatible service** Although this sounds quite technical, it's simply a description for an Internet-based email service such as Hotmail or Outlook.com. It is not necessary to install a separate connector in order to configure Outlook 2016 to connect to an account of this type.

- **Post Office Protocol (POP)** When connected to a POP account, Outlook downloads messages from your email server to your computer, and removes the original messages from the server after a specified length of time. You read and manage messages on your computer, and Outlook synchronizes with the server when it is connected.

- **Internet Message Access Protocol (IMAP)** When connected to an IMAP account, Outlook stores copies of messages on your computer, but leaves the originals on the email server. You read and manage messages locally, and Outlook synchronizes with the server when it is connected.

You can add one or more email accounts of any supported type to your Outlook profile, either during the initial setup procedure or at any time thereafter. You don't have to connect Outlook to an email account, but it's customary to do so. When you use Outlook without connecting to an email account, you can't send or receive messages, or synchronize your calendar, contacts, and tasks with Outlook installations on other computers. After you configure Outlook to connect to an email account, you can easily manage the information stored with that account by using the Outlook features specifically designed for each type of information.

Welcome to Microsoft Outlook 2016   ✕

Welcome to Outlook 2016

Outlook helps you manage your life with powerful tools for email, calendar, contacts, and tasks.

Let's get started. In the next few steps, we'll add your email account.

The wizard provides an easy-to-follow interface for connecting to an account

Configuring Outlook creates an Outlook Data File for each email account and an Outlook profile, which stores information about you and your email accounts. You can work with your profile from within Outlook or from the Mail control panel in Windows. Your profile includes information about your email account such as the user name, display name, server name, password, and the local data storage location.

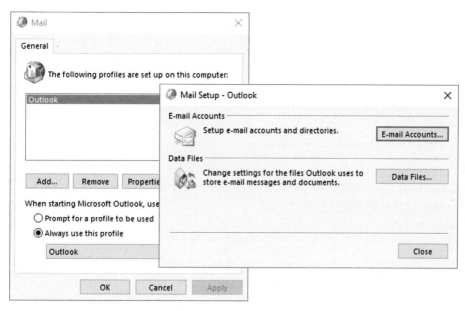

Outlook profile properties

You can connect to more than one email account per profile, to seamlessly manage all your email communications through Outlook. If you want to, you can create multiple profiles that link to different email accounts or to different sets of email accounts, but when using Outlook 2016, it is not necessary to create multiple profiles to manage multiple accounts.

A

Start the connection process

Before you can use Outlook to manage an email account, you must configure the app to connect to the account. When you start Outlook for the first time (or if Outlook hasn't yet connected to an email account in your computer user profile), the Microsoft Outlook Account Setup wizard guides you through the connection process.

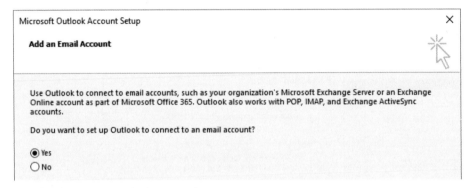

Start a connection to any supported email account

To start the email account connection process for the first time

1. Start Outlook. If you haven't yet completed the Outlook setup process, the Welcome To Microsoft Outlook 2016 splash page appears.

2. On the **Welcome to Outlook 2016** page, click **Next** to start the Microsoft Outlook Account Setup wizard.

3. On the **Add an Email Account** page of the wizard, click **Yes**, and then click **Next** to display the Auto Account Setup page of the Add Account wizard.

To start the email account connection process from within Outlook

1. Click the **File** tab to display the Info page of the Backstage view.

2. On the **Info** page of the Backstage view, click the **Add Account** button to display the Auto Account Setup page of the Add Account wizard.

> 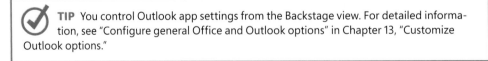 **TIP** You control Outlook app settings from the Backstage view. For detailed information, see "Configure general Office and Outlook options" in Chapter 13, "Customize Outlook options."

To start using Outlook without connecting to an email account

1. Start Outlook. On the **Welcome to Outlook 2016** page, click **Next** to start the Microsoft Outlook Account Setup wizard.

2. On the **Add an Email Account** page of the wizard, click **No**, and then click **Next**. Outlook displays a warning that its functionality is limited when not connected to an email account.

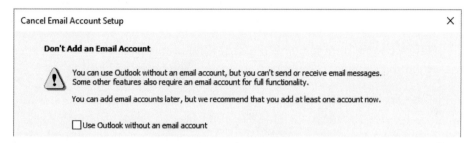

You can continue without connecting to an account, or go back

3. On the **Don't Add an Email Account** page, select the **Use Outlook without an email account** check box, and then click **Finish**. Outlook starts, and displays the Outlook Today page.

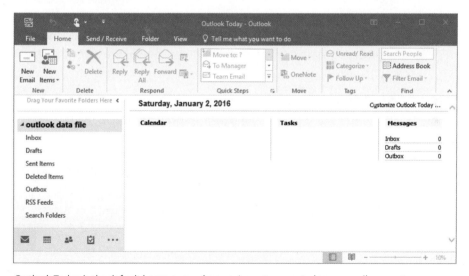

Outlook Today is the default home page when you're not connected to an email account

> **SEE ALSO** For information about configuring the Outlook Today page, see the sidebar "Outlook Today" in Chapter 11, "Track tasks."

Troubleshoot connection problems

The automatic account setup feature is very handy, but might not work every time. It is most successful when connecting to an on-premises Exchange account. When connecting to a remote Exchange server, to an Exchange account hosted by an external hosting company, or to a POP or IMAP account, manual configuration steps might be necessary.

Here are some common error messages and problems you could encounter when you connect to an Exchange account, and how to address them:

- **Server certificate does not match site** If Outlook encounters security issues associated with the electronic file (digital certificate) that validates the mail server's identity—for example, if the digital certificate does not match the name of your domain—Outlook notifies you of this problem and lets you choose whether to proceed.

  If a Security Alert message box appears, you can click the View Certificate button to display the digital certificate of the mail server and verify that you know and trust the company that issued the certificate. If you want, you can install the certificate on your computer by clicking the Install Certificate button and following the steps in the Certificate Import wizard.

  SEE ALSO For more information about digital certificates, see "Increase email security" in Chapter 5, "Manage email security."

- **Encrypted connection not available** This message might appear if your Exchange account is with a hosted service provider. Outlook first tries to establish an encrypted connection to the server. If this attempt is not successful, Outlook notifies you of this problem and asks whether you want to try to establish an unencrypted connection.

  If you click Next to establish an unencrypted connection, Outlook might inadvertently configure the connection to your Exchange account as it would a connection to an IMAP or POP account. This configuration can result in a loss of functionality related to information, such as appointments and tasks, stored on the Exchange server. The more likely solution to this issue is to click the Back button, click the Manual Setup Or Additional Server Types option, click Next, and then manually enter the server and connection information for your account.

If you encounter either of these errors when connecting to an Exchange account, verify that you are using the correct internal server address method. For example, if your email address is *jane@adatum.com*, you might address your email server as *mail.adatum.com* or by an internal address, such as *ADATUMExchange.adatum.local*.

To successfully troubleshoot your connection issues, you will likely need to manually configure your server settings. This requires that you have additional information from your server administrator about your email account, including the names of the incoming and outgoing servers, and whether either of the servers requires additional authentication.

A

Configure a connection automatically

The automatic connection process is a significant improvement over the manual account setup processes of the past, which required you to know and provide specific information about your email account, incoming and outgoing mail servers, and the ports to use for incoming and outgoing messages. For many accounts, you need to supply only three pieces of information—your name, your email address, and your email account password—and the Outlook Account Setup wizard handles the rest of the connection process for you.

Starting an automatic connection from the wizard

To connect to an email account that supports automatic connections

1. Display the **Auto Account Setup** page of the **Add Account** wizard.

2. Enter your name, email address, and email account password in the text boxes provided. Then click **Next** to search your available networks and the Internet for the specified domain.

> **TIP** The password characters you enter are hidden, so take care that the Caps Lock key is not inadvertently active when you enter the password.

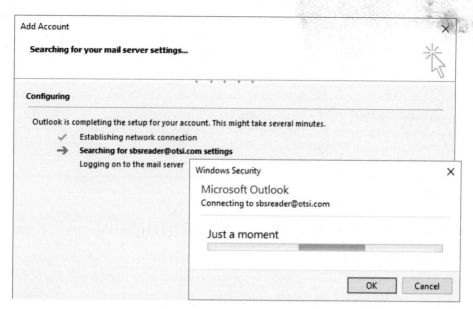

The wizard validates that it can log on to the email server

If the wizard locates an account matching the email address you entered, it attempts to log on by using the password you entered. If the connection is successful, a confirmation appears, along with additional account configuration options.

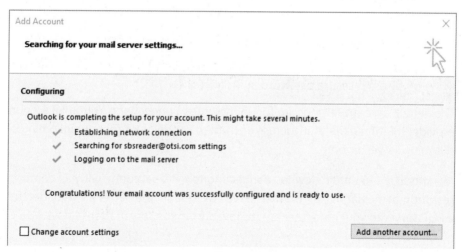

You can begin using the account now, or connect to additional accounts

A

3. Do either of the following:

- Click **Finish** to start using the account.

- Click **Add another account** to restart the wizard.

> ⚠️ **IMPORTANT** If the wizard is unable to complete the connection without further information, an error page appears. If this happens, click Back to return to the Auto Account Setup page. Then follow the procedure in "Configure a connection manually," next in this appendix.

Configure a connection manually

When manually configuring a connection to a POP or IMAP account, you must provide your name and email address, and the following information, which you can obtain from your email service provider:

- **Account type** Choose POP3 or IMAP from the drop-down list.

- **Incoming and outgoing mail servers** Server addresses are usually entered in the format *server.domain.com*.

- **Account user name** Many providers require that you enter the entire email address for this parameter rather than only the name before the @ symbol.

- **Account password** Outlook disguises the password characters as asterisks.

- **Logon authentication requirements** Some mail servers require that you log on by using secure password authentication.

The default account settings are for unencrypted connections. Your mail account provider might require that you use encrypted connections for your incoming server, outgoing server, or both.

It is important to note that when connecting to a POP account, you can control the retention of messages on the email server. By default, messages downloaded from a POP server to your computer are removed from the server after 14 days. You can choose to leave the messages on the server permanently, leave them there for a specified amount of time, or leave them there until you delete them from Outlook.

> **TIP** If you configure Outlook to connect to a POP account from a portable computer and experience difficulty sending email messages when connected to a public network (such as a hotel network), it might be because the network has blocked traffic on the default outgoing server port, port 25. If so, you can likely resolve the issue by changing the outgoing server port on the Advanced page of the Internet E-mail Settings dialog box for the account to port 80, 465, or 587.

After supplying the connection information for your email account, you can test the account settings to ensure that Outlook successfully connects to your incoming and outgoing servers.

To connect manually to an email account

1. Display the **Auto Account Setup** page of the **Add Account** wizard, click **Manual setup or additional server types**, and then click **Next** to display the Choose Service page.

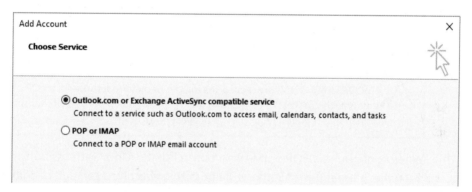

Connection processes vary by account type

2. Select your account type, and then click **Next** to display the Account Settings page for that type of account.

A

3. On the **Account Settings** page, enter or select the requested information.

Settings for a POP account

> ⚠ **IMPORTANT** In this procedure, the images depict the settings for a POP account. The process of completing the wizard is similar for IMAP accounts. Less information is required for Exchange ActiveSync accounts.

4. When configuring a POP or IMAP account, click the **More Settings** button to open the Internet E-mail Settings dialog box in which you can enter additional information, such as the name by which you want to identify the account, the email address you want to appear when you reply to a message, and outgoing server authentication information.

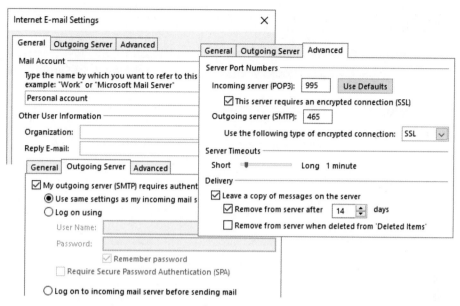

Pay special attention to the settings on the Advanced tab

5. In the **Internet E-mail Settings** dialog box, review the settings on each tab and configure any that are necessary. Then click **OK** to close the dialog box and return to the Account Settings page.

6. On the **Account Settings** page, click **Next** to test the connection.

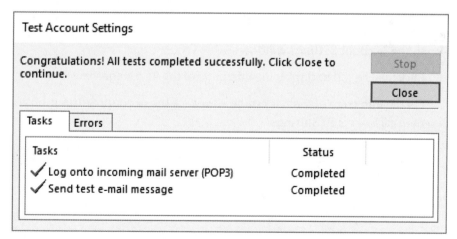

Testing confirms that you can send and receive messages with the current settings

7. Close the **Test Account Settings** dialog box, and then click **Finish** to start using the account.

Manage existing connections

You can manage Outlook settings for all the email accounts, RSS feeds, SharePoint lists, calendars, and address books you connect to from the Account Settings window.

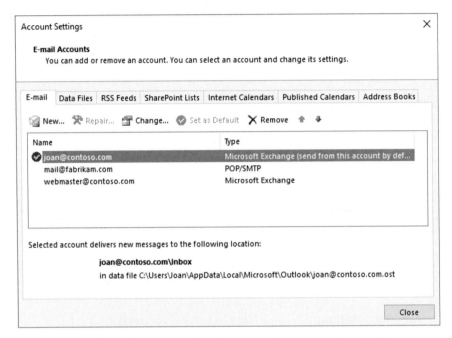

You can temporarily modify account settings if necessary for your current connection

To open the Account Settings window

1. Click the **File** tab to display the Info page of the Backstage view.

2. On the **Info** page of the **Backstage** view, click the **Account Settings** button, and then click **Account Settings**.

Manage all aspects of account connections

Appendix B

Keyboard shortcuts

Throughout this book, I provide information about how to perform tasks quickly and efficiently by using keyboard shortcuts. This section presents information about keyboard shortcuts that are built in to Microsoft Outlook 2016 and Microsoft Office 2016.

 TIP In the following lists, keys you press at the same time are separated by a plus sign (+), and keys you press sequentially are separated by a comma (,).

Outlook 2016 keyboard shortcuts

This topic provides a comprehensive list of keyboard shortcuts built into Outlook 2016. The content has been excerpted from Outlook Help and formatted in tables for convenient lookup.

Create Outlook items or files

Action	Keyboard shortcut
Create an item of the current module type	Ctrl+N
Create a message	Ctrl+Shift+M
Create an appointment	Ctrl+Shift+A
Create a meeting request	Ctrl+Shift+Q
Create a contact	Ctrl+Shift+C
Create a distribution list	Ctrl+Shift+L
Create a task	Ctrl+Shift+K

Action	Keyboard shortcut
Create a folder	Ctrl+Shift+E
Create a Search Folder	Ctrl+Shift+P
Create a fax	Ctrl+Shift+X
Create a new Office document	Ctrl+Shift+H
Post to the current folder	Ctrl+Shift+S
Post a reply in the current folder	Ctrl+T

Navigate in Outlook

Action	Keyboard shortcut
Switch to the Mail module	Ctrl+1
Switch to the Calendar module	Ctrl+2
Switch to the Contacts module	Ctrl+3
Switch to the Tasks module	Ctrl+4
Switch to the Notes module	Ctrl+5
Display the Folder List in the Folder Pane	Ctrl+6
Switch to the Shortcuts module	Ctrl+7
Switch to the Journal module	Ctrl+8
Switch to the next message (with message open)	Ctrl+Period
Switch to the previous message (with message open)	Ctrl+Comma
Move between the Folder Pane, the content area, the Reading Pane, and the To-Do Bar	Ctrl+Shift+Tab or Shift+Tab
Move between the Outlook window, the smaller panes in the Folder Pane, the Reading Pane, and the sections in the To-Do Bar	Tab
Move around message header lines in the Folder Pane or an open message	Ctrl+Tab
Move around within the Folder Pane	Arrow keys
Go to a different folder	Ctrl+Y

Action	Keyboard shortcut
Go to the Search box	F3 or Ctrl+E
In the Reading Pane, go to the previous message	Alt+Up Arrow or Ctrl+Comma or Alt+Page Up
In the Reading Pane, page up/down through text	Shift+Spacebar/Spacebar
Expand/collapse a group in the email message list	Right Arrow/Left Arrow
Go back to the previous/forward to the next view in the main Outlook window	Alt+B or Alt+Left Arrow/ Alt+Right Arrow
Select the InfoBar and, if available, show the menu of commands	Ctrl+Shift+W

Use the Outlook Backstage view

Action	Keyboard shortcut
Display the Info page of the Backstage view	Alt+F+I
Display the Save page of the Backstage view	Alt+F+S
Display the Save As page of the Backstage view	Alt+F+A
Display the Save Attachments page of the Backstage view	Alt+F+M
Display the Print page of the Backstage view	Alt+F+P
Display the Close page of the Backstage view	Alt+F+C
Display the Office Account page of the Backstage view	Alt+F+D
Display the Outlook Options dialog box	Alt+F+T
Close the Backstage view	Esc

 TIP After displaying a page of the Backstage view, press the KeyTips displayed on that page to use features and commands.

B

Locate Outlook items

Action	Keyboard shortcut
Find a message or other item	Ctrl+E
Expand a search to include all items of the current type	Ctrl+Alt+A
Expand a search to include items from the current folder	Ctrl+Alt+K
Expand a search to include subfolders	Ctrl+Alt+Z
Use Advanced Find	Ctrl+Shift+F
Search for text within an open item	F4
Find and replace text, symbols, or some formatting commands in the Reading Pane on an open item	Ctrl+H
Clear the search results	Esc

Manage Outlook items

Action	Keyboard shortcut
Save (except in Tasks)	Ctrl+S or Shift+F12
Save and close (except in Mail)	Alt+S
Save as (only in Mail)	F12
Undo	Ctrl+Z or Alt+Backspace
Delete an item	Ctrl+D
Print an item	Ctrl+P
Copy an item	Ctrl+Shift+Y
Move an item	Ctrl+Shift+V
Forward an item	Ctrl+F
Forward an item as an attachment	Ctrl+Alt+F
Flag an item for follow-up	Ctrl+Shift+G
Send or post or invite all	Alt+S

Action	Keyboard shortcut
Enable editing in a field (except in Mail or Icon view)	F2
Delete the selected category from the list in the Color Categories dialog box	Alt+D

Manage and format item content

 TIP The cursor must be inside a text box when you use these shortcuts.

Action	Keyboard shortcut
Check spelling	F7
Cut	Ctrl+X or Shift+Delete
Copy	Ctrl+C or Ctrl+Insert Note: Ctrl+Insert is not available in the Reading Pane
Paste	Ctrl+V or Shift+Insert
Delete the next word	Ctrl+Shift+H
Display the Format menu	Alt+O
Display the Font dialog box	Ctrl+Shift+P
Switch case (with text selected)	Shift+F3
Format letters as small capitals	Ctrl+Shift+K
Make letters bold	Ctrl+B
Add bullets	Ctrl+Shift+L
Make letters italic	Ctrl+I
Increase indent or create a hanging indent	Ctrl+T
Decrease indent or reduce a hanging indent	Ctrl+Shift+T
Underline	Ctrl+U

B

Action	Keyboard shortcut
Increase font size	Ctrl+] or Ctrl+Shift+>
Decrease font size	Ctrl+[or Ctrl+Shift+<
Clear character formatting	Ctrl+Shift+Z or Ctrl+Spacebar
Left-align text	Ctrl+L
Center text	Ctrl+E
Right-align text	Ctrl+R
Justify text	Ctrl+Shift+J
Apply styles	Ctrl+Shift+S
Remove paragraph formatting	Ctrl+Q
Insert a hyperlink	Ctrl+K
Edit a URL in the body of an item	Hold down Ctrl and click the mouse button

Work with the Mail module and email messages

Action	Keyboard shortcut
Switch to the Inbox	Ctrl+Shift+I
Switch to the Outbox	Ctrl+Shift+O
Choose the account from which to send a message	Ctrl+Tab (with focus on the To box), and then Tab to the Accounts button
Check names	Ctrl+K
Send a message	Alt+S or Ctrl+Enter
Reply to a message	Ctrl+R
Reply All to a message	Ctrl+Shift+R
Reply with a meeting request	Ctrl+Alt+R
Mark a message as not junk	Ctrl+Alt+J

Action	Keyboard shortcut
Display blocked external content (in a message)	Ctrl+Shift+I
Post to a folder	Ctrl+Shift+S
Apply Normal style	Ctrl+Shift+N
Check for new messages	Ctrl+M or F9
Go to the previous/next message	Up Arrow/Down Arrow
Open a received message	Ctrl+O
Delete and ignore a conversation	Ctrl+Shift+D
Open the Address Book	Ctrl+Shift+B
Add a Quick Flag to an unopened message	Insert
Display the Flag For Follow Up dialog box	Ctrl+Shift+G
Mark as read/unread	Ctrl+Q/Ctrl+U
Open the MailTip in the selected message	Ctrl+Shift+W
Find or replace	F4
Find the next instance of the current search term	Shift+F4
Show the properties for the selected item	Alt+Enter
Create a multimedia message	Ctrl+Shift+U
Create a text message	Ctrl+Shift+T
Mark for download	Ctrl+Alt+M
Clear the mark for download	Ctrl+Alt+U
Display Send/Receive progress	Ctrl+B (when a Send/ Receive is in progress)

Work with the Calendar module and calendar items

Action	Keyboard shortcut
Reply to a meeting request with a message	Ctrl+R
Reply All to a meeting request with a message	Ctrl+Shift+R

B

Action	Keyboard shortcut
Move between Calendar, TaskPad, and the Folder List	Ctrl+Tab or F6
Go to a date	Ctrl+G
Switch to Month view	Alt+= or Ctrl+Alt+4
Switch to Week view	Alt+Minus Sign or Ctrl+Alt+3
Switch to Work Week view	Ctrl+Alt+2
View from 1 through 9 days	Alt+key for number of days
View 10 days	Alt+0
Select the previous appointment	Shift+Tab
Go to the previous/next day	Left Arrow/Right Arrow
Go to the same day in the previous/next week	Alt+Up Arrow/Alt+Down Arrow
Go to the previous/next week	Alt+Up Arrow/Alt+Down Arrow
Go to the previous/next month	Alt+Page Up/Alt+Page Down
Go to the beginning/end of the week	Alt+Home/Alt+End
Go to the previous/next appointment	Ctrl+Comma or Ctrl+Shift+Comma/ Ctrl+Period or Ctrl+Shift+Period
Set up a recurrence for an open appointment or meeting	Ctrl+G

Navigate in the Date Navigator

Action	Keyboard shortcut
Go to the first/last day of the current week	Alt+Home/Alt+End
Go to the same day in the previous/next week	Alt+Up Arrow/Alt+Down Arrow

Navigate in Day view

Action	Keyboard shortcut
Select the time that begins/ends your work day	Home/End
Select the previous/next block of time	Up Arrow/Down Arrow
Select the block of time at the top/bottom of the screen	Page Up/Page Down
Extend/reduce the selected time	Shift+Up Arrow/Shift+Down Arrow
Move an appointment up/down	With the cursor in the appointment, Alt+Up Arrow/Alt+Down Arrow
Change an appointment's start/end time	With the cursor in the appointment, Alt+Shift+Up Arrow/Alt+Shift+Down Arrow
Move the selected item to the same day in the previous/next week	Alt+Up Arrow/Alt+Down Arrow

Navigate in Week view

Action	Keyboard shortcut
Go to the start/end of work hours for the selected day	Home/End
Go up/down one page view in the selected day	Page Up/Page Down
Change the duration of the selected block of time	Shift+Left Arrow, Shift+Right Arrow, Shift+Up Arrow, or Shift+Down Arrow; or Shift+Home or Shift+End

B

Navigate in Month view

Action	Keyboard shortcut
Go to the first day of the week	Home
Go to the same day of the week in the previous/next page	Page Up/Page Down

Work with the People module and contact records

Action	Keyboard shortcut
Dial a new call	Ctrl+Shift+D
Find a contact or other item (Search)	F3 or Ctrl+E
Enter a name in the Search Address Books box	F11
In Table or List view of contacts, go to the first contact that starts with a specific letter	Shift+letter
Select all contacts	Ctrl+A
Open a contact form for the selected contact	Ctrl+O
Update a list of distribution list members	F5
Open the Address Book	Ctrl+Shift+B
Use Advanced Find	Ctrl+Shift+F
Find a contact	F11
Close a contact	Esc
Send a fax to the selected contact	Ctrl+Shift+X
In a contact form, display the E-mail 1 information	Alt+Shift+1
In a contact form, display the E-mail 2 information	Alt+Shift+2
In a contact form, display the E-mail 3 information	Alt+Shift+3

Work in the Electronic Business Cards dialog box

Action	Keyboard shortcut
Open the Add list	Alt+A
Select text in the Label box when the field with a label assigned is selected	Alt+B
Open the Add Card Picture dialog box	Alt+C
Place the cursor at the beginning of the Edit box	Alt+E
Select the Fields box	Alt+F
Select the Image Align list	Alt+G
Select the color palette for background	Alt+K, then Enter
Select the Layout list	Alt+L
Remove a selected field from the Fields box	Alt+R

Work in Business Cards view or Address Cards view

Action	Keyboard shortcut
Select a specific card in the list	One or more letters of the name by which the card is filed or the field by which you are sorting
Select the previous/next card	Up Arrow/Down Arrow
Select the first/last card in the list	Home/End
Select the first card on the current page	Page Up
Select the first card on the next page	Page Down
Select the closest card in the previous/next column	Left Arrow/Right Arrow

B

Action	Keyboard shortcut
Select or cancel selection of the active card	Ctrl+Spacebar
Extend the selection to the previous/next card and cancel selection of cards after the starting point	Shift+Up Arrow/ Shift+Down Arrow
Extend the selection to the previous/next card, regardless of the starting point	Ctrl+Shift+Up Arrow/ Ctrl+Shift+Down Arrow
Extend the selection to the first/last card in the list	Shift+Home/Shift+End
Extend the selection to the first/last card on the previous page	Shift+Page Up/Shift+Page Down

Move between fields in an open card and characters in a field

 TIP To use the following keys, make sure a field in a card is selected. To select a field when a card is selected, click the field.

Action	Keyboard shortcut
Move to the previous/next field or control	Shift+Tab/Tab
Close the active card	Enter
Add a line in a multiline field	Enter
Move to the beginning/end of a line	Home/End
Move to the beginning/end of a multiline field	Page Up/Page Down
Move to the previous/next line in a multiline field	Up Arrow/Down Arrow
Move to the previous/next character in a field	Left Arrow/Right Arrow

Work with the Tasks module and tasks

Action	Keyboard shortcut
Accept/decline a task request	Alt+C/Alt+D
Find a task or other item	Ctrl+E
Open a selected item	Ctrl+O
Select all items	Ctrl+A
Delete the selected item	Ctrl+D
Switch between the Folder Pane, Tasks list, and To-Do Bar	Tab or Shift+Tab
Undo last action	Ctrl+Z
Flag an item or mark as complete	Insert

Work in the Timeline view when an item is selected

Action	Keyboard shortcut
Select the previous/next item	Left Arrow/Right Arrow
Select several adjacent items	Shift+Left Arrow or Shift+Right Arrow
Select several nonadjacent items	Ctrl+Left Arrow+Spacebar or Ctrl+Right Arrow+Spacebar
Open the selected items	Enter
Select the first/last item on the timeline (if items are not grouped) or in the group	Home/End
Display (without selecting) the first/last item on the timeline (if items are not grouped) or in the group	Ctrl+Home/Ctrl+End

B

Work in the Timeline view when a group is selected

Action	Keyboard shortcut
Expand/collapse the group tools	Enter or Right Arrow/Left Arrow
Select the previous/next group	Up Arrow/Down Arrow
Select the first/last group on the timeline	Home/End
Select the first item on the screen in an expanded group or the first item off the screen to the right	Right Arrow

Work in the Timeline view when a unit of time on the time scale for days is selected

Action	Keyboard shortcut
Move backward/forward in the increments of time shown on the time scale	Left Arrow/Right Arrow
Switch between active view, To-Do Bar, Search, and back to active view	Tab and Shift+Tab

Send and receive information

Action	Keyboard shortcut
Start a send/receive for all defined Send/Receive groups that include the F9 option	F9
Start a send/receive for the current folder	Shift+F9
Start a send/receive	Ctrl+M
Define Send/Receive groups	Ctrl+Alt+S

Use development tools

Action	Keyboard shortcut
Open the Visual Basic Editor	Alt+F11
Play a macro	Alt+F8
Create an InfoPath form	Click in an InfoPath folder, and then Ctrl+N
Choose an InfoPath form	Ctrl+Shift+Alt+T

Office 2016 keyboard shortcuts

This topic provides a list of keyboard shortcuts available in all Office 2016 programs, including Outlook. Additional keyboard shortcuts are available in other Office programs.

Display and use windows

Action	Keyboard shortcut
Switch to the previous/next window	Alt+Shift+Tab/Alt+Tab
Move to a pane from another pane in the program window If pressing F6 does not display the pane that you want, press Alt to put the focus on the ribbon, and then press Ctrl+Tab to move to the pane	F6 or Shift+F6
Copy a picture of the screen to the Clipboard	Print Screen
Copy a picture of the active window to the Clipboard	Alt+Print Screen

B

Use dialog boxes

Action	Keyboard shortcut
Move to the previous/next option or option group	Shift+Tab/Tab
Switch to the previous/next tab in a dialog box	Ctrl+Shift+Tab/Ctrl+Tab
Move between options in an open list, or between options in a group of options	Arrow keys
Perform the action assigned to the selected button; select or clear the selected check box	Spacebar
Select an option; select or clear a check box	The underlined letter
Open a selected list	Down Arrow or Alt+Down Arrow
Select an option from a list	The first letter of the list option
Close a selected list; cancel a command and close a dialog box	Esc
Run the selected command	Enter

Use edit boxes within dialog boxes

An edit box is a blank box in which you enter or paste an entry.

Action	Keyboard shortcut
Move to the beginning/end of the entry	Home/End
Move one character to the left/right	Left Arrow/Right Arrow
Move one word to the left/right	Ctrl+Left Arrow/Ctrl+Right Arrow
Select or unselect one character to the left/right	Shift+Left Arrow/ Shift+Right Arrow
Select or unselect one word to the left/right	Ctrl+Shift+Left Arrow/ Ctrl+Shift+Right Arrow
Select from the cursor to the beginning/end of the entry	Shift+Home/Shift+End

Use the Save As dialog box

Action	Keyboard shortcut
Open the Save As dialog box	F12
Open the selected folder or file	Enter
Open the folder one level above the selected folder	Backspace
Delete the selected folder or file	Delete
Move backward through options	Shift+Tab
Move forward through options	Tab
Open the Look In list	F4
Refresh the file list	F5

Undo and redo actions

Action	Keyboard shortcut
Cancel an action	Esc
Undo an action	Ctrl+Z
Redo or repeat an action	Ctrl+Y

Navigate the ribbon

Action	Keyboard shortcut
Activate or deactivate KeyTips	Alt or F10
Use a feature on the Quick Access Toolbar or ribbon	Press the KeyTip of the feature you want to use
Move to another tab of the ribbon	F10 to select the active tab, and then Left Arrow or Right Arrow
Expand or collapse the ribbon	Ctrl+F1

B

Action	Keyboard shortcut
Move the focus to the next/previous command	Tab/Shift+Tab
Move among the items on the ribbon	Arrow keys
Activate the selected command or control on the ribbon	Spacebar or Enter
Display the selected menu or gallery on the ribbon	Spacebar or Enter
Activate a command or control on the ribbon so that you can modify a value	Enter
Finish modifying a value in a control on the ribbon, and move focus back to the document	Enter
Get help on the selected command or control on the ribbon	F1

Move around in text or cells

Action	Keyboard shortcut
Move one character to the left/right	Left Arrow/Right Arrow
Move one line up/down	Up Arrow/Down Arrow
Move one word to the left/right	Ctrl+Left Arrow/Ctrl+Right Arrow
Move to the beginning/end of a line	Home/End
Move up/down one paragraph	Ctrl+Up Arrow/Ctrl+Down Arrow
Move to the beginning/end of a text box	Ctrl+Home/Ctrl+End

Move around in and work in tables

Action	Keyboard shortcut
Move to the previous/next cell	Shift+Tab/Tab
Move to the previous/next row	Up Arrow/Down Arrow

Action	Keyboard shortcut
Insert a tab in a cell	Ctrl+Tab
Start a new paragraph	Enter
Add a new row at the bottom of the table	Tab at the end of the last row

Access and use panes and galleries

Action	Keyboard shortcut
Move to a pane from another pane in the program window	F6
When a menu is active, move to a pane	Ctrl+Tab
When a pane is active, select the next or previous option in the pane	Tab or Shift+Tab
Display the full set of commands on the pane menu	Ctrl+Spacebar
Perform the action assigned to the selected button	Spacebar or Enter
Open a menu for the selected gallery item	Shift+F10
Select the first/last item in a gallery	Home/End
Scroll up/down in the selected gallery list	Page Up/Page Down
Close a pane	Ctrl+Spacebar, C
Open or close the Clipboard	Alt+H, F, O

Access and use available actions

Action	Keyboard shortcut
Move between options in a menu of available actions	Arrow keys
Perform the action for the selected item on a menu of available actions	Enter
Close the available actions menu or message	Esc

B

Find and replace content (when editing)

Action	Keyboard shortcut
Open the Find dialog box	Ctrl+F
Open the Replace dialog box	Ctrl+H
Repeat the last Find action	Shift+F4

Use the Help window

Action	Keyboard shortcut
Open the Help window	F1
Close the Help window	Alt+F4
Switch between the Help window and the active program	Alt+Tab
Return to the Help table of contents	Alt+Home
Select the previous/next item, hidden text, or hyperlink in the Help window	Shift+Tab/Tab
Perform the action for the selected item, hidden text, or hyperlink	Enter
Move back to the previous/forward to the next Help topic	Alt+Left Arrow or Backspace/Alt+Right Arrow
Scroll a few lines up/down within the current Help topic	Up Arrow/Down Arrow
Scroll one page up/down within the current Help topic	Page Up/Page Down
Stop the last action (Stop button)	Esc
Print the current Help topic If the cursor is not in the current Help topic, press F6 and then press Ctrl+P	Ctrl+P
In a Table of Contents, select the previous/next item	Up Arrow/Down Arrow
In a Table of Contents, expand/collapse the selected item	Right Arrow/Left Arrow

Glossary

add-in A utility that adds specialized functionality to an app but does not operate as an independent app.

address book A storage folder within your mailbox that contains contact records and contact groups.

appointment A block of time you schedule on your calendar that has a defined start time and end time, and to which you do not invite other attendees.

appointment window The app window that displays the form in which you enter information about an appointment.

arrangement A predefined combination of grouped and sorted messages.

Cached Exchange Mode A feature that stores and synchronizes a copy of a Microsoft Exchange Server account on a user's computer so that he or she can work offline, either by choice or due to a connection problem.

calendar A general reference to an appointment window, meeting window, or event window.

calendar item A general reference to an appointment, a meeting, or an event.

calendar item window A general reference to an appointment window, meeting window, or event window.

Calendar module The framework that provides the functionality to display and manage appointments, meetings, and events.

Calendar peek An interactive view of the current month's Date Navigator and the day's appointments associated with your default calendar, available from the Navigation Bar or the To-Do Bar.

category A name and associated color by which you can categorize, locate, group, and filter Outlook items.

client rule Or *client-side rule*. A rule that Outlook applies to messages after they arrive on your computer. See also *server rule*.

clip art Pre-made images that are distributed without copyright. Usually cartoons, sketches, illustrations, or photographs.

Clipboard A storage area shared by all Office apps where cut or copied items are stored.

contact A person about whom you save information, such as street and email addresses, phone and fax numbers, and webpage URLs.

contact card An interactive informational box that appears when you point to a message participant's name or presence icon. The contact card contains contact information and options. The expanded contact card also contains information about the person's position within the organization and distribution list memberships.

contact group A personal distribution list that you create within an address book, which can include contacts, other contact groups, Exchange Server distribution lists, mail-enabled Microsoft SharePoint libraries, and public folders.

contact index The alphabet bar located to the right of the contact list in People view, Business Card view, and Card view. Clicking a letter in this index scrolls the contact list to the first contact record that begins with that letter.

contact list The pane immediately to the right of the Folder Pane in the People module, which displays a list of contact records. Also, a SharePoint site list that stores contact information.

contact record A body of information you collect about a contact and store as an Outlook item.

contact record window The app window that displays the form in which you enter information about a contact to create a contact record.

content area The area to the right of the Folder Pane and below the ribbon, in which module content is displayed.

content pane The area of an email message in which you can enter and format message text, graphics, and other content.

contextual tab See *tool tab*.

conversation A means of organizing, viewing, and managing email messages that have the same subject line.

cursor A representation on the screen of the input device pointer location.

Date Navigator The small calendar displayed in the Folder Pane or in the Calendar peek that provides a quick and easy way of displaying specific dates or ranges of dates in the calendar.

delimited text file See *separated text file*.

desktop alert A notification that appears on your desktop when a new email message, meeting request, or task request is received in your Inbox.

dialog box launcher On the message window ribbon, a button in the lower-right corner of a group that opens a dialog box or pane containing features related to the group.

digital signature Data that binds a sender's identity to the information being sent. A digital signature may be bundled with any message, file, or other digitally encoded information, or transmitted separately. Digital signatures are used in public key environments and provide authentication and integrity services.

distribution list A group of recipients stored in Exchange Server that can be addressed as a single recipient. Administrators can create distribution lists that are available in the GAL. Users can create personal distribution lists called contact groups and add them to their personal address books.

document workspace A SharePoint site that is used for planning, posting, and working together on a document or a set of related documents.

domain On the Internet and other networks, the highest subdivision of a domain name in a network address, which identifies the type of entity that owns the address (such as .com for commercial users or .edu for educational institutions) or the geographical location of the address (such as .fr for France or .sg for Singapore).

draft A temporary copy of a message that has not yet been sent, located in the Drafts folder.

email Short for *electronic mail*. The exchange of electronic text messages and computer file attachments between computers over a communications network, such as a local area network or the Internet.

email message A message that is sent over a communications network such as a local area network or the Internet.

email server A computer that stores email messages for an organization.

email trail An email message and all responses to that message. When an individual message receives multiple responses, the email trail can branch into multiple trails. You can view all the branches of an email trail in Conversation view.

encryption The process of disguising a message or data in such a way as to hide its content.

event An activity that is not associated with a specific time, or an activity that occurs over a period of more than one day.

event window The app window that displays the form in which you enter information about an event.

filtering Displaying items that meet certain criteria; for example, filtering the Inbox to display only unread items. Filtering does not delete files, it simply changes the view so that you display only the files that meet your criteria.

Folders list A view that displays all mailbox folders, public folders, and connected SharePoint lists in the Folder Pane.

Folder Pane The pane that appears on the left side of the Outlook app window in every module. Its contents change depending on the module you're viewing. The Folder Pane can be minimized to display only folders that you designate as Favorites. Referred to in previous versions of Outlook as the *Navigation Pane*. See also *Navigation Bar*.

gallery A grouping of thumbnails that display options visually. Many galleries support the Live Preview feature.

Global Address List (GAL) The address book that contains all user, group, and distribution list email addresses in your organization. The administrator creates and maintains this address book. It may also contain public folder email addresses.

group An area of a ribbon tab that contains buttons related to a specific document element or function.

HTML In Outlook, an email message format that supports paragraph styles, character styles, and backgrounds. Most email programs support the HTML format.

HTTP A protocol used to access webpages from the Internet.

hyperlink A connection from a hyperlink anchor such as text or a graphic that you can follow to display a link target such as a file, a location in a file, or a website. Text hyperlinks are usually formatted as colored or underlined text, but sometimes the only indication is that when you point to them, the pointer changes to a hand.

InfoBar A banner near the top of an Outlook item window or the Reading Pane that displays information about the item.

information bar A banner across the top of the Outlook app window that displays information about the app and often contains commands related to changing the app status.

Information Rights Management (IRM) A policy tool that gives authors control over how recipients use the documents and email messages they send.

instant messaging (IM) The ability to see whether a person is connected to the Internet and to exchange messages. Most exchanges are text-only. However, some services allow attachments.

Internet Message Access Protocol (IMAP) A popular protocol for receiving email messages. It allows an email client to access and manipulate a remote email file without downloading it to the local computer. It is used mainly by corporate users who want to read their email from a remote location.

junk email Unsolicited commercial email (UCE). Also known as *spam*.

justifying Making all lines of text in a paragraph or column fit the width of the document or column, with even margins on each side.

keyboard shortcut Any combination of keystrokes that can be used to perform a task that would otherwise require a mouse or other pointing device.

Live Preview A feature that temporarily displays the effect of applying a specific format to text or graphics elements.

meeting request A message form linked to an Outlook calendar item. Meeting requests are generated by Outlook to manage meeting attendance.

meeting window The app window that displays the form in which you enter information to place a meeting on your calendar.

message header Summary information that you download to your computer to determine whether to download, copy, or delete the entire message from the server. The header includes the Subject, From, Received, Importance, Attachment, and Size fields.

message list The pane immediately to the right of the Folder Pane in the Mail module, in which messages and received items are displayed.

message window The app window that displays the form in which you create or respond to an email message.

Microsoft Office Clipboard See *Clipboard*.

Navigation Bar The bar located near the lower-left corner of the app window, above the status bar, that includes the navigation controls. It can be displayed as a compact vertical or horizontal bar that displays only module icons (compact view) or as a larger horizontal bar with text labels (standard view). See also *Folder Pane*.

offline address book A copy of an address book that has been downloaded so that an Outlook user can access the information it contains while disconnected from the server.

Outlook Today A single-screen dashboard that displays the calendar events and scheduled tasks associated with your default email account for the current day, which you display by clicking your mailbox in the Folder Pane or by clicking Shortcuts on the Navigation Bar and then clicking Outlook Today.

palette A collection of color swatches that you can click to apply a color to selected text or an object.

People module The framework that provides the functionality to display and manage address books.

People peek An interactive view of favorite contacts and a search box associated with your default address book, which you display by pointing to People on the Navigation Bar or by pinning it to the To-Do Bar.

permissions Rules associated with a shared resource on a network, such as a file, directory, or printer. Permissions provide authorization to perform operations associated with these objects. Permissions can typically be assigned to groups, global groups, or individual users.

phishing message A technique used to trick computer users into revealing personal or financial information. A common online phishing scam starts with an email message that appears to come from a trusted source but actually directs recipients to provide information to a fraudulent website.

phishing site A website that prompts users to update personal information, such as bank accounts and passwords, which might be used for identity theft.

Plain Text An email message format that does not support character or paragraph formatting. All email programs support the Plain Text format.

plain text messages Messages that don't support character or paragraph formatting in the message content.

point to To pause the cursor over a button or other area of the display.

Post Office Protocol (POP) A standard method that computers use to send and receive email messages. POP messages are typically held on an email server until you download them to your computer, and then they are deleted from the server. With other email protocols, such as IMAP, email messages are held on the server until you delete them. You can configure Outlook to manage the retention of messages on the POP server.

presence icon A colored icon that indicates the online presence and status of a contact.

print style A combination of paper and page settings that determines the way items print. Outlook provides built-in print styles, and you can create your own.

Quick Access Toolbar A customizable toolbar that displays frequently used commands and can be located above or below the ribbon.

Quick Step A feature with which you can perform up to 12 actions with an email message in your Inbox by clicking one command.

recall To instruct Outlook to delete or replace any unread copies of a message that was already sent.

recurring item A calendar item or task that occurs repeatedly on a specific schedule. You can specify an appointment, meeting, or event as recurring, and specify the frequency of recurrence. Outlook then creates a series of items based on your specifications.

redundant message A message whose content is wholly contained within another message. Redundant messages are moved by the Clean Up tool.

reminder A message that appears at a specified interval before an appointment, meeting, or task that announces when the activity is set to occur. Reminders appear any time Outlook is running, even if it isn't your active app.

resend To create a new version of a sent or received message.

resolving The process of matching a user name to the information on a network server, resulting in the user name being replaced by a display name and the name underlined.

ribbon A user interface design that organizes commands into logical groups, which appear on separate tabs.

Rich Text Format (RTF) An email message format that supports paragraph styles, character styles, backgrounds, borders, and shading, but is compatible with only Outlook and Exchange Server. Outlook converts RTF messages to HTML when sending them outside of your Exchange network.

rules Sets of criteria defining specific actions that Outlook takes when the criteria are fulfilled.

screen clipping An image of all or part of the content displayed on a computer screen. Screen clippings can be captured by using a graphics capture tool such as the Screen Clipping tool included with Office apps.

ScreenTip A note that appears on the screen to provide information about the app interface or certain types of document content, such as hyperlinks within a message.

Secure Multipurpose Internet Mail Extensions (S/MIME) A protocol that supports secure mail features such as digital signatures and message encryption.

separated text file A file that contains unformatted text organized into fields and records. Records are separated by carriage returns; fields are separated by a specific character such as a comma, tab, colon, or semicolon. Separated text files might have the file name extension .txt or .csv.

server rule Or *server-side rule*. A rule that Exchange applies when receiving or processing a message, before delivering it. See also *client rule*.

shortcut menu A menu that shows a list of commands relevant to a particular item. Sometimes referred to as a *context menu*.

sizing handle A small circle, square, or set of dots that appears at the corner or on the side of a selected object. You drag these handles to change the size of the object horizontally, vertically, or proportionally.

SmartArt graphic A predefined set of shapes and text used as a basis for creating a diagram.

spam Unsolicited commercial email (UCE). Also known as *junk email*.

status bar An app window element, located at the bottom of the app window, that displays indicators and controls.

tab A tabbed page on the ribbon that contains buttons organized in groups.

task list The pane immediately to the right of the Folder Pane in the Tasks module, in which tasks or flagged items are displayed.

task originator The person who creates a task, specifically when assigning the task to someone else.

task owner The person to whom a task is currently assigned. After a task has been assigned, the task originator can no longer update the information in the task window.

task window The app window that displays the form in which you enter information to create or manage a task.

Tasks module The framework that provides the functionality to display and manage tasks and flagged items.

Tasks peek An interactive view of the tasks associated with your default email account, which you display by pointing to Tasks on the Navigation Bar or by pinning it to the To-Do Bar.

Tasks view An arrangement of the Tasks module, displaying a list of tasks associated with a specific email account in the content area. See also *To-Do List view*.

third-party add-in A software program created by one company (the "third party") that extends the capabilities of an app created by another company.

thread In email and Internet newsgroup conversations, a series of messages and replies that are all related to a specific topic.

thumbnail A small representation of an item, such as an image, a page of content, or a set of formatting, usually obtained by scaling down a snapshot of it. Thumbnails are typically used to provide visual identifiers for related items.

title bar The horizontal bar at the top of a window that displays the window name and window-management buttons.

To-Do Bar An optional pane that can be displayed on the right side of the app window, to which you can pin the Calendar peek, Contacts peek, and Tasks peek.

To-Do List view The default arrangement of the Tasks module, displaying a list of incomplete tasks and flagged items for your default email account in the content area. See also *Tasks view*.

tool tab A tab containing groups of commands that are pertinent only to a specific type of document element such as a picture, table, or text box. Tool tabs appear only when relevant content is selected.

Uniform Resource Locator (URL) An address that uniquely identifies a location on the Internet. A URL is usually preceded by http://, as in http://www.microsoft.com. A URL can contain more detail, such as the name of a page of hypertext, often with the file name extension .html or .htm.

unique message A message that contains content that is not present in other messages. Unique messages are not moved by the Clean Up tool.

view Different ways in which Outlook items can be arranged in the Outlook module window.

View Shortcuts toolbar A toolbar located near the right end of the status bar that displays buttons for switching between views of the current module.

web beacon A graphic that links to a webpage and is embedded in a message for use as a signaling device.

work week The days and times you define within Outlook as available for work-related activities.

Index

About the author

Joan Lambert has worked closely with Microsoft technologies since 1986, and in the training and certification industry since 1997. As President and CEO of Online Training Solutions, Inc. (OTSI), Joan guides the translation of technical information and requirements into useful, relevant, and measurable resources for people who are seeking certification of their computer skills or who simply want to get things done efficiently.

Joan is the author or coauthor of more than three dozen books about Windows and Office (for Windows, Mac, and iPad), video-based training courses for SharePoint and OneNote, and three generations of Microsoft Office Specialist certification study guides.

Joan is a Microsoft Certified Professional, Microsoft Certified Trainer, Microsoft Office Specialist Master (for all Office versions since Office 2007), Microsoft Certified Technology Specialist (for Windows and Windows Server), Microsoft Certified Technology Associate (for Windows), and Microsoft Dynamics Specialist.

Joan currently lives in a small town in Texas with her simply divine daughter, Trinity; an ever-growing menagerie of dogs, cats, fish, and frogs; and the DeLonghi Gran Dama super-automatic espresso machine that runs the house.

Acknowledgments

I appreciate the time and efforts of Carol Dillingham, Rosemary Caperton, and the team at Microsoft Press—past and present—who made this and so many other books possible.

I would like to thank the editorial and production team members at Online Training Solutions, Inc. (OTSI) and other contributors for their efforts. Jaime Odell, Jean Trenary, Jeanne Craver, Kathy Krause, Susie Carr, and Val Serdy all contributed to the creation of this book.

OTSI specializes in the design and creation of Microsoft Office, SharePoint, and Windows training solutions and the production of online and printed training resources. For more information about OTSI, visit *www.otsi.com* or follow us on Facebook at *www.facebook.com/Online.Training.Solutions.Inc.*

I hope you enjoy this book and find it useful. The content of this book was guided in part by feedback from readers of previously published *Step by Step* books. If you find errors or omissions in this book, want to say something nice about it, or would like to provide input for future versions, you can use the feedback process outlined in the introduction.

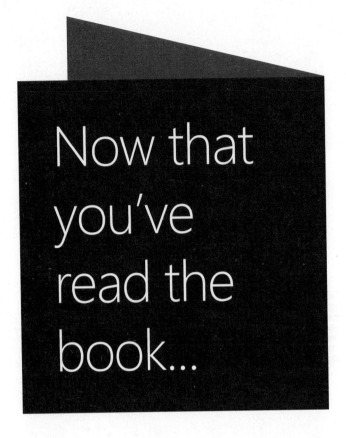

Now that you've read the book...

Tell us what you think!

Was it useful?
Did it teach you what you wanted to learn?
Was there room for improvement?

Let us know at http://aka.ms/tellpress

Your feedback goes directly to the staff at Microsoft Press,
and we read every one of your responses. Thanks in advance!

The quick way to learn Microsoft Outlook 2016!

This is learning made easy. Get more done quickly with Outlook 2016. Jump in wherever you need answers—brisk lessons and colorful screenshots show you exactly what to do, step by step.

- Get easy-to-follow guidance from a certified Microsoft Office Specialist Master
- Learn and practice new skills while working with sample content, or look up specific procedures
- Manage your email more efficiently than ever
- Organize your Inbox to stay in control of everything that matters
- Schedule appointments, events, and meetings
- Organize contact records and link to information from social media sites
- Track tasks for yourself and assign tasks to other people
- Enhance message content and manage email security

Step by Step

IN FULL COLOR!

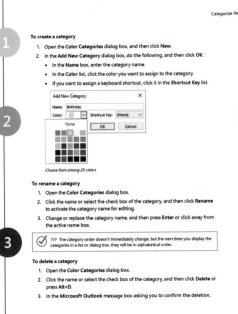

Download your *Step by Step* practice files from:
http://aka.ms/outlook2016sbs/downloads

1 Easy numbered steps

2 Colorful screenshots

3 Helpful tips and pointers

Microsoft Press

Celebrating over 30 years

ISBN 978-0-7356-9778-2

U.S.A. $34.99
Canada $43.99
[Recommended]

Microsoft Office/Outlook

53499

9 780735 697782